DICTIONARY OF PSYCHOLOGY AND ALLIED SCIENCES

Dedicated to

All Teachers & Students

who helped in improving the fields of psychology and allied mental health specialities

PREFACE

With the rapid unveiling of the aetiological factors and also with the changes in the classifications, the field of psychology has undergone a continuous change and refinements which need a dictionary for its completion. Moreover, the definitions of various terms is the backbone of understanding a subject, its research and its communication. The impetus for writing a dictionary has come largely from clinical practice and teaching. Both reveal the lack of focused knowledge concerning the overlapping territories between psychology, psychiatry, and neurology–a gap manifested in the paucity of literature on the subjects. My intention has been to provide a guide for students from a psychological, or sociological background, who may find several aspects of these branches which impinge on their interest usefully reviewed.

I have tried to produce a comprehensive text; it is a defining dictionary rather than an explaining one. The dictionary incorporates the revised nomenclature and the diagnostic terms have been arranged alphabetically.

All suggestions for the modification of this book are welcome and will be duly acknowledged.

M.S. Bhatia

CONTENTS

A

AA: Abbreviation for (1) Alcoholics Anonymous, (2) Achievement Age.

Abalienation: Loss or failing of the senses or mental faculties.

Abandonment: Discontinuation of treatment by the physician before he has been dismissed by the patient, obtained the consent of the patient to withdraw, or furnished another doctor to continue treatment.

ABBA design: An example of counterbalancing of the experimental conditions. The first condition (1) is followed by two trials of the second condition, (2) then by one of the first. The effect is to average out order effects.

Aberrant: Behaviour that deviates from what is normal, expected or desired.

Aberration: Pathological deviation from normal thinking. It is not related to a person's intelligence.

Ability: A capacity or skill or competence to perform an act without previous training. The term covers intelligence and specific aptitudes.

Ability test: Tests of potential–that is, of what an individual can learn with training. Compare achievement tests, personality tests.

Abiotrophy: Premature loss of vitality of cells or tissues. The concept of abiotrophy was used by Gowers as a possible explanation of dementia: precocious aging of the central nervous system was due to limited viability of the nerve cells concerned.

Ablutomania: Excessive interest in bathing and cleaning oneself. It is common in obsessive compulsive disorder.

Abnormal: A term applied to behaviour or people, who have been classed as not normal. A potentially controversial label because of problems defining normality. It is the rough equivalent of 'psycho-pathological' and may be defined according to a variety of criteria: (1) as behaviour which is different from the normal (i.e., unusual); (2) as behaviour which does not conform to social demands or culturally determined averages or norms; (3) as statistically uncommon behaviours, based on the assumptions of the normal distribution: (4) as behaviour which is maladaptive or painful for the individual' or (5) as the failure to achieve self-actualization, the humanistic view. These criteria have their own problems because they lead to classification of highly-regarded individuals like social reformers and artists as abnormal.

Abnormal behaviour: Behaviour which deviates from what is considered normal, culturally or scientifically, usually refers to maladaptive behaviour.

Abnormality or Psychological disorder: Any behaviour or state of emotional distress that causes personal suffering that is self-destructive, or that is unacceptable to the community.

Abnormal personality: A personality with traits which deviate markedly from what is generally accepted as normal. This deviation is a quantitative and not a qualitative one.

Abnormal psychology: The psychology of abnormal behaviour. This term has largely been replaced by clinical psychology when referring to the professional practice of abnormal psychology.

Aboiement: Involuntary production of abnormal sounds. It is often observed in schizophrenias, who may make many animalistic sounds.

Aboulia: See Abulia.

Above and below: Adler used this term to imply the unconscious notion existing in every psyche, male or female, of femaleness as a degradation and maleness as an ideal.

Abraham, Karl (1877–1925): First psychoanalyst in Germany; manic depressive psychosis, pregenital stages, character types, symbolism.

Abreaction: A process, used in some forms of psychotherapy, especially psychoanalytically oriented ones, by which repressed material, particularly a painful experience or a conflict, is brought back to consciousness. A therapeutic effect sometimes occurs through partial discharge or desensitization of the painful emotions and increased insight and also, by the development of new coping strategies, See also catharsis.

Abreaction, emotional: The discharge of emotion in the course of psychotherapy.

Abreaction, motor: The living-out of an unconscious impulse through muscular or motor expression.

Absence: A temporary loss of consciousness due to epilepsy without any convulsive phenomenon.

Abstinence: The act of refraining voluntarily from some activity or from the use of certain substances such as food or drugs. In psychoanalysis, abstinence refers to refraining from sexual intercourse. In classical psychoanalysis, it refers to one of the rules so called "rule of abstinence", though it is not clear what the patient should be made to abstain from. A Freudian phrase. " The treatment must be carried out in abstinence" refers specifically to the fact that analytical technique requires of the physician she demands. Friend also referred it to the need to ensure that the patient's suffering is not relieved too quickly.

Abstinence syndrome: In the area of alcohol or drug dependence, being without the substance on which the subject is dependent. It is equivalent to withdrawal symptoms and its appearance suggests the presence of physiological dependence or addiction.

Absorption: Engrossment with one object or idea with in attention to others.

Abstract attitude: Cognitive functioning that includes assuming a mental set voluntarily; shifting voluntarily from one aspect of a situation to another, keeping in mind simultaneously various aspects of a situation; grasping the essentials of a whole breaking it into its parts and solating them voluntarily, planning ahead ideationally, and/ or thinking or performing symbolically. A characteristic of many psychiatric disorders in the inability to assume the abstract attitude or shift readily from the concrete to the abstract and back again as demanded by circumstance. It is also known as categorical attitude and abstract thinning.

Abstracting disabilities: Difficulties in organizing and understanding the inputs once information has been recorded in the brain.

Abstraction: The process whereby thoughts or ideas are generalized and dissociated from particular concrete instances or material objects. Concreteness in proverb interpretation suggests an impairment of abstration, as in schizophrenia.

Abstract thinking: See abstract attitude.

Abstract thought: Thought which uses concepts which do not have an immediate material correspondence such as justice or freedom. In Piaget's theory of cognitive development, the capacity for abstract thought is only acquired after the age of about 12 years. It is an essential aspect of Piaget's formal operations stage.

Absurdity: In psychoanalysis, anything that is contradictory or incoherent or meaningless in a train of thought or a constellation of ideas.

Abulia: Lack of will or motivation, often expressed as inability to make decisions.

Abuse: (1) of substance, using them inappropriately in a way that is harmful to the individuals e.g., excessive alcohol consumption. See, addiction (2) inappropriate and harmful treatment of another person (child, elder, sexual, spouse). The most common form of abuse is child abuse.

Abused child: See battered child syndrome.

Acalculia: Loss of previously possessed faculty with arithmetic calculation: may follow parietal lobe damage.

Acanthesthesia: A type of paresthesia in which the patient experiences a sensation of pinpricks.

Acarophobia: Fear of small objects such as insect, worms, pins and needles seen in patients with alcoholism.

Acatalepsia: A mental deficiency characterized by the inability to reason or comprehend.

Acatamathesia: Inability to understand language. This is the perceptive (sensory) aspect of aphasia.

Acataphasia: A form of disordered speech in which statements are incorrectly formulated. The patient may express himself with words that sound like the ones he means to use but are not appropriate to his thoughts or he may use totally inappropriate expressions.

Accelerated interaction: An alternate term for marathon group session.

Accessible and inaccessible: A patient is said to be accessible if the psychiatrist or analyst succeeds in making rapport with him, and inaccessible if he fails. The term is pseudo-objective, since it implies that the capacity for rapport is a constant, identical in every examining physician. In general memotics are deemed to be accessible and psychotics inaccessible.

Accident proneness: Susceptibility to accidents based on psychological cause or motivations.

Accommodation: Loss of sensation of physical existence.

Acetylcholine: A neuro-transmitter which is particularly found at the motor end plate and is therefore involved in muscle action.

Achievement: The successful reaching of goal. Used particularly to refer to real life successes and when evaluating a person's life.

Achievement motivation: The motivation to accomplish valued goals and to avoid failure. This concept became important as motivation theory became less dominated by physiological drives. See also need for achievement. The concept was developed by McClelland.

Achievement test: Tests used to measure present knowledge or skills especially knowledge or skills developed through specific learning e.g., a statistics examination. Compare ability tests.

Achluophobia: Fear of the dark.

Acquisition: (1) A term used to indicate that a particular skill or ability has been gained by an animal or human being. When applied to language, this term is used to avoid drawing inferences about whether language has been learned or inherited. (2) The phase during a conditioning procedure in which the response is learned or strengthened.

Acquisition curve: The graphic representation of learning which shows that the strength of the learned response gradually increases with more and more learning trials.

Acrophobia: Fear of high places. Acting out: To express a wish, need or motivation particularly when it is unrecognized or unconscious in overt behaviour rather than words. Often the behaviour is aggressive and self-destructive and may be very uncharacteristic for the persons who may have no idea, why they behave in that way. In controlled situations, it may be therapeutic (e.g., children's play therapy). In psychoanalysis, the essence of concept is the replacement of thought by action and it implies that (a) the impulse being acted out has never acquired verbal representation, or (b) the impulse is too intense to be dischargeable in words, or (c) that the patient lacks the capacity for inhibition. Since psychoanalysis is a talking cure carried out in a state of reflection acting out is antitherapeutic. Acting out is characteristic of psychopathy and behaviour disorders and reduces the accessibility of these conditions to psychoanalysis.

Action theory: A theory concerned with the study of human goal directed behaviour and its social basis.

Active algolagnia: A synonym for sadism.

Active and passive: Friend made extensive use of the idea that there exists a polarity between activity and passivity; Masculinity, aggression, sadism and voyeurism being active and feminity, submissiveness, masochism and exhibitionism being passive. The situation is, however complicated by a further assumption that instincts can undergo reversal into their opposite, in particular that active instincts can become passive, sadism and voyeurism being usually cited as the examples of instincts capable of this reversal.

Active group therapy: A type of group therapy introduced and developed by S R Slavon and designed for children and young adolescents, with emphasis on emotional and active interaction is a permissive, non-threatening atmosphere. The therapist stresses on reality testing, ego strengthening and active interpretation.

Active therapist: Type of therapist, who makes no effort to remain anonymous but is forceful and expresses his personality definitively in the therapy setting. See also Passive therapist.

Act psychology: The origin of the concept lie in Brentano's doctrine of intentionality. It asserts that mind could not be reduced to a set of elements found in consciousness. It is the way in which that activity 'contains' or is 'directed towards' that result which manifests the true nature of mind not the results alone.

Actual neurosis: Friend, in his early writing, distinguished between psychoneuroses and actual neuroses, the former being due to psychological conflicts and past events the latter being the physiological consequences of present disturbances in sexual functioning. He further distinguished two forms of actual neurosis; neurasthenia, the result of sexual excess and anxiety neurosis, the result of unrelieved sexual stimulation.

Actualization: Realization of one's full potential. See also individuation.

Actualizing tendency: A term coined by Rogers (1954) to describe the process by which people seek to develop their various potentials and maximize their personal growth. Once their need for positive regard from others has been satisfied. See also self-actualization.

Acuity: The fineness of the discrimination that a sense organ can make. Most commonly used of vision.

Aculalia: Non-sense speech associated with marked impairment of comprehension.

Acute confusional state: (1) A form of delirium in which the most prominent symptoms are disorders of memory deficit and both retrograde and anterograde amnesia and clouding of consciousness (reduced clarity of awareness of environment and reduced capacity to shift, focus and sustain attention to environmental stimuli). See organic mental disorder. (2) An acute stress reaction is common in adolescence to new surroundings or new demand. The reaction is characterized by frustration; rage, inability to concentrate and feeling or estrangement, depersonalization, and loneliness; it is generally self-limited and subsides and the person adjusts to his situation. See also identity-crisis.

Acute reaction to stress: Very transient disorders of any severity and nature which occur in individuals without any apparent pre-existing mental disorder in response to exceptional physical or mental stress such as natural battle and which usually subside within hours or days. The acute reaction to stress may manifest a predominant disturbance of emotions e.g., panic states, excitability, fear, depression or anxiety; a predominant psychomotor disturbance e.g., agitation or stupor synonyms; catastrophic stress reaction, exhaustion delirium, combat fatigue, post-traumatic stress disorder.

Adaptation: The process of fitting or conforming to the environment by behavioural or psychic changes that promote an optimal level or functioning. The term has highly specific meanings in, (1) physiology— the adjustment of bodily organ to particular environmental demands, (2) evolutionary biology how a species is matched to the environments in which it has developed, and (3) psychology—the process by which an individual achieves the best balance feasible between conflicting demands. Piaget uses the term more specifically for the correspond to reality. In psychoanalytic view, adaptation tends to be regarded as a function which is imposed on the developing individual from without as a result of his experience of frustration.

Adaptational approach: An approach used in analytic therapy. Consonant with Sandor Rado's formulations on adaptational psychodynamics, therapy focuses on the maladaptive patterns used by patients in the treatment sessions, on how those patterns developed and on what the patients must do to overcome them and stabilize their functioning at self-reliant, admit levels. See also social adaptation.

Adaptive behaviour: Any behaviour that increases an organism's ability to adjust to a specific environment or situation.

Adaptive functioning: A composite term used to indicate a person's ability to function effectively in three major areas: social relations, occupational behaviour and use of leisure time. In DSM-IV's multiaxial classification. Axis V, is the clinician's determination of the patient's highest level of adaptive functioning in the previous year.

Addiction: A state of physiological or psychological dependence on some substance, usually a drug, resulting in tolerance of the drug such that progressively larger doses are required to obtain the same effect. Addictions are most clearly identified by a failure to function adequately when the substance is withdrawn. The commonest addictions are of socially accepted drugs such as nicotine and alcohol, though illegal drugs (e.g., heroin) and those initially taken as medical treatment (e.g., tranquillizers) cause more public concern. Colloquially the term has been stretched to cover need which have become exaggerated to a degree, that is damaging the individual e.g., addiction to television, violent exercise, or food.

Adjustment: Functional, often transitory, alteration or accommodation by which one can better adapt oneself to the immediate environment and to one's inner self. Also defined as a judgement heuristic in which subjective probability estimated at a certain point and are raised or lowered depending on the circumstances.

Adjustment disorder: Mild and transient disorders lasting longer that acute reactions to stress, which occur in individuals of any age without apparent pre-existing mental disorder. Such disorders are often relatively circumscribed or situation specific are generally reversible and usually last only a few months. They are usually closely related in time and content to stresses such as bereavement. Migration or separation experiences. In DSM III R category introduced for maladaptive reactions to identifiable life events or circumstances. The symptoms generally lessen as the stress diminishes or as the person adapts to the stress.

Adler, Alfred (1870–1937): Viennese psychiatrist and one of Freud's original followers. Adler broke off from Freud and introduced and developed the concepts of individual psychology, inferiority complex, overcompensation and masculine protest.

Administrative psychiatry: The branch of psychiatry that deals with the organization of the efforts of many people in clinical practice, in a programme or in a hospital or other facility to provide care and treatment. Its focus is on the management process formed by the interaction of health administration, clinical care of psychiatric patients, programme elements and the mental health organization itself with the attitudes, values and belief systems of the environment in which the structure exists.

Adolescence: Period of growth from puberty to maturity. The beginning of secondary sexual characteristics, usually at about 12, and the termination of adolescence is marked by the achievement of sexual maturity at about age 20. The period is associated with rapid physical, psychological and social changes. Research on adolescence has tended to emphasize the four developmental areas of competence, individuation, identity and self-esteem.

Adorno: Born Theodor Wiesengrund in Frankfurt at Main, Adorno (1903–1969) was a German Jewish Philosopher, an outstanding neo-Marxist intellectual and a founding father of the Frankfurt school. He made important contributions to musicology, aesthetics, sociology and social psychology.

Adrenaline: A sympathomimetic catecholamine formed from noradrenaline and the major hormones secreted by the adrenal medulla. It acts within the brain as a neurotransmitter. Its release during states of fear or anxiety produces many of the physiological changes associated with those emotions. It is also known as epinephrine.

Adultomorphic: The adultomorphic fallacy is attributing to infants and children, the thoughts and feelings which an adult would have under analogous conditions. The reference is usually to theories about the psychology of infants which the speaker believes overestimate their level of development.

Adynamia: Weakness or fatigability.

Aesthetics: The study of the nature of beauty, or of pleasing perceptual experiences.

Aetiology: The study of the cauzation. This term is particularly used in refer to the causes of illnesses and mental disorders.

Affect: The subjective and immediate experience of emotion attached to ideas of mental representations of objects. Affect has outward manifestations that may be classified as restricted, blunted, flattened, appropriate, or inappropriate. Psychoanalytically a distinction is made between (a) discharge affects, which accompany expression of a drive and (b) tension-affects, which accompany damming up of a drive. Affects are regarded as attached in ideas, and not vice versa. The concepts affects and emotion differ in that whereas the former regards them as affixed to ideas, the latter regards them as valid, independent experience.

Affect abnormal: A general term describing morbid or unusual mood states of which the most common are depression, anxiety, elation, irritability and affective lability. Affect appropriate. Emotional tone in harmony with the accompanying idea, thought, or speech.

Affect, blunted: A disturbance of affect manifested by a severe reduction in the intensity of externalized feeling tone. Observed in schizophrenia. It is one of that disorder's fundamental symptoms, as outlined by Eugen Bleuler.

Affect display: A set of physical changes which indicates an emotional state e.g., pilomotor response in cats, indicating fear and greeting smile in humans, indicating friendliness.

Affect-fantasy: Jung's term for an emotional laden fantasy.

Affect-flat: Absence or near absence of any signs of affective expression. This may occur in schizophrenia, dementia or psychopathic personality.

Affect, inappropriate: Emotional tone that is out of harmony with the idea, thought or speech accompanying it.

Affect, labile: Affective expression characterized by repetitious and abrupt shifts, most frequently seen in organic brain syndromes, early schizophrenia and some forms of personality disorders.

Affect restricted: Affective expression characterized by a reduction in its range and intensity.

Affect, shallow: A state of morbid sufficiency of emotional response presenting as an indifference to external events and situation, occurring characteristically in schizophrenia of the hebephrenic type but also in organic cerebral disorders, mental retardation and personality disorders.

Affectionless psychopathy: A term used by J. Bowlby to describe a syndrome in which an individual does not demonstrate any emotion, positive or negative, towards any other human being. Affectionless psychopaths were characterized by a lack of social conscience and a high level of delinquency.

Affective disorder: Any mental disorder in which disturbance of mood is the primary characteristic, disturbances in thinking and behaviour are secondary characteristics. In DSM-III the affective disorders include bipolar affective disorder, major depression, cyclothymic disorder, dysthymic disorder, and atypical affective disorders and in DSM-III (Revised), they are termed as mood disorders.

Affective domain: A traditional approach to understanding human personality, originating with the ancient Greeks, involving seeing the psyche as comprising to attitude theory in which an attitude is considered to consist of three major componentic cognitive, emotional and behavioural components.

Affective interaction: Interpersonal experience and exchange that are emotionally charged.

Affiliation: The process of joining or the sense of belonging to a group. Nearly everybody feels a desire to belong, so affiliation has been treated as a travel or motive.

Aftercare: After hospitalization, the continuing program of rehabilitation designed to reinforce the effects of therapy and to help the patient adjust to his environment.

Afterimage: An image which remains in the visual field after the original stimulus has ceased. After images usually occur, after particularly intense or prolonged stimulation of the retina.

Agape: (GK-brotherly love): Sometimes used in conjunction with Erose to contrast altruistic love (Caritas) with sensual love.

Agent: Many of the more puzzling aspects of psychoanalytical theory derived from the fact that one of its basis premises. PSYCHIC DETERMINISM, implicity denies the possibility that human beings can be agents who make decisions and are responsible for their own actions.

Age scale: A test in which items are grouped not by type of task but by the average age at which children pass-each item; scores are expressed as Mental Age (MA). See Stamford Binet intelligence scale.

Ageusia: Lack or impairment of the sense of taste. It may be seen in depressions.

Aggression: Forceful physical, verbal or symbolic action. May be appropriate and self-protective, including healthy self-assertiveness or inappropriate as in hostile or destructive behaviour. May also be directed towards the environment, towards another person or personality or towards the self, as in depression. It is used for behaviour (hitting), emotional state (feeling aggressive) and to an intention (wanting to harm). There are several classifications of different types of aggression, the most useful distinction being between instrumental aggression, an aggressive act performed in order to achieve some other objectives and hostile aggression, motivated by antagonistic feelings and emotions. In psychoanalytical usage it is a derivative of the Death Instinct.

Aggressive drive: Also known as the death instinct, it represents one of the two basic instincts or drives in psychoanalytic theory introduced by Freud; it operates in opposition to the life instinct or sexual drive in the dual-instinct theory. It is conceived of as an unconscious destructive drive or impulse directed at oneself or another that aims towards dissolution and death. It operates on the repetition compulsion principle, in contrast to sexual drive, which follows the pleasure pain principle, see also sexual drive.

Aging: Characteristic pattern of life changes that occur normally in humans, plants and animals as they grow older. Some age changes begin at birth and continue until death, other changes begin at maturity and end at death.

Agism: Systematic stereotyping of and discrimination against elderly people to create distance from their social plight and to avoid primitive fears of aging and death. It is distinguished from gerontophobia, a specific pathologic feat of old people and aging.

Agitated: Agitated depression and melancholia are psychiatric diagnostic terms referring to patients who are both deeply depressed and tense, restless and anxious.

Agitation: Excessive motor activity, usually non-purposeful and associated with internal tension, examples, inability to sit still, fidgeting, pacing, wringing of hands or pulling of clothes.

Agitation, catatonic: A state in which the psychomotor features of anxiety are associated with catatonic syndrome.

Agnosia: Inability to understand the importance of significance of sensory stimuli; it cannot be explained by a defect in sensory pathways or sensorium. In strict usage, the diagnosis of agnosia implies an organic cerebral lesion; however the term has also been used to refer to the selective loss or disuse of knowledge of specific objects due to emotional circumstances, as seen in certain schizophrenics, hysteries, and depressed patients.

Agoraphobia: Fear of open places; as phobic disorder characterized by a fear of leaving one's home. It may present with or without panic attacks. It is the commonest form of phobia, seen in clinical practice. Psychological treatments may attempt either to reduce the symptoms of the phobia or to resolve the underlying anxiety.

Agraphia: Loss or impairment of a previously possessed ability to write; may follow parietal lobe damage.

Agromania: Excessive interest in living alone or in rural seclusion, it is sometimes associated with schizophrenia.

Aichmophobia: Fear of pointed objects, usually expressed as a fear that the person will use the object against someone else.

Allurophobia: Fear of cats.

Aim-inhibition: A relationship is said to be aim-inhibited if the subject has no conscious erotic interest in the object. Common examples are friendships, platonic love and domestic affections between relatives. The concept assumes that, in the absence of inhibition, friendships would be overt homosexual relationships, platonic love would be consummated, and incest would occur.

Akathisia: A sate of motor restlessness manifested by the compelling need to be in constant movement.

It may be seen as an extrapyramidal side effect of butyrophenone or phenothiazine medication.

Akinesia: Lack of physical movement, as in the extreme immobility of catatonic schizophrenia.

Akinetic mutism: Absence of voluntary motor movement or speech in a patient who is apparently alert, as evidenced by following eye movements.

Akrasia: The technical term for weakness of will. Philosophers are interested in akrasia because although it is obvious enough that people act against their better judgement, yet when one looks carefully it seems impossible that they should do so.

Al-anon: An organization of relatives of alcoholics, operating under the structure of Alcoholics anonymous, to promote the discussion and resolution of common problems.

Alateen: An organization of teenaged children of alcoholic parents operating in some communities under the philosophic and organizational structure of Alcoholics Anonymous. It provides a setting in which the children may receive group support in achieving a better understanding of their parents problems and better methods for coping with them.

Alcoholic blackot: Amnesia experienced by an alcoholic concerning his behaviour during a drinking bout. The blackout usually indicates that reversible brain damage has occurred.

Alcoholic deterioration: Dementia and mental deterioration associated with chronic excessive alcohol use.

Alcoholic hallucinosis: The occurrence of hallucinations with a clear sensorium in a person with a history of heavy drinking and alcohol dependence. It usually follows a prolonged drinking bout. See also delirium tremens.

Alcoholics Anonymous (AA): An organization of alcoholics formed in 1935. It uses certain group methods such as inspirational supportive techniques to help rehabilitate chronic alcoholics.

Alcohol idiosyncratic intoxication: The DSM III term for a syndrome of marked alcohol intoxication with subsequent amnesia for the period of intoxication produced by the ingestion of quantities of alcohol that would be insufficient to induce intoxication in most people. In DSM-II, it was known as pathological intoxication.

Alcohol intoxication: The constellation of specific neurological, psychological, and behavioural effects produced by the recent ingestion of alcohol. Characteristically, the effects include slurred speech, motor ataxia, disinhibition of sexual or aggressive impulses, lability of mood, impairment of attention or memory and impairment of judgement.

Alcoholism: Excessive dependence on or addiction to alcohol usually to the point that the person's physical and mental health is threatened or harmed better termed as alcohol dependence syndrome.

Alcohol paranoid state: Paranoid state in alcoholics characterized by excessive jealousy and delusions of the spouse's infidelity. In DSM-III, this condition was called atypical paranoid disorder.

Aleatoric theory: A theoretical orientation employed in the understanding of cross time change in behavioural phenomena. From the aleatoric viewpoint, human activity is largely embedded within historically contingent circumstances.

Alexander, Franz: (Hungarian psychoanalyst, professor of psychoanalysis at the University of Chicago) chief contributions were in area of brief analytic and psychosomatic medicine.

Alexia: Loss of the power to grasp the meaning of written or printed words and sentences.

Alexithymia: A disturbance in affective and cognitive function which overlaps diagnostic entities but is common in psychosomatic, addictive and post-traumatic stress disorder. The chief manifestation is difficulty in describing or recognizing one's emotions, with a limited fantasy life and general construction in the affective life.

Algolagnia: Enjoyment of pain.

Algophobia: Fear of pain.

Alienation: The estrangement felt in a cultural setting one views as foreign, unpredictable, or unacceptable. For example, in depersonalization phenomens, feelings, of unreality or strangeness produce a sense of alienation from one's self or environment. In obsession where there is fear of one's emotions, avoidance of situations that arouse emotions, and continuing effort to keep feelings out of awareness, there is alienation of affect. Freudian psychoanalysis tends to concern itself with alienation from oneself or parts of oneself while existentialism and Marxism concern with alienation from others since, however self-alienation limits the capacity to relate to others and alienation from others limits the capacity to discover oneself, both above types of alienation are interdependents.

Alienist: Obsolete term for a psychiatrist who testifies in court about a person's sanity or mental competence.

All or none law: The principle which states that when a particular neurone is excited to fire a nerve impulse. The impulse is always the same size, and always travels at the same rate in the axon of that neurone.

All or none principle: The principle that a neurone either fires or it does not, with no variation in the strength of the electrical impulse. It was originally thought that all nerve cells operated according to the all or none principle, implying a necessity for digital processing models of brain functioning, and fostering some computer simulation approached to understanding cognition. However, more recent evidence has shown that all or none firing is uncommon within brain itself; and the cortical neurons may use variable coding.

Alliance: See therapeutic alliance, working alliance.

Alloplasty: Adaptation to stress by attempting to change the environment. See also autoplasty. Term was introduced by F. Alexander (1930).

Allport's group relation theory: Gordon W. Allport's theory that a person's behaviour is influenced by his personality and his need to conform to social forces. It illustrates the inter-relationship between group therapy and social psychology. For example, dealing with bigotry in a therapy group enhances the opportunity for therapeutic experiences because it challenges the individual patient's need to conform to earlier social determinants or to hold on to familiar but restrictive aspects of his personality.

Alpha male: A term used in ethology to describe a top-ranking or dominant male in a social group. See dominance hierarchy.

Alternating role: Pattern characterized by patiodic switching from one type of behaviour to another.

Altruism: Regard for an dedication to the welfare of others. The term was originated by August Comte (1798–1857), a French philosopher. In psychiatry, the term is closely linked with ethics and morals. Freud recognized altruism as the only basis for the development of community interest. Bleuler equated it with morality. There is dispute about whether truly altruistic behaviour ever occurs.

Alzheimer's disease: Presenile dementia; a chronic organic mental disorder of unknown cause characterized by progressive mental deterioration secondary to diffuse cerebral atrophy.

Ambiguous: Having more than one possible meaning. An ambiguous stimulus is one which can be interpreted in more than one way.

Ambitendence: A psychomotor disturbance characterized by an ambivalence towards a voluntary action, leading to contradictory behaviour; most frequently seen in catatonic schizophrenia.

Ambivalence: Presence of strong and often overwhelming simultaneous contrasting attitudes, ideas, feelings, and drives towards an object, person or goal. The term was coined by Eugen Bleuler, who differentiated three types—affective ambivalence, intellectual ambivalence and ambivalence of the will.

Ambivert: A person who has achieved a balance between extreme introversion and extreme extroversion as described by Eysenck.

Ambulatory schizophrenia: Schizophrenic mental illness that is sufficiently well compensated to so as not to require continuous hospitalization.

Amentia: Lack of intellectual development, as a result of inadequate brain tissue. In German speaking countries, it means a subacute delirious state while in U.K. a mental defect.

Ameslan: A standardized sign language used by deaf and dumb people in America. Several primate studies have involved the teaching of Ameslan to gorillas or chimpanzees, with a degree of success.

Ames room: A well-known visual illusion in which a room is constructed which when viewed from a particular viewing point, appears to be normal, but which in reality has one corner very much farther away from the viewer than the other. The appearance of equal distance is achieved by carefully balancing the perspectives of the room and the levels of the floor and ceiling. The effect is that people or objects of the same size appears to be of different sizes.

Amimia: A disorder of language characterized by an inability to gesticulate or to understand the significance of gestures. See also speech disturbances and learning disabilities.

Amnesia: Pathologic loss of memory; a phenomenon in which an area of experience becomes in accessible to conscious recall. It may be organic, emotional or of mixed origin and limited to a sharply circumscribed period of time. Two types are: retrograde: loss of memory for events preceding the amnesia proper and the condition(s) presumed to be responsible for it.

Anterogade: Inability to form new memories for events following such condition(s).

Amnesia, localized: Partial loss of memory; amnesia restricted to specific or isolated experience. It is also known as lacunar amnesia.

Amnesia, neurological: (1) Auditory amnesia: Loss of ability to comprehend sounds or speech. See also Wernicke's aphasia. (2) Tactile amnesia: Loss of ability to judge the shape of objects by touch. See also Astereognosis. (3) Verbal amnesia: Loss of ability to remember words. (4) Visual amnesia: Loss of ability to recall or recognize familiar objects or printed words.

Amok: A condition, usually associated with Malayan men, consisting of a sudden unprovoked outburst of wild rage, usually resulting in homicide.

Anaclitic: Literally, leaning on in psychoanalytic terminology, dependence of the infant on the mother or mother substitute for a sense of well-being (e.g., gratification through nursing). Normal behaviour in childhood, pathologic in later years, if excessive. Freud (1914) distinguished two types of object-choice (a) Narcissistic, which occurs when a person chooses an object on the basis of some real or imagined similarity with himself (b) Anaclitic object choice occurs when the choice is based on the pattern of childhood dependence on someone unlike himself. Homosexuality is narcissistic while heterosexuality is anaclitic.

Anaclite depression: A depression caused in infants between 6 and 18 months by prolonged separation from their mothers. The term was first used by Rene Spitz, and was an important concept in early studies of maternal deprivation.

Anaclitic therapy: A form of psychotherapy characterized by allowing the patient to regress. It is used mainly in the treatment of psychosomatic disorders.

Anagram: A puzzle or problem which consists of words with their constituent letters disarranged, such that all the necessary letters are present but in the wrong order. The letters may be randomly listed (GAANMRA) or rearranged to resemble other words (A granma). Anagrams are often used in laboratory problem solving tasks.

Anal character: A personality type that manifests excessive orderliness, miserliness and obstinacy. In psychoanalysis, a pattern of behaviour in an adult that is believed to originate in the anal phase of behaviour in an adult that is believed to originate in the anal phase of infancy, between one and three years. The term is usually used to refer to reaction formations against anal erotism in particular to compulsive obstinacy, orderliness and parsimony but can refer to their opposite viz., compulsive pliancy, untidiness and generosity.

Analytic psychology: The name given by the Swiss psychoanalyst Carl Gustav Jung to his theoretical system, which minimizes the influences of sexual factors in emotional disorders and stresses mystical religious influences and a belief in the collective unconscious.

Analogue: An object or phenomenon, which correspo-nds to another in at least some respects. The term is used in (i) theories of memory referring to information stored in the brain from which a representation or image of an object can be generated; (ii) in biology for characteristics of different species which have the same functions; and (iii) in electronics for information stores through a continuously variable quantity.

Analysis: See Psychoanalysis.

Analysis by synthesis: A term given to cognitive model in which the brain is seen as combining separate pieces of information about an event in order to make the best judgement about the nature of the event.

Analysis in depth: See Psychoanalysis.

Analysis of variance (ANOVA): A widely used statis-tical procedure for determining the significance of differences obtained on an experimental variable studied under two or more conditions. Differences are commonly assigned to three aspects; the individual differences among the subjects or patients studied, group differences, however classified (e.g., by sex), and differences according to the various treatment to which they have been assigned. The method can assess both the main effects of a variable and its interaction with other variables that have been studied simultaneously.

Analysis of transference: See Psychoanalysis.

Anamnesis: A patient's medical history particularly used in connection with the patient's own recollections.

Anancasm: Repetitious or stereotyped behaviour or thought usually used as a tension relieving device.

Anankastic personality: *Synonym* for obsessive compulsive personality. See compulsive personality under personality disorders.

Androgyny: A combination of female (feminine) and male (masculine) characteristics in one person. See also Bisexuality.

Anecdotal evidence: Information quoted in support of idea or theory which has been obtained purely from everyday experience or accounts, rather than from some form of systematic or controlled study.

Anergic schizophrenic: See Burned out schizophrenia.

Anesthesia: Absence of sensation.

Angel dust: A hallucinogenic-like substance abused the active agent of which is phencyclidine.

Angst: A mental disquiet or anguish considered by existentialists to be the inevitable outcome of a full appreciation of the implications of personal responsibility and personal choice.

Anhedonia: Inability to experience pleasure from activities that usually produce pleasurable feelings, contrast with hedonism.

Anima: In Jungian psychology, a person's inner being as opposed to the character or persons presented to the world. Further, the anima may be the more feminine 'soul' or inner self of a man, the animus the more masculine soul of a woman. See also Jung.

Animism: The attribution of living qualities to inanimate objects or phenomena; and frequently the attribution of conscious awareness. Animism is a powerful trend in human thought process which has been studied mostly in the thinking of young children. It is common place in everyday speech, e.g., referring to the family car as a person. and is demonstrated extensively in the belief systems of non-technological cultures.

Anniversary reaction: An emotional response to a previous events occurring at the same time of year. Often the events involved a loss and the reaction involves a depressed state. The reaction can range from mild to severe and may occur at any time after the event.

Anomaly: A noticeable deviation from what is expected or predicted.

Anomia: Inability to recall the names of objects.

Anomie: (Gk: Nomos=Law) A term popularized by Emile Durkheim (1858–1917) as a major cause for suicide. It refers to a sense of alienation and despair resulting from the loss or weakness of previously valued norms, ideals or goals.

Anorexia nervosa: A disorder marked by a severe and prolonged refusal to eat with severe weight loss, amenorrhea or impotence, disturbances of body image, and an intense fear of becoming obese. Most frequently encountered in girls and young women. May be associated with bulimia.

Anorgasmia: The inability to achieve orgasm in the female.

Anosognosia: Unawareness or nonacceptance of a neurological deficit.

Anthropology: The study of humans in relation to distribution, origin, classification and relationship of races, physical characteristics, environmental and social relations and culture.

Anthropomorphism: The attribution of human qualities such as personality emotions and motives to animals. Darwin and Lorenz supported this concept.

Antisocial personality disorder: A disorder characterized by the inability to get along with other members of society and by repeated conflicts with individual persons and groups. Common attributes include impulsiveness, egocentricity, hedonism, low frustration tolerance, irresponsibility, inadequate conscience development, exploitation of others, and rejection of authority and discipline. See also Dyssocial behaviour.

Antlophobia: Fear of floods.

Anxiety: Unpleasurable emotional state associated with psychophysiological changes in response to an intrapsychic conflict, in contrast to fear, the danger or threat in anxiety is unreal. Physiological changes consist of increased heart rate, disturbed breathing, trembling, sweating and vasomotor changes. Psychological changes consist of an uncomfortable feeling of impending danger, an overwhelming awareness of being powerless, the inability to perceive the unreality of the threat, prolonged feeling of tension, and exhaustive readiness for the expected danger. See also basic anxiety, fear.

Anxiety disorder: A disorder in which anxiety is the most prominent disturbance or in which the patient experiences anxiety if he resists giving in to his symptoms. In DSM-IV, the anxiety disorders include phobic disorder, anxiety state, obsessive compulsive disorder, post-traumatic stress disorder, and atypical anxiety disorder. See also anxiety state. Avoidant disorder. Free floating anxiety.

Anxiety, free-floating: See free floating anxiety.

Anxiety, generalized: See free floating anxiety.

Anxiety state: A disorder characterized by panic and anxious overconcern. Somatic symptoms are often prominent. Also known as anxiety neurosis.

Anwesenheit: (German word, means 'presence') is the experience in which the subject in clear consciousness, suddenly becomes aware of the presence of another person in the immediate vicinity, although the subject may in reality be alone or in the company of others. The extra person is not seen, heard or felt. The identity is often unknown but is sometimes felt to be a relative or close friend. It may be found in bereavement, temporal lobe epilepsy, sleep disorders, psychosis and drug-induced states (such as ergot derivatives, lisuride and pergolide). It is also reported by mountain climbers, polar explorers and ship wrecked sailors during periods of prolonged stress and physical danger, develop the feeling that an extreme member is with them.

Apathy: Want of feeling or affect or interest or emotional involvement in one's surroundings. It is observed in certain type of schizophrenia and depression.

Aphagia: A lack of eating which can be experimentally induced by lesions in the lateral hypothalamus. Animals with aphagia show no interest in solid food, to the point of starvation.

Aphasia: A disturbance in language function due to organic brain disorder. The disturbance cannot be explained on the basis of a defect in sensory pathways, in motor mechanism of phonation and articulation, or in sensorium. Aphasia may be classified as receptive, expressive or mixed (global). Specific types include (1) Motor (Broca's) aphasia; difficulty in speaking, with comprehension preserved; (2) Sensory (Wernicke's) aphasia; impaired comprehension, with speech relatively fluent (3) Conduction aphasia; preserved comprehension, with speech relatively fluent but with difficulty in correlating output with input, as in reading aloud or repeating spoken words (4) Anomic aphasia; difficulty in naming objects.

Aphonia: Inability to produce normal speech sounds. May be due to either organic or psychologic causes.

Apophanous idea: A delusional idea which suddenly appears in consciousness with no previous preparation, it is known as an autochthonous or sudden delusional idea.

Apophanous mood: A strange uncanny mood state in which the patient feels that there is something happening around him, but he does not know what it is. A delusional mood.

Apophanous perception: A new significance is attributed to a perception, usually is in the sense of self-reference in the absence of any emotional or rational cause.

Apophany: A state in which one or more psychological phenomena acquire a new delusional significance, i.e., primary delusional experiences or experiences of significance are occurring.

Apparent motion: A term used to describe visual illusions which provide an appearance of movement even when no such movement is actually occurring. Examples of this are found in the *phi phenomenon*, the water fall effect, and stroboscopic stimuli.

Appeasement: A ritualized gesture (including vocalizations and scents of submission). It is commonly the opposite of threat gestures such as crouching which reduces apparent size and hides markings of sex and species.

Apperception: Awareness of the meaning and significance of a particular sensory stimulus as modified by one's own experiences, knowledge, thoughts and emotions. See also perception.

Appetitive behaviour: Behaviour which is directed towards the satisfaction of some kind of desire, want, or need.

Applied psychology: A general term used to classify areas of psychology in which general theories are put in use to deal with practical, non-laboratory situations. Applied psychology traditionally includes clinical psychology, educational psychology, industrial and occupational psychology but also includes other fields where psychological theories may be put to use such as environment psychology or study skills.

Apprehension: (1) In *colloquial terms*, a feeling of unease or dread concerning some future event (2) In cognitive terms the mental grasping or full comprehension of a concept or idea.

Approach-avoidance conflict: A pattern of behaviour often seen when an organism is inclined or required to approach something which has simultaneously attractive and aversive qualities e.g., a parachute jump. The individual tends to oscillate between approach behaviour and avoidance behaviour, with approach behaviour typically dominant when the event or stimulus is more distant in time of space, and avoidance becoming more characteristic when the event or stimulus is closer.

Apraxia: Inability to perform a voluntary purposeful motor activity. The inability cannot be explained by paralysis or sensory impairment.

Aptitude: The ease with which a person will acquire a new set of skills or abilities. An individual is said to have an aptitude for a particular skill if she learns that skill more rapidly and with more ease than other individuals with the same prior knowledge of it.

Aptitude test: A test to assess the ease with which a person will acquire specified skills, i.e., a measure of aptitude for some kind of competence. See also attainment test.

Archetypes: Classic, powerful images which, according to Carl Jung, are held in the collective unconscious and recur frequently in folk art and mythology. Examples of Jungian archetyes are: the earth mother, the sea as a symbol of rebirth, the omnipotent father, the inaccessible virgin, the knave, etc.

Arithmetical retardation: Specific disorder in which the main feature is serious impairment in the development of arithmetic skills which is not explicable in terms of general mental retardation or inadequate schooling synonyms: dyscalculia, developmental arithmetic disorder.

Arithmomania: Obsession with numbers.

Arousal: A state which the sympathetic division of the autonomic nervous system is activated producing an alarm reaction, or a longer-term response to stress. Arousal is characterized by very high levels of adrenaline in the blood stream, and results in a general state of readiness to react in the organism. Depending on cognitive and environmental factors, this may result in anger, anxiety, exhilaration excitement, or if the arousal is frequent and prolonged and the energy is not dissipated by regular demanding exercise, in long term stress disorders.

Art therapy: Treatment procedure that uses the spontaneous creative work of the patient. For example, group members make and analyze drawings, which are often expressions of their underlying emotional problems.

Articulation: (1) Clear verbal expressions (2) Free movement through the action of a joint, sometimes extended to mean the assembly of joints and levers that make such movements possible, e.g., in robotics.

Artificial Intelligence (AI): Computer systems which can 'reason', and which, it is hoped by those involved, will eventually be able to produce the same kinds of outcomes as produced by human cognitive processes. Work on artificial intelligence has tended to concentrate on: (a) knowledge-based systems, known as 'expert systems', which are capable of limited decision making on the basis of input from a number of human experts; (b) man-machine interface research, such as the development of voice recognition systems; and (c) robotics, the development of sensing and manipulation processes. See also computer stimulation.

Ascetic syndrome: A syndrome, which appears in adolescents and young adults, leading to psycho-social withdrawal, severe sexual abstinence, practice of religious austerities, lack of concern with personal appearance and considerable loss of weight (J.S. Neki 1972).

Asch effect: A term used to describe conformity arising through awareness that, if the individual stated their own judgement, they would be responding differently from the rest of the group, and that others would be aware of that dissent. Asch's studies of conformity involves a subject members had been primed to give obviously wrong answers to a relatively simple problem and the real subject had to answer openly, after the majority had answered.

Asch, Solomon Eliot: Born in 1907, in Warsaw, His work has been seminal in the study of both conformity and impression formation. In both areas he has been concerned with how people make sense of information they receive. Apart from halo effects (a tendency for individual's judgements to be all in a favourable or all in an unfavourable direction), they also found the people were influenced by reports of the opinions of a large number of people, or the country's leading psychologists. See Asch effect.

Asneezia: It signifies absence of sneezing or inability to sneeze, was described as a hitherto unrecognized psychiatric symptom (Shukla, G.D., 1985). The patients tended to be older, poorer and poorly educated. The common psychiatric causes may be schizophrenia, endogenous depression, neurotic depression, hypochondriasis etc.

Asociality: An indifference to social values or customs, withdrawal from society, as seen in a recluse or a regressed schizophrenic.

Aspiration level: In a brilliant series of studies inspired by Lewin, Dembo and Hoppe conducted some of the first experimental studies in human motivation. This believes that the experience of success and failure depends upon the person's aspirations than on some objective standard of performance.

Assertivenes training: A procedure in which subjects are taught appropriate interpersonal responses involving frank, honest, and direct expression of feelings, both positive and negative.

Assimilation: One of two processes by which a schema in Piagetian theory is considered to develop. New information is said to have been assimilated when it fitted into existing schema and so can be understood in relation to earlier learning. Assimilation and accommodation are considered to be continuous cognitive processes, contributing to the generalized process of adaptation. See also equilibration.

Association: The linking of one thing with another in sequence. Associative learning which has been acquired as a result of the connection of a stimulus with a response.

Assortive mating: The tendency for organisms (including humans) to select as sexual partners those with characteristic similar to their own.

Assumption: An idea or set of ideas which is taken for granted in the formulation of an argument or theory.

Astasia-abasia: Incoordination in the erect position, and a resulting inability to stand or walk, with intact capacity for leg movements while sitting or lying down. In the absence of an organic lesion to the central nervous system, astesia-abasia is usually a manifestation of hysteria. Astasia, however can be a sign of organic cerebral pathology, especially involving the frontal lobes or corpus callosum.

Asthenic personality: A disorder characterized by lack of enthusiasm, fatigability, lack of capacity for enjoyment, and low tolerance for stress. Term omitted from DSM-III. See also Adynamia, Anhedonia.

Asyndesis: A disorder of language commonly seen in schizophrenia in which the patient combines unconnected ideas and images.

Ataque or Puerto Rican syndrome: Often characterized by anxiety, hyperventilation, and pseudoepileptic movements. There may also be hallucinations, screaming, some violence to others or the self, and mutism. Generally the episode is self-limited and may last only minutes. At other times, it is severe and extends to a few days, thereby causing difficulty in differentiating from acute schizophrenic episode or atypical psychosis.

Attachment: A close, emotionally meaningful relationship between two people in which each seeks closeness with the other and feels more secure in their presence. The attachment between mother and infant has been extensively studied and some writers apply the term only to the relationship of the infant to the mother. Attachment has been the subject of much research by John Bowlby. There is now much evidence that the quality of attachments in infancy affects exploration and play in the short term, and a wide range cognitive and social functions throughout childhood. However, it is no longer believed that infant always forms a major attachment exclusively to the mother. See also imprinting, monotropy.

Attachment disorder of infancy: The absence or disruption of behaviours that serve to anchor the infant to his mother and which produce abnormal reactions in the infants's behaviour.

Attachment learning: The theory that the presence of whom we are emotionally attached has a special effect on how we learn, especially in infancy.

Attainment test: A test designed to assess the knowledge and skills which an individual has obtained, either through experience or through following a prescribed course of training. See also aptitude test.

Attention: Concentration, the aspect of consciousness that relates to the amount of effort exerted in focusing on certain aspect of an experience activity or task.

Attention deficit disorder: A DSM-III category for a childhood mental disorder characterized by developmentally inappropriate short attention span and poor concentration. Hyperactivity (hyperkinesis) may or not be present. The category subsumes abnormal behaviour patterns that had been referred to be a variety of name including hyperactive child syndrome, strauss syndrome, and minimal brain dysfunction. See also Hyperactivity, Minimal brain dysfunction.

Attenuation: (1) The shortening or limiting of an object or event (2) A term used by Triesman to refer to the weakening of a signal being processed, as an essential part of a model of selective attention.

Attitude: A 'mental set' held by an individual which affects the ways that person responds to events and organizes his cognitions. Attitudes are commonly held to have three essential components or dimensions: a *cognitive dimension*, involving the beliefs and rationalizations which explains the holding of the attitude; *an affective dimension*, involving the emotional aspects of the attitude; such as likes dislikes, feelings of distaste, or affection and a conative, or behavioural dimension which involves the extent to which the individual is prepared to act on the attitude that he hold. See also prejudice, stereotype.

Attraction: (1) In general usage (e.g., Berschied and Walster 1978) it refers to a positive inner attitude felt by one person towards another (2) According to Byrne (1971) attraction refers specifically to the linking expressed by a subject for a stranger (3) Attraction also used to indicate growth of linking during acquaintance (4) It refers to the whole area of research into personal liking and hence to a variety of different forms of relationships (e.g., friendship, courtship and marriage) without concern for their possible differences in form, intensity and expressive nature of liking.

Attribution: The process by which an event or the behaviour of a person is understood in terms of suggested motives or influences. The judgement that a person or an event has a particular characteristic or quality.

Attributional error: The universal tendency to see one's own behaviour (particularly when it has undesirable consequences) as a rational response to the situation and other people's behaviour as originating in their characters. So, when I crash the car it is because of poor visibility and an icy road; but I attribute my friend's crash to the fact that he is careless and impatient. This is also known as the fundamental attribution error.

Attributional style: The theory that individuals tend to believe in particular kinds of causes for a wide range of effects. Styles may vary in the extent to which they incline towards stable causes (ones which are unlikely to change in the future), global causes (affecting lots of things) and internal external causes (such as character situation). So of two people who have failed an exam, one may attribute the cause to the room being noisy (unstable, specific and external), while the other may believe it is due to their being stupid (stable, global and internal). Martin Seligman believes that individuals who incline towards using a stable, global and internal pattern of attributions may become vulnerable to depression.

Attributional theory: An extensive and growing area of social psychology dealing with the ways that people attempt to account for their own and other people's behaviour. It is most concerned with the kinds of causes by which people come to account for their experiences-attributions about negative life events are considered to be particularly important. Although attribution theory has been used to improve and extend helplessness theory and is extensively used in cognition therapy strictly, attribution theory deals with how people come to have their beliefs about the causes of events and behaviour, while attributional theory deals with the different forms (or attributional styles) that such beliefs may take. See also Distinctiveness.

Atypical: A term throughout DSM as an adjective to describe unusual or uncharacteristic variations of different mental disorders. Included are atypical organic mental disorder, atypical psychosis, atypical anxiety disorder, atypical somatoform disorder, atypical dissociative disorder, atypical gender identity disorder, atypical paraphilia, atypical para noid disorder, atypical psychosexual dysfunction, atypical fictitious disorder with physical symptoms, atypical impulse control disorder, adjustment disorder with atypical features, atypical personality disorder, atypical conduct disorder, atypical eating disorder, atypical tic disorder, atypical stereotyped movements disorder and atypical developmental disorder.

Atypical child: A term describing a child with distorted personality development; often used in connection with brain-damaged or autistic children.

Atypical paranoid disorder: The DSM-III term for alcohol paranoid state. See also Alcohol paranoid state.

Authenticity: Quality of being authentic, real and valid in psychological functioning and personality, it applies to the conscious feelings, perceptions and thoughts that a person expresses and communicates. It does not apply to the deeper unconscious layers of the personality.

Authoritarian personality: A specific, rigid pattern of personality characterized by punitive approaches to social sanctions and high levels of prejudice towards outgroup members. Adorno showed that the cognitive styles of highly prejudiced right wing conservative had two distinctive traits (1) Rigidity—maintaining a belief system even in the face of direct evidence showing that it is untrue or inefficient; and (2) Intolerance of ambiguity – a tendency takes sides quickly and to be unable to cope with equivocal positions. Adorono concluded that this was due to defense mechanisms; highly prejudiced individuals had to protect themselves against ambiguities which might challenge their ideas. Also, they had often been brought up by cold and highly authoritarian parents producing a reaction formation; the child would displace its aggression towards authority figures onto minority groups in society. Adorno developed the F-scale (F for fascism), which measured authoritarianism through nine sub-traits. These were (1) Conventionalism (2) Authoritarian submissiveness (3) Authoritarian aggression (hostility towards those who challenge authority.)

Authoritative: A term used by *Baumrind* to describe a style of parenting or child rearing in which children are encouraged to participate in decision-making and to express their opinions, but the parent nonetheless has the final authority. This was in contrast with an authoritarian approach, in which the child is not encouraged to express an opinion; or a laissez faire approach in which the parent has little involvement in the process of decision-making.

Authority figure: A real or projected person in a position of power transferentially a projected parent.

Authority principle: The idea that each member of an organizational hierarchy tries to comply with the presumed or fantasized wishes of those above him while those below him try to comply with his wishes.

Autistic thinking: A form of thinking in which the thoughts are largely narcissistic and egocentric, with emphasis on subjectivity, rather than objectivity and without regard for reality the term is used interchangeably with autism and derelism. See also infantile autism, narcissism.

Autism: (1) Thought and fantasy determined entirely by the person's needs and wishes and not constrained by reality in any way. Daydreams are autistic, but the term is usually reserved for the more extreme and permanent removal from reality of schizophrenic thoughts. (2) A serious disorder appearing towards the end of infancy, in which the child withdraws from all social contact, which seems to be aversive and distressing. Activity is directed towards inanimate objects and may give evidence of quite high intelligence, but speech is usually minimal. Although it is often called infantile autism, or childhood autism, the condition can persist throughout the person's life. There is little agreement about cause, although a majority of those who work in the area probably believe in an organic predisposition and even less agreement about treatment. See also infantile autism.

Autochthonous: A term used to describe a state arising primarily from events within the individual – such as thirst, or hunger.

Autoerotism: A term used to onset without the participation of another person. The term, introduced by *Havelock Ellis* is at present used interchangeably with masturbation. It is also called autoeroticism. In psychoanalysis, autoerotism is considered a primitive phase in object relationship development preceding the narcissistic stage. In narcissism there is a love object in autoerotism.

Auto-erotism, erotic: Refer either to pleasurable activity in which the self is used as an object (e.g., Masturbation, Thumb sucking) or to a libidinal attitude, orientation or stage of development. In the former case, the words are being used objectively to describe observable behaviour, in the latter they are being used inferentially to describe a hypothesis about the patient's or infant's disregard of external object. According to classical instinct theory infants are autoerotically oriented i.e., their attitude towards their mother is based solely on self-love and their need for her is based on her capacity to provide them with gratification. When used is this sense autoerotic is synonymous with narcissistic (see Narcissism.) object theory is opposed to the idea of an autoerotic phase in infancy and takes the view that the infant is mother-related from the very beginning, that to quote Fairbairn (1952) the infant is object-seeking not pleasure seeking. According to this view autoerotic behaviour is substitutive, the subject using a part of himself as a symbolic equivalent of someone else.

Autogenic: Originating from the self; self-initiated e.g., autogenic training in which the individual is training to have internal control of their own relaxation.

Autohypnosis: Hypnosis which has been self-induced. Many forms of hypnotherapy concentrate on the development of the individual's own skills in autohypnosis, so that they can develop strategies for coping with stressful events.

Autokinetic effect: A visual illusion involving the apparent motion of a stationary dot of light, when it is perceived in a totally dark environment. The light appears to move in rapid jerks.

Automatic obedience: The phenomenon of undue compliance with instruction, a feature of command automatism associated with catatonic syndromes and the hypnotic state.

Automatic writing: Writing that is performed without conscious awareness by the writer. It is usually elicited under hypnosis, but it can be produced by sitting undisturbed for a long period and writing continuously with no attempt to control what is produced. After several hours the product may, or may not, give an uncensored glimpse into the unconscious.

Automatism: Automatic and apparently undirected non-purposive behaviour that is not consciously controlled. Seen in the psychomotor epilepsy.

Automysophobia: Fear of smelling bad or of being unclean.

Autonomous dysthymia: A depressive illness in which the mood is qualitatively changed and in which early morning awakening, diurnal mood variation, and overvalued or delusional ideas associated with the parent's basic worries usually occur. The illness may or may not be some external, but once it begins its course is relatively independent of the causal event and the environment.

Autonomous morality: The third of Kohlberg's three stages of moral development, in which the individual is considered to have reached a point where she arrives at moral judgements and decisions on the basis of her own reasoning, rather than simply by accepting the ideas laid down by society. In the first level of this stage, the individual accepts social rules and moral codes because she consideres them to have been democratically established for the common good; in the second level a more individual judgement is achieved and the person may eventually come to reject some commonly accepted social values which she feels to be unjust or immoral.

Autonomy: A state of independence and self-determination in the individual, considered to be the ultimate goal of humanistic and existentialist therapies.

Autoplasty: Adaptation to stress by changing intra-psychic processes. See also Alloplasty.

Auxilliary ego: In psychodrama, a person, usually a member of the staff, trained to act out different roles during a psychodramatic session to intensify the therapeutic situation. The trained auxiliary ego may represent an important figure in the patient's life. He may express the patient's unconscious wishes and attitudes or portray his unacceptable self. He may represent a delusion, hallucination, symbol, ideal, animal or object that makes the patient's psychodramatic world real, concrete and tangible.

Auxiliary therapist: Co-therapist. See also Co-therapy.

Average: A central value in a frequency distribution around which other values are distributed . Three kinds of averages are the mode, the median and the mean.

Aversive therapy: A form of behaviour therapy that involves the repeated coupling of an unpleasant or painful stimulus, such as an electric shock, with an undesirable behaviour pattern in an effort to eliminate the undesirable behaviour. It is also known as aversive conditioning.

Avoidance learning: The training of behaviour through a process of negative reinforcement, such that an aversive stimulus fails to take place in the behaviour is demonstrated. Avoidance learning is extremely resistant to extinction.

Avoidant disorder: In DSM-III, a term was used for a disorder of childhood or adolescence characterized by a persistent or excessive shrinking from strangers. In DSM-II, this condition was called withdrawing reaction.

Avoidant personality disorder: A personality disorder characterized by low self-esteem, hypersensitivity to rejection, and social withdrawal but a desire for affection and acceptance.

Awareness: A subjective state of being alert or conscious; cognizant of information received from the immediate environment.

Aypnia: Insomnia; inability to sleep.

B

Babbling: Vocalizations produced by infants, which include the full range of human phonemes. In verbal behaviour, Skinner argued that language acquisition occurred as a result of behaviour shaping, with infant babbling as the operants, conditioned through the *law of effect*.

Baby talk: The style of speech adopted by adults when talking to a baby, also called 'motherese'.

Backward conditioning: A variant of classical conditioning in which the *unconditioned stimulus* (UCS) precedes the *conditioned stimulus* (CS). There is not yet agreement over whether backward conditioning is possible. If it can occur, it is certainly difficult to achieve. See also trace conditioning, simultaneous conditioning, delayed conditioning.

Bad: When qualifying Object? Breast, Penis, Mother, Father, this referees to one of the two images or object-representations formed by splitting of the internalized object, breast etc. Bad in this context is omnibus word embracing 'frustrating', 'hateful', 'malevolent', persecuting,'. It is sometimes printed 'bad' in quotes.

Bad trip: A colloquialism for an acute panic reaction occurring is an unwanted adverse effect of hallucinogenic drugs, usually characterized by fear of death and of insanity and by various other abnormal experiences. e.g., distortions of body image, or sensations of breathlessness or paralysis. The reaction is extremely unpleasant but usually short lived and varies in intensity, occasionally leading to accidents and suicide attempts. See also: hallucinogens abuse.

Balance therapy: A theory put forward by Helder, suggesting that we need to maintain a state of cognitive equilibrium between the different attitudes that we hold, and that our social cognitions would, if necessary, become modified in order to create or perpetuate such a balance. Cognitive dissonance is a later variant of the theory.

Balanced design: An experimental design in which sources of variation such as practice, fatigue or sex of subjects are balanced so that they will not be responsible for differences between the groups. See ABBA.

Balanced scale: A test or questionnaire in which sources of basis in the items are counterbalanced. For example half of the items should be true and half false, so that any tendency to prefer to answer 'yes' does not distort the outcome.

Bandura, Albert: Born in 1925 in Alberta, Canada. He contributed by studying the 'causes of aggression' 'social learning theory'. 'Observational learning' 'modeling' 'self-efficacy' and 'self-inefficacy'.

Bandwagon effect: The tendency that all people have to believe a claim or hold an attitude if they believe that most other members of their group have that belief.

Barnum effect: An effect named after the circus entrepreneur, T.P. Barnum, whose motto in dealing with the gullible public was 'there' a fool born every minute'. Used to describe the widespread acceptance of certain common beliefs, e.g., astrological predictions which are written in such general terms that they can be readily applied to anyone, but which are read by the credulous as being an exact description of their own individual character or circumstance. In cognitive terms, if refers to the tendency for people to engage in selective perception, noticing only what they wish to believe and ignoring that which does not accord with their expectations.

Basal age: On tests graded by age, the highest age level up to which all of the items are passed. May be called 'basal mental age' in intelligence testing.

Baseline: A stable and reliable level of performance that can be used as a basis for assessing changes in behaviour caused by the introduction of an independent variable.

Basic anxiety: As conceptualized by Karen Horney the main spring from which neurotic trends get their intensity and pervasiveness. Basic anxiety is characterized by vague feelings of loneliness, helplessness, and fear of a potentially hostile world. See also Anxiety, Fear.

Basic fault: Term used by Balint (1952) to describe an aspect of the pathology of a certain type of patient whose whole development has been faulty and false. According to Balint, the basic fault can only be overcome if the patient is allowed to regress to a state of oral dependence on the analyst (see also oral) and experience a new beginning. The metaphor is presumably geological not moral.

Basic needs: The most compelling human needs such as food and the avoidance of pain. In Maslow's theory are at the base of a hierarchy of needs and other requirements, even for physical safety, will be ignored until they are satisfied.

Basic rule: The basic of fundamental rule of psychoanalysis governs the patient and not the analyst and is the injection that he do his best to tell the analyst whatever comes into his mind without reservation. The rule is a counsel of perfection, Resistance and Defence manifestating themselves clinically by failures to carry it out. See Free Association.

Basic trust: The development in an infant of total trust that the mother will provide for, protect and not harm the infant. It is the first of Erikson's eight stages of man, and is proposed as the most important task that the infant must complete. It is achieved as a result of the security provided by good mothering.

Bateson, Gregory (1904–1980): His studies on the processes of communication in mental disorder are fundamental. He also applied his anthropological expertise to psychiatry.

Battered baby: A term coined by C. Henry Kempe in 1962 in a paper which first alerted the medical profession to the widespread existence of infant who had been injured by their parents. See also child abuse.

Bayley infant development scales: Measures of infant development which assess infants (2–30 months) on mental and motor tasks. First development in the 1920s based on the work of Gesell, but still the most widely used infant assessment. The norms are based on normal infant and rely heavily on the ability of the infant to perform motor tasks, but the scale is now used almost exclusively to test children with motor impairments.

Beard, George M. (1839–1883): American psychiatrist who in 1869 introduced the term 'neurasthenia'.

Beers, Clifford W. (1876–1943): Author of "A Mind That Found itself" (1909) the book that is generally considered to have founded the mental hygiene movement, now the National Mental Health Association.

Behaviour: The movements or actions which a person or animal performs. If something is referred to as 'behaviour' it means that it is only concerned with actual behaviour, and not, for instance, with any cognitive aspects of a performance.

Behaviour, adaptive: Any behaviour that increases an organism's ability to adjust to a specific environment or situation.

Behaviour disorder: A general term used to cover a wide range of psychological disorders in which the behaviour of the person is the major concern. More specifically it applies to conditions such as psychopathy, addictions and hyperactivity. One feature of behaviour disorders is that they usually involve symptoms which are likely to bring the sufferer into conflict with society.

Behaviour genetics: The study of the ways in which an individual's genetic constitution contributes to the determination of behaviour.

Behaviour therapy/behaviour modification: Methods developed to alleviate psychological disorders which focus on changing behavioural problems by using techniques of classical conditioning, instrumental conditioning, operant conditioning and observational learning.

Behavioural assessment: An approach to the study of personality based on the direct observation of behaviour and the conditions under which certain behaviour occur.

Behavioural medicine: Psychological treatments designed to help people cope with physical health problems.

Behavioural perspective: A current viewpoint in psychology which has its roots in the older school of behaviourism; the emphasis is on the description, control and understanding of what people and animals do – their behaviour.

Behavioural ritualistic: Automatic behaviour of cultural or psychogenic origin.

Behaviour science: A scientific discipline dealing with any aspect of human behaviour, including interpersonal relationship, development, view and values experiences and activities. The behavioural sciences include sociology, psychology, anthropology and ethology.

Behaviour shaping: The production of novel behaviours through the systematic adjustment of reinforcement contingencies. In other words, by rewarding simple behaviours until they are established in the organism's repertoire of actions, and then rewarding only those variants of it which produce behaviour which is even closer to the desired outcome. Once that intern is established as a frequent behaviour pattern, only behaviour which is even closer to the desired outcome will be rewarded.

Behaviour therapy: (a) A psychiatric treatment modality that focuses on overt and objectively observable behaviour and uses various conditioning techniques derived form learning theory to modify the patient's behaviour directly. Behaviour therapy aims exclusively at symptomatic improvement, without addressing psychodynamic cauzation. A major worker in the field was Joseph Wolpe, who developed and popularized the technique of systematic desensitization. See also Assertiveness training, Aversive therapy, Behaviourism, Conditioning, Flooding, Implosion, Reciprocal inhibition and desensitization, shaping, symptoms substitution, systematic desensitization (b) Behaviourism: The school of psychological thought founded by John B. Waston in 1913 that regards only measurable and observable behaviour as the appropriate subject matter for human psychology. It holds that human behaviour can be described in terms of lawful principles that do not require consideration of unobservable mental events, such as ideas and emotions. See also behaviour therapy.

Beliefs: Cognitions, or thoughts, about the characteristics of objects.

Belle Indifference: Psychiatric diagnostic term describing the indifference with which Hysterical patients often seem to view conversion symptoms (see conversion hysteria) which should, on the face of it, be extremely distressing.

Bell's Mania: Acute delirious mania; probably a severe attack of mania with delirium due to exhaustion, malnutrition, drugs or intercurrent infection.

Belongingness and love needs: Needs for affection, affiliation and identification. In *Maslaw's theory* they are fulfilled after physiological and safety needs are satisfied.

Bender: Alcoholic jargon for a period of continuous drinking which lasts for a few days and stops because of money or physical exhaustion.

Bender Gestalt Test: A psychological test that measures the subject's ability to reproduce a set of geometric designs. It is useful for measuring vasomotor coordination and thus for detecting brain damage.

Bender, Lauretta (1897–1985): American psychiatrist who has done extensive work in the fields of child psychiatry, neurology and psychology.

Bereavement: Feeling of grief or desolation, especially at the death or loss of a loved one.

Berne, Eric (1910–1970): American psychiatrist who founded transactional analysis, which is used in both individual and group therapy. See also Ego state, Transaction, Transactional analysis.

Bestiality: Sexual deviation in which a person engages in sexual relations with an animal. See also Zoophilia.

Between group variance: A measure of the variation found among the means of a number of samples. The measure is divided by the within groups variance to give an F-ratio. These measures are usually computed within an analysis of variance. See also variance.

Biased sample: An error in the way that a particular sample has been selected, which results in that sample not being representative of the population as whole.

Biblioclast: One who destroys or mutilates books.

Bilingualism: The individuals who possess sufficient skills in a second language to permit a significant part of their social and/or intellectual activities to be conducted through the medium of the language. An important field of research is that of bilingualism in children, in particular how they affect their general learning capacities.

Biodynamics: System of psychoanalytic psychiatry introduced by J.H. Masserman.

Biofeedback: Provision of information to a subject regarding one or more of his physiological processes in the effort to enable the subject to gain some element of voluntary control over bodily functions that normally operate outside consciousness. See also Learned automatic control.

Biological clock: The idea that organisms contain a mechanism which maintains a fairly constant rate and which is responsible for controlling biological rhythms such as the sleep wake cycle. See biorhythm, circadian rhythm.

Biological determinism: The argument that human nature or human characteristics arise an inevitable consequence of human biological characteristics (See also reductionism).

Biological perspective: A current viewpoint in psychology in which the aim is to relate behaviour to functions of the body, the nervous and gendular systems in particular.

Biological rhythm: Periodic variation in physiological functions. A circadian rhythm shows a periodicity of about 24 hours. An ultradian rhythm has a cycle shorter than 1 day. An infradian rhythm is longer than 1 day.

Biopsychology: The study of the biological sources of individual functioning. The term usually has a slightly different emphasis at psychobiology but there is no universally agreed meaning for either lable.

Bipolar affective disorder: An effective disorder in which the patient exhibits both manic and depressive episodes.

Birth cry: A reflex cry which signals the start of breathing immediately after birth. It is possible for breathing to start without a birth cry.

Birth trauma: An attempt to explain psychological disturbance as resulting from the trauma of being born. Proposed by Otto Rank in the early days of psychoanalysis but was largely abandoned. Revived more recently in relation to concern about the technological nature of current methods of managing birth.

Bisexuality: Existence of the qualities of both sexes in the same person. Freud postulated that biologically and psychologically the sexes differentiated from a common core the differentiation between the two sexes was relative, rather than absolute and that regression to the common core occurs to varying digress in both normal and abnormal conditions. An adult person who engages in bisexual behaviour is one who is sexually attracted to and has sexual contact with members of both sexes. He is also known in lay terms as an AC-DC person. See also Androgyny, Heterosexuality, Homosexuality. Latent Homosexuality, Overt homosexuality.

Biswanger, Otto: (1852–1929) German neurologist and psychiatrist; originated concept of presenile dementia.

Bit: A term used in information theory to define a unit of information. A bit of information is not a vague amount but is precisely defined as the amount requires to choose between two equal alternatives; it halves the uncertainly. So if you were searching for a randomly chosen word in this dictionary. One bit would tell you which half it was in two bits would narrow it to a quarter and three bits to an eighth. Twelve bits would identify a specific word out of 4096. The word 'bit' is an abbreviation of 'binary digit'.

Black box: A term used to describe an approach to psychological theory in which the internal workings of the organism are regarded as unknowable, as if they take place inside a black box. One is left with the options of either (1) guessing what is going on in the box by observing the relationships between inputs to the box and its consequent behaviour, or (2) claiming that it is not important to know that goes on in the box, and that only the relationships between input and behaviour should be studied. The second approach was the one chosen by the behaviourists.

Blackout: In Britain, this word usually means a loss of consciousness or a loss of memory. As a technical term, it designates a loss of memory occurring after a few drinks of hard liquor, not sufficient to produce drunkenness. This marks the onset of the prodromal stage of alcohol dependence and is also known as a 'palimpsest'.

Black patch syndrome: A psychosis induced by sensory deprivation as a result of eye patches used after cataract surgery.

Blank screen: Neutral blackdrop on which the patient projects a gamut of transferential irrationalities. The passivity of the analyst allows him to act as a blank screen.

Bleuler, Eugen (1857–1939): Swiss psychiatrist known for his important studies in schizophrenia, which term he preferred over the earlier term dementia praecox. See also Affect, blunted; Altruism, Ambivalence; schizophrenia.

Blind spot: In psychiatry as area of a person's personality of which he is totally unaware. The unperceived areas are repressed, since their recognition would arouse painful or unpleasant emotions. In the course of group of individual psychotherapy, such blind spots often appear obliquely as projected ideas, intentions and emotions. See also projection, Scotoma.

Blocking: Interruption of a train of speech before a thought or idea has been completed. After a period of silence, which may last from a few seconds to minutes the person indicates that he or she cannot recall what he or she has been saying or meant to say. Blocking should be judged to be present only if the person spontaneously describes losing his or her thought or if upon questioning by the interviewer, the person gives that as the reason for pausing.

Blood brain barrier: An interface of the capillaries supplying blood to the brain with certain types of glial cells, namely astrocytes. This is a mechanism which interferes with or selectively prevents certain types of chemicals borne in the circulatory system from entering the brain. In general lipid soluble chemicals cross this barrier more readily than do water soluble substances.

Blunted affect: See Affect, blunted.

Body centered therapy: A relatively new term referring to a host of therapies whose common goal is the altering of self-image or personality through work with the physical body, either exclusively or as a major component of the therapy. The common therapies are bioenergetics (*Rolfing*), Feldenkrais method. Body centered psychotherapy (*Hakoni method*), Psychomotor therapy (Albert Pesos), Lomi work (Robert Hall et al.), the Alexander technique (Alexander, F.M.) also, related peripherally are dance and movement therapies and the traditional approaches like *Hatha Yoga* and such oriental martial art as *Tai Chi Ackado* and *Tai Kwando Body contact exploration maneuver:* See Rough manuscript.

Body contact exploration maneuver: Any physical touching of another person for the purpose of becoming more aware of the sensations and emotions aroused by the experience. The tech- nique is used mainly in encounter groups.

Body image: The idea that individual has of what their body is like. There is evidence of a physiological basis for a body image at birth, but an infant must learn which parts of the universe are not part of its own body. Later the body image extends beyond a representation of the body and comes to reflect an evaluation of bodily characteristics. The normal pattern is to overestimate such characteristics as head size and attractiveness. The body image is an important part of the self image.

Body language: A general term used to describe those aspects of non-verbal communication (NVC) which involve direct use of the body, such as gesture, posture and proxemics.

Body schema: The body schema is the internal representation which the individual has of his own body. According to Piaget, the very first schemes formed by the infant develops from the first 'me-not me' distinction. For the older person it includes ideas and memories of how the body is, has been and could be.

Bonding: The attachment and unity of two people whose identities are significantly affected by their mutual interactions. Bonding often refers to the attachment between mother and her child.

Bonhoeffer, Kart: (1868–1949) Berlin psychiatrist; symptomatic (organic) psychoses, acute exogenous reaction. *Bonhoeffer's sign* is the loss of normal muscle tone in chorea.

Borderline mental retardation: A condition in which the patient has an I.Q. of 70 to 80. See also Mental retardation.

Borderline personality disorder: A personality disorder classified in DSM marked by instability in various areas.

Borderline state: A state in which the symptoms are so unclear or transient that it is difficult to classify the patient as psychotic or nonpsychotic. It is also known as borderline psychosis.

Boredom: The emotion that ensues when an individual fails to find interests and activities which fully engage him. It may arise either as a external result of external limitations, e.g., solitary confinement, sensory deprivation, or monotonous work, as a result of internal inhibition. According to Fenichel (1954), neurotic boredom is a state of instinctual tension (See also instinct) in which the instinctual aim is missing. As a result the bored person seeks an object 'not in order to act upon it with his instinctual aim which he lacks'. He knows he wants something but does not know what it is hence the irritability and restlessness inseparable from boredom and absent in Apathy.

Bottomup processing: Perceptual processing which is initiated by the characteristics of the stimulus and leads on to higher forms of cognitive activity, as opposed to top down processing which begins from the higher levels.

Bouquet de maladies: The distinctive odour said to be characteristic of psychiatric patient.

Bovarism: Failure to differentiate phantasy and reality.

Bovina fames: (L. "oxlikehunger") Bulimia.

Bradykinesia: Slowness of motor activity with a decrease in normal spontaneous movement.

Bradylalia: Abnormally slow speech, common in depression.

Bradylexia: Inability to read at normal speed.

Brain: A general term to describe the complex of neural structures developed at the forward end of the spinal cord. In casual usage however, many psychologists refer to the brain when in fact they mean the cerebrum, or the cerebral cortex (e.g., split brain studies). Whether the whole brain or simply the cerebrum is meant must be deduced from the context.

Brain electrical activity mapping (BEAM): Computer enhanced analysis and display of electro-encephalographic and evoked response studies, a stimulus (e.g., flashing light) is presented to the patient and the responses are recorded electrically from scalp electrodes. Computers translate the information into a topographic, coloured display of electrical activity over the surface of the brain. Useful in diagnosing seizure disorder and seems to be helpful in looking at a typical psychiatric presentation. See also brain imaging.

Brain imaging: Any technique that permits the in-vivo visualization of the substance of the central nervous system. The best known of such techniques is computerized axial tomography (CT), commonly called the CAT scan. However, two newer methods of brain imaging, positron emission tomography (PET) and Magnetic Resonance Imaging (MRI) also yield a series of two-dimensional images (or slices) of brain regions of interest. A number of other related techniques, such as ultrasound, angiography in its various forms, radionuclide scans, regional cerebral blood flow (RCBF) measurements, brain electrical activity maping (BEAM) and its variant and even the older pneumoencephalogram (PEG) also provide images of some aspect of the central nervous system, but are generally more limited in the structure visualized in degree or some other parameter, than CT, PET and MRI.

Brain storming: A technique for developing new ideas, commonly used in advertising work and other problem-solving situation. A group undertakes a period of intensive concentration in which any idea at that comes to mind-regardless of how apparently inappropriate it might be-is noted. There is an agreement but to reject or ridicule any suggestion. At the end of the period of time, all the ideas thus generated are examined for their potential values as a solution to the problem in hand. Some recent research indicates that groups will produce more ideas if the individuals work on their own and then pool their suggestions.

Brainwashing: The technique of operating total control over a person's environment with a consistent application of deprivation, debilitation and dread (the three Ds), so that the victim become amenable to adopting a completely new belief system or ideology. The process may depend on some form of identification. It usually refers to systematic efforts to indoctrinate non-believers.

Brain waves: Overall electrical activity of the brain which can be detected outside the skull by an electroencephalogram.

Breeder hypothesis: Given by Farris and Dunham in 1939 that low social class leads to schizophrenia.

Breuer, Josef (1842–1925): Viennese physician with wide scientific and cultural interests. His collaboration with Freud in studies of cathartic therapy was reported in studies on Hysteria (1895). He withdrew as Freud proceeded to introduce psychoanalysis, but he left important ideas on that discipline, such as the concepts of the primary and secondary processes.

Bribe: In psychoanalysis a compromise. The symptoms of a neurosis are regarded as symbolic repressed impulses.

Brief psychotherapy: A form of psychotherapy in which the sessions are limited to 10 to 15 in number and during which time attempts to modify behaviour occur. The approach is used in both individual and group settings.

Brief reactive psychosis: A DSM category for a psychosis of less than 1 week's duration with sudden onset after a major stress.

Brigham, Amariah (1798–1849): One of the original thirteen founders of the American Psychiatric Association (1844) and the founder and first editor of its official journal, now the American Journal of Psychiatry.

Brill, A.A. (1874–1948): First American analyst (1908): Freud gave him permission to translate several of his most important works. He was active in the formation of the New York in the forefront of propagators of psychoanalysis as a lecturer and writer.

Briquet's syndrome: See Somatization disorder.

Brooding compulsion: See Intellectualization.

Bruxism: Grinding of the teeth, occurs unconsciously while awake or during stage 2 sleep. May be secondary to anxiety, tension or dental problems.

Bulimia: Episodic eating binges or excessive intake of food or fluid, generally beyond voluntary control. Characteristic are self-induced vomiting and purging following eating, which is of the binge eating variety. The resulting loss of body fluids and electrolytes may lead to severe disturbance such as EKG abnormalities and tetany. Sometimes seen as a symptom in anorexia nervosa.

Fig. 1. Classification of Body Build

Burned out schizophrenic: A chronic schizophrenic who is apathetic and withdrawn, with minimal florid psychotic symptoms but with persistent and often severe schizophrenic thought processes. He is also known as an anergic schizophrenic.

Burnout: A stress reaction developing in person working in an area of unrelenting occupational demands. Symptoms include impaired work performance, fatigue, insomnia, depression, increased susceptibility to physical illness and reliance on alcohol or other drugs of abuse for temporary relief.

Burrow, Trigant L. (1875–1951): American student of Freud and Jung who coined the term *'group analysis'* and later developed a method called phyloanalysis. Much of Burrow's work was based on his social views and his opinion that individual psychotherapy places the therapist in too authoritarian a role to be therapeutic. He formed groups of patients, students and colleagues who living together in a camp, analyzed their interactions. See also consensual validation, Lifwynn foundation, Phyloanalysis, Third nervous system.

Bystander apathy: A rather moralistic label applied by social psychologists to the phenomenon that onlookers fail help in emergencies even though they may be upset by what is happening. Concern about bystander was aroused by the case of kitty Genovese who was stabbed to death in New York in 1964.

C

C.A.: Abbreviation for chronological age. See also Intelligence quotient.

Cacedemonomania: A condition in which the patient thinks he is possessed by a devil or other evil spirit.

Cacergasia: Inadequate functioning of body or mind.

Cachinnation: Inordinate laughter without apparent cause; it is common in hebephrenic schizophrenia.

Cacosomnia: Sleeplessness.

Cacothymia: Any mental affection with depravation of the morals.

Camptocormia: (Kamptos, curved, kormos, trunk) it constitutes a rare psychogenic syndrome characterized by a frontal flexion of the vertebral column with passive dropping of both arms a variable degree of genuflexion, producing a simian appearance. Unsteady gait is often found. Souques (1916) and Rosanoff-Saloff (1916) were first report the cases in French soldiers.

Cannabis: See Marihuana.

Cannon-Bard theory: A theory of emotion put forward in the 1920s in which it was stated that the psychological experience of emotion, and the physiological reactions produced by the body (see autonomic nervous system) were completely independent of one another. Compare James-Lange theory, interactionism, and see also alarm reaction.

Capgras' syndrome (delusion of doubles): Belief that a person known to the patient has been replaced by an exact double. Usually the person implicated is a close relative, particularly spouse. The common causes are functional psychiatric disorders (schizophrenia, paranoid state, affective disorders etc.) and organic illnesses (temporal lobe epilepsy, brain tumor, delirium etc.).

Cardiac neurosis: A group of cardiovascular symptoms, frequently associated with dysfunctions in other physiological systems, presenting as autonomic manifestations of an anxiety state. Common complaints like palpitations, thoracic apical pain, breathlessness, dizziness on postural change or effort, sweating and flushes and fatigue, may the underlying anxiety and panic attacks. The syndrome was first described during military campaigns in the 19th and early 20th centries and has been known under a variety of names e.g., irritable heart (Da Costa, 1871), 'effort syndrome' (Lewis, 1917) and 'neurocirculatory asthenia' (Oppenheimer, 1918) *Synonyms*: Cardiovascular neurosis: Da Costa's syndrome: effort phonia; effort syndrome; irritable heart; neurocirculatory asthenia; soldier's heart.

Care and protection proceedings: Intervention by court on behalf of a child when the parents or caretakers provide inadequately for the child's welfare.

Carebaria: Senzation of discomfort or pressure in the head.

Caregiver: Any person involved in the identification or prevention of illness or in the treatment or rehabilitation of the patient; includes the psychiatrist and other members of the traditional treatment team as well as community workers and other non-professionals.

Caretaker: A general term given to refer to the person who looks after a child thus avoiding the assumptions inherent in the use of terms like mother or parent, and allowing for a wider range of possibilities. Despite the apparent opposite, the term 'caregiver' is used with identical meaning.

Castration: Removal of the sex organs. In psychologic terms, the fantasized loss of the genitals. Also used figuratively to denote state of impotence, powerlessness, helplessness or defeat.

Castration complex: In psychoanalytic theory, a group of unconscious thoughts and motives that are referable to the fear of losing the genitals, usually as punishment for forbidden sexual desires.

Castration threat anxiety: A Freudian concept, referring to the anxiety experienced by the young boy during the Oedipus complex. As the young boy's sexual interest is directed towards his mother, and his father is perceived as a rival for the mother's love, and the child develops fear that the father (being bigger and more powerful than he) may deal with the competition by castrating him. See also phallic stage.

Catalepsy: Condition in which a person maintains the body position which he is placed. It is a symptom observed in severe cases of catatonic schizophrenia. It is also known as waxy flexibility and cerea flexibilities. See also command automatism.

Cataphasia: See Verbigeration.

Cataplexy: Temporary sudden loss of muscle tone, causing weakness and immobilization. It can be precipitated by a variety of emotional states, and it is often followed by sleep.

Catastrophic anxiety: The anxiety associated with organic mental disorders when the patient is aware of his defects in mentation. The anxiety can be overwhelming.

Catastrophic stress: A reaction to exceptionally severe physical or mental stress, characterized by a breakdown of coping behaviour, intense anxiety and shock. The term has also been applied to the state of agitation and helplessness exhibited by patients with cerebral damage when confronted with tasks beyond their competence (Goldstein, 1878–1965) See also acute reactions to stress.

Catastrophe theory: A mathematical theory which deals with changes of state which are sudden, substantial and not easily reversible. Like walking off a cliff. Many psychological phenomena look this, with examples ranging from spontaneous reversal of perception of a Necker cube, through experiences of insight (aha) to the sudden onset of a phobia. It is always difficult to record significant psychological phenomena in a form that can be entered into a mathematical equation and we do not know whether catastrophe theory will be useful to psychology.

Catathymia: A situation in which elements in the unconscious are sufficiently affect laden to produce changes in conscious functioning.

Catathymic crisis: A suddenly occurring isolated and nonrepetitive act that develops from a state of intolerable tension.

Catatonic behaviour: Marked motor anomalies, generally limited to disturbances in the context of a diagnosis of a non-organic psychotic disorder.

Catatonic excitement: Excited motor activity, apparently purposeless and not influenced by external stimuli.

Catatonic negativism: An apparently motiveless resistance to all instructions or attempts to be moved, when passive, the person may resist any effort to be moved; when active he or she may do the opposite of what is asked-for example, firmly clench jaws when asked to open mouth.

Catatonic posturing: Voluntary assumption of an inappropriate or bizarre posture, usually held for a long period of time. Example: A patient may stand with arms outstretched as if he were Jesus on the cross.

Catatonic rigidity: Maintenance of a rigid posture against all efforts to be moved.

Catatonic stupor: Marked decrease in reactivity to environment or/and reduction in spontaneous movements and activity, sometimes to the point of appearing to be unaware of one's surroundings.

Catatonic waxy flexibility: The person's limbs can be 'moulded' into any position, which is than maintained. When the limb is being moved, it feels to the examiner as if it were made of pliable wax.

Catchment area: A geographic area for which a mental health program or facility has responsibility for its residents.

Categorical Attitude: See abstract attitude.

Catharsis: Release of ideas, thoughts and represses materials from the unconscious accompanied by an affective emotional response. It is commonly observed in the course of both individual and group psychotherapy, See also Abreaction, Converzational catharsis, Repression.

Cathexis: In psychoanalysis, a conscious or unconscious investment of psychic energy in an idea, a concept, an object or a person.

Cattell Infant Intelligence Scale: Psychological test assessing general motor and cognitive development in infants aged 3 months to 2.5 years.

Causalgia: Burning pain that may be either organic or psychic in origin.

Causality: The conception that events can be explained as the necessary consequences of prior events the latter being the causes and the former the effects. Psychoanalysis is generally regarded as a causal theory, since it explains present events, symptoms, etc., in term of the prior experiences of the subject. Its habit of explaining of the present Conscious mental event in terms of the conception of causality since it is assumed that the unconscious 'cause' was there first and contains the dynamic of the past. Freud's concept of *Psychic Determinism* is based on the assumption that unconscious processes can be the cause of conscious ones, but not vice versa. Some aspects of psychoanalytical theory, notably those centering round the Interpretation of Dreams and the use of Symbols, are concerned with meaning and the grammar of unconscious thinking and not with cauzation.

Ceiling effect: An effect when a test is too easy so that all of the subjects score near the top (or ceiling) of the scale. The result is that the test is unable to distinguish between individuals who are more, or less, competent. The opposite is known as a 'floor effect'.

Censor, Censorship: In Freud's first formulations the mental agency responsible for Dream distortion and Repression was called the censor. The censor is the theoretical ancestor of the Super-ego.

Centration: A *Piagetian term* which refers to the pre-operational child's tendency to focus on one central characteristic of a problem, to the exclusion of other features. For example judging the volume of a of liquid purely by a single dimension such as height, rather than taking into account other dimensions such as width. Centration is considered by Piagetians to be a manifestation of egocentricity, which can lead to the inability to decentre and the inability to conserve number and volume.

Centripetal: In psychiatry, connoting treatment or approaches that focus on minute analysis of the psyche.

Cephalalgia: Headache, this term was included in DSM-II but was omitted from DSM-III.

Cerebral electrotherapy (CET): A treatment using low intensity pulses of direct electrical current. It is used primarily in the treatment of depression, anxiety and insomnia. Not to be confused with electroconvulsive therapy.

Cerebration: Mental activity.

Cerea flexibilitas: The waxy flexibility often present in catatonic schizophrenia in which the patient's arm or leg remains in the position in which it is placed.

Character analysis: Psychoanalytic treatment that concentrates on character defenses.

Character assassination: Term used by Leslie Farber (1967) to describe the misuse of psychoanalytical theory to disparage, character and impugn motives. This is done by either (a) interpreting behaviour in terms of Infantile motive without reference to the modifications of them produced by Sublimation, education, sophistication etc. or (b) labeling character traits by reference to whatever psychiatric condition displays them in caricature form.

Character defense: A trait of personality that serves an unconscious defensive purpose.

Character disorder: A pattern of personality characterized by maladaptive, inflexible behaviour.

Character neurosis: A psychoanalytical concept derived from a typology constructed from the interpretation of character traits as their derivations of phases of development, or the analogues of particular symptoms. Thus the former would include the hysterical or obsessional character. According to this concept, the manifestations of character neurosis are intermediate between normal character traits and neurotic symptoms (Jones, 1938). See also personality disorder.

Charcot, Jean M. (1825–1893): French neurologist noted for describing hysteria and treating it by means of hypnosis. Freud based much of his early work on Charcot's pioneer studies in hysteria.

Charles Bonnet syndrome: It was named in 1938 by Morsier, after the man who first described and later himself developed the condition. It is characterized by vivid and complex visual hallucinations that are recognized as nureal and occur in the absence of any other psychiatric symptoms. The syndrome has most frequently been described in elderly people and is commonly associated with visual impairment.

Chi Square: A statistical technique in which variables are categorized in order to determine whether a distribution of scores is due to chance or to experimental factors.

Child abuse: The significant failure of a responsiable person to care for a child appropriately. Physical injury, sometimes called non-accidental injury or NAI, was the first form to be widely recognized (see battered baby syndrome) and is still the commonest form to be reported. However it is now recognized that other forms of child abuse may be at least as common, though often they are more difficult to identify. The major forms of abuse can be grouped under the headings of physical, emotional and sexual and in each case the abuse may be active or passive. See failure to thrive and sexual abuse.

Child analysis: Application of psychoanalytic to the treatment of the child.

Childhood: Portion of a person's life span between infancy and puberty.

Childhood Psychosis, atypical: A variety of infantile psychotic disorders which may show some, but not all of the features of infantile autism. Symptoms may include stereotyped repetitive movements, hyperkinesis, self-injury, retarded speech development, echolalia and impaired social relationship. Such disorders may occur in children of any level of intelligence but are particularly common in those with mental retardation.

Childhood schizophrenia: In DSM-III, called pervasive developmental disorder. See also pervasive developmental disorder.

Child rearing styles: A generalized term used to refer to characteristic ways of handling or dealing with one's children. The 1960s saw considerable amount of research into the effects of child-rearing or parenting styles, much of which proved inconclusive.

Chronobiology: The science or study of temporal factors in life stages and disorders, such as the sleepwalking cycle, biologic clocks and rhythms, etc.

Chronophobia: Fear of time; sometimes called prison neurosis, since almost all prisoners are affected by it in some fashion. It is characterized by panic, anxiety and claustrophobia.

Chunking: The process by which according to Miller, short term memory can be extended. Miller's theory that short term memory was of limited capacity to able to deal with only 7 plus-or minus 2 items at a time. However by grouping items of information into meaningful chunk's that capacity could be extended considerably (e.g., the figures 1.0.6.6 would form four units treated separately, but just one 'chunck' if perceived as the date 1066). See also short term memory.

Circadian rhythm: A term used to describe bodily cycles that last for approximately 24 hours, e.g., of temperature and of alterness. Many individuals show pronounced circadian rhythm, becoming attuned to their daily cycle. Distruption of such cycles, such as occurs when traveling from one time-zone to another, can produce an uncomfortable period of readjustment, known as jet lag. Extensive research by Kleitman and other has investigated natural human periodicity in cue-free environments such as caves in which lighting and temperature are kept constant. Physiological correlates of diurnal rhythms (e.g., fluctuations in body temperature) and the relationship between circadian rhythms and performance have been studies in this way. Circadian rhythms are also known as diurnal rhythms when referring to functions which occur during the day, and nocturnal rhythms for night-time activities. There is controversy over whether circadian rhythms are controlled by a biological clock.

Circumstantiality: Disturbance in the associative thought and speech processes in which the patient digresses into unnecessary details and inappropriate thoughts before communicating the central idea. It is observed in schizophrenia, obsessional disturbances, and certain cases of dementia. See also Tangentiality.

Clairvoyance: The perception of objects or events which are beyond the known reach of the senses. It is a particular form of extra-sensory perception distinguished by the fact that it is practiced by medium, a person supposed to have special powers to communicate with and receive messages from distinct or dead people. Clairvoyance is classified as a branch of parapsychology.

Clang association: Association or speech directed by the sound of a word, rather than its meaning. Punning and rhyming may dominate the person's verbal behaviour. It is seen most frequently in schizophrenia or mania. Also known as clanging.

Classical concept: A term referring to the classification of human concepts following work by J.S. Bruner and others on the development of thinking. Classical concepts are those in which the identifying properties of the concept are shown by every member of that class. So, for instance, all the cards of the suit 'diamonds' in a pack will show the diamond symbol, will be rectangular, etc. By contrast, although 'having four legs' would be an identifying property of the concept tables not all members of the class would posses that property.' Tables' would therefore be a probabilistic concept rather than a classical concept.

Classical conditioning: See conditioning.

Claustrophobia: A phobic fear or avoidance of closed a simple or specific phobia.

Client-centered psychotherapy: A nondirective form of psychotherapy originated by Carl Rogers in which the therapeutic process focuses on the patient's own thinking and feeling, which the therapist merely helps to clarify through understanding and empathy. The client-centered approach was developed as a reaction against the authoritativeness and interpretation of the more traditional psychotherapies, based on a humanistic approach.

Climacteric: The menopause and postmenopausal period in woman. It is sometimes used to refer to the same age period.

Clinical interview: A method of investigation based on informal contact between the researcher and the individual(s) which he or she is studying. Use of the clinical interview technique avoids the main problem of artificiality in research, but sometimes at the cost of objectivity and reliability. It has been frequently used in psychology, for instance by Piaget in his studies of cognitive development in children.

Clinical psychologist: See psychologist, clinical.

Clinical psychology: That branch of psychology which is concerned with the use of insights and method obtained from theoretical psychology and clinical experience to assist those with problems in living, or with psychological difficulties. Over the last 25 years the profession has shifted from providing assessment as requested by psychiatrists to functioning as independent therapists. Clinical psychologists may use a range of techniques such as cognitive therapy and biofeedback. The major specialisms are defined in terms of the client groups, i.e., general adult, child, mental handicap, neurology and elderly. However, clinical psychologists are increasingly to be found in community bases or working alongside general medical practitioners and are beginning to be employed in industry.

Clouding of consciousness: Any disturbance of consciousness in which the person is not fully awake, alert and oriented.

Cluster suicides: Multiple suicides, usually among adolescents, in circumscribed period of time and area. Thought to have an element contagion.

Cocaine: Alkaloid obtained from leaves of the coca plant. It is an effective local anesthetic when applied topically. Its systemic effects include striking central nervous system stimulation, manifested by garrulousness, restlessness, excitement and feelings of increased muscular strength and mental capacity. Its potent euphoric and mood elevating effects were eloquently described by Sigmund Freud in reference to his own self-administered experiences with it.

Codes of language: A description of styles of language use, which distinguishes two main 'codes' of language. *Elaborated codes*, which involve a wide vocabulary and extensive use of nouns explicit descriptions, and *restricted codes*, involving a more restricted vocabulary, a preference for pronouns, and the use of implicit description in preference to explicit. These codes were first described by Bernstein, who argued (a) that *elaborated codes* were used far more by middle-class than by working class individuals, and (b) that the *language codes* used would facilitate or inhibit cognitive development owing to elaborated codes less dependent on context and therefore more amenable to abstract conceptualization. Bernstein's work was heavily criticized, notable by Labour.

Coding: Also referred to as encoding, the term is generally taken to refer to ways in which information is represented cognitively e.g., for storing in memory of for association with other information. Memories may be coded in a variety of ways, using many different modalities (e.g., kinaesthetic, or enactive coding, visual or iconic coding , auditory coding). See also representation, schema.

Coefficient of correlation: A statistical term referring to the relation between two sets of paired measurements. Correlation coefficients—which may be positive, negative, or curvilinear, depending on whether the variations are in the same direction, the opposite direction, or both directions, can be computed in a variety of ways. The most common is the product moment method referred to as 'r'.

Another method is rank correlation (p). Correlation coefficients are intended to show degree of relation, but causal relationship between variables.

Coexistent culture: Alternative system of values, norms and pattern for behaviour. The group therapy experience often leads to an awareness of other systems as legitimate alternatives to one's own system.

Cognition: Mental process of knowing and becoming aware. One of the ego functions, it is closely associated with judgement. Groups that study their own processes and dynamics use more cognition than the encounter groups, which emphasize emotions. It is also known as thinking.

Cognitive-appraisal theory of emotions: A theory which states that the emotions we feel result from evaluations, or appraisals of information received from the situation, from evaluations of information received from the situation, from the body and from memories of past encounters with similar situations. See reapproval.

Cognitive behaviour therapy: A method of psychological therapy derived from behaviour therapy but extended to take account of the patient's cognitions. The objective is to modify both maladaptive behaviours and maladaptive beliefs. See also cognitive therapy.

Cognitive complexity: Reflects a style of thinking (cognition) and described the number of dimensions and the relationship among dimensions on which a person places stimulus information in the process of translating a stimulus into response. The use of several more less independent dimensions of perceptions, judgement and behaviour is called differentiation. The degree of cognitive complexity identified for any individual reflects the degree of differentiation and or integration which he or she displays.

Cognitive consistency: The tendency to avoid contradictory cognitions about social reality.

Cognitive development: The way that cognitions develop during childhood. The major and most detailed theory of cognitive development is that produced by Piaget, though his theory is largely restricted to the ways thinking and understanding change through childhood. One of Piaget's most important contributions was to establish that the thought and logic of young children is not an inferior version of adult thinking, but has its own rules and is well adapted to the needs of the child. Cognitive development is not just a process of getting better at adult modes of cognition, but is a complex progression through different kinds of thinking and understanding.

Cognitive dissonance: A concept put forward by Festinger, in which the main proposal is that each individual strives to maintain consistency between the differing cognition. Should a noticeable inconsistency arise, this will produce a state of cognitive dissonance, which the individual experiences as uncomfortable and attempts to correct. Dissonance is reduced by adjusting one of the beliefs or attitudes involved in the inconsistency, so that the conflict disappears.

Cognitive framework: Categories and their perceived interrelationships used in social perception, induced are implicit personal theories, relationships among traits, and stereotypes.

Cognitive learning: A change in the way information is processed as a result of experience that a person or an animal has had. See imitation.

Cognitive map: An internal representation of a specific or general area, which forms a plan or outline that can guide behaviour. The idea of cognitive maps was put forward by Tolman following work in which he demonstrated that rats which had been allowed to explore mazes freely would perform better when subsequently reinforced, than ones which had not had such an experience. Tolman used the concept of cognitive maps in which cognition might be involved in learning at a time when learning was largely conceptualized as a reflexive, stimulus-response process. Later research on cognitive maps in humans demonstrated, for instance the way that areas familiar to an individual would be perceived as larger and more complex than distant ones. Some cognitive theorists, among them Tolman, have argued that cognitive mapping forms the basis of all internal representations.

Cognitive perspective: A current viewpoint psychology which emphasizes information processing in the study of mind and behaviour. See information processing theory.

Cognitive processes: Specific mental operations occurring in perception, learning or problem solving.

Cognitive psychology: The branch of psychology which is concerned with the study of cognition. Cognitive psychology is generally taken to include the study of perceptual processes, attention, memory, imagery, language, concept formation, problem solving, creativity, reasoning, decision making, cognitive development and cognitive styles.

Cognitive-response approaches: Views of attitudes which stress the importance of the active information done by people in the formation of attitudes.

Cognitive restructuring: See cognitive therapy/ cognitive behaviour therapy.

Cognitive slippage and derailment: Thought which is marked by a series of ideas which depart from a logical framework; it is characteristic of many schizophrenic patients.

Cognitive-structural school: Psychologists who argue for the importance of active interaction between the developing organism and the environment in determining behaviour and cognition, Jean Piaget is a representative of this school.

Cognitive styles: Distinctive patterns of cognitive which characterize individuals work on cognitive styles has included investigation of convergent and divergent thinking, field dependence, and forms of intelligence.

Cognitive therapy: In its narrow sense, an approach to the treatment of depression developed by Aaron Beck. Beck sees depression as resulting from a combination of a negative evaluation of the self, a negative view of present experiences and events and negative expectations of the future. The sufferer than uses faulty logic to maintain this outlook. The therapist must be very active to modify the way the patient thinks, insisting on correct logic and challenging unrealistically pessimistic assumptions. Beck has described specific techniques to be used in cognitive therapy but the term is now beginning to be used for a wide range of less well defined approaches based on similar principles.

Cohesion: See group cohesion.

Cohesiveness: Refers to the forces that hold a group together. It is based upon the attraction that the members of the group feel for each other and/or the sharing of the common group goal.

Coitus: Sexual intercourse.

Coitus interruptus: Sexual intercourse that is interrupted before the man ejaculates.

Cold turkey: Abrupt, withdrawal from opiates without the benefit of methadone or other drugs. The term was originated by drug addicts to describe their chills and consequent gooseflesh. Abstinence-oriented therapeutic communities use this type of detoxification. See also Detoxification.

Collaboration: A term used by Harry Stack Sullivan to connote sensitivity to the needs of another person.

Collective Experience: The common emotional experiences of a group of people. Identification, mutual support, reduction of ego defenses, sibling transferences, and empathy help integrate the individual member into the group, in the setting of group psychotherapy, it accelerates the therapeutic process. S.R. Slavson, who coined the phrase, warned against letting the collective experience submerge the individuality of the members or give them an opportunity to escape from their own autonomy and responsibility.

Collective unconscious: Psychic contents outside the realm of awareness that are common to mankind in general. Jung who introduced the term believed that the collective unconscious is inherited and derived from the collective experience of the species. It transcends cultural differences and explains the analogy between ancient mythological ideas and the primitive projections observed in some patients who have never been exposed to those ideas.

Collegial marriage: A relationship in which comradeship and sharing are emphasized; husband and wife assume responsibility for different roles in the marriage with each respecting the individualibilities and interests of the other.

Coma: A state of profound unconsciousness from which the person cannot be roused, with minimal or no detectable responsiveness to stimuli. It is seen in severe in injury or disease of the brain, in such systemic conditions as diabetic ketoacidosis and uremia, and in intoxications with alcohol and other drugs. In psychiatry, coma may be seen in severe catatonic states and in hysteria.

Coma vigil: Coma in which the eyes remain open. It is typically seen in acute organic brain syndromes associated with systemic infection.

Combact fatigue: A disabling physical and mental reaction to stress of military battle.

Combined therapy: A type of psychotherapy in which the patient is in both individual and group treatment with the same or two different therapists. In marriage therapy, it is the combination of married couples group therapy with either individual sessions with one spouse or Conjoint therapy, Co-therapy, Family therapy, Marriage therapy, Quadrangular therapy.

Command automatism: Condition closely associated with catalepsy in which suggestions are followed automatically.

Command negativism: See Negativism.

Commitment: A legal process for admitting a mentally ill person to a psychiatric treatment program. The legal definition and procedure vary from state to state although commitment usually requires a court or judicial procedure. Commitment may also be voluntary.

Communication disorder: A form of speech or writing that impairs tne communication because of aberrancy of rate, content, of form but not because of failure to follow semantic or syntactic rules. Examples include pressure of speech, tangentiality, echolalia, and preservation. See also Language disorder.

Community: See Therapeutic community.

Community mental health: The attempt to bring public health principles to the area of mental health. Community mental health stresses crisis intervention in psychiatric emergencies; it attempts to make inexpensive specialized psychotherapy available to poor people; it attempts to resolve community problems that lead to psychological disorder.

Community mental health center: A community or neighbourhood mental health facility or a group of affiliated agencies that severe as a locus for the delivery of the various services of community psychiatry. See also community psychiatry.

Community psychiatry: Psychiatry focusing on the detection, prevention and early treatment of mental disorders and social deviance as they develop in the community rather than as they are perceived and encountered at large centralized psychiatric facilities. Particular emphasis is placed on the environmental factors that contribute to mental illness.

Community psychology: The subfield of psychology emphasizing application of psychological principles, ideas and points of views to help solve social problems and to help individuals adapt to their work and living groups.

Companionship marriage: A relationship in which male and female roles are not regarded as fixed; husbands and wives freely assume the rights and obligations of their partners, depending on the situation.

Comparison level (CL): The social exchange theory, a subjective standard for judging whether the outcomes experienced in a social relationships are satisfactory. Compare comparison level for alternatives (*Clalt*).

Comparison level for alternatives (Clalt): In social exchange theory, an individual's standard used for judging the outcomes that would be received in the next best alternative relationship, or in simply being alone, when outcomes in the present relationship fall below the Clalt, a person will leave the relationship in favour of the alternative. Compare comparison level (CL).

Compensation and overcompensation: A defence mechanism in which an individual substitutes one activity for another in an attempt to satisfy frustrated (see frustration) motives. It usually implies failure or loss of self-esteem in one activity and the compensation for this loss by efforts in some other realm of endeavour.

Compensation neurosis: An ill-defined, heterogenous assortment of neurotic symptoms with a marked somatic tint (anxiety irritability, postural dizziness, headache, poor concentration, visual difficulties, sleep disturbances, sexual problems, intractable pain), all atributed by the patient to the effects of an accident or other injury (especially involving the head) and presented as a motive for litigation aimed at compensation. The condition first described by Charcot (1873) and by Oppenheim (1889), has been claimed to occur more frequently in men, in the less educated and less skilled occupational groups, and in people with pre-existing emotional difficulties. Although the 'secondary gain' motive often features prominently as a unifying theme for the variable symptomatically, the psychological cauzation of the complaints may be overinterpreted and the possible contribution of organic factors overlooked. The nosological status of the condition remains, therefore, uncertain. *Synonyms*: accident neurosis; litigation neurosis: traumatic neurosis; post-traumatic neurosis.

Competency to stand trial: Ability to be tried in a court of law. A person is competent to stand trial when at the time of the trial he (1) understands the nature of the charge and the potential consequences of conviction and (2) is able to assist his attorney in his defense. See also Durham rule, insanity, M' Naughten rules.

Competition: Struggle for the possession or use of limited goods, concrete or abstract. Gratification for one person largely precludes gratification for another.

Complex: A group of interrelated ideas, mainly unconscious, that have common emotional tone. A complex strongly influences the person's attitudes and behaviour. The term was introduced by Jung, who called it a feeling-toned idea.

Complimentarity of interaction: A concept of bipersonal and multipersonal psychology in which behaviour is viewed as a response to stimulation, and interaction replaces the concept of reaction. Each person in an interactive situation plays both a provocative role and a responsive role.

Complimentary role: See Role.

Compromise: A mental mechanism whereby a conflict is evaded by disguising the repressed wish to make it acceptable in consciousness.

Compulsion: Uncontrollable, repetitive and unwanted urge to perform the act. It serves as a defense against unacceptable ideas and desires, and failure to perform the act leads of to overt anxiety. See also Obsession, Repetition compulsion.

Compulsive personality disorder: A personality disorder characterized by rigidity, over conscientiousness, extreme inhibition, inability to relax and the performance of repetitive patterns of behaviour. A DSM-III term used to replace the DSM-II term obsessive-compulsive personality.

Computer simulation: The use of computers to replicate human thought strategies and patterns of behaviour. Research on computer simulation has involved the study of the use of heuristics in reasoning, and of probhalistic judgements in decision-making. It is hoped by those involved that such research will eventually throw light on human cognitive processes in industrial psychology; computer simulation often provides a safer, cheaper, or more ethical way of examining what will happen to the process being simulated, under a variety of conditions. See also artificial intelligence.

Conation: That part of person's mental life concerned with his strivings, motivations, drives and wishes as expressed through his behaviour.

Concept: The concepts used in psychoanalytical theory can be classified according to the underlying assumptions of Fictions which are being used to organize the facts into theoretical formulations. For example: (1) *Principle concepts*: which assume that mental life is actuated by, usually, the Conflict between opposing forces actuated by principles, e.g., Eros and Thanatos. Life and Death instincts,

Sex and Aggression, the Reality and Pleasure principles (2) *Structural concepts:* These assume that mental processes are localizable on a diagram e.g., id, ego and Super-ego, Ego-Boundary layers or strata of mental content by which Memories, Impulses, Phantasies, etc., are imagined to be at varying distances from the surface. In this instance hypothesis about the accessibility of Unconscious phenomena to Consciousness are formulated in terms of their distance from it, it usually being assumed that the longer ago the further down (3) *Economic Concepts:* These assume the existence of some form of mental Energy, Quanta of which may be attached to Structures (bound energy) or may move from one structure to another (free energy), e.g., Libido, Aggression, Destrado, Cathexis (4) *Dynamic concepts:* Those which describe mental activity in terms process, derive and development, e.g., Instinct, Drive, Impulse, Sublimation (5) *Faculty concepts:* These are hangovers from pre-Freudian psychology; e.g., Memory, Insight, both of which can be, but often are not restated in dynamic terms i.e., remembering forgetting and (perhaps) introspection.

Concept formation: The name given to the process by which concepts are developed and distinguished. A considerable amount of research on cognitive development has emphasized concept formation.

Conception: An abstract mental idea of anything. Also the act of becoming pregnant.

Concordance: A term used in studies of twins to indicate the degree of similarity a particular trait. See also Discordance.

Concrete operational stage: This is the third of Piaget's *four stages of cognitive development,* characterized by the child's fascination with the materials world and his strong inclination to collect facts and statistics. Children in the concrete operation stage were considered unable to deal fully with abstract concepts, and able to deal with those aspects of experience which had a material equivalent or which could be represented in a concrete fashion. The stage was considered to last from approximately 7 to 11 years of age. See also sensorimotor stage, pre-operational stage, formal operational stage.

Concrete thinking: Thinking characterized by actual things and events and immediate experience, rather than by abstractions. Concrete thinking is seen in young children; in those who have lost or never developed the ability to generalize as in certain organic mental disorders, and in schizophrenics. See also Abstract thinking.

Concrete word: A word for which a visual image is easily formed, Compare abstract word.

Condensation: A mental process in which one symbol stands for a number of components; often present in dreams.

Conditional positive regard: A concept introduced by Carl Rogers, which refers to the satisfaction of the basic need for positive regard in human beings. The term 'conditional positive regard' refers to approval, love or respect given only as a result of the individual behaving in appropriate', or socially acceptable ways. A person who has encountered nothing bit conditional positive regard throughout their life will according to Rogers, become unable to satisfy the need for self-actualization. Autonomous action, or exploration of their own potential, necessitates taking a certain amount of risk, in that it could conceivable result in social disapproval. The formation of a relationship which provides unconditional positive regard for the individual provides the security for such self-realization to take place and this is the goal of Rogerian client-centered therapy.

Conditioned reflex: A physiological reflex, or automatic response which is produced in response such a reaction, but has come to do so as a result of the process of classical conditioning.

Conditioned reinforcer: An event or stimulus which has acquired the property of strengthening a learned (conditioned) response, such that the learning is less likely to become extinguished. See also secondary reinforcement.

Conditioned response: A response which is produced in specific conditions, as a result of being associated, through a training process, with a particular stimulus, known as a conditioned stimulus. The training process consists of repeatedly pairing a novel stimulus with one which will elicit the desired response automatically. After a while, the new stimulus will come to elicit the response independently, at which point the response is said to have become a conditioned response. See classical conditioning.

Conditioned stimulus: A stimulus which brings about a response as a result of repeated association with an unconditioned stimulus. See also classical conditioning, conditioned response.

Conditioning: Procedure resulting in the acquisition or learning of more or less permanent changes in behaviour. There are two main types of conditioning, also called *Pavlovian conditioning* and *respondent conditioning*, a neutral stimulus is repeatedly paired with a stimulus (the unconditioned stimulus) that naturally elicits a response (the unconditioned response) until the neutral stimulus (the conditioned stimulus) comes to elicit that response (now the conditioned response) by itself. Operant conditioning also known as instrumental conditioning, is a conditioning procedure developed by B.F. Skinner in which a spontaneously emitted behaviour (an operant behaviour) is either rewarded (reinforced) or punished and as a result, then occurs with a frequency that is either increased (in the case of reinforcement) or decreased (in the case of punishment). See also behaviour therapy.

Conditions not attributable to a mental disorder: A DSM-III category gives to a person who may or may not have a mental disorder but who has a

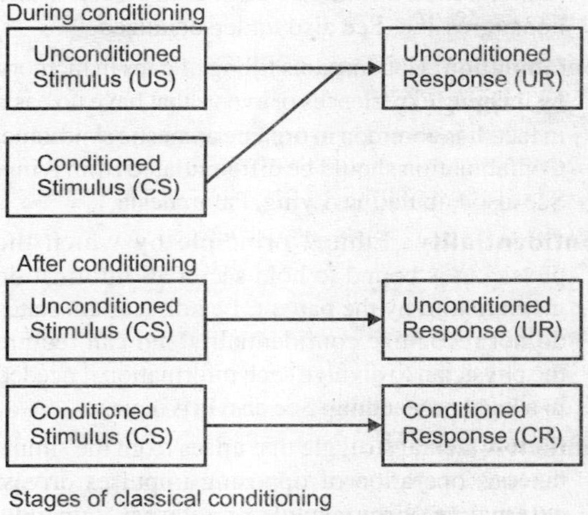

Fig. 2. Classical Conditioning (Pavlovian)

problem which may require intervention by a psychiatrist. Included are martial problem, occupational problem, phase of life problem, malingering, bereavement, antisocial behaviour, borderline intellectual functioning, and non-compliance with medical treatment.

Conditions of worth: A concept put forward by Carl Rogers concerning the way in which the individual's self-concept is affected by the conditional positive regard which he or she has experienced throughout life. Conditions of worth are an internalized set of values by which the individual assesses their own behaviour. In individuals who have experienced only conditioned positive regard throughout life, such conditions of worth may come to represent unrealistic high standards of conduct, giving the individual a negative self-concepts, and inhibiting the expression of their need for self-actualization.

Conduct disorder: In DSM a childhood disorder characterized by antisocial behaviour. The conduct disorders include undersocialized, aggressive and nonaggressive and socialized aggressive and nonaggressive. See also undersocialized.

Confabulation: Unconscious filling of gaps in memory by imaging experiences or events that have no basis in fact. It is common in organic amnestic syndrome. Confabulation should be differentiated from lying. See also Fabulation, Lying, Paramnesia.

Confidentiality: Ethical principle by which the physician is bound to hold secret all information given to him by the patient. Legally certain states do not recognize confidentiality and can require the physician to divulge such information if needed in a legal proceeding. See also Privilege.

Conflict: A mental struggle that arises from the simultaneous operation of opposing impulses drives, external (environmental) or internal demands. Termed intrapsychic when the conflict is between forces within the personality; extrapsychic, when it is between the self and the environment.

Conflict-free area: Part of one's personality or ego that is well integrated and does cause any conflicts, symptoms or displeasures.

Conformity: The social process by which people in a group or in a social situation engage in behaviour which appears to be socially acceptable, that is, to go along with the social expectations apparent at the time. Conformity is often divided into compliance (conforming while inwardly disagreeing) and internalization (conforming as a result of internal agreement with the behaviour). *Normative conformity* refers to the process of conforming as a result of the existence of strong social norms directing the accepted behaviour; *informational conformity* is the process by which an individual may conform to others on the grounds that they are better informed about the situation; while ingratiational conformity refers to conformity with the specific purpose of the individual's achieving social approval, or a feeling of belonging. The classic experiment in the field was conducted by *Solomon Asch*, who constructed groups of people to pretend to misjudge the length of a line and found that subjects in the group who had not received this instruction felt under strong pressure to conform. Conforming to group pressure is sometimes called the *Asch effect*.

Confrontation: A communication that deliberately invites another to self-examine some aspect of behaviour in which there is discrepancy between saying and doing.

Confusion: A term usually employed to designate a state of impaired consciousness associated with acute or chronic cerebral organic disease. Clinically it is characterized by disorientation, slowness of mental processes with scanty association of ideas, apathy, lack of initiative, fatigue and poor attention. In mind confusional states rational responses and behaviour may be provoked by rendering the subject unable to retain contact with the environment. The term is also employed loosely to describe disordered thinking in the functional psychoses; this latter usage is not recommended. See also confusion, reactive, consciousness, clouded. *Synonym*: confusional state.

Confusional state, acute: Short lived transient psychotic condition, lasting hours or days. Unless specified as 'reactive' confusion, the term refers to organic states e.g., delirium or twilight state. *Synonyms*: acute psycho organic syndrome; acute organic reaction.

Confusional state, subacute: Transient organic psychotic condition in which the symptoms, usually less florid than the acute state, last for several weeks or longer, during which time they may show marked fluctuations in intensity. *Synonyms*: amentia; subacute delirium; subacute psycho-organic syndrome.

Confusion reactive: Mental disorders with clouded consciousness, disorientation (though less marked than in organic confusion) and diminished accessibility often accompanied by excessive activity and apparently provoked by emotional stress. *Synonyms*; psychogenic confusion, psychogenic twilight state.

Congenital: Referring to conditions present at birth, including hereditary conditions and those resulting from prenatal development or the process of birth itself.

Congruence: A general term used to refer to behaviour, attitudes or ideas which are in accord and not in conflict with other such behaviour attitudes or ideas.

Conjoint therapy: A type of marriage therapy in which a therapist sees the partners together in joint sessions. That situation is also called triadic or iriangular therapy, since two patients and one therapist work together. See also Combine therapy, Family therapy, Marriage therapy, Quadrangular therapy.

Conjugal paranoia: See Paranoia, conjugal.

Conscience: The morally self-critical part of one's standards of behaviour, performance and value judgements. Commonly equated with the superego.

Conscious: One division of Freud's topographic theory of the mind, the conscious refers to that portion of mental functioning that is within the realm of awareness at all times. More generally, the term means having present knowledge of oneself, one's acts and one's surroundings and thus refers to the functioning of the sensorium. See also Preconscious, unconscious.

Consciousness: The awareness of one's own mental processes, or the state of having this awareness. The state of being aware of one's perceptions, thoughts, and feelings is vivid and undesirable but extremely difficult to study. The major issue is whether consciousness has any function or whether as the behaviourists claim it is just a by-product of behaviour. As developments like information theory have provided a language for describing private mental events, psychologists are returning to the study of phenomena like consciousness, See also unconscious, sensorium.

Consciousness, clouded: A state of impaired consciousness representing mild stages of disturbance on the continuum from full awareness to coma. Disorders of awareness, orientation and perception are associated with cerebral or other physical organic disease. Although the term has been employed to cover a wider range (including the restricted perceptual field following acute emotional stress) it is best used to designate the early stage of an organically determined con-fusional state. See also confusion; consciousness.

Consciousness, narrowing (restriction) of the field of: A form of disordered consciousness in which the field is restricted to and dominated by a small group of ideas and emotions to the virtual exclusion of other content. This condition occurs in extreme fatigue and hysteria; it also may be associated with some forms of cerebral disorders, especially the twilight states of epilepsy. See also: consciousness; consciousness clouded; twilight state.

Consensual validation: The continuous comparison of the thoughts and feelings of group members towards one another that tend to modify and correct interpersonal distortions. The term was introduced by Harry Stack Sullivan to refer to the dyadic therapeutic process between doctor and patient. Previously, Trigant Burrow had referred to consensual observation to describe the process, which results in effective reality testing.

Consensus: A common or generalized agreement, usually concerning social norms or acceptable behaviour; also used to refer to agreement between theories or ideas.

Conservation: The ability to recognize that volume, number or mass do not change when the physical appearance of the way that they are presented changes. In *Piagetian theory* the ability to conserve is developed towards the end of the preoperational stage. Prior to that time if the child is presented with, say, two identical balls of clay and one of them is rolled into a sausage shape, the child will say that the longer one contains more clay. Piaget considered this to arise from the process of centration; the child's tendency to focus on a single, central attribute of objects rather than taking several different aspects of its appearance into account. More recent studies (e.g., Donaldson), however, have demonstrated that the language used to the child and the social situation of the experiments may have produced the result, and that children may be able to conserve at a much earlier age than Piaget suspected.

Conservatorship: In most jurisdiction this status means that the conservatee is under the control of another person or persons (conservator) with respect to discal or contractual affairs but not with respect to the physical person or body (as with consent to medical or surgical treatment).

Consistency: The extent to which a particular response occurs whenever a particular stimulus or situation is present; a factor important in making attributions, See consensus information, distinctiveness.

Consistency paradox: The gap between the belief that personality traits are consistent across situations and the fact that people don't always behave as their traits would predict.

Consistency theories: A group of theories about attitudes which focus on the individual's attempt to maintain consistency among the numerous attitudes he or she holds. See balance theory.

Constancy scaling: The process by which the perceptual system adjusts to distance, by mentally 'scaling up' objects which are far away, such that they are not perceived as being smaller. It is considered that constancy scaling may provide an explanation for certain visual illusions. e.g., the Ponzo illusion.

Constitution: A person's intrinsic psychological or physical endowment. Used broadly, it includes an aggregate of characteristics that have developed from the interation of hereditary and environment influences. More narrowly used it indicates characteristics that are purely hereditary or genetically determined.

Constitutional types: Constellations of morphologic, physiologic, and psychologic traits as earlier proposed by various scholars. Galen: Sanguine, melancholic, pyknic (stocky), asthenic (slender), athletic and dysplastic (disproportioned) types, Sheldon; ectomorphic (thin), mesomorphic (muscular) and endomorphic (fat) types, based on the relative preponderance of outer, middle or inner layers of embryonic cellular tissue.

Construct: A term used in personal construct theory to define concepts in a precise way. It is proposed that our cognitive system is made up of bipolar constructs as illness-health and honest-dishonest. A large part of the theory is concerned with the relationships between constructs, e.g., a particular individual may have the idea that honest people tend also to be healthy.

Constructive memory: The general term given to memory for meaningful material which has been affected by the individual's own pre-existing schemata, values or attitudes. Since *Bartlett*, it has been observed that people rarely remember events or information accurately, but instead tend to adapt their memories to make more sense and accord with their own cognitions and cognitive styles, which is known as constructive memory.

Constructive processes: Modifications of the material to be remembered which take place at the time of input. Compare reconstructive processes.

Consultation-liaison psychiatry: Clinical psychiatry that is carried out on the medical or surgical wards of a general hospital. The psychiatrist collaborates closely with non-psychiatric physicians in the total care of the patient.

Contagion: Force that operates in large groups or masses. When the level of psychological functioning has been lowered, some sudden upsurge of anxiety can spread through the group speeded by a high degree of suggestibility. The anxiety gradually mounts to panic, and the whole group may be simultaneously affected by a primitive upheaval.

Context: A general setting or environment in which an event or a phenomenon occurs. There is evidence to suggest that memory is highly context dependent and that re-establishing a context will provide cues which facilitate the retrieval of memories. Similarly, the context of a communication or an utterance may be an important influence on how it is understood. See state dependent learning.

Context bound: Limited to one particular setting and not applicable to others. The phrase context-bound is particularly used to refer to Bernstein's descriptions of restricted codes of language users is closely tied to the specific situation in which the utterance is made, owing to its reliance on pronouns rather than nouns and on nuances of tone of voice. Thus, Bernstein argued serves to inhibit abstract conceptualization in the restricted language code user.

Contextualism: Emphasizes the importance of contextual factors in the explanation of social, psychological and historical events.

Continuity: The expected consistency of various characteristics as the individual develops. Most development psychologists expected the intelligence quotient to stay reasonably constant as the child grew older, but it is not recognized that its continuity has been overestimated. In fact there is remarkably little continuity in any kind of measurable characteristics over anything more than short time periods. Most psychologists seem, like most other people to believe in continuity and some are producing more sophisticated models of development to account for the lack of continuity in their data.

Contract: Explicit, bilateral commitment to a well-defined course of action. In group or individual therapy the therapist patient contract is to attain the treatment goal.

Control: The term is used in three contexts (1) the process of keeping the relevant conditions of an experiment constant (2) causing an independent variable to vary in a specified and known manner (3) using a spontaneously occurring and discoverable fact as a check or standard of comparison to evaluate the facts obtained after the manipulation of the independent variable.

Control group: In an experimental design, the group in which a condition or factor being tested is deliberately omitted. For example, in a study measuring the effects of a new drug, the control group may be given a placebo, instead of the drug. See also Experimental group.

Conventional level: Type of thinking about moral issues in which value is placed on maintaining the conventional order and satisfying the expectancies of others. Compare preconventional level, post-conventional level.

Conventional morality: This is the second of the three stages of moral development proposed by Kohlberg. Individuals at this stage consider that society's rules are by definition moral. In the early part of the stage the individual adopts moral codes in order to avoid social sanctions. In the second part of the stage, such moral codes or rules are seen as intrinsically right because they facilitate the smooth operation of society, and therefore should not be challenged. See also autonomous morality, pre-moral stage.

Convergent thinking: Problem solving which works consistently towards a defined solution; a way of thinking that assumes there is single right answer and that the way to reach that answer is to work directly towards it. It has been pointed out that within the educational system students are trained in convergent thinking and that intelligence tests depend entirely on convergent thinking ability. Rather less justifiably it is then assumed that convergent thinking is opposed to creativity and is inferior to creative or divergent thinking. It could be argued that the reason that most people use convergent thinking most of the time is because it works for most problems.

Conversational catharsis: Release of repressed or suppressed thoughts and feelings in group and individual psychotherapy as a result of verbal interchange.

Conversion: A defense mechanism, operating unconsciously, by which intrapsychic conflicts that would otherwise give rise to anxiety are, instead, give symbolic external expression. The repressed ideas or impulses and the psychologic defenses against them, are converted into a variety system. These may include such symptoms as paralysis, pain or loss of sensory function.

Conversion disorder: A somatoform disorder in which the patient experiences an involuntary limitation or alteration of physical function that is an expression of psychological conflict or need, not physical disorder. See also Hysterical neurosis.

Conversion symptom: A loss or alteration of physical functioning that suggests a physical disorder but that is actually a direct expression of a psychological conflict or need. The disturbance is not under voluntary control, and is not explained by any physical disorder (this possibility having been excluded by appropriate investigation). Conversion symptoms are observed in conversion disorder, and may occur in schizophrenia.

Conviction: A firm and settled belief.

Convulsive disorder: See Epilepsy.

Convulsive therapy: A form of therapy involving a group of techniques that induces seizures. In the strictest sense the seizures are patterned electrical discharges that are termed central seizures and that can be measured by use of an electro-encephalograph.

Cooperative therapy: See Co-therapy.

Coping mechanisms: Ways of adjusting to environmental stress without altering one's goals or purposes; includes both conscious and unconscious mechanisms.

Coprolalia: The use of vulgar or obsence language. It is observed in some cases of schizophrenia. The word is derived from the Greek words 'kopros' (excrement) and lalia (talking). See also Gilles de la Tourette's disease.

Coprophagia: Eating of fifth or feces.

Coprophilia: Excessive interest in filth or feces or their symbolic representations.

Corrective emotional experience: Reexposure under favourable circumstances to an emotional situation that the patient could not handle in the past. As advocated by Franz Alexander, the therapist temporarily assumes a particular role to generate the experience and facilitate reality testing.

Correlation: The extent to which two measures vary together, or a measure of the strength of the relationship between two variables. It is usually expressed by a coefficient which varies between +1.0, perfect agreement and –1.0 a perfect inverse relationship correlation coefficient of 0.0 would mean a perfectly random relationship. The correlation coefficient signifies the degree to which knowledge of one score or variables does not necessarily indicate a causal relationship between them; the correlation may follow because each of the variables is highly related to a third yet unmeasure factor.

Cotard's syndrome (Nihilistic delusions): Delusions of negative to a varying degree. May have their body or self has disappeared and they no longer exist, even that the whole universe no longer exists. Frequently a depressive symptoms but many have a basis in organic brain disease.

Co-therapy: A form of psychotherapy in which more than one therapist treat the individual patient or the group. It is also known as combined therapy, cooperative therapy, dual leadership, multiple therapy, and three-cornered therapy.

Counselling: The term has two rather opposed meanings (i) counseling is a form of therapy derived from the non-directive counseling of Carl Rogers in which the client is supported while they gain insight into their problem and work on finding their own solution. Within this use, people who offer therapy but who have no formal qualification or whose therapy is carried out a part of another job (e.g., priests), usually call themselves counselors (ii) Counselling is also guidance on practical personal problems such as vocational choices, problems in studying etc. These counselors are much note active in providing information, offering advice practitioners are called counseling psychologist.

Counterbalancing: A strategy used it the design of those experiments in which it is possible that the order of presentation of the conditions of the study could produce an unwanted effect, such as a *practice effect or a fatigue effect*. Counterbalancing involves systematically varying the order of presentation of the conditions, such that, for example half of the group of subjects would have conditions. A followed by condition B, while the other half would have condition B first, followed by condition A. See also order effects.

Counter-conditioning: In behaviour therapy, the conditioning of a response which is incompatible with an existing undesirable behaviour. Some one who is afraid of spiders might be trained to relax whenever they think of a spider, so that first reaction prevents them from feeling fear.

Couples therapy: See marriage therapy.

Couvade syndrome: Husband (usually) developed extreme anxiety and various physical symptoms as of pregnancy, when wife is pregnant. May have morning sickness, abdominal pains, constipation, food cravings etc.

Creativity: The ability to produce novel products or solutions to problems. Creativity has been studied as a counterpart to intelligence, represented by divergent and convergent thinking abilities respectively. However, it is difficult to devise tests, as a creative response is by definition unpredictable, so correct answers cannot be specified in advance. In fact there is no agreed way of measuring how creative any particular achievement may be. Also it is probably even less appropriate than with intelligence to think of creative as a quality of which an individuals has a certain measurable amount. Despite these difficulties E. Paul Torrance has produced a test of reactivity that seems to work quite well (it includes classic items like 'how many uses can you think of for a brick'). He claims that results from the test show that school education reduces the child's creativity. The classic theory of creativity is that it requires preparation (doing the group-work), incubation (a period of subconscious processing), inspiration (a sudden insight), and verification (checking the solution works). More recent theories, for example Edward de Bono's, usually come down to claiming that creativity results from a random element in thinking. It seems unlikely that Leonardo da Vinci's output could be accounted for in this way. So the present state of the field is that we have no plausible theory of how creativity happens, no reliable way of measuring the creativity of a person, and no real characteristics of the individual or because of particular kinds of circumstances. We clearly need a creative solution to these problems, but we do not have much idea of how to achieve this.

Criminal responsibility: Legal term meaning the ability to formulate a criminal intent at the time of an alleged crime. A person cannot be convicted of a crime if it can be proved that he lacked criminal responsibility by reason of insanity. See also competency to stand trial, Durham rule, Insanity, M'Naughten rules.

Crisis: A state of psychological disequilibrium, turning point in a person's life.

Crisis intervention: A brief therapeutic approach used in emergency rooms of general or psychiatric hospitals that is ameliorative, rather than curative, of acute psychiatric emergencies. Often treatment factors focus on environmental modification although interpersonal and intrapsychic factors are also considered. Individual, group, family, or drug therapy is used within a time limited structure of several day to several weeks. See also Hot line.

Crisis-intervention group psychotherapy: Group therapy aimed at decreasing or eliminating an emotional or situational crisis.

Crisis, therapeutic: See Therapeutic crisis.

Criterion: A standard or yardstick by which a judgement or evaluation is made. One use of the term is for the level of probability required for a statistical result to be regarded as significant. The usual criterion is a probability level of less than .05.

Critical period: A time period during the development of the individual in which a particular function can readily be acquired. Outside of the specific time it will be difficult or impossible to acquire the function.

The function may result from physical development (maturation) or from prepared learning. Imprinting in ducklings is a well known example, and in human infants it three dimensional vision is about achieved by the age about two years then it will never be acquired. On a strict definition, critical periods should be well defined time during development and the function should be impossible to achieve either before of after this period. However, outside of physical growth processes, examples of strict critical periods are rather rare. It is now known than even imprinting can be obtained well after the end of the normal critical period. In human development it is now more common to speak to sensitive periods. But even this looser term as often been applied too enthusiastically. For example it is not very helpful to refer to a critical or sensitive period for language acquisition when language can be acquired at any time during a period of at least 12 years and possibly more.

Cross-cueing: The process observed in split-brain patients by which one hemisphere of the brain transmits information to the other. In a typical experiment a subject may be shown an object to one side of the brain only. Later the object is shown to the other side of the brain, and the subject is asked questions about it. Although in such patients the corpus callosum has been cut so no direct transmission of information between the cerebral hemispheres is possible, subjects may produce feedback on the correctness of the answer offered by an imperceptible nod, frown, or other physical signal. This is recognized by the other side of the brain, so that the question can be answered correctly. Cross-cueing of this nature can often be extremely rapid and subtle.

Cross-cultural study: A study which involves the comparison of people from different cultures.

Cross-model transfer: The transferring on information from one sensory mode to another. For instance figure ground perception learned as a result of experienced with tough may also be applied when the subject is using vision. This kind of transfer is found frequently with subjects who have acquired a new sensory function; e.g., people blind from birth who have obtained their sight through an operation performed in adulthood.

Cross-cultural psychiatry: The comparative study of mental illness and health among various societies around the world.

Crowd psychology: The psychology of crowd and mass behaviour is a psychology of history both in its subject matter and its models and in its initial aim of reforming the theory and practice of politics.

Crystallized intelligence: The type of intelligence involved in an plying what has been learned; reflects one's cultural exposure and is composed largely of knowledge and skills. Compare fluid intelligence.

Cue: Something which gives an idea or a hint about something. A cue in *memory theory*, for instance, is a remembered item which connects with further information, allowing the individual to retrive more. In *perception*, a cue is the item of information which is used by the brain to direct the interpretation of specific stimuli; a *depth cue* is that part of the information which indicates how for away something is.

Cue-dependent forgetting: The inability to retrieve information stored in memory because of insufficient internally or externally generated cues.

Cult: A system of beliefs and rituals, as for the cure of disease or suffering, based on dogma or religious teaching; the devoted adherents to such a system.

Culture: A general term used to describe the set of accepted ideas, practices, values and characteristic which develop within a particular society or people.

Although most modern societies are multicultural to some degree, the word culture is often, though not accurately, used interchangeably with 'society'.

Cultural deprivation: Restricted participation in the culture of the larger society.

Cultural determinism: The view that patterns of behaviour are determined by cultural rather than biological or other factors. Some customs, attitudes, values or role perceptions remain *unchanged* over several generations.

Cultural diffusion: The spread of cultural traits through contact across societies.

Culture fair tests: Tests that reduce cultural bias by incorporating knowledge and skills common to many different cultures and socio-economic groups.

Culture free and culture fair tests: During the 1960s and early 1970s considerable efforts were made to develop psychometric tests. e.g., I.Q. and personality tests, which would avoid cultural bias by being free from reference to culture altogether. In practice the diversity of cultures was so great that such tests proved impossible to develop. Researchers had to content themselves with the attempt to establish tests which instead of being completely free of cultural influences, allowed a fair assessment of those from other cultures. Such culture fair tests are psychometric which do not provide an advantage to members of one culture over another. In which do not provide an advantage to members of one culture over another. In practice, however culture-fair tests are extremely difficult to achieve owing to cultural diversity which not only produces differences in background knowledge and skills, but also in motivation and attitudes to tests. It is very difficult for those compiling the tests to be fully aware of their own cultural assumptions. It could also be argued that since the culture itself if not fair, a biased test will give more accurate prediction. e.g., a test which gives an advantage to middle class academic values will more accurately predict which children will do best in school.

Cultural psychiatry: Branch of psychiatry concerned with mental illness in relation to the cultural environment. Symptoms regarded as psychopathological in one cultural setting may be acceptable and normal in another.

Cultural relativism: The view that patterns of understanding found in different cultures are as good as each other. This view point has implications for method, philosophic position, the evaluation of values and for attitude towards culture change.

Culture shock: A state of social isolation, anxiety and depression resulting ehen a person is suddenly placed in an alien culture or reenters his or her own culture after a prolonged absence, or has divided loyalities to two or more cultures. It is common among immigrants, but can occur also when life circumstances change radically within a society.

Culture-specific syndromes: Forms of disturbed behaviour specific to certain cultural systems that often do not conform to western nosologic entities, commonly cited syndromes are:

Syndrome	*Culture*	*Symptoms*
amok	Malay	Acute indiscriminate homicidal mania.
Dhat	Indian sub-continent	Anxiety or depression, somatic symptoms produced by a belief of passive semen in urine.
koro	Chinese, S.E. Asia	Fear of retraction of penis into abdomen with the belief that this will lead to death.
latah	S.E. Asia	Startle-induced disorganization, hypersuggesti-

		bility, automatic obedience, and echo-praxia.
Possession syndrome	S.E. Asia	Dissociative states produced by a belief of being possession by a godess or evil spirit.
piblokto	Eskimo	Attacks of screaming, crying, and running naked through the snow.
windigo	Canadian Indians	Delusions of being Indians possessed by a cannabalistic monster (windigo), attacks of agitated depression, oral sadistic fears and impulses.

Cunnilingus: Use of the mouth or tongue to stimulate the female genitalia.

Current material: Data from present interpersonal experiences. See also Genetic material.

Cybernetics: The scientific study of regulatory mechanisms.

D

Da Costa's syndrome: Chest pain, palpitations, and light-headedness occurring as a somatic manifestation of pathological anxiety. It is also called neurocirculatory asthenia and soldier's heart.

Dance therapy: A therapeutic modality that uses body movement as a form of nonverbal expression to rehabilitate people with mental or physical disorders. It was pioneered by Marian Chase in 1940.

Daydreaming: The activity of engaging in fantasies or imaginative speculations during quiescent waking periods. Some research suggests that daydreaming may be instrumental in promoting positive mental health for the individual, perhaps through the clarification of goals and ambitions.

Day hospital: A hospital setup in which a patient spends the day in the hospital and returns home at night. See also Night hospital. Partial hospitalization, Weekend hospital.

Day residue: Any element of a dream that is clearly derived from some event of the previous day. The day residue is often useful in deciphering meaning from the dream.

Deaggressification: The process by which infantile aggressive Energy (see also Aggression) loses its primitive, aggressive quality when the impulses to which it is attached participate in Sublimation. See Neutralization, Autonomous. Function of the EGO.

Death instinct: Freudian concept, also called Thanatos, of an unconscious drive toward dissolution and death, operating in opposition to the life instinct (Eros) see also instinct, Life instinct.

Decay theory of memory: The theory that information in memory eventually disappears if it is not reactivated; it appears to be more plausible for short-term than long-term memory.

Decent ration: The process by which an individual is able to step out of his own mental perspective, and to take another person's point of view. According to Piaget, the ability to "decent ire" only emerge during the pre-operational stage, and forms a part of the gradual reduction of egocentrism which Piaget saw as central to cognitive development.

Decision theory: Any theory which attempts to explain how decisions are made. In practice the term is most often applied to theories which apply mathematical models to human decision processes.

de Cleramhault's syndrome (Pure erotomania): Delusional belief that another person (the object) often of unattainably higher social status loves the patient (the subject, usually a female) intensely. 'Primary' or 'Pure' erotomania, is an isolated phenomenon whereas 'secondary' type is much common in the setting of paranoid, manic or other disorder.

Decoding: Technical term for the process of understanding spoken language.

Decompensation: The deterioration of existing defenses, leading to an exacerbation of pathologic behaviour.

Decomposition: In psychiatry, the division of a person into separate personalities or identities, as seen in the paranoid schizophrenic who splits the persecutor into separate entities.

Deductive reasoning: Reasoning from the general to the particular; drawing a conclusion that follows necessarily from certain premises.

Deep structure: A term coined by the linguist Noam Chomsky to describe the universal properties of basic grammar, supposedly common to all languages. It was the similarities of deep structure which allowed for chomsky's proposed innate language acquisition device; a theoretical construction by which he explained the infant's readiness to acquire human language.

Defect: A lasting and irreversible impairment of any, particular psychological function (e.g., 'cognitive defect') of the general development of mental capacities ('mental defect') or of the characteristic pattern of thought, feeling and behaviour constituting the individual personality. A defect in any one of the se areas can be either innate or acquired. A characteristic defect state of the personality, ranging in its manifestations from loss of intellectual and emotional vigour, or mild eccentricities of behaviour, to autistic withdrawal or affective blunting, has been held by Kraepelin (1856–1926) and Bleuler (1857–1939) to be a hallmark of the outcome of schizophrenic illness (see also: personality change), in contradistinction from manic-depressive psychosis. The ubiquity of outcome into defect in the schizophrenic disorders is not supported by more recent research, not is its irreversibility.

Defence: A general designation for all the techniques which the ego makes use of in conflicts which may lead to neurosis–Freud (1922). The function of defence is to protect the Ego and defences may be instigated by (a) Anxiety, due to a bad Conscience (Super-ego threats); or (b) realistic dangers. The concept of defence is usually stated in terms which imply that the human ego is beset by threats to this survival emanating from the Id, the super-ego and the outside world, and that is, therefore, perpetually on the defensive. But the concept is better regarded less negatively and taken to include all techniques used by the ego to master, control canalize and use forces which may lead to Neurosis. The concept also implies that neurosis is due to a failure of defence, according to this view the Inhibitions resulting from successful Repression are not neurotic symptoms. Anna Freud (1937) lists nine defences: Regression, Repression, Reaction-Formation, Isolation, Undoing, Projection, Introjection, Turning Against the Self & Reversal plus a tenth, Sublimation,' which pertains rather to the study of the normal than to that of neurosis-Splitting and Denial are also usually listed as defences. Since psychoanalysis holds that anxiety is a spur to development, some perhaps all, of the defences play a part in normal development and it is usually assumed that certain defences belong to specific stages of development, e.g., introjection, projection, denial and splitting to the Oral phase, reaction-formation, isolation and undoing to the Anal phase. See also Technique.

Defence mechanism: Unconscious process acting to relieve conflict and anxiety arising from one's impulses and drives. See also compensation, Conversion, Denial, Displacement, Dissociation, Idealization, Incorporation, Intellectualization, Introjection, Projection, Rationalization, Reaction formation, Regression Repression, Sublimation, Substitution, Symbolization, Undoing.

Defensive emotion: Strong feeling that serves as a screen for a less acceptable feeling, one that would cause a person to experience anxiety if it appeared. For example expressing the emotion of anger is often more acceptable to a patient than expressing the fear that his anger covers up. In that instance, anger is defensive.

Deficiency motive: A motivation that arises because of a perceived deficiency of some kind. The deficiency can range from physiological (e.g., food) to higher needs, such as that for recognition. Deficiency motives are distinguished from 'abundancy motives' in which it is judged that the organism is trying to acquire more of the material than is needed for comfortable survival.

Degeneration: In neurophysiology, the deterioration of neural tissue which occurs through lack of stimulation, injury, or lack of nutrients. In stimulus deprivation studies, some damaged perceptual functioning which was originally thought to result from cognitive deficits was later found to be caused by neural degeneration.

Deindividuation: The process by which individuals come to feel that they are simply part of a corporate entity, such as group or crowd members. Deindividuation involves the individual's surrendering the immediate perception of independence and autonomy, and feeling as though they have merged anonymously with the other people involved. It is commonly found in military units in action and in mobs.

Deinstitutionalization: Change in locus of mental health care from traditional, institutional setting to community-based services. Sometimes called transinstitutionalization because it often merely shifts the patients from one institution (the hospital) to another (such as a prison).

Deixis: The notion of deixis refers to linguistic expressions which signal the contextual existence of persons, objects and similar orientational features. Deictic words include personal pronouns, adverbials of time and place and expression signaling an honorific dimension.

Deja entendu: Illusion that what one is hearing one has heard previously. See also Paramnesia.

Deja pense: A condition in which a thought never entertained before is incorrectly regarded as a repetition of a previous thought.

Déjà vu: Illusion of visual recognition in which a new situation incorrectly regarded as a repetition of a previous experience. See also Paramnesia.

Delayed conditioning: A form of classical conditioning in which the conditioned stimulus is presented several seconds before the conditioned stimulus, but with both coming to an end at the same time.

Body comparison with simultaneous conditioning or trace conditioning, delayed conditioning is considered to be the most effective.

Delay-learning phenomenon (or delayed association): Denotes any case where associative learning depends on bridging a long interval between events.

Delinquent act: Antisocial action by children or young people, mostly offences against property and larceny, but also including violent and sexual crimes, truancy from school, early drinking and drug abuse, and, generally refusal to conform to social rules.

Delirium: An acute, reversible organic mental disorder characterized by confusion and some impairment of consciousness. It is generally associated with emotional liability, hallucinations or illusions, and inappropriate, impulsive, irrational, or violent behaviour.

Delirium tremens: An acute and sometimes fatal reaction to withdrawal from alcohol, usually occurring 72 to 96 hours after the ceszation of heavy drinking. Its distinctive characteristic is marked autonomic hereactivity (tachycardia, fever, hyper-hidrosis, dilated pupils), which is usually accompanied by tremulousness, hallucinations or illusions, and delusions. See also Formication.

Delirium Verborum: Delirious state in which the patient is excessively talkative.

Delusion: A false belief that is firmly held, despite objective and obvious contradictory proof or evidence and despite the fact that other members of the culture do not share the belief. Types of delusion include *Bizzare delusion*. False belief that is patently absurd or fantastic. *Delusion of control*. Delusion that a person's thoughts, feelings, or actions are not his own bur are being imposed on him by some external force. *Delusion of grandeur*. (grandiose delusion). Exaggerated concept of one's importance, power, knowledge, or identity, *Delusion of jealousy* (delusion of infidelity). Delusion that one's lover is unfaithful. *Delusion of persecution.* Delusion that one is being attacked, harassed, cheated, or conspired against. *Delusion of poverty.* Delusion that one is or will be without material possessions. *Delusion of reference.* Delusion that events, objects, or the behaviour of others have a particular and unusual meaning specifically for oneself. *Encapsulated delusion.* Delusion without significant effect on behaviour., *Fragmentary delusion.* Poorly elaborated delusion, often one of many with no apparent interconnection. *Nihilistic delusion* (delusion of negation) Depressive delusion that the world and everything related to it have ceased to exist. *Paranoid delusion.* Delusion of persecution and grandiose delusion. *Religious delusion.* Delusion involving the Deity of theological themes. *Sexual delusion.* Delusion centering on sexual identity, appearances practices, or ideas, *Somatic delusion.* Delusion pertaining to the functioning of one's body. *Systematized delusion.* A group of elaborate delusions related to a single event or theme.

Delusion, mood-congruent: See Mood congruent psychotic features

Delusion mood incongruent: See Mood incongruent psychotic features

Demand characteristics: The sum total of cues (derived from the manner in which the subject is solicited. The manner in which he is treated by the experimenter, the scuttlebutt about the experiment, the experimental instructions, and, most important, the experimental procedure itself) that communicates the purpose of the experiment and the nature of the behaviour expected of the subject. Subjects may confirm the investigator's hypothesis an effort to behave appropriately rather than responding directly to the independent variable under investigation. By extensions, as applied to non-experimental settings, the tendency of individuals to live up to what is implicitly expected of them, a factor that may play a major role in the outcome of treatment.

Dementia: An organic mental disorder characterized by general impairment in intellectual functioning. Frequent components of the clinical syndrome are failing memory, difficulty with calculations, distractibility, alterations in mood and affect, impairment in judgement and abstraction reduced facility with language, and disturbance or orientation. Although generally irreversible because of under lying progressive degenerative brain disease, dementia may be reversible if the cause can be treated. Treatabie causes of dementia include brain tumour, subdural hematoma, normal-pressure hydrocephalus, vitamin B_{12} deficiency, liver disease, syphilis, poisoning with bromides or other toxins (metals), Uremia, hypothyroidism, hyoeradrenocorticism, hypercalcemia, and lung carcinoma; all have been reported to produce dementia in their clinical pictures See also Amentia.

Dementia precos: Obsolete term for schizophrenia.

Dementia subcortical: First described by S.A.K. Wilson (1912). Dysfunction of subcortical structures results in abnormalities in speed of information processing attention and concentration, memory, word list generation, abstraction, categorization, judgement, problem resolutions, strategy formulation and visuospatial abilities. The common causes are Parkinson's disease, Huntington's vhorea. Progressive supranuclear palsy (PSP) Wilson's disease, idiopathic basal ganglion calcification, spinocerebellar degeneration etc.

Denial: A defense mechanism, operating unconsciously, used to resolve emotional conflict and allay anxiety by disavowing thoughts, feelings, wishes, needs, or external reality factors that are consciously intolerable.

Denotative meaning: The specific or symbolic meaning of an utterance or term. The denotative meaning of something is that which is simply and necessarily contained in the use of that term, without any of the additional associations or implications which is listener may understand. See also connotative meaning.

Dependence, drug: See drug dependence.

Dependence on therapy: Patient's pathological need for therapy, created out of the belief that he cannot survive without it.

Dependency: A state of reliance on another, as for security, love, protection, or mothering.

Dependency needs: Vital needs for mothering, love, affection, shelter, protection, security, food, and warmth. May be a manifestation of regression when they reappear openly in adults.

Dependent personality disorder: A personality disorder characterized by lack of self confidence, a tendency to have others assume responsibility for significant areas of one's life, and a subordination of one's own needs and wishes to those of the others on whom on is dependent. Solitude is extremely discomforting to a person with the disorder.

Dependent variable: The variable which is measured as an indicator of the outcome of an experiment. If you set up an experiment to assess the effect of coffee on speed of essay writing, the dependent variable would be the measure of writing speed. The dependent variable is so named because, if the experimental hypotheses is valid, its value will depend on the condition of the independent variable which has been set up.

Depersonalization: Senzation of unreality concerning oneself, parts of oneself, or one's environment which occurs under extreme stress or fatigue. It is seen in schizophrenia, depersonalization disorder, the schizotypal personality disorder. See also Ego boundaries.

Depersonalization disorder: In DSM, a dissociative disorder characterized by a feeling that one's reality is temporarily lost. Also known as depersonalization neurosis.

Depression: A mental state characterized by feeling of sadness, loneliness, despair, low esteem, and self reproach. The term refers either to a mood that is so characterized or to an affective disorder. Accompanying signs include psychomotor retardation or at times agitation, withdrawal from interpersonal contact and vegetative symptoms, such as insomnia and anorexia. See also Anaclitic Dysthymic disorder, Grief, Major depression.

Depressive position: A Kleinian concept, it describes the position reached (in her scheme of things) by the infants (or by the patient in analysis) when he realizes that both his Love and Hate are directed towards the same object–the mother becomes aware of his ambivalence and concerned to protect her from his hate and to make reparation for what damage he imagines his hate has done. Since Klein's system includes the death instinct and innate hostility and envy of the mother, his crisis is conceived as playing an essential part in every infants' development regardless of the quality of its mothering, and its outcome is held to determine all later development. Healthy and neurotic persons are considered to have passed the depressive position while persons with depressive problems are fixated at it and persons with schizoid and paranoid problems have failed to reach it. See paranoid-schizoid position. See Segal (1964).

Deprivation emotional: Relative lack of environmental or interpersonal experience during the early development years. See also Sensory deprivation.

Depth psychology: The psychology of unconscious mental processes. Also a system of psychology in which the study of such processes plays a major role, as in psychoanalysis.

Derealization: Sometimes changed reality or that one's surrounding have altered. It is usually seen in schizophrenics, See also Ego boundaries.

Dereism: Mental activity that follows a totally subjective and idiosyncratic system of logic and fails to take the facts of reality or experience into consideration. See also Autistic thinking.

Descriptive psychiatry: A system of psychiatry focusing primarily on the study of observable symptoms and behavioural phenomena, rather than underlying psychodynamic processes. Kraepelin's systematic description of mental illness was an early example. See also Dynamic psychiatry.

Desensitization: A procedure which will reduce the responsiveness of the subject. Used mostly for behavioural techniques which reduce or eliminate inappropriate emotional responses, usually anxiety. The basic procedure is to present weak forms of the feared stimulus while using stronger forms of a stimulus is then gradually increased in strength without triggering the fear response. The standard procedure is called 'systematic desensitization' and is an example of counter conditioning.

Desexualization: The process by which infantile libidinal energy loses its primitive, erotic quality when the Pregenital impulses to which it is attached participate in sublimation and Ego Development. See Libidinal Development, Infantile, Neutralization, Autonomous, Functions of the Ego.

Designer drugs: Addictive drugs that are synthesized or manufactured to give the same subjective effects as well known illicit drugs. Since the process is a covert operation there is great difficulty in tracing the manufacturer to check the drugs for adverse effects.

Destrudo: Rarely used term for the energy of the death instinct and therefore analogous to the libido of the life-instinct.

Detachment: A behaviour pattern characterized by general aloofness in interpersonal contact; may include intellectualization, denial and superficiality.

Determinism: Concept that nothing occurs by chance alone; instead, things result from specific causes or forces. This school of thought denies the notion of free will.

Determinism, Psychic: The assumption made Freud that mental phenomena have causes in whatever sense physical ones do. See Freud's views on causality, determinism and free will and their relation to the scientific thought of this time. He seems to have held that demonstration of the existence of unconscious mental processes proved the assumption of determinism, since it made it possible to assert that conscious processes were the effects of unconscious ones. He did not however, regard consciousness as a mere epiphenomenon, but as a regulator capable of a 'more stable control and guidance of the flow of mental processes'–Jones Copcit. The assumption of psychic determinism, at least as usually stated, leaves no place in analytical theory for a self or agent initiating action or defence or for the use of explanations other than causal ones.

Detoxification: Treatment by the use of medication, diet, rest, fluids and nursing care to restore physiologic functioning after it has been seriously disturbed by the over use of alcohol, barbiturates or other addictive drugs.

Development: The processes of change over the life span. One aspect is physical development which is strongly influenced by generic tendencies. The other is psychological development which is much more directly influenced by environmental factors.

Development disorder: A handicap or impairment originating before the age of 18 which may be expected to continue indefinitely and which constitutes a substantial impairment. The disability may be attributable to mental retardation, cerebral palsy, epilepsy, or other neurologic conditions and may include autism.

Developmental norms: The expected level of performance of children at a specific age. For example, in a given population the norms for the number of words spoken might be 50 at 18 months, 400 at three years etc. Developmental norms can be used to give a precise indication of how uncommon any unusual performance as being exceptionally poor is only the first step in deciding whether any further action is desirable.

Developmental Psychology: The psychological study of development. Some distinction is made between developmental psychology which is the study of the laws and processes of development, and child psychology which is more focused on empirical techniques for studying children at specific ages. However the terms are often used fairly interchangeably, and the phrase 'experimental child psychology' has come into use to preserve the distinction. Major theories of development have been propounded by Freud, Gesell and Piaget, among others. All of the large scale theories were established in the first half of this century, and most are restricted to childhood. However, there is reason to believe that development continues throughout adulthood. The field of life span developmental psychology has to therefore become active in recent years but as yet has no major theory as a basis. In fact developmental psychology in general seems to be proceeding quite adequately at present without much reliance on overall theories of development. Instead there are theories to deal with restricted areas such as attachment and language and a focus on a number of more or less practical issues. The areas of greatest current interest include: the growth of cognitive and social competence; the nature-nurture or generic-environment debate, the question of continuity; applications to education and to parenting;

the importance of play and creativity and most recently the family.

Deviation: Departure from the average or norm.

Dhat syndrome: It is a culture-bound sexual neurosis quite common in the south east Asia in which a patient presents with somatic complaints along with feeling of physical and mental exhaustion attributed to the passage of a whitish discharge with urine (Dhat) believed to be semen by the patient, although there is no objective evidence of such discharge. It was first described by N.N. Wig (1960).

Diagnosis: The process of determining, through examination and analysis, the nature of a patient's illness.

Diagnostic and statistical Manual of Mental Disorder: A handbook for the classification of mental illnesses. Formulated by the American Psychiatric Association. It was first issued in 1952 (DSM-I). The second edition (DSM–II) issued in 1968, correlates closely with the eighth edition of the World Health Organization's International classification of Diseases. The third edition (DSM-III) issued in 1980, departs more widely from that classification. The revised edition DSM III came in 1987 (DSM-III-R) and fourth edition in 1992 (DSM-IV).

Dialogue: Verbal communication between two or more persons.

Dichotic listening task: A method of investigating selective attention by presenting two different messages through the two sides of headphones, and asking the subject to attend to one only. Dichotic listening tasks are usually, monitored by asking the subject to engage in 'shadowing'-speaking the attended message out loud as they listen.

Differential diagnosis: The determination of which of two or more diseases with similar symptoms is the one that afflicts the patient.

Differential reinforcement: Procedure in which desirable behaviour is reinforced and problematic or less desirable behaviour is extinguished or punished.

Diglossia: (Fwerguson, 1959) It refers to a situation in which two varieties of a language are used in different social functions or domains within a speech community.

Dipsomania: Compulsion to drink alcoholic beverages.

Disability: Defined by the Federal Government as "Inability to engage in any substantial gainful activity by reason of any medically determinable physical or mental impairment which can be expected to last or has lasted for a continuous period of not less than 12 full months."

Disconnection syndrome: Term coined by Norman Geschwind (1926–1984) to describe the interruption of information transferred from one brain region to another.

Discordance: A research term used in studies of twins to indicate the degree of dissimilarity between the two members of each pair with respect to a particular trait. See also Concordance.

Discovery learning: A form of educational practice studied particularly by J.S. Bruner, in which students operate mainly by deduction and inference, with guidance and resources being provided by the teacher. Discovery learning emphasizes the student's own activity and enquiry, rather than the teacher's transmission of information.

Discrimination: Process of distinguishing between different but often similar stimuli and reacting appropriately. The term also refers more specifically to the occurrence of operant behaviour in environments in which the behaviour has been reinforced but not in those in which it has not been reinforced. See also Discriminative stimulus.

Discriminative Stimulus: An environmental even correlating with the operation of a certain reinforcement matrix, such that behaviour that has been reinforced in the presence of the stimulus but not in it absence tends to occur only when the stimulus is present.

Disembedded thought: Thinking which is not applied in a relevant context, but is required to take place independent of context. Many of the criticisms put forward of piagetian approaches to the understanding of the child's cognition centre around the idea that the child was required to engage in disembedded tasks; and that when the tasks were out in an appropriate social context, children were noticeably more successful at them.

Disengagement: A theory of ageing put forward by Cummings and Henry in 1961, in which it was proposed that the elderly undergo a process of systematic disengagement or withdrawal from society, reducing the amount of participation in and integration with society. The process was thought of as a way of coping with the deaths and illnesses of partners and friends, and as a possible preparation for approaching death Cunnings and Henry proposed that this behaviour had a possible biological origin. The theory has been heavily criticized, mainly on the grounds that social pressure on old people to withdraw from society is high, and that for many, society affords few alternatives to withdrawal. Social exchange process have been suggested as possible alternative models.

Disinhibition: Freedom to act according to one's inner drives or feelings, with less regard for restraints imposed by cultural norms or one's supergo; removal of an inhibitory constraining, or limiting influence, as in the escape from higher cortical control in neurologic injury, or in uncontrolled firing of impulses when a drug interferes with the usual limiting or inhibiting action of GABA within the central nervous system.

Disintegrative psychosis: A Heterogeneous group of conditions usually commencing at the age of three or four years when, after general premonitory symptoms, the hitherto normal child develops, over a few months, loss of speech and of social skills accompanied by hyperactivity, stereotyped motor behaviour, a severe impairment of emotional response, and usually but not necessarily, of intellectual capacity. Clinical evidence of neurological disease is uncommon but the psychosis may result from a variety of illness which damage the brain (e.g., measles encephalitis). The outcome is poor, most children becoming mentally retarded and incapable of speech. Comment: The syndrome was originally described as 'dementia infantilis' by Heller in 1930. *Synonyms*: Heller's syndrome; childhood onset pervasive developmental disorder.

Disorganized schizophrenia: A DSM–III term replacing hebephrenic schizophrenia. See also Hebephrenia.

Disorientation: Impairment of awareness of time, place, and the position of the self in relation to other persons; confusion. It is characteristic of organic mental disorders.

Displaced aggression: Aggressive behaviour which is directed towards a target which is not the original source of frustration. Typically, aggression becomes displaced because the original target is unreachable, or because it would be inexpedient for the individual to direct aggression towards the original. For instance, it may be dangerous for someone to express directly the aggressive feelings generated by an unpleasant boss, and such feelings may become displaced onto family member instead.

Displacement: A defence mechanism of channeling undesired or inexpedient impulses to alternative outlets. An example would be the application of aggressive tendencies to becoming the best chess player in the college. When the outcome of displacement is regarded as socially desirable the process is also called sublimation.

Display: A pattern of social behaviour that is species-specific and forms a part of the communicative system within or between social groups or between individuals.

Disposition: A tendency to behave in a particular way, when used by developmental or clinical psychologists the term implies an inherited tendency, and is used interchangeably with predisposition. When used in the context of motivation and personality it is a general term for any relatively stable behavioural tendency and no genetic basis is implied.

Dispositional attribution: Believing that a person's behaviour is caused by his character or personality, rather than the situation that he is in. People are usually more likely to make dispositional attributions about the behaviour of other people and to account for their own behaviour in terms of the situation they were in. See also attribution error, situational attribution.

Dissociation: The splitting off of clusters of mental contents from conscious awareness, a mechanism central to hysterical conversion and dissociative disorders; the separation of an idea from its emotional significance and affect as seen in the inappropriate affect if schizophrenic patients.

Dissociative disorder: A mental disorder characterized by a sudden, temporary alteration in consciousness, identity, or motor behaviour. In DSM–III the dissociative disorders include psychogenic amnesia, psychogenic fugue, multiple personality, and depersonalization disorder.

Dissonance: A state in which a cognitive discrepancy is produced between two events such that one cognition is in direct contradiction to another. Typically, such cognitive dissonance results in attitude change, such that the dissonance is reduced.

Distinctiveness: A concept in attribution theory which concerns how unique an event or behaviour is. Distinctiveness is one of three major criteria used to formulate attributions for any given situation. The other criteria are consistency and consensus.

Distortion: Misrepresentation of reality. In psychoanalysis, it also refers to the process of modifying unacceptable unconscious mental elements so that they are allowed to enter consciousness in a more acceptable but disguised form.

Distractible speech: Pattern of speech in which the person repeatedly changes subjects in response to nearby stimuli.

Distractibility: Inability to maintain attention; shifting from one area or topic to another with minimal provocation. Distractibility may be a manifestation of organic impairment or it may be a part of a function disorder such as anxiety states, mania or schizophrenia.

Distributed practice: A procedure during learning in which time gaps are interspersed during the practice. For example, if you were trying to learn the contents of a chapter, you would take a short break at the end of each page. This approach has been found to lead to more effective learning than massed practice in which no breaks are taken.

Distribution: The pattern made by a set of scores when grouped according to frequency. Theoretical distributions are the pattern that would be produced by scores that conformed precisely to a mathematically defined function. The most important of these is the normal distribution, but each statistic has its own distribution.

Distributive analysis and synthesis: Therapeutic application of Adolf Meyer's psychobiological school psychiatry. Systematic investigation of the patient's entire past experience yields a constructive synthesis of his assets and liabilities and leads to an effort to enable him to adapt to his environment.

Divergent thinking: Thought which ranges far more widely than is conventional. Tests of divergent thinking are often included in creativity tests, as it is assumed that highly creative individuals will be able to utilize novel frameworks more readily than those with a more conventional style of cognition. See convergent thinking.

Dix, Dorothea Lynde (1802–1887): Foremost nineteenth century American crusader for the improvement of institutional care of the mentally ill.

Doctor-patient relationship: Human interchange that exists between the person who is sick and the person who is selected because of training and experience to heal.

Dogmatism (closed mindedness): A somewhat unfashionable term, related to the idea of close mindedness or the inability to form new cognitive systems of various kinds.

Dominance: A predisposition to play a prominent or controlling role when interacting with others. In neurology the (normal) tendency of one-half of the brain to be more important than the other in medicating various functions (cerebral dominance). In genetics, the ability of one gene (dominant gene) to express itself in the phenotype of an individual, even though that gene is paired with another (recessive gene) that would have expressed itself in a different way.

Dominance hierarchy: A concept first proposed in 1922 by Schjelderup-Ebbe, after observation of a consistent order of precedence among hens when given restricted access to food supplies. Dominance hierarchies became popular as ethological concepts throughout the 1950s and 1960s and were considered to present a basic model of social organization for most social animal, but the existence of linear dominance hierarchies has been increasingly called into question by ethologists in recent years.

Dopamine: A neurosynaptic transmitter found in the brain, specially associated with some forms of psychosis and abnormal movement disorders.

Double bind: According to Bateson, et al. (towards a theory of schizophrenia, 1956) the childhood of future schizophrenics is characterized by, repeated experiences of being put into a double bind by, typically, their mothers. This experience consists in being made the object of incompatible, contradictory emotional demands in a situation in which there is no avenue of escape and in which no other member of family rescues the child from bind by either compensating for or correcting the mother's behaviour or by elucidating it to the child. The schizophrenic's response to a double bind is to lose the capacity to distinguish the logical status of thoughts. In other words, his defence against confusion, and his own and his mothers ambivalence, is to lose the capacity to understand those nuances which enable one to have insight into motives and to appreciate discrepancies between overt and concealed meanings. In any language, a double bind is an impossible position. Strictly speaking the double bind is not a psychoanalytical concept, since it refers to an interpersonal situation and not to an internal conflict, or developmental process. Although, originally formulated as a theory of schizophrenia, it has been adduced as an explanation of neurotic behaviour. The possibility that an analyst may put a patient into a double bind has also been envisaged.

Double-blind study: A study in which one or more drugs and a placebo are compared in such a way that neither the patient not the persons directly or indirectly involved in the study known which is being given to the patient. The drug being investigated and the placebo are coded.

Down's syndrome: An abnormality of an autosomal chromosome, associated with mental retardation and characteristic physical features. In most cases the anomaly consists in trisomy of a chromosome of the G group; the remainder may exhibit D/G translocation. G/G translocation or mosaicism. The incidence of Down's syndrome has been estimated as close to 1 in 550 live births, with a relationship to late maternal age. The degree of mental retardation varies but the IQ level on standard tests in rarely above 70. Physical features include characteristic 'mongoloid' facies, single palmar creases, a large fissured tongue, hypotonia, retarded growth and congenital cardiac and gastrointestinal defects. The condition was originally described by John Langdon Haydon Down (1828–1896). *Synonyms*; Mongolism, Langdon Down's disease; autosomal trisomy G; congenital acromicria trisomy 21.

Drane's test: in a patient with monocular blindness (of organic origin), if prism is placed before defective eye, it will not impair reading; whereas in a patient with blindness of functional (hysteria or malingering) origin, it will impair reading.

Drawing test: Any of a variety of psychological tests in which the subject is asked to draw certain familiar objects, such as people trees, and houses. Altitudes and feelings are often revealed in the way the subject depicts those objects.

Dread: Anxiety related to a specific danger.

Dream: Mental activity during sleep in which thoughts, emotions, and images are experienced as though real. It is associated with rapid eye movement (REM) sleep. The dream was regarded by Freud as providing an outlet for the discharge in disguised form of unconscious and often acceptable impulses and wishes.

Dream analysis: Finding hidden meanings in disguised symbolic form by interpreting the content of dreams. Dreams analysis is a particular tool of the psychoanalytic schools of thought proposed by Freud and Jung. It is considered to form an important set of clues to the unconscious mind, because dreaming is thought to express levels of unconscious wish fulfillment expressive of the individual's deepest conflicts and desires.

Dream work: A term used by Freud to mean the complex process by which unconscious wishes and fantasies are disguised in dreams, appearing in symbolic form.

Dreamy state: An altered state of consciousness, likened to a dream situation, that develops suddenly and from which the patient usually recovers within a few minutes. It is accompanied by visual, auditory and olfactory hallucinations and is most commonly associated with temporal lesions.

Drive: A hypothetical construct used to explain motivated behaviour. It refers to a basic urge that produces a state of psychic tension that motivates the person into action to alleviate the tension. The term is currently preferred over Freud's term "instinct". See also Aggressive drive, sexual drive.

Drive-reduction theory: The theory that motivation occurs, and behaviour is energized mainly or entirely as a result of the need to alleviate or reduce drives. It is a rather negative theory in that it assumes that all drives produce tension or arousal and that the organism is always motivated to minimize drive states. The failure to encompass enjoyment and activities which deliberately increase arousal (like exploration and sky diving) was one reason for the decline of the theory.

Drug abuse: The self-administration of a medicinal or pleasurable substance in a quantity or manner that impairs health or social functioning. The term has prorative overtones so it is advisable to restricts its use to indicate the malevolence of an individual, or of his or her behaviour.

Drug abuse, nondependent: Self-administration of a drug without dependence (as defined in 'drug dependence' below), to the detriment of one's health or social functioning. Drug abuse may be secondary to a psychiatric disorder. The term, and the concept on which it is based, have been contested in the light of evidence that dependent and nondependent abuse of drugs cannot be reliably distinguished.

Drug dependence: A state, psychic and sometimes also physical, resulting from taking a drug, characterized by behavioural and other responses that always include a compulsion to take a drug on a continuous or periodic basis in order to experience its psychic effects, and sometimes to avoid the discomfort of the absence. Tolerance may or may not be present. A person may be dependent on more than one drug. *Synonyms*: drug addiction; toxicomania.

Drug Tolerance: Repeated use of some substance or drug, often narcotics, so that larger and larger doses are required to produce the same physiologic and /or psychologic effect obtained previously by a smaller dose.

Drug withdrawal syndrome: State associated with the discontinuation of the taking of a drug, ranging from severe, as specified for alcohol (delirium tremens), to less severe states characterized by one or more symptoms such as convulsions, tremor, anxiety, restlessness, gastrointestinal and muscular complaints, and mild disorientation and memory disturbance. *Synonym*: abstinence syndrome.

Drunkenness, pathological: Acute psychotic episode induced by relatively small amounts of alcohol. These are regarded as individual idiosyncratic reaction to alcohol, not due to excessive consumption, and without conspicuous neurological signs of intoxication. *Synonym*: alcohol idiosyncratic intoxication.

Dualism: The view that the mind is a separate entity that exists apart from the body and other aspects of material reality.

Dual leadership: See Co-therapy.

Dual-memory theory: A model of memory first proposed by William James, in 1890, and later developed by (among other) Miller and Atkinson and Shiffrin. Dual memory theory postulates two independent memory systems, a limited-capacity, immediate or short-term memory, and a large-capacity, long-term memory. The Atkinson & Shiffrin model proposes that short-term memory forms a first state to long-term memory storage, and that material is transferred from STM to LTM by means of rehearsal. See also levels of processing.

Dual-Sex Therapy: A specific form of psychotherapy developed by William Masters and Virginia Johnson, in which treatment is focused on a particular sexual disorder. The crux of the program is the round-table session, in which both a male therapist and a female therapist are present with the patient couple. Special exercise are prescribed for the couple, the overall goal being to diminish fears of sexual performance and to facilitate communication in sexual and non-sexual areas.

Durham rule: Federal court ruling in 1954 holding that "an accused is not criminally responsible if his unlawful act was the product of mental disease or mental defect." It has since been replaced by the American Law Institute formulation of insanity, which states that "a person is not responsible for criminal conduct if at the time of such conduct as result of mental disease or defect he lacks substantial capacity either to appreciate the wrongfulness of his conduct or to conform his conduct to the requirements of law." See also Competency to stand trial, Insanity M'Nughten rules.

E

Eating disorder: A disorder characterized by a marked disturbance in eating behaviour. In DSM, the eating disorders include anorexia, bulimia, pica, and rumination disorder of infancy.

Ecdemomania, ecdemonomia: Morbid impulse to travel or wander about.

Echolalia: Repetition of another person's words or phrase. Observed in certain cases of schizophrenia, particularly the catatonic types. The behaviour is considered by some authors to be an attempt by the patient to maintain a continuity of thought processes. See also Communication disorder, Gilles de la Tourette's disease.

Echopraxia: Repetition of another person's movements. It is observed in some cases of catatonic schizophrenia.

Echul: A culture specific syndrome described in native Americans in Southern California consisting sexual anxiety and convulsions related to severe stress, such as death and spouse.

Ecology: The study of environment, with an underlying assumption that environment characteristics are responsible for the ways organisms function.

Ecological validity: The extent to which controlled experimental results can be generalized beyond the confines of the particular experimental context of a variety of contexts in the real world.

Ecomania: Morbid attitude towards the members of one's family.

Encounters: One who obtains gratifications through listening to sexual accouters; eavesdropper; the audible counterpart of voyeur.

Ecouteurism: Sexual pleasure obtained from sounds or listening to sexual or toilet activities of others.

Ecstasy: State of rapturous delight.

ECT: See electroconvulsive therapy.

Ectomorphic: Thin; one of Sheldon's constitutional types. See also constitutional types, Endomorphic, Mesomorphic.

Educable: Capable of achieving a fourth-grade academic level. The term describes the mildly mentally retarded (I.Q. of 50 to 70.) See also Mental retardation. Trainable.

Educational psychology: One of the major professions of psychologists. In Britain practitioners are employed within the educational system to deal with psychological issues concerning children in school, and to assess and monitor the progress of children with special needs. They are usually based in Schools Psychological Services or Child Guidance Clinics. In some areas the work is largely taken up with assessing children who are having difficulties in school and making recommendations about which kind of educational setting they need. Other areas have been able to develop much more varied work ranging from therapy with individual children and their families, through curriculum development and teacher training, to consulting with the school on more effective management structures. Training courses usually last for two years and award master's degree, but require the applicant to have a good psychology degree, training as a teacher, and two years of teaching experience before starting the course.

Effort after meaning: A term used by Bartlett to describe the ways in which individuals attempt to organize their memories, and to make sense of them; if necessary, altering the content of the specific information in order to do so.

Ego: One of the three components of the psychic apparatus in the Freudian structural framework. The other two components are the id and supergo. Although the ego has some conscious components, many of its operations are automatic. It occupies a position between the primal instincts and the demands of the outer world; therefore, it mediates between the person and external reality. In so doing , it performs the important functions of perceiving the needs of the self, both physical and psychological, and the qualities and attitudes of the environment. It evaluates, coordinates, and integrates those perceptions so that internal demands can be adjusted to external requirements. It is also responsible for certain defensive functions to protect the person against the demands of the id and the superego. It has a host of functions, but adaptation to reality is perhaps the most important one psychiatric usage of the term should not be confused with common usage which connotes self love. See also Reality testing.

Ego-alien: Refers to aspects of a person's personality that he views as repugnant, unacceptable, or inconsistent with the rest of his personality. It is also called ego-dystonic. See also Ego-syntonic.

Ego analysis: Intensive psychoanalytic study and analysis of the ways in which the ego resolves for attempts to deal with intrapsychic conflicts, especially in relation to the development of mental mechanisms and the maturation of capacity for rational thought and action. Modern psychoanalysis gives more emphasis to considerations of the defensive operations of the ego than did earlier techniques, which emphasized instinctual forces to a greater degree.

Ego boundaries: A concept introduced by Federn that refers to the ability of the intact ego to differentiate the real boundaries prevent repressed unconscious material from overwhelming the ego. When that happen, the person experiences depersonalization and derealization. Boundaries are said to be weakened in schizophrenia and dissociative states.

Egocentric: Self-centered; selfishly preoccupied with one' own need; lacking interest in others.

Egocentricity or egocentrism: A central concept in Piagetian theory, egocentricity refers to the idea that children take their own perspective as central, and tend to assume that other people have the same understandings, motives and needs as the child. It is not a moralistic concept, and has nothing in common with selfishness or egotism; but instead in concerned with the child's perception of association and causality. The process by which child gradually comes to differentiate itself from the external world, through the development of the body-schema to recognized that objects have permanent existence; and to be above to decentre and see things from another's viewpoint are, for piaget, significant milestones in the reduction of egocentricity. When used of adults the term does have implications of selfishness though perhaps in should just imply a delayed cognitive development.

Egocentric speech: Speech which is simply involved in monitoring and directing the child's internal thought processes and has no communicative function. According to Piaget, this is a significant part of the child; acquisition of speech; it forms a valuable tool of thought, which the child practices as it performs mental operations on the external world.

Ego-coping skill: adaptive method or capacity developed by a person to deal with or overcome a psychological or social problem.

Ego-defense: See defense mechanism.

Ego-dystonic: Aspects if a person's behaviour, thought, and attitudes viewed as repugnant or inconsistent with the total personality. Contrast with ego-syntonic.

Ego-dystonic homosexuality: A psychosexual disorder in which a person has unwanted and distressful homosexual arousal and wishes to acquire or increase heterosexual arousal. A DSM-III term replacing sexual orientation disturbance.

Ego ideal: The part of the personality that comprises the aims and goals for the self; usually refers to the conscious or unconscious emulation of significant figures with whom one has identified. The ego ideal emphasizes what one should be or do in contrast to what one should not be or not do.

Ego instinct: In Freud's formulations prior to 1920, there were two groups of instincts–the self preservative or ego instinct and the reproductive or sexual instinct.

Egoism: A tendency to give an excessively high priority to one' own needs and wishes and a correspondingly low priority to those of other people. See egotism for a comparison.

Ego libido: Libido which is invested in the ego. It is not always clear whether this refers to the energy available for ego functions or self-love.

Egology: A term devised by S. Rado to mean study of the ego, the "I".

Egomania: Morbid self-preoccupation or self-centeredness. See also Narcissism.

Ego-model: A person after whom another person patterns his ego.

Egormorphism: The attributing of one' own need, desires, motives, etc., to someone else.

Egopathy: Hostile behaviour due to psychopathically exaggerated sense of self-importance.

Ego psychology: The study and elucidation of those slowly changing functions known as psychic structures which usually shape, channel, and organize mental activity into meaningful and tolerable patterns of experience. The usual structures referred to in this sense are memory, speech, locomotion, cognition, drive, restraint, discharge, and the capacity to make judgements and decisions.

Ego state: In Eric Berne's structural analysis, a state of mind and its related set of coherent behaviour patterns. There are three ego states; parent, adult and child.

Ego strength: Ability to retain reality and manage the forces of the bid and supergo.

Ego-syntonic: Aspects of a person's behaviour, thoughts, and attitudes viewed as acceptable and consistent with the total personality. Contrast with ego-dystonic.

Egotism: A constant tendency overvalue oneself and therefore to undervalue other people. The difference from egoism in that egotists tend not to be interested exploit them. Egotistical attitudes tend to be clearly displayed whereas egoism may need to be concealed to be effective.

Einstellung: A term coined by the Gestalt school of psychology of refer to the kinds of mental sets which can influence problem-solving by inducing a rigidity of thought which precludes the perceptions of alternative strategies or solutions.

Eidetic image: Unusually vivid and apparently exact mental image, may be a memory, fantasy, or dream.

Egotization: The process by which a mental process or function becomes part of the self, structure or deaggressified and desexualized.

Eitingon, Max (1881–1943): Austrian psychoanalyst. An emissary of the Zurich school, he gained fame as the first person to be analyzed by Freud in a few sessions in 1907. Later, he became the first chief of the Berlin Psychoanalytic clinic, a founder of the Berlin Psychoanalytic Institute, and founder of the Palestine Psychoanalytic Society.

Ejaculatory incompetence (impotence): Inability to reach orgasm and ejaculate during sexual intercourse despite adequacy of erection.

Ekbom's syndrome (delusion of infestation): Delusion that body and/or surroundings are infested with insects, parasites etc. "Evidence of this is gathered. Often paranoid or depressive or sometimes organic brain disorder may cause it.

Elaborated code: A term used by Bernstein to refer to the form of language commonly used by middle-class families, characterized by an extensive use of nouns, explanations, and synonyms. Bernstein's use of the term code is continuous, as are many other parts of his theory. This is due mainly to the theory having been associated with the verbal deprivation of class difference in language use, which argue that restricted language use implies restricted cognitive possibilities. See code of language, restricted code.

Elaboration: An unconscious process or expansion and embellishment of detail, especially with reference to a symbol or representation in a dream.

Elation: An effective state of joyous gaiety which, when intensified and out of keeping with life circumstances, is a dominant symptom of mania and hypomania. *Synonym*: hyperthymia.

Elective mutism: A childhood mental disorder in which a child who is able and willing to speak to select persons persistently refuses to speak in other social or school situations.

Electra complex: The female analogue of the Oedipus complex in the male, it is an infrequently used term to describe unresolved developmental conflicts influencing a woman's relationships with men. Term was given by Jung. Most theories, including Freud, have rejected the use of the term.

Electroconvulsive therapy (ECT): A treatment, usually for depression, that involves the application of electric current to the brain for a fraction of a second through scalp electrodes, including a convulsive reaction and unconsciousness.

Elopement: In psychiatry, escape; absenting oneself from a mental hospital without permission.

Elusion: Term used by Laing (1961) to describe the process by which a person may avoid confrontation with himself and others by impersonating himself i.e., by playing at the role that he in fact has. It counterfeits truth by a double pretence, i.e., by pretending that phantasy is real and then pretending that reality is a phantasy.

Emancipated minor: Legal term for a minor who exercise general control over his or her life and hence has the legal rights of an adult.

Embodied and unembodied: Terms used by Laing (1960) to describe two states if being, the embodied state being possessed by persons with primary ontological security who feel they began when their bodies began die, the unembodied being that possessed by persons who lack primary ontological security and have a sense of being detached from their bodies.

Emergency reaction, or "fight-or-fight" response: The pattern of bodily changes accompanying fear and anger which help the organism deal with threatening situations. Compare relaxation response. See sympathetic system.

Emic vs. etic: Conceptions derived from the internal logic of an emic, universal conceptions, cutting across cultures are etic (Pike, 1954).

Emotion: The experience of subjective feelings which have positive or negative value for the individual. Beyond this statement the definition must depend on the particular theory of emotion being held. Most current theories regard emotions as a combination of psychological response with a cognitive evaluation of the situation. The idea that emotions are the source of actions has become less popular and in fact the term has only a remote link with any idea of motion, having come into English from the French word emouvoir, "to excite". Some definitions would reserve the term emotions for fairly intense and fairly brief experiences. It is certainly useful to distinguish emotions from states, like hunger, sexual desire, and frustration) , which may give rise to emotions, and from behaviours such as aggression, which may indicate the presence of an emotion but which are not themselves emotion.

Emotional deprivation: See deprivation, emotional.

Emotional disorder: Lay term for mental illness or mental disorder, in common usage it does not specifically imply an affective or schizophrenic disorder.

Emotional insight: See Insight.

Emotional liability: Excessive emotional responsiveness, characterized by stable and rapidly changing emotions.

Emotional support: Encouragement, hope, and inspiration given to one person by another.

Empathy: The intellectual and emotional awareness and understanding of another person's state of mind. It involves the projection of oneself into another person's frame of reference. It is important ability in a successful therapist or a helpful group member. See also sympathy.

Empiricism: A philosophical school of thought highly influential in psychology, which argues that only that which can be directly observed or measured can be meaningfully studied.

Enactive representation: According to Bruner, the first mode of representation developed by the young child. Enactive representation involves the storing of information in the form of kinaesthetic senzations, such as the way that most adults would recall the sensation of a fairground waltzer or helkter-skelter. In the world of the infant, such "muscle memories" would be adequate to cope with most of the information encountered by the child, as the child develops and its world widens, further forms of representation are added to its repertoire, such as iconic representation and symbolic representation.

Encapsulated elusion: See Delusion.

Encephalopathy: Any of the metabolic, toxic, neoplastic, or degenerative diseases of the brain.

Encoding: The processing of information in such a way that it can be represented internally, for memory storage.

Encopresis: A disorder, most common in children in which the main manifestation is the persistent voluntary or involuntary passage of formed faces of normal or near-normal consistency, into places not intended for that purpose, in the individual's own sociocultural setting. Sometimes the child has failed to gain bowel control, and sometimes the child has gained control but becomes encopretic again later. There may be a variety of associated psychiatric symptoms, and there may be smearing of faeces. The condition would not usually be diagnosed under the age of four years.

Encounter group: A form of sensitivity training that emphasizes the experiencing of individual relationships within the group and that minimizes intellectual and didactic input. It is a group that focuses on the present, rather than concerning itself with the present or outside problems of its members. J.L. Moreno introduced and developed the idea of the encounter group in 1914. See also Body contact exploration maneuver Sensitivity training group.

Endogenous: A term introduced into psychiatry by Mobius in 1893 for the purposes of etiological, clinical classification to designate those mental disorders caused primarily by hereditary and constitutional factors, originating within the soma or the central nervous system. The precise meanings of endogeny and exogeny are, however, too arbitrary to justify more than a provisional distinction. For example, a brain tumour although arising within the central nervous system would give rise to an 'exogenous' mental disorder, while a psychogenic psychosis would be an 'endogenous' mental disorder, while a psychogenic psychosis would be an 'endogenous' disorder (Jaspers, 1946). The distinction, therefore, is of mainly historical significance.

Endomorphic: Obsese, one of Sheldon's constitutional types. See also Ectomorphic, Mesomorphic.

Endorphin: A naturally produced chemical with morphine-like action; usually found in the brain and associated with the relief of pain. May be the body's own protection against pain. The highest concentration is in the pituitary gland.

Engineering psychology: The application of psychology to man-machine interact ion. It includes the selection and training of people to operate machines, and advice on the design of machines so that they can be efficiently used by human operators.

Engram: A memory trace a neurophysiologic process that accounts for persistence of memory.

Engulfment: Term used by Laing (1960) to describe a form of anxiety suffered by persons who lack primary ontological security in which relationships with others are experiences as overwhelming threats to their identity.

Enkephalins: One of the major families of endogenous opioids, the other being the endorphins. The enkephalins are pentapeptides; their two natural forms (met- and leu) differ from each other only in terminal aminoacid; see endorphins.

Enlightenment effects: The effects of a given psychological theory on those who came to understand its premises and predictions. The most celebrated form of enlightenment effect is the self fulfilling prophecy initially described by Morton.

Enuresis: A disorder, most common in children, in which the main manifestation is a persistent involuntary voiding of urine by day or night which is considered abnormal for the age of the individual. Sometimes the child will have failed to gain bladder control and in other cases he or she will have gained control and then lost it. Episodic or fluctuating enuresis should be included. The disorder would not usually be diagnosed under the age of four years.

Environment: The total external context in which an individual operates. The concept of environment is usually used to include physical surroundings and their characteristics and social contexts and interactions, but it may be used more specifically in include all the different dacets of the physical but to exclude the social. See ecology.

Environmental determinism: The view that behaviour, personality, or psychological characteristics originate as a direct consequence of individual learning and environment influences, and are not significantly influenced by innate factors.

Environmental psychology: The study of the ways that the environment influences and channels individual behaviour. Environmental psychology includes the study of such factors as territoriality and personal space, ergonomic design, and the physical attributes of surroundings.

Environmentalism: The doctrine that all significant determinants of behaviour are to be found in the environment. Strict behaviourism is one version of environmentalism. See heredity-environment controversy.

EPI: The Eysenck Personality inventory; a questionnaire designed to assess people on the two character traits of extroversion and neuroticism. These were proposed as the two main underlying individual differences in personality; each representing several second-order traits.

Epidemiology: In psychiatry, the study of the incidence, prevalence, control, and distribution of mental disorders within a particular population.

Epigenesis: A term introduced by Erikson to refer to the stages of ego and social development.

Epilepsy: A neurological disorder resulting from a sudden, excessive, disorderly discharge of neurons in either a structurally normal or a diseased cerebral cortex. It is characterized by the paroxysmal recurrence of short-lived disturbances of consciousness, involuntary convulsive muscle movements, psychic or sensory disturbances, or some combination thereof. It is termed idiopathic epilepsy when there is no identifiable organic cause.

Epileptic dementia: A form of epilepsy that is accompanied by progressive mental and intellectual impairment. Some believe that the circulatory disturbances during epileptic attacks cause nerve cell degeneration and lead to dementia.

Epileptic psychosis, acute: A term describing the acute psychotic manifestations, usually lasting from several days to a few weeks, that are liable to occur in an epileptic independently of seizures and of ictal or postictal confusional state. These manifestations, which usually take the form of an acute paranoid reaction, are encountered mostly in people with seizures of temporal-lobe origin, usually during spontaneous periods of remission or remissions produced by anticonvulsive treatment. They are often accompanied by the disappearance of interictal electro encephalogram (EEG) discharges ('forced normalization'). The fact that such manifestations are not necessarily related to seizures, occur in only some epileptics, indicates that the strict relation suggested by the term 'acute epileptic psychosis' cannot be demonstrated. Preference should therefore, be given to the expression 'acute psychotic episode in an epileptic' or acute psychosis in an epileptic'.

Epileptic psychosis, chronic: Chronic hallucinatory paranoid psychosis occurring in subjects with epilepsy, particularly temporal-lobe epilepsy. It is characterized by religious or mystical delusions and tends to occur in subjects whose seizures are tapering off, whether spontaneously or in response to treatment. Chronic epileptic psychosis is rare and it is difficult to distinguish from the 'functional' paranoid psychoses, although in the epileptic variety affect and social integration are sometimes well-preserved. The relationship between epilepsy and chronic psychosis is neither simple nor clear. On the one hand, the psychotic phenomena are directly related to epilepsy of the temporal lobe, probably of the dominant hemisphere, occur in inverse proportion to the presence and frequency of temporal lobe seizures; and are independent of the presence of associated brain lesions. This is all evidence in favour of the epileptic nature of the psychotic manifestations. On the other hand, it would be more appropriate to use the expression 'chronic psychosis in an epileptic individual' since numerous factors–organic, psychological (the reliving of previous experience during some seizures), sociological (rejection by society, low status of the epileptic) and pharmacological (long-term anti-convulsant therapy, which disturbs folic acid metabolism) may play a part in the cauzation of the psychoses observed in epileptics.

Epileptic twilight state: A transient psychic change occurring during or after an epileptic seizure, usually one of temporal lobe origin, and characterized by reduced alertness with narrowing of the field of consciousness resulting in a 'hazy' and 'blurred' perception of the surroundings. Such states may be classed as intermediate between confusional states, in which dissolution of consciousness is more complete, and dreamy states, in which fantasy is prevalent.

Epinephrine: One of the catecholamines secreted by the adrenal gland and by fibres of the sympathetic nervous system. It is responsible for many of the physical manifestations of fear and anxiety. Also known as adrenaline.

Episodic: Term used to describe an illness in which there are sustained disturbances clearly distinguished from previous functioning.

Episodic memory: A long-term memory store containing memories of the specific things that have happened to a person (reminiscences). Compare semantic memory.

Epistemology: The theory of knowledge; the study of the method and grounds of knowledge.

Epistemophilia: Pleasure in gaining knowledge. There is a tendency to regard the thirst for knowledge as either a derivative of scopophilia, i.e., as an extension of sexual curiosity or as a sublimation of oral drives.

Equality rule: A rule employed as a standard in making judgements of fairness in social relationships; requires that outcomes be do tributed equally among participants in a relationship.

Equilibration: In Piagetian theory, the process by which schemata are developed to take account of new information. If new information which is encountered fails to fit into an existing schema, the individual is thrown into a state of cognitive discomfort known as disequilibrium. Though the two process of assimilation and accommodation, the schemata are adapted or adjusted such that the new information can be handled and the cognitive balance is restored. This is the process of equilibration.

Equity theory: A theory of social behaviour which suggests that individuals attempt to establish perceived equality of the outcome/input ratios in relationships.

Erben's test: It is based on the physiological principle that during fine movement agonists and contracting antagonists act in synergy so that movements can be executed with precision during gross movement; agonists along contract and antagonist relaxed in a patient with organic illness. Tremors may also be associated. In testing the muscle power in a patient with functional hemiparesis, antagonists muscles contract when patient is told to move part and there are no tremors.

Eremophobia: Fear of being by oneself.

Ergasia: Adolf Meyer's term for a person's total activity, as opposed to the functioning of part of the whole.

Erikson, Erik (1902-): German born, Psychoanalyst and child analyst noted for his theory of ego development and psychosexual development which he conceptualized in terms of social adaptation as it relates to Freud's formulations. See also Epigenesis, Psychosocial development. Author of major studies of Luther and Gandhi.

Erogenous zone: An area of the body particularly susceptible to erotic arousal when stimulated, especially the oral, anal, and genital areas. Sometimes called erotogenic zone. Eros: See life instinct, sexual drive.

Erotic: Consciously or unconsciously invested with sexual feeling; sensually related.

Erotolalia: Sexual obscene speech, especially in reference to the use of such speech during sexual intercourse as a means of enhancing gratification.

Erotomania: Pathological preoccupation with sexual activities or fantasies.

Erythrophobia: Fear of blushing.

ESB: The usual abbreviation for a form of direct electrical stimulation of the brain which appears to function as a powerful reinforcer of behaviour and to give highly pleasurable sensations. Experiments conducted in the 1960s seemed to imply that there was a direct 'pleasure centre' in a particular region of the hypothalamus. For instance, stimulation of this area in rats, given as a reward for level-pressing, produced an extremely high response rate; and in terminally-ill cancer patients produced reports of feeling 'wonderful' or 'happy' (Campbell). It was though that this might be the root of all motivational states. However, the 'pleasure centre' concept presents some difficulties; for instance, unlike other forms of learning, it extinguishes very quickly, so the status of ESB is now rather unclear.

ESP: See Extrasensory perception.

Essentialism: The opposite of existentialism. Freudian psychoanalysis is an essentialist theory since it explains phenomena in terms of essences i.e., in terms of forces underlying the phenomena.

EST: Electroshock therapy. See also Electroconvulsive therapy (ECT).

Ethnocentrism: Conviction that one's own group is superior to other groups. It impairs one's ability to evaluate members of another group realistically or to communicate with them on an open, equal, and person-to-person basis.

Esteem needs: One level of the hierarchical model of human needs proposed by Maslow. Esteem needs include the need for achievement and social recognition and are considered to achieve importance once physiological, safety, and social needs have been met. See also self-esteem.

Ethical: To do with rights and wrongs. Owing to the scope of psychological interests and the potential for psychological damage, ethical issues have become of great importance in modern psychology. They include such aspects of psychological practice as the use of deception in experimental work; the investigation of characteristics which are potentially threatening to the self-concept (of Milgram's work on obedience); the use of animals in research; and questions of confidentiality in professional practice. Professional psychological associations usually have specially committees which evaluate and provide guidance on ethical issues.

Ethnography: A method of unstructured observational research developed by anthropologists for studying the workings of human cultures 'from within'. It involves the researcher's participation (participant observation) in the everyday lives of the group under study.

Ethnology: A science that concerns itself with the division of mankind into races and their origin, distribution, relations and characteristics.

Ethnomethodology: The study of the everyday methods of practical reasoning used in the production and interpretation of social action.

Ethogenics: A theory and associated methodology for the analysis and explanation of social interaction.

Ethologism: The appeal of concepts and findings derived from ethological studies of the behaviour of non-human animals as a source of immediate diagnosis of the dilemmas of the human condition and of prescriptions for change. Term was coined by Callan (1970).

Ethology: The study of behaviour in the natural environment. Ethological studies of animal behaviour have been conducted throughout the 20th century, and were systematized by the work of Konrad Lorenz and Niko Tinbergen. More recently, the ethological approach has been applied to the study of human behaviour, most notably in the fields of mother-infant interaction and non-verbal communication.

Etiology: The study of the causes of disease.

Euergasia: Word used by Adolf Meyer to mean normal mental functioning.

Eugenics: A set of political beliefs based on the idea that intelligence and personality are fixed inherited characteristics determining role and position in society. Eugenicists believe that breedings should be restricted among those of the 'lower' classes of society, and that those of subnormal intellect or undesirable personality should be sterilized to prevent the spread of such genetic characteristics.

Eunuch: Male whose testes have been removed before puberty.

Euphoria: An exaggerated feeling of well being that is inappropriate to apparent events. It may be induced by drugs such as opiates, amphetamines, and alcohol.

Euphorohallucinogen: A substance capable of producing euphoric hallucinations. See also hallucinogenic drug.

Euthymic: Normal mood.

Evasion: Act of not facing up to or of strategically eluding something. It consists of suppressing an idea that is next in a thought series and replacing it with another idea closely related to it. Evasion is also known as paralogia and perverted logic.

Event-related potential: Electrical activity produced by the brain in response to a sensory stimulus or associated with the execution of a motor, cognitive, or psychophysiologic task. See also evoked potential and electroencephalogram.

Evoked potential: Electrical activity produced by the brain in response to a sensory stimulus; a more specific term than event-related potential. See also electroencephalogram.

Exaltation: Feeling of intense elation and grandeur.

Executive ego function: A psychoanalytic term for the ego's management of the mental mechanisms in order to meet the needs of the organisms. See also ego.

Exhibitionism: A paraphilia in which a man exposes his genitals to females in a socially inappropriate fashion. The condition rarely occurs in women.

Existentialism: Philosophical theory which gives priority to phenomenology and ontology over cauzation, which rejects explanations in terms of essences imagined to actuate behaviour from within in favour of study of the phenomena themselves.

Existential psychiatry (existentialism): A school of psychiatry evolved from orthodox psychoanalytic thought; stresses the way in which a person experiences the phenomenologic world and takes responsibility for existence. Philosophically, it is holistic and self-deterministic in contrast to biologic or culturally deterministic points of view.

Existential psychotherapy: A type of therapy that puts the emphasis on here-and-now interaction and on feeling experiences, rather than on rational thinking. Little attention is given to patient resistances, and the therapist is involved on the same level and to the same degree as the patient. It is based on existential philosophy which holds that a person has the responsibility for his own exis- tence. See also Phenomenology.

Exorcism: A magical practice in which mystical incantations are invoked to remove demons that are alleged to have entered the mind.

Experiencing: Feeling emotions and sensations, as opposed to thinking; being involved in what is happening, rather than standing back at a distance and theorizing.

Experiment: A form of empirical investigation or study in which variables are manipulated in order to discover cause and effect. An experiment will involve at least one independent variable, which will be set up in such a way as to produce changes in a dependent variable.

Experimental design: The logical framework of an experiment which maximizes the probability of obtaining or detecting real effects and minimizes the likelihood of ambiguities regarding the significance of the experimentally observed differences.

Experimental group: A group whose main purpose is concerned with sharing whatever happens in spontaneous fashion.

Experimental neurosis: Laboratory studies can induce apparently neurotic behaviour in animals by training them to perform a task and then gradually making it impossible. First studied by Pavlov and presented as a basis for controlled study of neurosis in humans. Subsequently doubts were raised about whether the mental states of the animals were really similar to those of neurotic humans and the research was abandoned. A similar process occurred more recently with the study of learned helplessness.

Experimental philosophy: That branch of philosophy which, during the 18th and 19th centuries, became increasingly concerned with the study of the human mind, and which drew on empirical observations for its conclusions. Experimental philosophy became transmuted into psychology towards the end of the 19th century; the 'founding fathers' of psychology, Wilhelm Wundt, Herman Ebbinghaus and William James were simultaneously the last of the experimental philosophers.

Experimental psychology: Those branches of psychology which are firmly based in laboratory experimentation. The term is used to cover such areas as learning memory and perception. It has now been largely replaced by the wider area of cognitive psychology.

Experimenter bias: Experimenter expectations that are inadvertently communicated to patients or subjects. Such expectations may influence experimental findings.

Experimenter effects: Experimental problems producing a biased result brought about by the influence of the experimenter, for example, through subjects responding to the person who conducts the experiment. Experimenter effects may occur indirectly, because of the personal characteristics of the experimenter (e.g., their age, sex or other such feature) or directly, as a result of the beliefs or unconscious bias being transmitted to the subjects, and producing a self-fulfilling prophecy. The latter is usually controlled by using the double blind technique.

Expert witness: A status conferred on a witness based on appropriate qualifications, training and experience which acknowledges that competence and authority of the witness in a particular area of expertise. Expert witnesses are permitted to offer opinions in court related to their area of expertise which would not be permitted a witness without such status.

Explosive disorder, intermittent: A disorder of impulse control in which the person recurrently strikes out in an extremely angry and hostile fashion; the outbursts generally contrast sharply with the person's normal behaviour. See also Explosive disorder, isolated.

Explosive disorder, isolated: A disorder of impulse control in which the person has a single episode characterized by failure to resist a violent impulse against others. See also Explosive disorder, intermittent.

Explosive dysphasia: See Dysphasia.

Extended family therapy: A type of family therapy that involves family members, beyond the nuclear family, who are closely associated with it and affect it.

External validity: The applicability of the generalizations that may be made from the experimental findings beyond the occasion with those specific subjects, experimental conditions, experimenters, or measurements.

Extinction: The weakening of a reinforced operant response as a result of ceasing reinforcement. See also operant conditioning. Also, the elimination of a conditioned stimulus without the conditioned stimulus. See also respondent conditioning.

Extra psychic conflict: Conflict that arises between the person and his environment. See also intrapsychic conflict.

Extrapyramidal syndrome: A variety of signs and symptoms, including muscular rigidity, tremors, drooling, shuffling gait (parkinsonism); restlessness (akathisia); peculiar involuntary postures (dystonia); motor inertia (akinesia) and may other neurologic disturbances. Results from dysfunction of the extrapyramidal system. May occur as a reversible side effect of certain psychotrophic drugs, particularly phenothiazines. See also tardive dyskinesia.

Extrasensory perception (ESP): Experiencing of an external event by means other than the five senses. Telepathy–perception of another person's thoughts–and clairvoyance–perception of outside events–are two kinds of extrasensory perception. See also Parapsychology.

Extroversion: The state of one's energies being directed outside oneself. It is also spelled extraversion. See also Introversion.

Eyebrow flash: A recognition signal which consists of rapidly raising the eyebrows as a greeting to an individual who is recognized. The eyebrow flash seems to be common to all human cultures, and to some other species. It therefore is considered to be innate.

Eye contact: Mutual gaze, or the amount of time which two people spend looking at each other simultaneously. Eye contact is sometimes taken as an indicator of intimacy; eye-contact with unknown individuals tends to be avoided. It is powerful signal in all primates, including human beings; prolonged eye contact with neutral or hostile facial expression is taken as a threat gesture, and tends to be responded to by either aggressive or avoidance behaviour.

Eysenck, Hans Jurgen: Born in Germany in 1916. He is a major personality theorist. His main contributions were 'three factors theory of personality' (Extroversion/introversion, neuroticism, psychoticism), EPI (Eysenck Personality Inventory) 'MMQ' (Maudsley Medical Questionnaire), 'MPI' (Maudsley Personality Inventory).

F

Fabulation: A term used by Adolf Meyer to mean fabrication. See also Confubulation.

Face validity: The appearance of validity a test that "seems right" ; face validity is not necessarily true validity.

Facial affect programme: A strategy of including behavioural change through making the individual aware of the sensations arising from facial expressions which are different from those that he/she uses habitually. It is thought that encouraging the continued use of positive facial expressions, as opposed to those normally used, will provide positive feedback both through social interaction and through muscular interpretation. See facial feedback hypothesis.

Facial electromyography: A technique for measuring the degree of tension in facial muscles by recording the electrical discharge of the muscles. By mapping the muscle tensions occurring in different expressions a systematic and objective measure of facial expression can be obtained.

Facial expression: Characteristics patterns of arrangements of the muscles in the face, which provide important non-verbal clues in social interaction. Facial expression may be used either to express understanding, attitudes, emotions, or as specific cultural signals with clearly defined meanings. Some researchers have found that basic emotional expressions seem to be common to all human cultures, and are also found in blind babies, which would seem to imply that they are innate. However, other facial expressions show cultural variability, and seem to be acquired through social interaction.

Facial feedback hypothesis: The idea that our experience of emotion arises at least in part from our interpretations of the arrangement of our facial muscles. So mood changes may be affected by the altering of the facial expression, which will provide feedback leading to a change in the emotion that the person experience. The effect is used in studies of mood when subjects are asked to make, say, a depressed face as a part of a procedure for changing their mood.

Factitious disorder: A mental disorder characterized by the voluntary production of unreal physical or psychological symptoms. Unlike malingering, there is no apparent goal or obvious benefit in factitious disorder. See also Malingering, Munchausen syndrome, Somatoform disorder.

Factor analysis: A statistical technique that examines population clusters to extract patterns of commonality.

Failure to thrive, FTT: A condition of poor growth in infants, usually defined as being below the third centile (i.e., in the bottom 3% for the stage, sex, and population). In some cases there is a psychological problem which accounts for the poor growth but in the majority of cases there is no organic cause and the condition is called "non-organic failure to thrive". FTT was once believed to be a direct result of emotional deprivation and in its extreme form was called "deprivational dwarfism". It is now widely recognized that the basic problem is that the child does not receive enough food to sustain appropriate growth, though this in turn in likely to result from emotional or other difficulties of the parent, the child, or both.

Falling out: Seen among black Americans, but also called "blacking out" by Bahamians and "indisposition" by Haitians in Maimi. The patient simply collapse but without biting the tongue or incontinuance of urine or faeces. This is accompanied by lack of ability to speak or move, even though the individual hears and understands.

Falsifiable hypothesis: A hypothesis stated in sufficiently precise fashion that it can be tested by acceptable rules of logic, empirical and statistical evidence, and thereby found to be either confirmed or disconfirmed. As unfalsifiable hypothesis is one that is so general and/or ambiguous that all conceivable evidence can be "explained" by it.

Family neurosis: Mental disorder person's psychopathology is unconsciously interrelated with that of the other members of his family.

Family romance: It is the childhood phantasy that one's apparent parents are not one's real one's and that one is really of noble or royal birth.

Family therapy: An approach to psychological treatment in which the whole family is the focus, rather than an individual patient. Earlier approaches were derived from psychoanalysis and treated the family as if it had psychological processes similar to those of individuals. Recently, methods have been developed from systems theory, which recognize that, while the behaviour of a competent may seem strange when it is in isolation, it will make much more sense in the context of the complete system. Applied to individuals, and recognizing that families are one of the most significant systems within which most people function, this approach has led to a new way of looking at psychological disturbance. It assumes that in many cases the 'symptoms' shown by an individual are a meaningful response to their circumstances. More specifically, disturbed behaviour likely to be an attempt to regulate relationships, or solve problems, within the family. The literature contains many examples of spectacular success using 'systemic family therapy' but there has been little systematic evaluation of the techniques.

Fantasy: Daydream: fabricated mental picture of a situation or chain of events. A form of thinking dominated by unconscious material and primary processes, it seeks wish fulfillment and immediate solutions to conflicts. Fantasy may serve as the matrix for creativity or for neurotic distortions of reality.

Fantasy and phantasy: In modern use fantasy and phantasy, inspite of their identity in sound and in ultimate etymology, tend to be apprehended as separate words, the predominant sense of the former being 'caprice, whim, fanciful invention', and that of the latter is imagination, visionary notion.

Father surrogate: Father substitute. In psychoanalysis, the patient projects his father image onto another person and responds to the person unconsciously in an inappropriate and unrealistic manner, with the feeling and attitudes that he had towards his real father.

Fatigue effect: An experimental effect about brought by the subject's being tired, bored, or otherwise affected by the duration of the experimental procedure. It can contaminate experimental results because it may appear that subjects are less good at later tasks when in fact they are just getting tired. See counterbalancing, order effects.

Fausse reconnaissance: False recognition. See also Paramnesia.

Faute de mieux: Literally," for want of anything better", connoting in psychiatry a person's choosing a homosexual relationship when no partner of the opposite is available.

Fear: A primitive, intense emotion in the face of threat, real or imagined, which is accompanied by physiological reactions resulting from arousal of the sympathetic nervous system and by defensive pattern of behaviour associated with avoidance, fight or concealment.

Fear, guilty: Rado's term for the fear that dire consequences are in store for one because of a misdeed (or forbidden impulse). Guilty fear is thus a derivative of the dread of conscience. It is a prominent feature of the obsessive syndrome where it opposes the patient's defiant range and leads, ultimately, to repression of the latter. See attack, obsessive.

Fear, impulse: A fear that arises within the individual, more or less directly from an instinctual sources. It is contrasted with real object in the environment. The fear of being in a dark place is a real or "reality" fear. The fear of imminent collapse and death, while in excellent health, is an impulse fear.

Fear of:

Air: Aerophobia

Animals: Zoophobia

Anything new: Kaino (to) phobia; neophobia

Bacilli: Bacillophobia

Bad men: Pavor sceleris; scelerophobia

Barren space: Cenophobia; kenophobia

Bearing a monster: Teratophobia

Bees: Apiphobia; melissophobia

Being alone: Autophobia; eremiophobia; monophobia

Being beaten: Mastigophobia

Being buried alive: Taphephobia

Being enclosed: Clithrophobia

Being laughed at: Catagelophobia

Being locked in: Claustrophobia; clitrophobia

Being looked at: Scopophobia

Being touched: (h) Aphephobia; haptephobia

Birds: Ornithophobia

Blood: Hematophobia; homophobia

Blushing: Ereuthophobia; erythrophobia

Brain disease: Meningitophobia

Burglars: Seelerophobia

Cats: Ailurophobia; geleophobia; neophobia

Change: Kainophobia; Kainitophobia; neophobia

Childbirth: Maieusiophobia

Choking: Anginophobia; pnigophobia

Cold: Cherimaphobia; psychropophobia

Comets: Cometophobia

Confinement: Caustrophobia

Contamination: Coprophobia; molysmophobia; mysophobia; scatophobia

Corpses: Necrophobia

(Crossing a) bridge or river: Gephyrophobia

(Crossing a) street: Dromophobia

Crowds: Demophobia; Ochlophobia

Cumbersome Pseudoscientific terms: Hellenologophobia

Dampness: Hygrophobia

Darkness: Achluphobia; nyctophobia; scotophobia

Dawn: Eosophobia

Daylight: Phengophobia

Death: Necrophobia; thanatophobia

Definite disease: Monopathophobia

Deformity: Dysmorphophobia

Demons: Demonia; demonomania; entheomania

Depths: Bathophobia

Devils: Demonophobia; stanophobia

Dirt: Mysophobia; rhypophobia; rupophobia

Disease: Nosophobia; pathophobia

Dogs: Cynophobia

Dolls: Pediophobia

Dust: Amathophobia

Eating: Cibophobia; phagophobia; sitophobia

Electricity: Electrophobia

Emptiness: Kenophobia

Everything: Pamphobia (obs); panphobia; panophobia; pantophobia

Examination: Examination phobia

Excrement: Coprophobia; scatophobia

Eyes: Ommatophobia

Failure: Kakarrthaphobia

Fatigue: Kopophobia

Fearing: Phobophobia

Feathers: Pteronophobia

Female genitals: Eurotophobia

Fever: Fibriphobia; pyrexiophobia

Filth: Mysohobia; rhypophobia; rupophobia

Filth (personal): Automysophobia

Fire: Pyrophobia

Fish: Ichthyphobia

Flash of lightning: Selaphobia

Flogging: Mastigophobia

Floods: Antlophobia

Flutes: Aulophobia

Flying: Aviophobia

Fog: Homichlophobia

Food: Cibophobia; phagophobia; sit (i) ophobia

Forests: Hylophobia

Frogs: Batrachophobia

Functioning: Ergasiophobia

Ghosts: Phasmophobia

Girls: Parthenophobia

Glass: Crystallophobia; hyelophobia

God: Theophobia

Gravity: Barophobia

Hair: Trichopathophobia; trichophobia

Heat: Thermophobia

Heaven: Siderophobia; uranophobia

Heights: Acrophobia; hyposophobia
Hell: Hadephobia; sygiophobia
Heredity: Patroiophobia
High objects: Batophobia
Horses: Equinophobia
Houses: Domatophobia; oikophobia
Humiliation: Catagelophobia
Ideas: Ideophobia
Impending death: Meditatio mortis; thanatophobia
Infinity: Apeirophobia
Injury: Traumatophobia
Innovation: Neophobia
Insanity: Lyssophobia; maniaphobia
Insects: Acarophobia; entomophobia
Jealousy: Zelophobia
Justice: Dikephobia
Knives: Aichmophobia
Large objects: Megalophobia
Left: Levophobia; sinistrophobia
Light: Photophobia
Lightning: Astraphobia; astrapophobia; keraunophobia
Loneliness: Erem (i) Ophobia; monophobia
Machinery: Mechanophobia
Many things: Polyphobia
Any things: Gamophobia
Materialism: Hylephobia
Medicine (s): Pharmacophobia
Men: Androphobia
Metals: Metallophobia
Meteors: Meteorophobia
Mice: Musophobia
Mind: Psychophobia
Mirrors: Eisoptrophobia; spectrophobia

Missiles: Ballistophobia
Moisture: Hygophobia
Money: Chrematophobia
Motion: Kinesophobia
Myths: Mythophobia
Naked body: Gymnophobia
Naming, being named: Onomatophobia
Needles: Belonephobia
Neglecting duty: Paralipophobia
Negro(es): Negrophobia
Night: Noctiphobia; nyctophobia
Northern lights: Auroraphobia
Novelty: Kainophobia; kainotophaobia; neophobia
Odor: (personal): Bromidrosiphobia
Odor(s): Olfactophobia; osmophobia; osphresiophobia
Open space(s): Agoraphobia; agyiophobia
Pain: Algophobia; odynophobia
Parasites: Parasitophobia; phobanthropy
Places: Topophobia
Pleasure: Hedonophobia
Points: Aichmophobia
Poison: Iophobia; toxi(co) phobia
Poverty: Peniaphobia
Precipices: Cremnophobia
Public places: Agoraphobia
Punishment: Poinephobia
Rabies: Cynophobia
Railroads or trains: Siderodromophobia
Rain, rainstorms: Ombrophobia
Rectal excreta: Coprophobia
Rectum: Proctophobia
Red: Erythrophobia
Responsibility: Hypengyophobia

Ridicule: Catagelophobia

Right: Dextrophobia

Rivers: Potamophobia

Robbers: Harpaxophobia

(The) Road: Rhabdophobia

Ruin: Atephobia

Scared things: Hierophobia

Scabies: Scabiophobia

(Receiving a) Scratch: Amychophobia

(The) Sea: Nautophobia; thalassophobia

Self: Autophobia

Seman: Spermatophobia

Sex: Genophobia

Sexual intercourse: Coitophobia cypri (do) phobia

Shock: Hormephobia

Ships: Nautophobia

Sin: Hamartophobia

Sining: Enosiphobia; peccatiphobia; scrupulosity

Sitting: Thassophobia

Sitting down: Kathisophobia

Skin lesion: Dermatophobia

Skin (of animals): Doraphobia

Sleep: Hypnophobia

Small objects or animals: Microbiophobia; microphobia

Smothering: Pnigerophobia

Snakes: Ophidiophobia

Snow: Chinophobia

Solitude: Erem (i) Ophobia; monophobia

Sounds: Acousticophobia; phonophobia sourness; Acerophobia

Speaking: Lal (i) Ophobia

Speaking aloud: Phonophobia

Spiders: Arachneophobia

Stairs: Climacophobia
Standing up: Stasiphobia
Standing up and walking: Stasibasiphobia
Stars: Siderophobia
Stealing: Kleptophobia
Stillness: Eremiophobia
Stories: Mythophobia
Strangers: Xenophobia
Streets: Agoraphobia; agyiophobia
String: Linonophobia
Success: Polycratism
Sunlight: Heliophobia
Talking: Lal(i) Ophobia
Tapeworms: Taeniophobia
Taste: Geumaphobia
Teeth: Odontophobia
Thinking: Phronemophobia
Thirteen: Triskaideakaphobia
Thunder: Astra(po) phobia; brontophobia; tonitrophobia
Time: Chronophobia
Travel: Hodophobia
Trembling: Tremophobia
Trichinosis: Trichinophobia
Tuberculosis: Phthisiophobia
Tuberculophobia
Vaccination: Vaccinophobia
Vehicles: Amaxophobia
Veneral disease: Cypridoophobia; cypriphobia
Voids: Kenophobia
Vomiting: Emerophobia
Walking: Basiphobia
Water: Hydrophobia; nautophobia
Weakness: Asthenophobia

Wind: Anemophobia

Women: Gynophobia; horror feminae

Work: Ponophobia

Writing: Graphophobia

Febriphobia: Pyrexeophobia; fear of fever Fechner, Gustav Theodor (fek'ner) (1801–87) German physicist. Psychologist, philosopher.

Fechner's Law: A principle in psychophysics, which states that the sensation experienced by an individual increases as a logarithmic function of the stimulus intensity. In other words, that the physical increase in stimulation required for a perceived increase in intensity is not constant, but systematically greater for higher intensities. For example switching a light on may be perceived as a substantial increase in brightness when the room was previously dark, but may be hardly noticeable during bright sunlight. See also Weber's Law, relative threshold, absolute threshold.

Federn, Paul: (1871–1950), Austrian psychoanalyst, one of Freud's earliest followers, and the last survivor of the original Wednesday Evening Society. He made important original contributions to psychoanalysis, such as the concepts of flying dreams and ego feelings and he was instrumental in saving the minutes of the Vienna Psychoanalytic Society for subsequent publication.

Feeble mindedness: Obsolete term for mental retardation.

Feedback: In a given system, the return, as input, of some form of information regarding the output; it is used as a regulatory mechanism. In psychiatry, it often refers to the verbally or otherwise expressed response to a person's behaviour by another person or a group.

Fellatio: Use of the mouth or tongue to stimulate the male genitalia.

Feminine identity: Inner sense of gender affiliation with females, see also Gender identity. Masculine identity.

Feminism in boys: Adoption by preadolescent boys of appearance, clothes and behaviour typical of the female sex. Early effeminate behaviour in boys can be precursor or predictor of adult homosexuality.

Ferenczi, Sandor: (1873–1933) Hungarian psychoanalyst, one of Freud's early followers, and a brilliant contributor to all aspects of psychoanalysis. His temperament was more romantic than Freud's, and he came to favour more active and personal techniques, to the point that his adherence to psychoanalysis during his last years was questioned.

Fetishism: A paraphilia in which sexual excitement and gratification are achieved by substituting an inanimate object such as shoe, piece of underwear, or other article of clothing for a human love object.

Field dependence/independence: As aspect of cognitive style concerned with whether a person is dominated by context when making judgements (field dependence) or whether they can ignore distracting contextual information (field independence). It may be tested by the accuracy with which a subject can judge the orientation of a line when it is surrounded by a frame at a different angle, or when the subject is in a chair which can be tilted away from the vertical. Large individual differences have been found, which seem to relate to other areas of cognitive functioning.

Field theory: Conceptual approach to the study of personality formulated by Kurt Lewin. The person and his environment together constitute the life space, a complex field of forces acting on the personality and determining behaviour. The fundamental focus of the theory is on an operational analysis of the causal determinants of human behaviour. Lewin expressed his concepts in geometric and mathematical terms borrowed from physics in an attempt to provide a framework suitable to the scientific study of human behaviour. Field theory has been applied by various individual and group psychotherapists and has received particular attention in areas of social psychology and group process.

Fight or fight response: See alarm reaction.

Figure-ground organization: The tendency, which is built into our visual perception, to organize incoming information (which arrives in the form of light waves of varying intensities and wavelengths) into meaningful units, or figures, set against a background. Figure-ground organization was intensively studied by the Gestalt psychologists, who identified several principles of perceptual organization which served to make up figure-ground discrimination. These were collectively known as the Laws of Pragnanz, and included the principle of closure, and the principle of "good gestalt".

Figure-ground perception: This is a general term used to refer to those aspects of perception which derive from figure-ground organizations. So, for instance, it would include areas such as pattern perception, which is dependant upon the organization of visual information into figures against background.

Filter models: Theoretical models put forward to suggest plausible mechanisms by which cognitive processes may take place. The best known filter models were put forward to explain the process of selective attention, by psychologists such as Broadbent, Triesman, and Deutsch. Each of these represented a more or less complex attempt to explain the way in which incoming information is channeled such that only a selected part of it is received, rather than the overwhelming whole.

First mental-health revolution: The trend toward human treatment for mental patents, beginning in the late eighteenth century.

Fixation: The arrest of psychosexual development at

any stage before complete maturation; a close and paralyzing attachment to another person, such as one's mother or father. See also Anal phase, Oral phase, Phallic phase, Regression.

Fixed action pattern: Complex sequences of behaviour that are genetically pre-programmed so that all members of the species show the behaviour when it is needed. Neither learning nor practices are needed for the behaviour to be performed perfectly. Fixed action patterns have been intensively studied by ethologists, and involve sequences of behaviour which have been inherited as a complete unit.

Fixed-interval reinforcement: A reinforcement schedule in which reinforcements, or rewards, are given only after a set period of time since the last reinforcement became available. After a suitable acquisition period, this method of administering reinforcement tends to produce a high level of responding around the time of the reinforcement, and a low rate of responding at other times. It has low resistance to extinction.

Fixed-ratio reinforcement: A reinforcement schedule in which reinforcements, on rewards, are only given after a set number of response had been made since the last reinforcement. Fixed-ratio reinforcement schedules produce a very rapid response rate, but have a low resistance to extinction.

Fixed-role therapy: A method of treatment derived from personal construct theory in which the client agrees to adopt particular ways of behaving which are clearly different from (though not opposite to) his or her usual style. The method seems particularly effective in undermining a belief that only one kind of behaviour is possible.

Flagellantism: The process by which sexual partners are aroused and gratified by whipping or being whipped. It is also known as flagellation.

Flagellation: A masochistic or sadistic act in which one or both participants derive stimulation, usually erotic, from whipping or being whipped.

Flexibilitas cerea: See cerea flexibilitas.

Fliess, Wilhem (1858–1928): Berlin nose and throat specialist who shared an early interest with Freud in the physiology of sex and entered into a prolonged correspondence that figures importantly in the records of Freud's self analysis. Freud was influenced by Fliess'S concept of bisexuality and his theory of the periodicity of sex functions.

Flight into health: Phrase used to describe the rapid symptomatic recovery sometimes displayed by patients who wish to avoid psychoanalytical investigation. Probably a manic defence.

Flight into illness: Phrase used to describe the escape from conflict achieved by developing symptoms.

Flight of ideas: A nearly continuous flow of accelerated speech with abrupt changes from topic to topic, usually based on understandable associations, distracting stimuli, or plays on wards. When severe, the speech may be disorganized and incoherent. Flight of ideas is most frequently seen in Manic episodes, but may also be observed in some cases of Organic Mental Disorders, Schizophrenia, other psychotic disorders, and occasionally, acute reactions to stress.

Flocillation: Aimless plucking or picking, usually at bed clothes or clothing. It is common in senile psychosis and delirium.

Flooding (implosion): A behaviour therapy procedure for phobias and other problems involving maladaptive anxiety, in which anxiety producers are presented in intense forms, either in imagination or in real life. The presentations are continued until the stimuli no longer produce disabling anxiety.

Fluid intelligence: A general relation-perceiving capacity which represents one's potential intelligence somewhat independent of socialization and education. Compare crystallized intelligence.

Focal conflict theory: Theory elaborated by Thomas French in 1952 that explains the behaviour of a person as an expression of his method of solving currently experienced personality conflicts that originated very early in his life, he constantly resonates to those early life conflicts.

Focal Person (FP): The individual who is being studied in social psychology experiments.

Focal therapy: An approach to psychotherapy in which a specific focus (problem) is identified early in the therapy and efforts are concentrated on this focus for the remainder treatment. The method was developed as part of the attempt to make psychotherapy shorter and more cost-effective.

Folie a deux: A condition in which two closely related persons, usually in the same family, share the same delusions. In DSM-III-R called induced psychotic disorder in recognition of the well known clinical fact that not all such instances involve shared delusions; they can also be manic, depressive, etc.

Forensic psychiatry: The branch of psychiatry that is concerned with the legal aspects of mental illness.

Forensic psychology: The application of psychology to legal matters. Includes work on reliability of witnesses, evidence given by children, the consequences for children of possible court actions, and the causes of criminal behaviour.

Foreplay: The sexual play that precedes sexual intercourse. It is also called forepleasure.

Fore-pleasure and end-pleasure: The terms enable the pleasure associated with erotic activity to be divided into (a) that associated with mounting tension, fore-pleasure, and (b) that associated with reduction of tension, end-pleasure, the former being a tension-affect, and latter a discharge-affect.

Forgetting: Broadly speaking, theories of forgetting can be stored into seven major approaches; decay theory (the idea that memory traces gradually decay overtime, unless strengthened by being retrieved); interference theory; amnesia brought about through physical causes; motivated forgetting; lack of appropriate cues for retrieval; lack of the relevant context for retrieval; and inadequate processing during storage (see levels of processing theory).

Formal operational stage: The last of piaget's four stages of cognitive development. In the formal operational stage, the individual has become capable of abstract thought and can conceptualize possibilities which are outside of direct experience. Piaget considered this to be the highest form of cognitive, and one which is shown only in human beings, and from the age of about 12 years at the earliest. The proceeding stages he viewed as steps towards this point, which, on the basis that ontogeny recapitulates phylogeny, illustrated the stages by which abstract logic must have evolved. See also sensorimotor stage, pre-operational stage, concrete operational stage, genetic epistemology.

Formal thought disorder: A disturbance in the form of thought. The boundaries of the concept are not clear and there is no consensus as to which disturbances in speech or thoughts are included in the concept. For this reason, "formal thought disorder" is not used as a specific descriptive term in DSM-II. See loosening of associations, incoherence, poverty of content of speech, neologisms, perseveration, blocking, echolalia, changing.

Formication: A tactile hallucination involving the sensation that tiny insects are crawling over the skin. It is most commonly encountered in cocainism and delirium tremens.

Foulkes, S.H. (1923–1989): English psychiatrist and one of the organizers of the group therapy movement in Great Britain. His work combines Moreno's ideas–the here-and-now, the sociogenesis, the social atom, the psychological network-with psychoanalytic views. He stressed the importance of group-as-a-whole phenomena. See also Group analytic psychotherapy, Network.

Free association: Investigative psychoanalytic technique devised by Freud in which the patient seeks to verbalize without reservation or censorship the passing contents of his mind.

Free-floating anxiety: Severe, pervasive, generalized anxiety that is not attached to any particular idea, object, or event. It is observed particularly in anxiety disorders, although it may be seen in some cases of schizophrenia.

Free recall: In memory experiments, retrieval of stored items in any order by the subjects. See retrieval.

Free will: The idea that, contrary to the claims of determinism, the decisions and actions of agents are not foreordained whether by the fate or by God's knowledge or by laws psychology or neuro-physiology.

Frequency distribution: A statistical description of raw data in terms of the number of cases that fall into each interval within a set of data. Frequency or frequency polygram.

Freud, Anna (1895–1982): Austrian psychoanalyst and daughter of Sigmund Freud, noted for her contributions to the development theory of psychoanalysis and its applications to preventive work with children.

Freud, Sigmund (1856–1939): Born on 6th May in Freiberg, Moravia. Austrian psychiatrist and the founder of psychoanalysis. With Josef, Breuer, he explored the potentialities of cathartic therapy, then went on to develop the analytic technique and such fundamental concepts of mental phenomena as the unconscious, infantile sexuality, repression, sublimation, and super go, ego, and id formation and their applications throughout all spheres of human behaviour. See also aggressive drive, Altruism, Bisexuality. Cocaine, Conscious, Death instinct, Dream, Drive, Ego, Free association, Hypnoid state, id, infantile sexuality, Instinct, Interpretation of dreams, Inversion, Latent homosexuality, Life instinct, Minutes of the Vienna Psychoanalytic Society, Oedipus complex, Parapraxis, Penies envy,

Preconteria, Superego, Three Essays on the Theory of sexuality, Unconscious, Vienna Psychoanalytic, Society, Wednesday Evening Society.

Freudian slip: A mistake which can be interpreted as revealing unconscious wishes, fears, etc. Freud argued that all apparently accidental happenings reveal something of the unconscious.

Frigidity: In the female, lack of sexual response or feeling, ranging from complete lack of arousal to incomplete climax. See also Anorgasmia, Impotence.

Frotteur: A person who becomes sexually aroused by rubbing up against someone, usually without specific genital contract, as in a crowd.

Frustration-aggression hypothesis: The proposal, particularly associated with Leon Berkowitz, that aggression is always caused by some kind of frustration. It also tends to be assumed that frustration always leads to aggression. This theoretical model has achieved widespread popularity, and is supported by comparative studies of overcrowding in animals as well as by studies of human behaviour.

Fugue: A dissociate disorder characterized by a period of almost complete amnesia during which the person actually flees from his immediate life situation and begins a different life pattern. Apart from the amnesia, metal faculties and skills are usually unimpaired. See also Psychogenic amnesia.

Fulfillment: Satisfaction of a need or wish.

Functional: Referring to changes in functioning not attributable to known organic alterations.

Functional fixedness: A form of einstellung, or mental set, in which the individual is unable to deviate from using objects in a manner consistent with the normal functioning. So, for instance, in a problem-solving exercise, functional fixedness may prevent someone from realizing that something like a jug usually used to contain liquids, could also be turned upside-down and used as a support.

Functionalism: The claim that psychological phenomena are best understood in terms of their functions rather than their structure- which would be the claim of structuralism. Concepts such as adaptation and role, and therapeutic methods such as systemic family therapy represent a functionalist approach.

Furor therapeutics: Disparaging term for therapeutic enthusiasm. According to Freud, furor therapeuticus is against the long-term interests of patients being analysed.

Fusion: A term used in psychoanalysis to mean the joining together of instincts.

Future shock: One of several theories about the stress imposed by transitions and life events. The idea was introduced in a book with that title by Alevin Toffler to describe what he claimed were the traumatic effects of our present rapid progress into the future. Toffler proposed that people could be protected against the effects of change by maintaining some areas of stability in their lives.

G

GABA (Gamma aminobutyric acid): The major neurotransmitter in the brain implicated in several psychiatric and neurologic conditions, mostly notably Huntington's disease. See also disinhibition.

Galton, Sir Francis 1822–1911): Born in Sparkbrook, Birmingham, England, he was a Pioneer in the study of individual differences and in the application of statistical techniques to psychological problems. His important contributions were "The art of travel", Inquiries into human faculty, "Hereditary genius" and "word Association Test".

Galvanic skin response (GSR): Also known as galvanic skin resistance, this is a highly sensitive measurer of arousal, registering even such slight increases in arousal as are produced by a disturbing thought or as slight pain. It refers to the electrical resistance of the skin, which changes as a result of increases in the rate of sweating. GSR detectors form an important component in polygraphs, which record a range of physiological indicators of psychological events, and may be used as lie-detectors.

Gambler's fallacy: A belief that if a chance event occurs, then it is less likely to occur on the next trail. If red comes up several times running on a roulette wheel there is a (mistaken) tendency to believe that black is more likely on the next throw. This universal tendency has been of interest to cognitive theorists as it is a failure to follow probabilistic logic and so may shed light on how humans assess probability. It may best be seen to reflect the fact that genuine instances of "random' sampling without replacement' are uncommon in real life and not as a failure to judge probabilities acutely. The gambler's fallacy is therefore a normally effective strategy which becomes inappropriate in certain, rather artificial, circumstances.

Gambling, pathological: See Pathological gambling.

Game: The psychological uses of this term are similar to the ordinary meaning except that the idea of playfulness is usually absent. So a game is an activity within defined limits in which all of the participants operate according to agreed rules. Much of social interaction can be regarded as a game, with plenty of scope for problems when the rules and the limits of the game are not made explicitly. Eric Berne was one of the first to explore this concept in this book Games People Play. 'Game theory' is a specific approach which express the rules of the game in mathematical terms so that the possible strategies can be precisely identified and their consequences predicted. See also zero-sum game.

Gamophobia: Fear of marriage.

Ganser syndrome: Ganser in 1987, described two prisoners who developed brief bouts of mental illness characterized by disturbed consciousness, Hallucinations, sensory changers of hysterical kind and characteristic answers to questions. These episodes terminated abruptly with subsequent amnesia for the episode and complete recovery, Enoth and Trethowan (1979) listed the four essentials diagnostic features as approximate answers, clouding of consciousness, somatic conversion and visual and/or auditory hallucinations (pseudo-hallucinations). The condition is not confined to prisoners. The causes have been listed as schizophrenia, neurosyphilis, alcoholism, Kotdskogg's psychosis, cerebrovascular disease, depression, mental retardation, trauma and artefactual illness.

Gaslight phenomenon: A type of imposed psychosis, described Barton and Whithead in which a presentation of metal illness is found, on further enquiry, to have been induced or imposed on the patient by some other person for the other person's gain. Among these gains is removal of the patient to a hospital.

Gaze: Reactions to others depend on how they are perceived and how their behaviours is interpreted. It follows that how much people look and when and where they look are crucial for their social performance.

Geisteswissenchaftliche psychologie: Originally referred to psychology as it explores the transindividual, objective mind and its products, then its relations to individual, subjective minds hence the alleged foundation of Giesteswissenschaften (i.e., the humanities, historical and cultural sciences). It was coined by E. Spranger.

Gegenhalten: Neurological term for active but involuntary resistance to passive movement of the extremities.

Gelatio: Regid state of the body in catalepsy.

Gender identity disorder: A psychosexual disorder in which the person feels discomfort and inappropriateness about his or her anatomical sex. See also transsexualism.

Gender role: The public declaration of gender identity-that is, the image of malenmess or femaleness that the person presents to others. It may or may not coincide with gender identity.

Gender role disorder: A condition in which conflict, worth resulting distress, is experienced between the external appearance and orientation of assigned sex on the one hand, and biological sex and/or gender identity on the other. Cultural; factors may be prepotent. Transsexualism exemplifies the condition.

Gene: The basic unit of heredity. It is composed of DNA and is contained within the cell chromosome.

General adaptation syndrome (GAS): A long-term response to stressful stimulation identified by Selye in 1949. It is characterized by extremely high levels of adrenaline in the bloodstream, but without rapid heart and pulse rates normally associated with adrenaline release. The general adaptation system has been shown to result in increased susceptibility to illness, possibly through a decline in the number of white blood cells and antibodies produced by the body.

General intelligence factor (G): The idea of one overall capacity of intelligence suggested by Galton and Spearman. Many psychologists consider this to be a contentious view, arguing that intelligence is a combination of many different skills and attributes. Most intelligent tests are based on the assumption that a generalized intelligence factor, or "g", can be calculated as a result of the administering of a set of specialized sub-tests, and it is a consequence of this belief that the Intelligence Quotient, or IQ, has been so widely applied.

General adaptational syndrome (GAS): Hans Selye's term for the responses of the body to major stress, passing through the alarm reaction, resistance and, finally, exhaustion.

Generalization: Process by which a behaviour occurs in a setting in which it had not previously being reinforced.

Generalized anxiety disorder: A DSM-III classification of anxiety disorder characterized by severe generalized anxiety not attached to any particular idea, object or event. See also Free-floating anxiety disorder.

General problem-solver (GPS): A computer program designed in early 1970's, which emphasized the use of heuristics in tackling specific problems; and which formed the prototype for many subsequent attempts at computer simulation, within the general field of artificial intelligence.

General systems theory: Theoretical framework viewing phenomena from the standpoint of the systems (groups of organized interacting components) involved in the phenomena. In psychiatry, it emphasizes an integrated, holistic view of personality and behaviour.

Generalization: The process by which a learned response will occur in more situations than those in which it was first learned; it will also be applied to similar situations.

Generalization gradient: The relationship between the strength of a given response and the similarity of the triggering stimulus to the original stimulus. When electing a generalized response, a stimulus which is very similar to the original will produce a strong response, while one which is less similar will evoke weaker response.

Genetic(s): In the singular, concerning the origin of something. Used particularly to refer to the development of abilities and characteristics of children (see genetic epistemology) but also applies to the development of characteristics in a species or the development of the species itself. See ontogeny and phylogeny. In the plural, genetics refers to the study of genes and their actions. See behaviour genetics.

Genetic counseling: Presentation and discussion, generally with a prospective parental couple, of factors involved in the inheritance of pathological conditions as they relate to the couple's genetic endowment.

Genetic engineering: The process of altering genetic characteristics through microscopic surgical or chemical intervention; usually taking the form of inserting a new section of chromosome into an existing one, such that when the chromosome is replicated, the new portion is also replicated and becomes part of the organism's overall genotype.

Genetic epistemology: The little for a theory of the growth of knowledge and understanding. It is usually reserved for Jen Piaget's theory charting the development of the child's cognitive functioning through a series of stages.

Genetic material: In psychiatry, data out of the patient's personal past history that are useful in developing an understanding of the psychodynamics of his present adaptation. See also current material.

Genetic psychology: The psychology of development (not of genetics). It covers the psychological development of both individuals and species but the term is no longer widely used.

Genital phase: The final stage of psychosexual development. It occurs during puberty. In this stage the person can achieve sexual gratification from general-to-genital contact and has the capacity for a mature, affectionate relationship with someone of the opposite sex. See also Phenotype.

Geriatrics: Branch of medicine that deals with the aged and the problems of aging Geriatric psychiatry is also known as geropsychiatry. See also Gerontology.

Geronotology: The scientific study of aging.

Gestalt psychology: A form of psychology popular in Europe in the first half of the twentieth century, which gathered support in opposition to the mechanistic approach of the behaviourist school in America. Gestalt psychology emphasizes the holistic nature of the human being and opposes stimulus response reductionism, on the grounds that ' the whole is more than the sum of its parts', and that there are many aspects of perception, memory and learning processes which cannot be understood in terms of collections of smaller units, but which are complete and unitary in themselves. The Gestalt emphasis on cognitive psychology provided an important background to the 'cognitive revolution' of the 1960s and 1970s.

Gestalt principles of perception: An attempt to describe the important features of perceptual functioning through a set of principles which are consistent with the gestalt emphasis on wholes. See law of Pragnanz.

Gestalt therapy: Type of psychotherapy that emphasizes the treatment of the person as a whole–his biological component parts and their organic functioning, his perceptual configuration, and his interrelationships with the outside world. Gestalt therapy, developed by Frederic S. Perls, can be used in either an individual or a group therapy, setting. It focuses on the sensory awareness of the person's here and now experiences, rather than on past recollections or future expectations. Gestalt therapy uses role playing and other techniques to promote the patient's growth process and to develop his full potential.

Gesture: A mode of non-verbal communication in which information is conveyed by movement, usually (but not always) of the hands and arms. Gestures tend to vary considerably from one culture to another, and the same sign may have a very different meaning even in neighbouring countries.

Giles de ta Tourette's disease: A rate illness that has its onset in childhood; First described by a Paris physician, Gilles de la Tourette, the disease is characterized by involuntary muscular movements and motor in coordination, accompanied by echolalia and coprolalia.

Glick effect: Positive correlation between dropping out of school and subsequent marital instability (Marriage drop-out).

Globus hystericus: A symptom in which the person is disturbed by the sensation of a lump in his throat. It is manifestation of anxiety.

Glossolalia: Gibberish-like speech, or speaking in tongues.

Goal: The place, condition or object that satisfies a motive.

Go-around: Techniques used in group therapy in which the therapist requires each member of the group to respond to another member, a theme, or an association. This procedure encourages the partici pation of all members in the group.

God complex: A belief sometimes seen in therapists that one can accomplish more than is humanly possible or that one's word should not be doubted. The God complex of the aging psychoanalyst was first discussed by Ernest Jones, Freud's biographer. See also Mother Superior complex.

Goffman, Erving: Born in 1922 in Manville, Alta, Canada he was a sociologist who has had an enormous, influence on thinking and studies of the self (and self representation) institutionalization, roles and social interaction.

Gradient of generalization: The amount of stimulus generalization depends on how similar the test stimuli are to be the stimuli present during learning. See stimulus generalization.

Gradients of texture: One of the principal monocular cues for depta perception, consists of a gradation in the fineness of detail which can be seen at increasing distances from the viewer.

Grandiose delusion: Delusion of grandeur. See also Delusion.

Gray out syndrome: A psychosis that occurs in pilots flying in the stratosphere, out of sight of the horizon.

Grief: Alteration in mood and affect consisting of sadness appropriate to a real loss. Normally, it is self-limited. See also depression.

Grief reaction: A response by a bereaved person to the loss, that characteristically proceeds from a phase of shock and bewilderment, via a depressive preoccupation with the deceased, to a gradual period of resolution. Deviations from this sequence are common and morbid patterns of grieving may constitute a frank depressive illness. *Synonyms:* Bereavement reaction; brief depressive reaction related to bereavement; uncomplicated bereavement.

Group analytic psychotherapy: Term applied by S.H. Foulkes to the early group procedure he developed in 1948. Interventions dealt primarily with group, rather than individual, forces and processes, and the group was used as the principal therapeutic agent. Foulkes is considered a pioneer in the field of group psychotherapy.

Group cohesion: The mutual bonds formed between members of a group as a result of their concerted effort for a common interest and purpose. Until cohesiveness is achieved the group cannot concentrate its full energy on a common task.

Group dynamics: Phenomena that occur in groups; the movement of a group from its inception to its termination. Interactions and interrelations among members and between the members and the therapist create tension, which maintain a constantly changing group equilibrium. The interactions and the tension they create are highly influenced by individual members' psychological make-up, unconscious instinctual drives, motives, wishes and fantasies. The understanding and the effective use of group dynamics are essential in group treatment. It is also known as group process. See also Lewin, Kurt; psychodynamics.

Group norms: Standards of behaviour or thought expected of group members, a person in a group must follow the norms set by the group or suffer the social consequences. See conformity.

Group pressure: Demand by group members that individual members submit and conform to group standards, values, and behaviour.

Group process: See Group dynamics.

Group psychotherapy: Application of psychotherapeutic techniques to a group of patients, using interpatient interactions to effect changes in the maladaptive behaviour of the individual members.

See also Activity group therapy, Psychoanalytic group psychotherapy. Repressive inspirational group psychotherapy.

Group relations theory: See Allport's group relations theory.

Group test: A psychometric test which is administered to several people at once, by a single tester; such as some of the school-type intelligence tests.

Group think: The conformity of opinion that arises under certain conditions in decision-making groups; often due to the reluctance of some members of the group to voice criticism.

Growth motive: A term used in humanistic models of personality to describe the tendency of human beings towards personal growth development, not only through the acquisition of new skills and experience, but also through cognitive reevaluation and an increased sense of personal control and autonomy. Humanistic psychologists consider this to be a very basic motive in the human being, and fundamental to an understanding of mentally healthy behaviour.

Grubelsucht: Brooding over trifles; seen most commonly in obsessive compulsive neurosis and depressive psychoses.

Guardianship: In most jurisdictions, in the context of mental illness, a person under guardianship by reason of mental illness is under the total control of another person or persons and in the status of a ward with respect to the both his body (as in consenting to surgery) and fiscal or contractual affairs.

Guilt: Emotional state associated with self-reproach and the need for punishment. In psychoanalysis, guilt refers to a neurotic feeling of culpability that stems from a conflict between the ego and the superego. It begins developmentally with parental disapproval and becomes internalized as conscience in the course of superego formation.

Guilt has normally psychological and social functions, but special intensity or absence of guilt characterizes many mental disorders, such as depression and antisocial personality, respectively. Some psychiatrists distinguish shame as a less internalized form of guilt. According to classical theory, the neurotic sense of guilt arises as infantile sexual and aggressive wishes. Guilt differs from anxiety is that (a) anxiety is experienced to an act already committed and (b) the capacity to experience guilt is contingent on the capacity to internalize objects whereas the capacity to experience anxiety is not.

Gustatory hallucination: See Hallucination.

H

Habeas corpus: Legal term for the right to petition a court to decide whether confinement has been undertaken with due process of law.

Habit: In behaviourist terms, a habit is described simply as a learned stimulus-response sequence; in cognitive psychology it is seen as a set of automatic routines and sub-routines in which the individual engages, and which, owing to frequent exercise, requires little conscious cognitive input. The learning process involved in acquiring a habit is likely to involve classical conditioning, but will not be habituation.

Habit, complaint: Kanner's term for hypochondriasis is in children.

Habituation: A very basic form of learning which involves gradually ceasing to respond to a non-significant stimulus which is repeatedly experienced. Ceasing to notice the ticking of a clock is a typical example. Habituation can be distinguished from fatigue by the fact that a small change in the stimulus will result in the response reappearing, a process called 'dishabituation'. Habituation is essential in allowing organisms to concentrate on those properties of stimuli which have significance for them, and to avoid having the cognitive system overloaded with irrelevant information. So, far example, car drivers do not habituate to the sight of red at the top of a traffic light, but they are likely to have difficulty in remembering the colour of the stripes the poles are painted.

Habromania: General term for morbid gaiety.

Halfway children: R. Geist's term for chronically ill children and adolescents who are neither well nor sick as to require continuous intensive inpatient care.

Halfway house: A specialized residence for patients who do not require full hospitalization but who need an intermediate degree of care before returning to independent community living.

Halloween effect: Hyperactivity and other behavioural and cognitive disfunction in response to ingestion of sugar, such as candy given to children in the "trick-or-treat" ritual of Halloween.

Hallucination: A false sensory perception occurring in the absence of any relevant external stimulation of the sensory modality involved. Examples include: Auditory hallucination. Hallucination of sound, Gustatory hallucination. Hallucination of taste. Hypnagogic hallucination. Hallucination occurring while falling asleep (ordinarily not considered pathological). Hypnopompic halluncination. Hallucination occurring while awaking for sleep (ordinarily not considered pathological). Kinesthetic hallucination. Hallucination of bodily movement. Lilliputian hallucination. Visual sensation that persons or objects are reduced in size; it is more properly regarded as an illusion (see also Micropsia). Olfactory hallucination. Hallucination involving smell. Somatic hallucination. Hallucination involving the perception of a physical experience localized within the body. Tactile (haptic) hallucination, Hallucination involving the sense of touch. Visual hallucination. Hallucination involving sight.

Hallucination, effective: A hallucination in which the content is either grandiose or self-deprecatory or involves other features common to a depressive syndrome, such as guilt, disease, or poverty.

Hallucinogen: A drug which induces hallucinogens are psilocybin and LSD (lysergic acid diethylamide), but there are many others, including mescaline and that contained in the fly agaric mushroom. Traditionally, hallucinogens have formed an integral part of religious and social ceremonies in many parts of the world. In the west they are normally used as recreational drugs, although there have been several instances of artists and creative writers utilizing their effects to obtain special insights for their work, and one or two investigations of their usefulness in certain kind of therapy. Term is used synonymously with psychotomimetic.

Hallucinosis: A state in which a person experiences hallucinations without any impairment of consciousness.

Halo's effect: The improvement in anxiety may sometime spuriously improve depression is known as Halo's effect. It is also used in statistics as a source of error where the patient answers to fit with previously chosen answers (say in a questionnaire). See Hawthorne effect also. An effect in which people or objects who are judged positively on one characteristic are also judged positively on others. For instance, a person who is judged to be physically attractive is more likely to be perceived as being more amusing, or intelligent, than a physically less attractive individual of similar personality.

Handedness: The term for specialization in use of one hand which develops in humans during the first years of life. Often the preferred foot or the preferred eye are not on the same side as the preferred hand. Handedness is thought by some to related to hemisphere dominance. Since the right cerebral hemisphere controls the left side of the body and vice versa, people who are right-handed are thought to be left-hemisphere-dominant, while left handed people to be right hemisphere dominant.

The evidence relating handedness to cerebral dominance is at times contradictory, despite the plausibility of the idea.

Haplology: Rapid speech in which syllables are left out. It is seen in certain manias and in schizophrenic conditions.

Haptic hallucination: See hallucination.

Harmon's Diaphragm test: It helps in differentiating monocular blindedness of organic in nature from functional type. In this test, if both eyes are open, a patient with organic type of blindness will be unable to tell with which eye objects are seen or the patient will be able to see contralateral half of letters whereas in blindness of functional origin, patient sees all letters or those on ipsilateral side.

Hawthorne effect: The phenomenon that when changes are introduced into a work environment in order to bring about an increase in productivity, there may be a temporary increase in productivity just because changes have been tried. An entirely useless change may therefore appear to work unless the effects are tested over a reasonable period. Hawthorne effects illustrate the importance of social factors and expectations in the working environment.

Healthy identification: Modeling of oneself, consciously or unconsciously, on another person who has a sound psychic make-up. The identification has constructive results. See also imitation.

Hebephrenia: A complex of symptoms considered a form of schizophrenia. It is characterized by wild or silly behaviour or mannerisms, inappropriate affect, frequent hypochondriacal complaints, and delusions and hallucinations that are transient and unsystematized. Hebephrenic schizophrenia is listed in DSM III as disorganized schizophrenia. See also schizophrenia.

Hecker Ewald: (1843–1909) German psychiatrist known from his studies in hebephrenia (a term he coined).

Hedonism: In philosophy, hedonism is the idea that pleasure or happiness is the highest good. In psychology, it is the idea that it is fundamental to human beings to seek pleasure and to avoid pain, and that this in itself is a valid explanation of much behaviour.

Heider, Fritz: Born in 1896 in Vienna, he was the center of a variant of gestalt psychology. His main contributions were 'The psychology of interpersonal relations', and 'Studies on topics the analysis of action of desire and pleasure', the structure of sentiments, the concepts of ought and value, of request and command of benefit and harm.

Helplessness theory: An approach to human functioning deriving from Seligman's studies of learned helplessness in animals. Some animals were found to react to unpleasant situations over which they had no control by ceasing all attempts to change the situation. Their state of passivity and apathy was felt to resemble depression and so a theory that depression results from experiences of helplessness was proposed by Seligman in the mid 1970s. Subsequently the theory has been revised and integrated with attribution theory.

Hemispheric dominance: The observation that in most individuals, one side of the brain is more influential or has greater control over the body that the other side, thus possibly producing right or left handedness, etc.

Herd instinct: Desire to belong to a group and to participate in social activities, Wilfred Trotter used the term to indicate the presence of a hypothetical social instinct in humans. In psychoanalysis, herd instinct is viewed as a social phenomenon, rather than as an instinct.

Here-and-now approach: A technique that focuses on understanding the interpersonal and intrapersonal responses and reactions as they occur in the ongoing treatment session. Little or no emphasis is put on past history and experience.

Heredity: The processes by which part of the biological potential of the parent is transmitted to the offspring. In sexual reproduction this involves half of the genetic material of each parent combining to form the complete genetic structure of the offspring. See also chromosome, gene.

Heritability estimate: A figure which purports to state the proportion of influence exerted by genes on the individual's development. Despite the fact that many developmental geneticists and psychologists (e.g., Hebb) have demonstrated unequivocally how inseparable genetics and the environment are, such figures continue to be constructed. The most well-known 'heritability estimate' is that of 80% genetic influence on the variation in intelligence, put forward by Jensen in 1969 on the basis of Cyril Burt's fraudulent data on twin studies. Controversy concerns not so much the estimate of 80% as the conclusions to be drawn from any estimate of heritability.

Hermaphrodite: A person who has both female and male gonads, usually one sex dominating.

Hermeneutic interpretative theory: The theory of human understanding in its interpretive aspect. A hermeneutic is a set of practices or recommendations for revealing an intelligible meaning of an otherwise unclear text or text analogue.

Hermeneutics: The study of meanings in social behaviour and experience. It is concerned with meanings on a number of level, which range through the conscious and unconscious, personal, and social to the cultural and sociopolitical levels. Rather than simply looking at the generalities of behaviour, or at statistical information, hermeneutics is concerned with the interpretation of experience, and the ways in which various forms of symbolism are used to convey meaning in human life.

Heroin: The illicit opioid most commonly used by narcotics addicts. Larger and larger amounts of the drug are craved to achieve the same narcotic and analgesic effects. Injected intravenously, it produces a more rapid onset of euphoria than does morphine. Although on a weight basis it is about 2.5 times as potent as morphine. It does not produce more euphoria, greater physical dependence, or fewer side effects. It's popularity in illicit trade may be related to its small bulk and ease of manufacture.

Heterogeneity: Dissimilarity in the genotypical structure of individuals originating through sexual reproduction.

Heterolalia: The substitution of meaningless or inappropriate words for those meant or untended, malapropism.

Heteronomous morality: The second of Piaget's stage of moral development, this is also known as the 'moral realism' stage. At this point, morality is considered to be subject to the laws of others; in other words, the child accepts as right and proper the rules given by authority.

Heterosexuality: Sexual attraction or contact between opposite-sex persons. The capacity for heterosexual arousal is probably innate, biologically programmed, and triggered in very early life, perhaps in part by olfactory modalities, as seen in lower animals. See also Bisexuality, Homosexuality.

Heterozygous: Possessing different allelic forms of a gene at a given locus in homologous chromosomes.

Hidden observer: The term given to the experience of a dispassionate 'inner self' which observes the individual in stressful situations, or during day to day living. Such an experience is particularly common during hypnosis, in which the hidden observer is felt to have experiences which are parallel to, but not the same as the hypnotized self. In psychotherapy, the objective part of the therapist which comments on his or her feelings and involvement with the patient is called the 'observing ego'.

Hierarchy: A structured form of organization constructed in levels, with each level overshadowing or dominating the lower ones. The idea of hierarchy is used in many different ways; a hierarchy of concepts, for instance, refers to the ways in which concepts may be stored in the brain, such that general concepts contain within themselves smaller constituent units. The analysis of organizations is almost always formulated in terms of hierarchies.

Hierarchy of needs: Maslow's hierarchy of human needs refers to the idea that human needs become important in systematic progression. Lower, more 'basic' needs such as food and security are important first, and 'higher' needs such as for beauty and self actualization only become important once the lower levels have been satisfied. The theory applies both developmentally and to the mature person. According to Maslow children must be adequately satisfied at one level before they start to develop motivations at the next level, so the higher stages are not reached for several years and self-actualization may take atleast 30 years to achieve. Adults may be stuck at a lower level if they have never experienced sufficient satisfaction at that level, but even those who have progressed higher may cease to be motivated at the upper levels if they are seriously threatened in a more basic way. For example, the need for dignity ceases to matter is you look up and find you are in danger of being run down by a bus.

Higher-order need strength: The concept was derived from Maslow theory according to which needs exist in a hierarchy of prepotency from lower (Physiological i.e., safety) to higher (Social; e.g., self esteem and self actualization) and from Alderfer's modification which posits three levels of needs existence, relatedness and growth. This concept was based on the work of Hackman and Oldham (1980).

Historical psychology: Psychology concerned with cross-time alterations on transformations in patters of human conduct and their psychological bases.

Historicism: A term indicating the tendency to regard all cultural phenomena, including philosophies and world views, as the result of historical development. Humanistic psychology; An approach to psychology which includes love, involvement and spontaneity instead of systematically excluding them. It aims at the liberation of people from the bonds of neurotic control whether these derive from the structure of society or from the psychological condition of individuals.

Histrionic personality disorder: A condition which the patient, usually an immature and dependent person, exhibits unstable, over reactive, and excitable self dramatizing behaviour that is aimed at gaining attention and is at times seductive although the person may not be aware of that aim. It was termed hysterical personality in DSM-II.

Holism: An approach to the study of the individual in totality, rather than as an aggregate of separate physiologic, psychologic and social characteristics.

Holistic: Complete, treating its subject matter as a coherent and indivisible unit. For instance, a holistic approach to medicine would involve dealing with the whole person, including their own experiences, stresses, and understanding of the situation, rather than simply treating the symptom.

Holophrastic: Using single word to express a combination of ideas. Schizophrenics may use holophrastic language.

Homeostasis: The tendency to maintain a constancy and stability of bodily processes to ensure optimal functioning; the state of bodily equilibrium and the processes whereby such equilibrium is maintained.

Homosexuality: Sexual attraction or contact between same-sex persons. Some authors distinguish two types; Overt and latent. See also Ego-dystonic homosexuality, Inversion, Lesbianism.

Homosexual panic: The sudden, acute onset of severe anxiety, precipitated impulses. See also Homosexuality.

Hoover's test: It is for unilateral leg paralysis, capitalizes on psychological principle that when supine patients try to lift one leg against resistance, there is compensatory downward thrust of other leg which can be detected by examiner's hand under heel. This is present only in paralysis or paresis of organic in nature and not in hysterical paresis.

Horney, Karen (1885–1952): Psychiatrist and psychoanalyst whose theories of the genesis of neurosis emphasized environmental and cultural factors and thus departed from the biological-instinctual framework of orthodox Freudian thought. See also Basic anxiety.

Hospitalism in children: A syndrome closely related to anaclitic depression, developing in infants in hospital who are separated from their mothers or mother-surrogates for long periods of time. It is characterized by listlessness, unresponsiveness, emaciation and pallor, poor appetite and disturbed sleep, febrile episodes, lack of sucking habits, and an appearance of unhappiness. The disorder is reversible if the mother, or mother surrogate, and child are reunited within 2–3 weeks. *Synonym*: reactive attachment disorder of infancy.

Hostile aggression: Aggression in which the objective is to inflict harm on the other, as opposed to instrumental aggression which is undertaken for some other purpose. See aggression.

Hsieh-Ping: A culture-specific trance like state seen in Taiwan, characterized by tremor, disorientation, delirium, and ancestor identification and often accompanied by visual or auditory hallucinations. The seizure, may last from, 30 minutes to several hours.

Humanistic psychology: An approach within psychology which emphasizes the whole person and their scope for change. Humanistic psychologists reject the reductionist approach of many researchers, which action simply as collections of separate mechanisms; and they also argue against the dehumanization and 'objectifying' of human behaviour produced by trivial laboratory investigations and behaviouristic attitude with psychology. Instead, they argue that psychologists should take more account of the whole person, including attitudes, values, and responses top social situations (including experiments). To attempt to study people in a regimented way, is, they think, to ignore the essence of what it is to be human. There are many humanistic psychologists, of whom Carl Rogers is perhaps the most famous. Humanistic psychology is also closely link with the phenomenological approach within psychology.

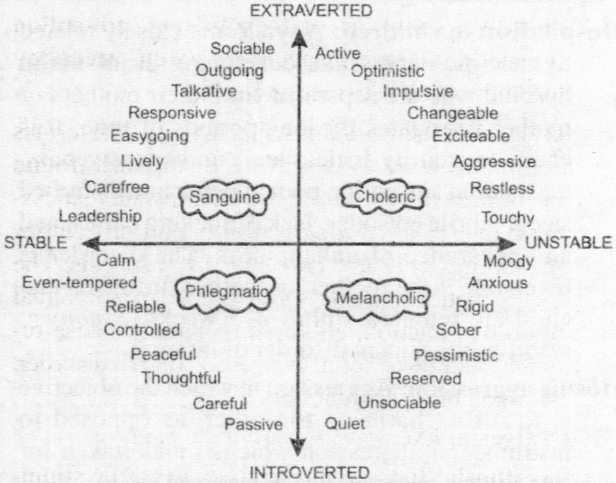

Fig. 3. The theory of the Humours & Eysenck Personality Inventory.

Humanistic Theory: A group of diverse theories that share a holistic conceptualization that emphasis the uniqueness, value, dignity, and worth of each human being as an individual. Human behaviour is considered understandable only in terms of the meaning of experiences for the individual person; it represents a complex interplay of numerous physical, psychological, and sociocultural factors.

Humiliation: Sense of disgrace, dishonour, and shame; it is often experienced by depressed patients.

Humour: A stimulus, a response or a disposition. Commonly it is referred to the excitement of amusement, the expression of amusement and temporary and habitual conditions of the mind.

Hydromania: Impulse to commit suicide by drowning.

Hygiene factors: Factors in the working environment, identified by Hertzberg, which are to do with the working conditions of the individual, such as shift organization, staff facilities, and organizational structure. In investigations of job satisfaction, Hertzberg found that bad hygiene factors contributed considerably to job dissatisfaction, but that incentives known as 'motivators' (e.g., promotion prospects, a sense of goals etc.) were necessary to produce job satisfaction itself.

Hyperactivity: Increased muscular activity. The term is commonly used to describe a disturbance found in children that is manifested by constant restlessness, over-activity, distractibility and difficulties in learning. It is also known as hyperkinesis. The hyperkinetic syndrome is also referred to as minimal brain dysfunction, although its precise cause remains unknown. See also attention deficit disorder. Minimal brain dysfunction.

Hyperalgesia: Excessive sensitivity to pain.

Hyperesthesia: Increased sensitivity to tactile stimulation.

Hyperkiness: Excessive, unintentional motor activity of the limbs or any part of the body, appearing spontaneously or in response to stimulation. Hyperkinesis is a feature of a variety of organic disorders of the central nervous system but may also appear in the absence of a demonstrable localized lesion.

Hyperkinetic syndrome of childhood: Disorders in which the essential the features are short attention-span and distractibility. In early childhood the most striking symptom is disinhibited, poorly organized and poorly regulated extreme overactivity, but in adolescence this may be replaced by underactivity. Impulsiveness, marked mood fluctuations and aggressiveness are also common symptoms. Delays in the development of specific skills are often present and disturbed, poor relationships are common. *Synonym*: attention deficit disorder with hyperactivity.

Hyperlexic: Hyperlexic children are those who learn to read extremely quickly, with little apparent difficulty. The opposite of dyslexic.

Hypermnesia: Exaggerated degree of retention and recall. It can be elicited by hypnosis and may be seen in certain prodigies; it may be a feature of obsessive-compulsive disorder, some cases of schizophrenia, and manic episodes of bipolar affective disorder.

Hyperorexia: Extreme appetite. See also Bulimia.

Hyperphrenia: (Hyperfragia) (1) Excessive mental activity, such as occurs in the manic phase of manic depressive psychosis or in the severe preoccupations association with the neuroses. (2) Intellectual capacity for above the average.

Hyperpragia: Excessive thinking and mental activity, generally associated with the manic phase of bipolar affective disorder.

Hypersomnia: Excessive time spent asleep. It is not related to narcolepsy.

Hyperventilation: Excessive breathing generally associated with anxiety. A reduction in blood carbon dioxide produces symptoms of light-headedness, palpitations, numbness and tingling periorally and in extremities, and occasionally syncope.

Hypervigilance: The continual scanning of the environment for signs of threat.

Hypesthesia: Diminished sensitivity to tactile stimulation.

Hypnagogic: Referring to the semiconscious state immediately preceding sleep; may include hallucinations, which are of no pathologic significance.

Hypnagogic imagery: Vivid visual imagery which is experienced during the transition from walking to sleep. It often makes the form of an unusually clear image of an object that has been subject of intense concentration during the day, but the most common image is of falling. Hypnopompic imagery, which is rarer, is a similar kind of imagery which occurs during waking.

Hypnoanalysis: The use of hypnosis is psychoanalysis to gain access to unconscious processes that the patient cannot reveal by means of ordinary therapeutic maneuvers.

Hypnodrama: Psychodrama under hypnotic trance. The patient is put into a hypnotic trance and encouraged to act out various past experiences.

Hypnoid state: A term introduced by Freud describing an alteration of consciousness that occurs characteristically in hysteria during periods of emotional stress. It is characterized by heightened suggestibility, and it provides a basis for hysterical somatic symptom formation.

Hypnopompic: Referring to the state immediately preceding awakening; may include hallucinations, which are of no pathologic significance.

Hypnosis: Artificially induced alteration of consciousness characterized by increased suggestibility and receptivity to direction. See also Mesmerism–an early term for hypnosis.

Hypnotherapy: A type of therapy that makes use of hypnosis. See also symptom substitution.

Hypochondriasis: A somatoform disorder characterized by excessive, morbid anxiety about one's health. The term is derived from the belief that the state was caused by some dysfunction in the hypochondrium, especially the spleen. Hypochondriacal patients express predominant disturbance in which the physical symptoms or complaints are not explainable on the basis of demonstrable organic findings and are apparently linked to psychological factors. Also known as hypochondriacal neurosis.

Hypomania: A psychopathologic state and abnormality of mood falling somewhere between normal euphoria and mania. It is characterized by unrealistic optimism, pressure of speech and activity, and a decreased need for sleep. Some people show increased creativity during hypomanic states, while others show poor judgement irritability, and irascibility. See also bipolar disorder.

Hypothesis: An idea which is not proven, or which is advanced as a tentative suggestion or possible explanation. In terms of formal experimental method, an hypothesis is an idea, derived logically and consistently from a specific psychological theory, which contains an explicit prediction which can be verified or refuted by some kind of empirical investigation, usually an experiment. See null hypothesis.

Hypothetico-deductive method: The technique of investigation outlined by Popper as being central to the scientific method. It consists of investigating by means of the formulation of an explicit hypothesis containing an explicit prediction as to what would happen in a given situation. An empirical investigation would then be set up to test the hypothesis, i.e., to see if the prediction were true. If the hypothesis were retained because the prediction worked, that would be taken as support for the theory from which the hypothesis was derived. If, on the other hand, the hypothesis were refuted, that would be taken (in an idealized world) as evidence against the original theory; and an alternative explanation would have to be found.

Hysteria: A mental disorder in which motives, of which the patient seems unaware, produce either a restriction of the field of consciousness or disturbances of motor or sensory function which may seem to have psychological advantage or symbolic value. It may be characterized by conversion phenomena or dissociative phenomena. In the conversion form the chief or only symptoms consist or psychogenic disturbance of function in some part of the body. E.g., paralysis, tremor, blindness, deafness or seizures. In the dissociative variety the most prominent feature is a narrowing of the field of consciousness which seems to serve an unconscious purpose and is commonly accompanied or followed by a selective amnesia. There may be dramatic but essentially superficial changes of personality sometimes taking the form of a fugue. Behaviour may mimic psychosis or, rather, the patient's idea of psychosis. *Synonyms*: hysterical neurosis; conversion hysteria.

Hysterical anaesthesia: Functional disorder characterized by the absence of tactile sensation in an area of the body. It is observed in certain cases of conversion disorder.

Hysterical neurosis: A DSM-II diagnostic category for a neurosis involving a sudden impairment of function in response to emotional stress. In the conversion type there is functional impairment in one of the special senses or in the voluntary nervous system; the dissociative type is manifested by an alteration in state of consciousness or by such symptoms as amnesia, disorientation, fugue, somnambulism, or multiple personality. In DSM-III they are also called conversion disorder and dissociative disorder.

Hysterical personality: See Histrionic personality disorder.

Hysterical psychosis: A term applied to a psychotic reaction to stressful circumstances occurring predominantly, but not exclusively, in individuals with hysterical personality traits. The illness is usually short-lived and may take one of several forms; stupor twilight state, pseudodementia, Ganser's syndrome, fugue, and a schizophrenia-like state. Some culture bound psychiatric syndromes e.g., Latah, also have marked hysterical features.

I

Iatrogenic illness: A disease accidentally caused or aggravated by a physician.

ICD: International Classification of Diseases.

Iconic representation: The coding or representing of memories by utilizing sensory images (from the Greek 'icon' meaning; image'). Iconic representation is usually used to refer to visual imagery, and was considered to the second mode of representation to develop, according to Bruner. See also enactive representation, symbolic representation.

Iconomania: Morbid impulse to worship and/or collect images.

Id: Part of Freud's structural theory of mental functioning. The id is that part of the psychic apparatus that operates unconsciously, harbours the innate, biological, instinctual drives; and is the source of psychic energy (libido). If follows the pleasure principle, seeks immediate reduction of drive tension without regard for external reality, and is under the influence of the primary-process mental activity that characterizes the unconscious. See also Ego, Superego.

Idea: The memory of past perceptions. An idea depends upon an image in the same way as a perception depending upon a sensation.

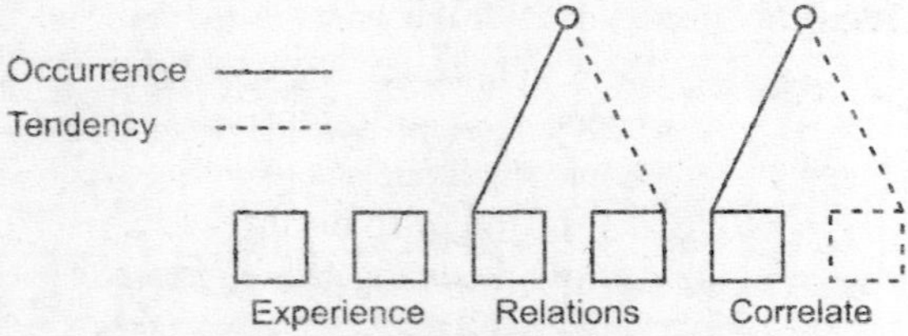

Fig. 4. The development of new idea.

Ideal: An image or representation of oneself as one would like to be. Derived from societal values and significant others the ideal self is composed of wished for (but possibly unattainable) modes of behaviour, values, traits, aspects of personal appearance etc. A disparity between ideal self concept (i.e., image of oneself as one really) is taken to be a sign of poor mental health and its reduction a primary goal of psychotherapy (See Riogers).

Idealization: A mental mechanism whereby a person consciously or unconsciously overestimates an admired attribute or aspect of another person.

Idea of reference: Misinterpretation of incidents and events in the outside world as having a direct personal reference are frequently seen in paranoid patients. If present with sufficient frequency or intensity or if organized and systematized, they constitute delusions of reference. See also Delusion.

Ideation: The process concerned with the highest function of awareness, the formation of ideas. It includes thinking, intellect and memory.

Ideational shield: An intellectual, rational defense against the anxiety that a person would feel if he became vulnerable to the criticisms and rejection of others. As a result of his fear of being rejected, he may feel threatened if he criticizes another person, an act that is unacceptable to him. In both group and individual therapy, conditions are set up that allow the participants to lower the ideational shield.

Idea fixed: A fixed idea that is recurrent and most often associated with obsession states.

Identification: A defence mechanism, operating unconsciously, by which person patterns himself after some other person. Identification plays a major role in the development of one's personality and specifically of the superego. To the differentiated from imitation or role modeling, which is a conscious process.

Identification with the aggressor: An unconscious process by which a person incorporates within himself the mental image of a person who represents a source of frustration from the outside world. A primitive defense, it operates in the interest and service of the developing ego. The classic example of this defense occurs towards the end of the oedipal stage, when a boy, whose main source of love and gratification is his mother, identifies with his father. The father represents the source of frustration, being the powerful rival for the mother, the child cannot master or run away from his father, so he is obliged to identify with him. See also psychosexual development.

Identity: A person's global role in life and the perception of his sense of self. Problems with identity are common during adolescence, in schizophrenia, and in the borderline and schizotypal personalities. See also Gender identity, identity disorder, sexual identity.

Identity crisis: A loss of the sense of the sameness and historical continuity of one's self and inability to accept or adopt the role one perceives as being expected by society; often expressed by isolation, withdrawal, extremism, rebelliousness, and negativity, and typically triggered by a combination of sudden increase in the strength of instinctual drives in a milieu of rapid social evolution and technologic change. See also psychosocial development.

Identity disorder: In DSM-III a disorder characterized by a chaotic sense of self; a loss of the sense of personal sameness, usually involvirg a social role conflict as perceived by the person himself. It is common in adolescence, when the adolescent feels unwilling or unable to accept or adopt the role he believes is expected of him by society. It is often manifested by isolation, withdrawal, rebelliousness, negativity, and extremism.

Identity formation: The process of forming an identity. The identifications made throughout development plays an important role, and adolescents in particular will try out different kinds of identity and use feedback from others to decide which to retain and which to abandon.

Idealogy: Any false, categorically mistaken, ensemble of ideas whose falsity is explicable, wholly or in part, in terms of the social role or function they, normally unwittingly, serve.

Idioctonia: Suicide.

Idiographic: Attempting to understand the functioning of individuals, as opposed to the search for general laws of behaviour. Idiographic approaches to human personality examine characteristics which are considered to be common to all individuals, but which, in their operation, make each person unique. So, for instance, personal construct theory represents an ideographic approach; whereas the psychometric approaches, which are concerned with comparing people with one another, do not. See also nomothetic.

Idiopathic: Without known cause.

Idiosyncratic: Special to that particular individual; characteristic of that person but not of most people.

Idiot Savant: A mentally retarded person who is able to perform unusual mental feats in sharply circumscribed intellectual area, such as complicated calculations or puzzle solving.

Idiotropic: Egocentric; introspective.

I-It: Philosopher Martin Buber's description of damaging interpersonal relationships. If a person treats himself or another person exclusively as an object, he prevents mutuality, trust, and growth. When pervasive in a group. I-It relationships prevent human warmth, destroy cohesiveness, and retard group; process. See also I-Thou.

Illinois test of psycholinguistic ability: Psychological test assessing various aspects of language ability in children 2 to 10 years of age.

Illogically: Pattern of speech or thinking in which conclusions that are reached do not follow logically. It may take the form of unwarranted or faulty inferences.

Illogical thinking: Thinking that contains clear internal contradictions or in which conclusions are reached that are clearly erroneous, given the initial premises. It may be seen in individuals without mental disorder, particular in situations in which they are distracted or fatigued. Illogical thinking was psychopathological significance only when it is marked, as in the examples noted below, and when it is not due to cultural or religious values or to intellectual deficit. Markedly illogical thinking may lead to, or result from, a delusional belief or may be observed in the absence of a delusion.

Illuminism: A state of hallucination in which the patient carries on converzations with imaginary supernatural creatures.

Illusion: Perceptual misinterpretation of a real external stimulus.

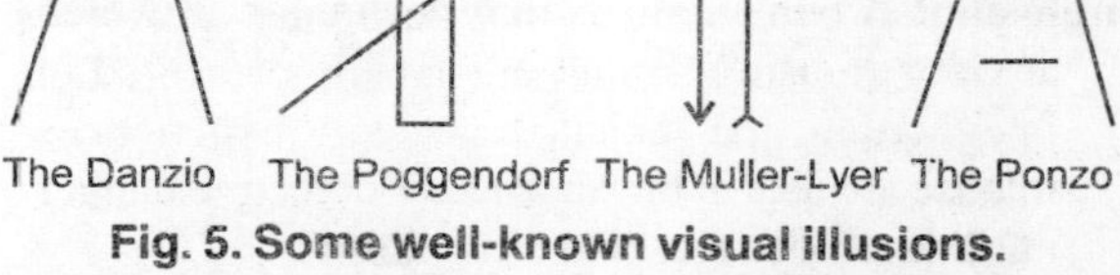

The Danzio The Poggendorf The Muller-Lyer The Ponzo

Fig. 5. Some well-known visual illusions.

Image: A revived experience of a percept recalled from memory.

Imago: A Jungian term referring to an idealized, unconscious mental image of a key person in someone's early life.

Imbecile: See Mental Retardation.

Imitation: The copying of a specific action or sequence of behaviour. Imitation forms a learning process which is very common amount all mammals, and especially humans. It provides an extremely rapid form of learning and mechanism of early socialization. See also identification.

Immediate memory: A term occasionally used instead of short term memory.

Immunization: Hardening of a person's attitude on a particular subject by giving him or her a mind exposure to an opposing attitude; exposure makes the originally held attitude resistant to change by strong further arguments.

Impasse: see therapeutic impasse.

Impetus: In psychoanalytic psychiatry, the force or energy behind a particular drive.

Implicit personality theory: The ideas about how personality traits are grouped together often taken for granted in everyday living. For example, traits like ambitious may automatically be grouped with aggressive and energetic; or kind could be grouped with gentle and peaceable. This means that individuals who are known to have one particular characteristic are often reacted towards as if they also possessed the full range of associated traits. They are treated in accordance with the unspoken and assumed theory of personality held by the people whom they encounter. See also personal construct theory.

Implosion: A behaviour therapy technique in which anxiety arousing stimuli are vividly presented in imagination; the patient repeatedly experiences intense anxiety in the absence of objective danger until the anxiety response is extinguished.

Implosion therapy: Otherwise known as flooding, this refers to a technique in behaviour therapy in which the phobic individual receives direct and extended exposure to the feared stimulus, until they become relaxed with it. For instance, some who has had a car accident and become frightened of going out may be repeatedly shown film of cars approaching them. As they become used to this, the fear dies away and, through classical conditioning, a more relaxed attitude becomes associated with the stimulus. See also systematic desensitization.

Imposter Phenomenon (IP): The phenomenon characterized by the feeling of discrepancy between a person's public image as someone successful and his private perception of himself as someone unworthy. Even as his successes accumulate, the victim of IP can not accept them as evidence of his talents and abilities. To conceal his 'secret', an IP victim may adopt a number of strategies, single or combined. These can be classified into a workaholic, the magical thinker, thé shrinking violet, the charmer, the chameleon and the genie. Two American Psychologists Pauline Clance and Suzanne Imes, from Gerogia state University coined the term.

Impotence: The inability to achieve or maintain a penile erection of sufficient quality to engage in successful sexual intercourse. Two types are described by Masters and Johnson; in Primary impotence, there has never been a successful sexual coupling; in Secondary impotence, failure occurs following at least one successful union. Compare with orgasmic dysfunction.

Impression formation (or person formation): The way in which we perceive or understand other persons.

Fig. 6. Imprinting.

Imprinting: The process involving following of the mother which occurs during a critical period shortly after birth in some species, mostly notable in ducks and geese. The 'following' behviour can be elicited by any moving object during the hours, perhaps days, after birth, and the animal seems to have a strong innate tendency to learn about and in some way identify with the object. The learning is very resistant to change, and later in life social and sexual behaviour will be directed at animals or objects which resemble the imprinted stimulus. Attempts have been made to explain the bonding of human infants to their mothers as a form of imprinting but the two processes are quite different, and it seems that the main thing they had in common at the time the theory was proposed was that neither could be satisfactorily explained.

Improvization: In psychodrama, the acting out of situations without prior preparation.

Impulse: A psychic striving or urge to person an action. See also Drive, Instinct.

Impulse control: Ability to resist an impulse, drive, or temptation to perform some action.

Impulse control disorder: A mental disorder in which there is weak impulse control. The impulsive behaviour is usually irresistible, pleasurable, and aimed at obtaining immediate gratification, without regard for the consequences of the behaviour. Examples of impulse; control disorder are pathological gambling, kleptomania, pyromania, intermittent and isolated explosive disorders, the substance use disorders, and the paraphilias.

Impulsion: The blind following of internal drives without regard for social acceptance or pressure from the superego. Impulsion is normally seen in young children. In adults it is common in those weak defensive organizations; in such cases it tends to be a symbolic phenomenon.

Imu: A psycho reactive phenomenon seen among the Ainu, consisting of hyperkinesias, catalepsy, echolalia, echopraxia, and command automatism. Imu occurs exclusively in adult females.

Inadequate personality disorder: Personality disorder characterized by ineffective responses to physical, social, and emotional demands; instability; poor judgement; impaired coping ability; and generalized ineptness, despite the absence of any actual physical or mental deficit. This category has been eliminated from DSM-III.

Incentive: An aspect of motivation that result from expectation of reward or punishment (Hull, 1931).

Incentive theory: A theory of motivation that distinguishes between the expectation that a goal can be achieved (incentive motivation) and the strength of the need for the goal (drive motivation). The amount of effort made to achieve a goal is a function of both kinds of motivation. So high drive alone may be ineffective if paired with low incentive: I would very much like a million pounds but do not expect success so I am not doing anything about it. Equally, high incentive (I am sure I could get spasm for dinner if I tried) will not generate goal (or spasm) seeking if my drive is low because I do not like the stuff. Practically, the theory indicates that if an organism is not working for a goal it is necessary to know whether to increase need (life will be really wonderful if I can get A-level psychology), or incentive (there is still enough time to look up all the terms I do not understand).

Incest: sexual activity between close blood relatives. Common patterns are father-daughter, mother-son and between siblings. Incest may also be homosexually oriented.

Incidence: Research term meaning the number of cases of a disease whose onset occurs during a specific period of time. See also Prevalence.

Incoherence: Speech that, for the most part, is not understandable, owing to any of the following: a lack of logical or meaningful connection between words, phrases, or sentences; excessive use of incomplete sentences' excessive irrelevancies or abrupt changes in subject matter; idiosyncratic word usage; distorted grammar. Mildly ungrammatical construction or idiomatic usages characteristic of particular regional or ethnic backgrounds, lack of education, or low intelligence should not be considered incoherence; and the term is generally not applied when there is evidence that the disturbance in speech is due to aphasia. Incoherence may be seen in some Organic Mental Disorders, Schizophrenia, and other psychotic disorders.

Incompetence: A legal term indicating that thought processes are inadequate for sound judgement and may lead to maladaptive of normal behaviour. Legally, an incompetent person cannot be held responsible for his actions.

Incongruences: In Rogers' self theory, mismatches between the self as perceived and the ideal self the person would like to be.

Incorporation: A primitive unconscious defence mechanism in which the psychic representation of another person are assimilated into oneself through a figurative process of symbolic oral ingestion. It represents a special form of introjection and is the earliest mechanism of identification.

Independent variable: The variable that an experimenter sets up to cause an effect in an experiment. An independent variable may have two or more conditions, and subjects' responses to each of them are studied. Independent variables may be existing features of the subjects (males vs. females) or be created by the experiment (dark vs. light conditions). It is called Independent because it is not affected by the experimental procedures. See dependent variable.

Indexical expressions: A term used by philosophers and social scientists in referring to expressions, statements or utterances which can be understood only with reference to the context in which they can occur. The most obvious examples are such as 'here', 'there', 'now', 'then' etc.

Indigenous psychology: The study of man as he conceives himself in terms of his collective representations. The term 'indigenous' emphasizes cultural views, theories, conjectures, assumptions and metaphors; draws attention to what is generally available to man in his attempts to make sense of and organize his psychological life.

Individual psychology: System of psychiatric theory developed by Alfred Adler, it stresses compensation and overcompensation for feelings of inferiority in a person's strivings to adapt to the social milieu. It emphasizes the interpersonal nature of a person's problems, and it is applied by some practitioners to group psychotherapy and counseling.

Individual therapy: The traditional dyadic therapeutic technique in which a psychotherapist treats one patient during a given therapeutic session. Newer techniques deal with more than one patient. See also Family therapy, Group psychotherapy.

Individuation: Jungian term denoting a process whereby the person molds and develops a healthy integrated individual personality through maximum differentiation and development of each system of the personality. See also Actualization.

Induced psychosis: Mainly delusional psychosis, usually chronic and often without florid features, which appears to have developed as a result of a close, if not dependent, relationship with another person who already has an established similar psychosis. The mental illness of the dominant member is most commonly paranoid. The morbid beliefs are induced in the other persons and given up when the pair are separated. The delusions are at least partly shared. Occasionally, several people are affected. *Synonyms*: folie a deux; folie communique, folie impose; folie induite; induced paranoid disorder; psychosis of association; symbiontische Psychose.

Induction: Making general laws from knowledge of particular cases. Inductive reasoning is being used when results from a sample are utilized to make statements about a population, and is fundamental to the operation of empirical psychology. Inductive reasoning has also been studied as part of the subject matter of cognitive psychology. It can be contrasted with deduction.

Industrial psychology: The application of psychology to industrial situations. Industrial psychologists may study the effects of environmental influences on people at work; of organizational influences, such as the effects of different management structures or styles; of social relationships within an industrial setting; or of sources of stress and industrial accidents.

Industrial therapy: Current organization of outside industrial working conditions within a unit in a psychiatric hospital. The main purpose is preparation of patients for their return to the working community.

Ineffability: An ecstatic state in which the person insists that his experience is inexpressible and indescribable, that it is impossible to convey what is like to one who never experienced it.

Infancy: The childhood period of helplessness and marked dependency; generally the first year of life.

Infantile autism: A syndrome beginning in infancy and characterized by withdrawal and self-absorption, failure to develop attachment to a parental figure, ineffective communication and mutism, preoccupation with inanimate objects, and an obsessive demand for sameness in the environment. It is also known as Kanner's syndrome. See also Autistic thinking.

Infantile dynamics: Psychodynamic integrations, such as the Oedipus complex, that are organized during childhood and continue to exert an unconscious influence on adult personality.

Infantile sexuality: Freudian concept regarding the erotic life of infants and children. Freud observed that, from birth, infants are capable of erotic activities. Infantile sexuality encompasses the overlapping phases of psychosexual development during the first 5 years of life and includes the oral phase (birth to 18 months), when erotic activity centers on the mouth; the anal phase (ages 1 to 3), when erotic activity centers on the rectum; and the phallic phase (ages 2 to 6), when erotic activity centers on the genital region. See also psychosexual development.

Infant psychiatry: That aspects of child psychiatry which deals with the diagnosis treatment, and prevention of maladaptive psychological functioning in infants.

Inferiority complex: Concept originated by Alfred Adler that everyone is born with a feeling of inferiority or inadequacy secondary to real or fantasied organic or psychological deficits. How the inferiority or feeling of inferiority is handled determines a person's behaviour in life. See also Masculine protest.

Information-processing: An approach which analysis cognitive process in terms of the manipulations of information that are involved. As computers have become capable of progressively more sophisticated operations, information processing has become accepted as a plausible approach to understanding perception decision making, etc. The approach is more directly involved with computers when they are used to run models of particular cognitive process (called a simulation) to see how the model would work in practice.

Information-processing theories of intelligence: Theories holding that intelligence should be measured in terms of such function as sensory processing, coding strategies, memory, and other mental capacities. See information-processing theory.

Information-processing theories of memory: Models of memory which say that human beings process information for storage in stages. See sensory register, short-term memory (STM), long-term memory (LTM), information processing theory.

Information theory: System dealing with the transmission, reception, and distortion of communicated messages.

Informed consent: Permission to perform a medical or research procedure which includes; (1) a rational understanding of the nature of the proceedings; (2) the foreseeable risks; (3) the expected benefits (4) the consequences of withholding consent; (5) available alternative procedures; and (6) that consent is voluntary.

Infradian rhythm: See Biological rhythm.

Inhibition: The depression or arrest of a function. In psychoanalysis, the conscious or unconscious confining or restraining of an impulse or desire. It often refers to the operation of the superego.

Initial insomnia: Falling asleep with difficulty. Usually seen in anxiety disorder.

Innate: Literally, inborn. It means unlearned, or present at birth, and is used synonymously with inherited or genetic.

Innate releasing mechanism (IRM): A term used by Tinbergen to refer to the stimulus which triggered off an instinctive behaviour. Examples are the moving shape which stimulates peeking in a young herring-gull chick and that which provokes 'freezing' in turkey chicks. The behaviour released by an IRM has direct survival value, either in avoidance of predators or in obtaining food. Currently the term sign stimulus is preferred to refer to these signals, as it avoids the implicit assumption about internal mechanisms contained within the term IRM.

Inner-directed person: A person who is self motivated and autonomous and is not easily guided or influenced by the opinions and values of other people. See also Other-directed person.

Insanity: Legal concept denoting a mental disturbance, due to which a person lacks criminal responsibility for an alleged crime and hence cannot be convicted of the crime. See also. Competency to stand trial, criminal responsibility. Durham rule, M'Naughten rules.

Insanity defence: A legal concept that a person cannot be convicted of a crime if he lacked criminal responsibility by reason of insanity, which term is defined as a matter of law. The promise is that where an alleged criminal lacks the mens rea because of insanity, such a person lacks criminal responsibility and cannot be convicted. Standards which the courts in Anglo-American law have established to define insanity have changed over the last century and continue to change.

Insecurity: Feelings of helplessness, unprotectedness, and inadequacy in the face of manifold anxieties arising from uncertainty regarding one's goals, ideals, abilities, and relations to others.

Insight: Conscious recognition of one's own conditions. In psychiatry, it more specifically refers to the conscious awareness and understanding of one's own psychodynamics and symptoms of maladaptive behaviour. It is highly important in effecting changes in the personality and behaviour of a person, Intellectual insight refers to knowledge of the reality of a situation without the ability to successfully use the knowledge to effect an adaptive change in behaviour. Emotional insight refers to a deeper level of understanding or awareness that is more likely to lead to positive change in personality and behaviour.

Insomnia: Difficulty in falling asleep or difficulty in staying asleep. See also Initial insomnia, Middle insomnia, terminal insomnia.

Insomnia of nonorganic origin: Disorders of initiating or maintaining sleep, not associated with somatic disorders or dysfunctions and most commonly attributable to anxiety, tension, affective psychoses or adverse environmental factors.

Instinct: A basic, inborn urge or drive. Freud postulated the existence of two opposing primal instincts; a life instinct (eros) and a death instinct (Thanatow). An extensive array of human instincts has been proposed, including possessive instinct, mastery instinct, and herd or social instinct. Because of its implications of a fixed, essentially unalterable, largely hereditary response or psychic tendency that does not involve learning or reason, the term has become ambiguous and controversial when applied to human behaviour. It is exceedingly difficult if not impossible, to demonstrate convincingly that any given human activity is, in fact, instinctual. Many modern psychoanalysts prefer the term "drive" for what Freud termed "Instinct". See also Drive.

Instinctive behaviour: Behaviour which occurs as a result of the direct action of genes. Such behaviour typically shows certain distinctive characteristics. These are stereotype (the behaviour, being fixed and not modifiable by the individual); there is a complex sequence of behaviour, not just a reflex response; it arises in individuals reared apart from their own species; it does not require prior learning or practice; it is species-specific. Such behaviour, would appear to be relatively common in fish and birds, but rather less so among the higher animals.

Institutionalization: The effect on a person of living for a long time in an institution. Institutions like mental hospitals are likely to develop procedures which are very different from those in the outside world. As the inmate adapts to the regime they may develop patterns of motivation and behaviour which would prevent thém from functioning successfully in the outside world. Ironically, the phenomenon operates most clearly in just those institutions, like mental hospitals and prisons, that are supposed to improve the client's ability to function within society. It has been suggested that the reason that staff in institutions fail to take the process of institutionalization into account is that they themselves are subject to it.

Instrumental aggression: Aggression which occurs because it will result, directly or indirectly, in a desired outcome for the individual showing the aggression.

Instrumental conditioning: See conditioning.

Instrumental learning: Learning which occurs as a direct result of the beneficial or pleasant consequences which it has for that individual. Often used synonymously with operant conditioning.

Insulin coma therapy (ICT): A form of shock treatment in which large amounts of insulin are given to a psychotic, usually a schizophrenic, producing profound hypoglycemia and resulting in a coma. Introduced by Manfred Sakel in 1933, it declined in use drastically after the introduction of antipsychotic drugs.

Intake: The initial interview between a patient and member of a psychiatric team. The term is usually used in connection with admission to a mental health facility.

Integration: The useful organization and incorporation of both new and old data, experience, and emotional capacities into the personality. Also refers to the organization and amalgamation of functions at various levels of psychosexual development.

Intellectualization: An unconscious defense mechanism in which reasoning or logic is used in an attempt to avoid confrontation with an objectionable impulse and thus defend against anxiety. It is also known as brooding compulsion and thinking compulsion.

Intellectual sub average functioning: An I.Q. more than two standard deviations below the test mean obtained on an intelligence test.

Intelligence: The capacity for learning and the ability to recall, integrate constructively, and apply what one has learned; the capacity to understand and to think rationally.

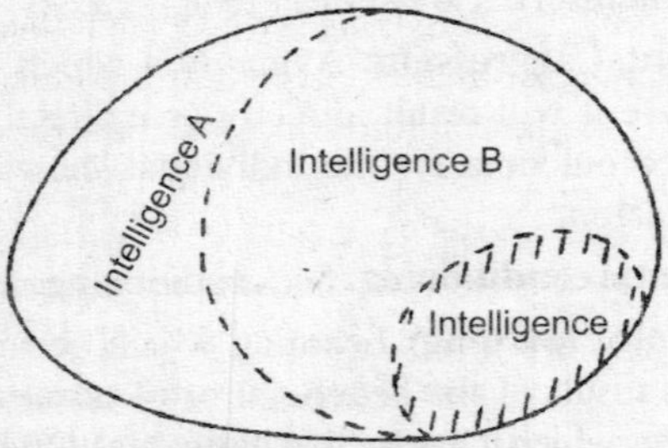

Fig. 7. A possible model of intelligence A, B and C.

Intelligence A, B, C: Classifications developed by Hebb and Vermon in an attempt to express the relatie contributions of experience and inheritance to an individual's intelligence. The term intelligence A was used to describe the total potential intelligence of an individual, given that particular genotype and an ideal environment from conception. Intelligence B was conceived as an unknown proportion of intelligence A, which was that amount of their potential which the individual had been able to realize throughout their life. Intelligence C referred to the unknown proportion of intelligence B which would be measured using an intelligence test. In formulating this model, Hebb was applying the genetic distinction between genotype and phenotype and arguing that, to talk of the relative contributions of genetic and environment as if they were alternatives or could be quantified, was inherently misleading.

Intelligence quotient (I.Q.): A numerical measure of mental capability determined by dividing a mental age (M.A.) score achieved on a specific test, such as the Stanford-Binet Test, by the patient's chronological age (C.A.) and multiplying by 100.

Intelligence test: A standardized set of task from which intelligence can be estimated. All tests should have been fully assessed for reliability and validity, but a great variety is now available, to some extent reflecting problems that have been identified during the history of mental testing. Of the most widely used tests, the Stanford Binet is a direct descendant of the original test devised by Binet to give a single measure of IQ. The Wechsler provides 12 sub-scales measuring different aspects of intelligence. Raven's Progressive Matrices attempts to eliminate cultural bias by having items and even administration which do not depend on using language. The recently developed British Ability Scale is an attempt to incorporate later psychological work on intelligent performance such as Piaget's ideas.

Interaction: A situation in which one thing reciprocally affects another, such that an exchange takes place. The term is used particularly in reference to social interaction.

Interactionism: The interactionist perspective within physiological psychology is a direct contrast to the traditional reductionist approaches. Rather than seeing physiology as the direct cause of behaviour, an interactionist perspective emphasizes the ways in which environment, cognition and physiology may all have a reciprocal effect on one another, such that each may influence the other in achieving a given effect. Within this approach, physiological variables which are usually regarded causes may equally well be seen as results.

Interego: Stekel's proposed substitute for the Freudian term superego.

Interference: The concept in memory theory that information may become lost or distorted because of the storage of additional information. The interference theory of forgetting was a popular approach in memory research throughout the 1950s and 1960s; and centered round the idea that memories could become displaced because of the storage of similar information. Interference was considered to be of two kinds; proactive interference, in which material which had been learned first interfered with the acquisition of later information and retroactive interference, in which information which had been acquired at a later stage interfered with the retrieval of previously learned material.

Intermission: In psychiatry, the interval between attacks of a particular syndrome. When it is not certain that the symptoms will return, the interval is called a remission. See also Remission.

Intermittent reinforcement: Any schedule of reinforcement in which the response is not always reinforced.

Internationalization: Making something part of oneself. Freud was concerned with the child internalizing the moral values of its parents, as expressed in their system of rewards and punishments. The term is now used more broadly, particularly in areas like conformity studies, where its use distinguishes subjects who have fully adopted and internalized the values from those who express them for expediency.

Internal-external scale: A scale originally devised by Rotter in the 1950s to measure whether a person believes the causes of events to originate within themselves (emotions abilities effort) or without (powerful other people, luck). See locus of control for one use of such a scale, and attribution theory for another.

Internal validity: The extent to which an individual item in a test measures the same thing as the other items. See validity.

International classification of diseases (ICD): The World Health Organization's official list of disease categories subscribed to by all WHO member nations, who may, however, assign their own terms to each category.

Interpersonal attraction: The degree to which people are drawn towards each other; influenced by proximity, attitude similarity, physical attractiveness.

Interpersonal conflict: See Extrapsychic conflict.

Interpersonal psychiatry: Dynamic-cultural system of psychiatry based on Harry Stack Sullivan's interpersonal theory, which proposes that each person must be viewed as an entity interacting with the sociocultural and interpersonal environment. Since the emphasis is on interactive experiences, group psychotherapy conducted by practitioners of this school focuses on the patient's interactive transactions with one another.

Interpersonal skill: Effectiveness of adaptive behaviour in relation to other persons; ability to express feeling appropriately, to be socially responsible and responsive and to work in harmony with others.

Interposition: A monocular cue for depth; near objects block portions of faraway objects.

Interpretation: The process of elucidating and expounding the meaning of something obstruse, obscure etc. (i) Content interpretations–refers to unconscious impulses and phantasies without reference to the defensive processes which have been keeping them unconscious. (ii) correct interpretations – are those which both (a) explain adequately the material being interpreted and (b) are formulated in such a way and communicated at such a time that they have actually , for the patient (iii) Direct interpretations – are based solely on the analyst's knowledge of symbolism without reference to the patient's associations (iv) Dream interpretations—the activity of discovering the latent content of meaning of a dream by analysis of its manifest content (v) Mutative interpretations —which alter the patient (vi) Premature interpretations—are true interpretations communicated to the patient before they can make sense to him (vii) Transference interpretations–relate the patient's behaviour and associations to his relationship to the analyst.

Interpretation of dreams: The title of a book by Freud. Published in 1899 this work a major presentation not only of Freud's theories about the meaning of dream's–subject hitherto regarded as outside scientific interest–but also of his concept of a mental apparatus that is topographically divided into unconscious, preconscious, and conscious areas.

Interpropositional logic: The capacity to a judge whether or statements (propositions) are logically connected to one another regardless, whether the statements are true; develops in formal operational stage.

Interval psychosis: Postoperative delirium, the major psychiatric complication observed in surgical intensive care units.

Intervening variable: Something intervening between an antecedent circumstance and its consequence, modifying the relation between the two. For example, appetite can be intervening variable determining whether or not a given food will be eaten. The intervening variable may be inferred rather than empirically detected.

Interview: A converzation between a professional and a subject designed to provide the professional with a certain kind of information. The nature of the interview will be influenced by its function which may be evaluation of the subject (for a job), therapeutic, or research. The form of the interview may be fully specified in advance (structured interview), be planned in more or less detail, or be conducted without any prior consideration of what information is wanted and how it is to be obtained. Research has shown interviews to be an inaccurate method of selecting, but this may be because the interviews studied had not been carefully constructed.

Intrapersonal conflict: See Intrapsychic conflict.

Intrapsychic ataxia: See Ataxia.

Intrapsychic conflict: State of tension arising from the clash of two or more incompatible or opposing forces–for example, wishes, needs, motives, thoughts–operating within oneself. It is also known as intrapersonal conflict. See also Extrapsychic conflict.

Introjection: The unconscious, symbolic internationalization of a psychic representation of a hated or loved external object with the goal of establishing closeness to and constant presence of the object, anxiety consequent to separation or tension aring out of ambivalence toward the object is diminished; in the case of a feared hated object, internationalization of its malicious or aggressive characteristics serves to avoid anxiety by symbolically putting those characteristics under one's control.

Intropunitive: Turning anger inward toward oneself. It is commonly observed in depressed patients.

Introspection: The process of self examination, or looking within one's experience in order to gain insight into psychological phenomena. Although notoriously unreliable in many respects, introspection can at times provide valuable insights which could at other times be missed.

Introspectionism: A school of thought, prevalent in the early years of psychology as an independent discipline from philosophy, in which investigations were conducted though systematic, and often detailed, introspection by one or two highly trained psychologists. Although often castigated as 'armchair psychology' by the early behaviourists, this technique established some important theoretical perspectives, such as those outlined in James's principles of psychology; which in many cases are still of use to modern psychology. With the advent of behaviourism in the first part of the twentieth century, introspectionism as a technique became disregarded; but of recent years it has re-emerged to a limited extent within the phenomenological school of modern psychologists.

Introversion: A preoccupation with one's self, accompanied by lack of interest in the outside world. See also Extroversion.

Introvert: An individual inclined towards a solitary, reflective life-style. Introversion is a personality dimension regarded as the opposite of extraversion. It was proposed by Carl Jung and incorporated into the Eysenck Personality Inventory. Eysenck sees introversion as rising from a higher level of cortical arousal resulting in a lower level of inhibition to the same stimulus. Introverted individuals, he argues, do not get bored as easily as extraverts, and so are better at tasks requiring sustained or which involve relatively little change in stimulation.

Introverted personality disorder: See schizoid personality disorder.

Intuitive substage: In Piaget's theory of cognitive development. The second of two substages of the preoperational stage, from roughly 4 to 7 years of age; it is characterized by unsystematic reasoning based on perceptual appearances. Compare preconceptual substage.

Inversion: Term for homosexuality used by Freud, who distinguished three types; absolute, amphigenous, and occasional. See also Homosexuality, Latent homosexuality, overt homosexuality.

Involutional melancholia: Depression occurring in the middle age in persons, who generally have no history of previous mental illness. Characteristic manifestations include delusions of sin, guilt, or poverty; an obsession with death pre-occupational with somatic particularly gastrointestinal function; despair, dejection, agitation, anxiety, and insomnial and in some cases, paranoid ideation. It is also known as involutional psychosis. The term involutional melancholia is not used in DSM – III but is replaced by the diagnosis major depression, single episode, with melancholia or with mood congruent psychotic features.

Involutional paranoid state: A DSM–II term characterized by delusional formation in the involutional period. In DSM–III this is subsumed under a typical paranoid disorder or paranoia.

Ipsative: Assessed or measured by comparison with the self. Ipsative scales involve the individual using his or her own values or behaviour as the yardstick by which comparisons and evaluations are made.

Irresistible impulse test: The rule that a person is not responsible for a crime if he acts through an irresistible impulse which he was unable to control because of a mental disease. Still accepted in some states, but rejected by most. Introduced in 1922 in USA.

Irrumation: Fellatio.

Isakower phenomenon: Hypnagogic experience first described by Isakower (1938) in which the subject imagines soft, doughy masses to be moving towards his face. Isakower interpreted this phenomenon as a revival of the infant's experience of being at the breast.

Isolated explosive disorder: See explosive disorder, isolated.

Isolation: In psychoanalysis, a defense mechanism involving the separation of an idea or memory from its attached feeling tone. Unacceptable ideational content is thereby rendered free of its disturbing on unpleasant emotional charge. See also Alienation, Relatedness.

Isonome: A signal or pathway in the brain that has similar effects on several different agencies.

Isophilic: Term used by Sullivan to mean liking or feeling affectionate towards people of the same sex, without the sexual or erotic aspects of homosexuality.

I-Thou: Philosopher Martin Buber's conceptior. that a person's identity develops from the true sharing by persons. Basic trust can occur in a living partnership in which each member identifies the particular real personality of the other in his wholeness, unity, and uniqueness. In groups, I-Thou relationships promote warmth cohesiveness, and constructive group process. See also I-It.

J

Jamais Vu: False feeling of unfamiliarity with a real situation that one has experienced; it is a paramnestic phenomenon. See also Paramnesia.

James-Lange theory: An early theory of emotion which argued that the experience of emotion arose from the perception of physiological changes in the body, brought about by the emotional stimulus. In other words: the physiological changes occurred first, and the emotion was simply the perception of those changes. See also alarm reaction; Cannon-Bard theory.

Janet Pierre (1859–1947): The last great representative of the French school of psychiatry; known for his concept of psychological automatism and for his interest in cases of multiple personalities. He was the first to use the term la beel indifference. See also Psychasthenia.

Japanese illusion test: This is to test analgesia of organic and functional in origin. Patient is asked to cross both hands palm-to-palm, interlock fingers and invert. Patient with organic illness shown consistent responses to testing of anaesthetic hand.

Jealousy: Differs from envy in that in involves three parties; the subject, an object whom the subject loves and a third party who arouses anxiety in the subject about his security of tenure of the second party's affections, subject and an object whose good fortune or possessions the subject envies.

Jealousy is related to possessiveness of the other; envy to comparison of the self with the other.

Jet lag: A syndrome in which the individual's circadian rhythms becomes out of phase with the surrounding environment, as a result of the rapid crossing of time zones during long distance travel. This produces feelings of extreme fatigue, and in some cases disorientation, sometimes lasting for several days until the individual adjusts fully to a new time system.

Jhin Jhinia: A culture-specific syndrome that is said to occur in epidemic form in India, consisting of bizarre and seemingly involuntary contractions and spasms.

Jones, Ernest (1879–1958): Welsh psychoanalyst and one of Freud's early followers. He was an organizer of the American Psychoanalytic Association in 1911 and of the British Psychoanalytical society in 1919 and a founder and long-time editor of the Journal of International Psychoanalytical Association. A profile author, he is most noted for his three volume biography of Freud. See also Rationalization.

Judgement: Mental act of comparing or evaluating choices within the framework of a given set of values for the purpose of electing a course of action. If the course of action chosen is consonant with reality or with mature adult standards of behaviour, judgement is said to be intact or normal; judgement is said to be impaired if the chosen course of action is frankly maladaptive, results from impulsive decision based on the need for immediate gratification, or is otherwise not consistent with reality as measured by mature adult standards.

Jung, Carl Gustav (1875–1961): Swiss psychiatrist and psychoanalyst originally associated with Freud. Jung later founded the school of analytic psychology. See also Affect-fantasy, Analytic psychology, Anima, Imago, Collective unconscious, individuation, Persona.

Jungian: Pertaining to the psychoanalytic system developed by Carl Jung sometimes also referred to as analytical psychology.

Juramentado: A culture specific syndrome described in the Malays and Moros consisting of marked agitation and assault or stabbing of anyone, they encounter, followed by a stupor and, upon awakening, amnesia for the episode.

K

Kanner's syndrome: See infantile autism.

Kelly George, A. (1905–1966): A Physicist mathematician, sociologist, educationist and eventually clinical psychologist, influenced psychology with his major work. 'The psychology of personal constructs'. Kelly emphasized that Personality is equivalent to 'Psychology' and not just one part of it.

Key word method: A mnemonic technique for learning the meanings of technical or foreign terms, which involves identifying a key familiar word derived from the sound of the unknown one. By forming a visual image linking this key word with the meaning of the word to be learned, the information is acquired; the visual image forming a link between the perceived sound of the new word and its meaning.

Kibbutz: An Israeli community in which property and responsibility are held in common by all members of the kibbutz (kibbutzniks). Many kibbutzim have communal child rearing systems, which were intensively studied in the 1960s. The then current theoretical ideas on mother-infant bonding implied that children would become psychologically damaged if not kept with their mother, Little evidence of this was found among the communally-reared children of the kibbutzim.

Kin selection: A concept put forward in sociobiology, kin selection involves the idea that an individual may protect their genes for the future by protecting not just their offspring, but other relatives who share them. Since siblings share on average 50% of their genes, the individual can ensure that a proportion of the genes survive by protecting his or her siblings. The concept is used to explain behaviour which is apparent altruistic, such as the self-sacrificing behaviour of workers ants.

Kinesics: The study of body posture movement and facial expressions.

Kinesiology: The study of body movement, especially in the context of its communicative function.

Kinesthetic sense: The sense by which muscular motion, tension, position and posture are perceived, proprioception.

Kirkbride, Thomas, S. (1809–1883): American psychiatrist, one of the 13 original founders of the American Psychiatric Association. He is noted for his 1854 manual advocating reform in the design of institutions for the mentally ill.

Klazomania: Compulsory shouting, usually a motor discharge phenomenon based on mesencephalic or other central nervous system irritation.

Klebedenken: Adhesive, sticky, preservative, thinking seen in schizophrenia.

Klebenbleiben: A type of language disturbance occurring in schizophrenia in which the speaker repeats the topic on different words, elaborates it, qualifies it, explains it, but cannot leave it.

Klein, Melanie (1882–1969): British pioneer in the psychoanalysis of children. Noted for her work on early childhood development, particularly infantile aggression and the origins of the superego in the early infancy.

Kleine-Levin syndrome: Periodic episodes of hypersomnia; first appears in adolescence, usually in boys and is accompanied by bulimia.

Kleptomania: An outmoded term for a morbid, often sudden and usually irresistible impulse to steal without an apparent need. The impulse tends to recur. The objects are mostly of little or no value but may carry symbolic significance. It has been described to occur more frequently in women and to be associated with depression, neurotic illness, personality disorder or mental retardation. *Synonym*: shop lifting (pathological).

Koro: An acute delusional syndrome seen in Malaya and South China in which the patient suddenly becomes actually anxious that his penis is shrinking and may disappear into his abdomen, in which case he will die.

Korsakoff's psychosis: An organic mental disorder seen in long-term alcoholics. Its major characteristic feature is a profound memory impairment, particularly for recent events, for which the patient attempts to compensate by confabulation. The official DSM-III term is alcohol amnestic disorder. See also Wernicke's encephalopathy.

Kraepelin, Emil (1865–1926): German psychiatrist noted for his pioneering work in psychiatric nosology and classification systems. He differentiated between manic depressive psychoses and dementia precox (schizophrenia). One of the last representatives of the predynamic school of psychiatry, he is often considered the father of descriptive psychiatry. See also Descriptive psychiatry.

Krafft_Ebing, Richard Von (1840–1903): Neuropsychiatrist and student of sexual pathology, remembered for his now classic psychopathia sexualis, a pioneering study of sexual aberrations, published in 1886.

Kretschmer, Ernest (1888–1964): German psychiatrist noted for his theories of the relation of physique to character and personality. See also constitutional types.

L

La belle indifference: An inappropriate attitude of calm or lack of concern about one's disability. It is seen in patients with conversion disorder. See also Hysterical neurosis Literally "beautiful indifference".

Labelling: When a label is applied to someone there is tendency for that person to be seen, both by others and often by themselves as having all of the characteristics implied by the label, and being nothing more than that. So labeling someone as schizophrenic or depressive can cause them to be treated as less than a whole person, since all of other behaviour is likely to be interpreted in terms of the illness, as schizophrenic or depressed behaviour. This can be resisted by instating on referring to 'a person with depression' rather than 'a depressive'. But the tendency remains difficult to avoid. The study of labelling and its implications is an important part of social psychology, and has been so ever since the discovery of the self-fulfilling prophecy.

Labeling theory: A perspective on deviance which tends to see the deviant as a victim of a society which categorizes him as criminal or mad in an arbitrary or despotic way.

Labile: Unstable; characterized by rapidly changing emotions.

Labile affect: See Affect Labile.

Laconic speech: Condition characterized by a reduction in the quantity of spontaneous speech. Replies to questions are brief and unelaborated, and little or no unprompted additional information is provided. It is also called poverty of speech. Occurs in major depression, schizophrenia and organic mental disorders.

Lacunar amnesia: See Amnesia, localized.

Laissez-faire: Leaving people to get on with thing in their own way. It is used to indicate a style of leadership in which most of the responsibility for action is left with the group, rather than assumed by the leader. Groups with laissez-faire leadership tend not to be as productive as others, but some findings suggest that they continue to operate better than other groups when the leader is absent.

Language: The complex system of communication which involves the organization of word into meaningful combinations. Although most people would agree that the use of language is a distinctively human attribute, the lack of a precise definition of what exactly language is, makes it difficult to decide whether such phenomena as bird songs, bee dances, or whatever can be taught to chimpanzees in this line, should be called language. It is generally accepted, however, that language involves symbolic representation, and that there are distinct rules concerning acceptable combinations of the elements of language (usually word) which do not permit all possible combinations to be regarded as meaningful. Language can be studied on a number of levels, which may be broadly classified as lexical (concerning the word units themselves and their referents); syntactic (concerning the rules for combining words into meaningful utterances); and sematic concerning the meaning of what is said. The use of analogy and metaphor in language means that the lexical characteristics of an utterance may not be identical with its semantic characteristics (e.g., describing someone as 'burning' with enthusiasm). Psychologists have also studied social aspects of language use; such as the impact of accents or sexiest language, and recently much research attention has been devoted to discourse analysis; looking at the way that language is used in complete conversations.

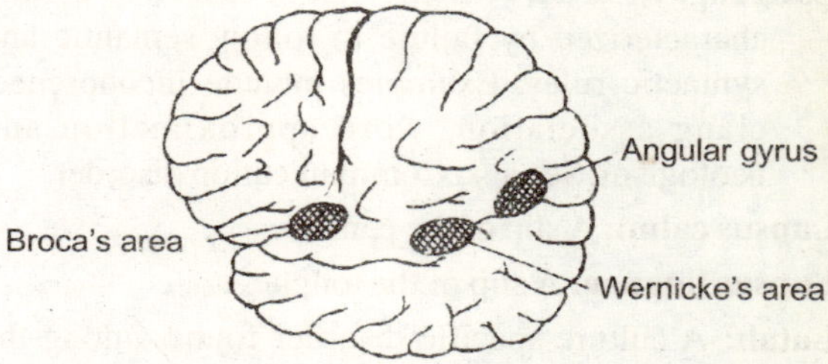

Fig. 8. Language areas of the cerebral cortex.

Language acquisition device: A mechanism proposed by Chomsky to explain the extreme rapidity with which young children develop speech. He proposed that the young infant is born with an innate language acquisition device, which enables it to extract basic rules of grammar from the speech heard around them. Moreover, this occurs as a more or less automatic process; all that is required is that the child hears or experiences language used by others. In view of an increasing body of research indicating that human interaction forms a fundamental part of speech acquisition, later theorists have modified this concept, preferring instead to talk of a language acquisition system, or LAS; which allows for rather more active involvement on the part of the child than simply passive decoding.

Language areas: Specific parts of the cerebral cortex, usually (though not always) located on the left hemisphere, and mediating the functions of language. There are three main language areas; Broca's area, which is largely responsible for speech production and the formulation of appropriate words, Wernicke's area, which is concerned with the comprehension of speech, and the angular gyrus, which receives information concerned with the written word from the visual cortex and converts it into sound-equivalent representations for decoding in Wernicke's area.

Language disorder: Disturbance of speech or writing characterized by failure to follow semantic and syntactic rules. Examples include incoherence, clang association, word approximation and neologism. See also Communication disorder.

Lapsus calmi: A slip of the pen.

Lapsus linguae: A slip of the tongue.

Latah: A culture-specific disorder found among the Malaysian people and characterized by either a sudden onset of unusual and inappropriate motor and verbal manifestations or by an echo reaction, in which the victim is compelled to imitate any words or actions to which he is exposed. In both forms the affected person cannot control or inhibit his behaviour.

Latency phase: Period of psychosexual development after the phallic phase and succeeded by the genetal phase, extending from about age 5 to the beginning of adolescence. During the latency phase there is an apparent ceszation of sexual preoccupation and a blockade of libidinal inpluses, and boys and girls are inclined to choose friends and join groups of their own sex. See also Anal phase, Genital phase. Infantile sexuality, Oral phase, phallic phase, psychosexual development.

Latency content: The hidden (unconscious) meaning of thoughts or actions, especially in dreams or fantasies. In dreams, it is expressed in distorted, disguised, condensed, and symbolic form.

Latent homosexuality: Unexpressed conscious or unconscious homoerotic wishes that are held in check. Freud's theory of bisexuality postulated the existence of a constitutionally determined, although experientially influenced, instinctual masculine-feminine duality. Normally, the opposite-sex component is dormant, but a breakdown in the defenses of repression and sublimation may activate latent instincts and result in overt homo-eroticism. Many writers have questioned the validity of theory of a universal latent homo-eroticism. See also bisexuality, Homo-sexuality, Overt homosexuality.

Latent learning: A system of learning first demonstrated in 1932 by Tolman, who presented clear empirical evidence that even laboratory rats could form internal, cognitive representations of a complex maze; and that learning need not necessarily show immediately in behaviour but might remain latent until it was advantageous to use it. Latent learning was important as a concept because it provided a counter to the behaviourist argument that learning and changes in behaviour were synonymous.

Latent schizophrenia: Condition characterized by clear schizophrenic symptoms without a history of prior overly psychotic schizophrenic episodes. In DSM-III the condition was subsumed under the category of schizotypal personality disorder.

Laterality: Specialization of function on one side. Used both of handedness and of the specialization of function in either the left or right hemisphere of the brain.

Lateral thinking: Thinking which involves a 'sideways leap' from conventional attempts to solve a problem, and which reaches a solution by adopting novel tactics or by reformulating the problem in an unusual manner. Lateral thinking has been promoted since the 1960 by de Bono, and involved a search for originality and flexibility in mental operations which would counteract sterile and hidebound problem-solving practices, both in management and in day to day problem-solving. Divergent thinking has a similar meaning. See also creativity.

Law of effect: The principle developed by Thorndike, that a response which was followed by a pleasant consequence would be more likely to be repeated. This idea was developed and amplified by B.F. Skinner, in his work on operant conditioning.

Law of effort: A principle developed as a result of investigations into imprinting in ducklings, in which it was observed that the more effort a duckling had to put into following its imprinted 'parent' around, the stronger the attachment bond would become.

Law of exercise: The principle developed by J.B. Watson, on association learning, which stated that a learned connection between a stimulus and a response would be established by the repetition of their association. In other words, if they occurred together often enough, they would become associated together, and the learning would have occurred. This concept was later developed more fully by Pavlov in his research on classical conditioning.

Law of mass action: A principle formulated by Lashley as a result of investigations into the role of the association cortex in learning. He found that much of the cerebral cortex appeared to have non-localized functioning, but instead seemed to function as a mass; the more there was of it, the more effective the learning; or alternatively the greater the amount destroyed, the greater the learning impediment. See also equipotentiality.

Law of Pragnanz: The principle by which meaningfulness or organization of visual stimuli occurred, according to the Gestalt psychologists. The law of Pragnanz is concerned with the ways that perceptual organization occurred through the subsidiary principles of proximity, similarity, closure and good gestalt, such that meaningful figures against backgrounds are seen, rather.

Laxative habit: Reliance on, and abuse of purgatives as a means of controlling weight, often occurring in association with 'binge eating' in bulimia.

Leadership role: Stance adopted by the therapist in conducting group therapy. There are three main leadership roles: authoritarian, democratic, and laissez-faire. Any group-social, therapeutic, training, or task oriented- is strongly influenced by the role practiced by the leader.

Learned autonomic control: The learned regulation by a person of physiological responses that are under autonomic nervous system control. Experimental psychologist Neal E. Miller, using biofeedback training techniques demonstrated that such visceral response are subject to learning.

Learned helplessness: A concept demonstrated experimentally by Martin Seligman. He showed that animals which had received unpleasant experiences about which they could do nothing, were less ready to undertake action when in a similar situation where a relatively simple response would avert an unpleasant experience. Instead, the animals would remain passive, and do little to help themselves, not even struggling. Seligman drew parallels between the behaviours shown by animals in this condition and the behaviours associated with depression in humans. From these parallels he developed helplessness theory, which proposes that (some) depression may result from a belief of having no control over bad events. Subsequently the theory was revised by Seligman and others in terms of attribution theory.

Learning: A relatively permanent change in knowledge behaviour or understanding that results from experience. Innate behaviours, maturation and fatigue are excluded. Learning has been claimed as the core phenomenon of psychology though in practice, the field often seems to have operated by producing a theory and then defining learning as being whatever that theory explains. Specialist areas include modeling and imitation, motor skills, insight, formation of schemata creativity, habituation and conditioning. The learning of specific skills such as language have become areas of study in their own right.

Learning curve: The graph that is obtained when a measure of competence is plotted against the number of leaning trials the animal or person has had. The learning curve has a characteristic shape but this is usually achieved rather artificially by averaging together a large number of learning curves while the individual curves may be much less regular.

Learning disability: A syndrome affecting school age children of normal or above normal intelligence characterized by specific difficulties in learning to read (dyslexia), write (dysgraphia), and calculate (dyscalculia). The disorder is believed to be related to slow developmental progression of perceptual motor skills. See also minimal brain dysfunction.

Learning set: A generalized style of learning, or state of preparedness to solve problems in certain ways, which has been acquired through experience with similar types of problems. Possession of a learning set means that the individual is likely to look for that kind of solution in preference to any alternative strategy. Where problems are similar, learning sets may be advantageous, but, may prove a hindrance to the individual faced with a problem which requires a novel approach.

Learning theory: An approach to the understanding of human behaviour that emphasizes the way in which learning comes about. According to learning theory, learning itself represents a change in behaviour resulting from practice. Through the application of certain laws of learning, that theory of behaviour attempts to explain the basic process that are necessary for learning to occur.

Lesbianism: Female homosexuality. About 600 B.C. on the island of Lesbos in the Aegean Sea, the poetess

Sappho encouraged young women to engage in sexual activities with one another. Lesbianism is also known as Sapphism. See also Bisexuality, Homosexuality, Latent homosexuality. Overt Homosexuality.

Lethologica: Temporary inability to remember a proper noun or name.

Levels of processing: A theory of memory put forward by Craik and Lockhart, which argues that information may be processed at a number of levels, depending on how it is organized, linked with other memories, tied in with emotional experience, and so on. Information which has been only superficially processed or accepted passively will be readily forgotten, and this is used to explain the phenomena of rapid forgetting previously characterized as short-term memory. Information which has been processed more deeply will be retained for a longer period of time.

Lewin, Kurt (1890–1947): German psychologist who emigrated to the United States in 1933. Two of his chief theoretical contributions are the field approach (field theory) and group dynamics, each of which has been useful in the experimental study of human behaviour in a social situation. See also Field theory.

Libido: A term originally used by Freud to refer to sexual energy which is derived from the id and is available to power mental and physical activity LaterFreud regarded libido as a general life energy. In common usage, the connotation of sexual energy is still associated with the term.

Lie detector: A popular name for a device measuring bodily indications of the arousal presumed to accompany lying; also known as a polygraph.

Life-event: An event result in a major change in the life situation of a person. There is evidence that all life events, even those that are fundamentally positive, impose a stress. Holmes and Rahe have produced a 'Life Events Scale' which gives weightings to different events, ranging; from 100 for death of a spouse down to 12 for Christmas and 11 for minor violations of the law. The scale can be used to provide a total score for all of the life events experienced during, say, the last year. People experiencing a slot of change will obtain a high score, and high scores may indicate that a person is at higher risk of illness or accidents. Negative life events may also some people more prone to depression.

Life instinct: All the constructive tendencies of the organism that aim at the maintenance and perpetuation of the individual and species. Freud introduced the dual-instinct theory, which postulates the existence of two opposing instincts; the life instinct (eros, sexual drive) and the death instinct (Thanatos, aggressive drive). See also Aggressive drive, Death instinct. Sexual drive.

Life lie: A contrary-to-fact conviction around which a person structures his life philosophy and attitudes.

Lifwynn Foundation: An organization established by Trigant Burrowin 1972 as a social community in which the participants examined their interactions in the daily activities in which they were engaged.

Limbic system: An area in the brain associated with the control of emotion, eating, drinking, and sexual activity.

Linguistic: To do with language. The term linguistics is used to refer to the study of language itself.

Linguistic relativity hypothesis: Sometimes also known as the Sapir-Whorf hypothesis, this is the idea that thinking is dependent on the language used by the individual. In other words, that the possession of words for each concept shapes a person's ;thought. In the 'strong' form of the hypothesis, words are seen to determine thought entirely; but a 'weak' form has become more generally accepted, which states that the words available serve to facilitate and amplify thought, and to indicate relationships between concepts, rather than actually to determine them.

Locus of control: A concept at the core of a social learning theory developed by Rotter in the 1950s. It refers to the belief that a person has about where social reinforcements originate: whether they are internal to the person, or external. Someone with an internal locus of control will tend to believe that marks on an easy depend on the amount of effort and ability applied to writing it. Someone with an external locus of control will tend to attribute the marks to luck, predestination, or the whims of the person doing the marking. LOC can be measured using a variety of short self-report scales and has been found to relate meaningfully to how people behave in a great variety of situations. Such evidence supports the construct validity of the scales, writings in the area often imply that an internal locus of control is preferable. It is true that an internal LOC is more likely to result in the individual making efforts to improve their situation but whether this is useful depends on whether events are actually under their control or not. A similar but not identical concept was developed more or less independently in attribution theory. See internal-external scale.

Logic: A set of rules by which conclusions can be reliably deducted from initial statements (propositions). Logic can be applied without regard for the truth of professions. For example, 'all students work hard and those who work hard pass their exams, therefore all students pass their exams' is sound logic. The fact that it is not true that all those who work hard pass their exams, means that the conclusion is not necessarily true, although it could be, by accident. Logic has been of interest in psychology because it can be regarded as perfect reasoning and is therefore a starting point for analyzing how people reason. It turns out that people are much more sophisticated and rather less rigid in their thinking than logic that has been invented, and there is not too much similarity between the two processes.

Logorrhea: Copious, pressured, coherent speech; uncontrollable, excessive talking. It is observed in manic episodes of bipolar affective disorder. Logorrhea is also known as tachylogia, verbomania, volubility and garrulousness. See also Pressure of speech.

Logo therapy: Existential analysis based on spiritual values rather than psychobiological laws.

Long-term memory (LTM): A term used to describe memories other than those which remain for a few seconds only. According to the two process theory of memory, any information which is retained for any length of time above a few seconds is deemed to have been stored in long-term memory; while that which lasts just for a brief interval (such as a telephone number which has just been looked up) is considered to have been stored in short in short-term memory. Many modern researchers question this commonly accepted distinction, arguing that it is unnecessary and that it fails to discriminate between information retained for varying periods of time. One alternative to this approach has been the levels of processing theory, which argues that the decisive factor in how long information is retained is how deeply it has been organized and processed and that there is no need to postulate separate memory stores.

Loosening of association: A characteristic schizophrenic thinking or speech disturbance involving a disorder in the logical progression of thoughts, manifested as a failure to adequately verbally communicate. Unrelated and unconnected ideas shift from one subject to another. See also Tangentiality.

Love: An act of full attention and giving that accepts and attaches to someone as he or she is, thereby enhancing the potential of what that person can become. Psychoanalysis have as much difficulty defining such a protean concept as do others. It appears in the literature as (a) eros a personified force or principle (b) an instinct or group of instincts liable to come into conflict with either self preservative (See self preservation) or destructive instincts. (c) an affect more often contrasted with hate than with fear; and (d) a capacity or function liable to inhibition, perversion and sublimation (a) genital love-is not synonym for sexual desire but the form of love of which a person who has reached the genital level is capable (b) Love-object-is an object whom he is indifferent (c) Oedipal love-is love for a parent or for a parent–substitute.

Love need: A term used by some humanistic psychologists to refer to the need for affection or positive regard from others, which is seen as a fundamental part of human nature.

LSD (lysergic acid diethylamide): A potent psychotogenic drug discovered in 1942. LSD produces psychotic-like symptoms and behaviour changes, including hallucinations, delusions, and time space distortions.

Luria, Alexander Romanovich (1902–1977): Russian neuropsychologist who developed a treatment for aphasia, combining physical and psychologic techniques for victims of brain trauma.

Lust Dynamism: A term used by Sullivan to describe clearly stated sexual desires and abilities.

Lying: To make statements that one knows consciously are false with intent to deceive should be differentiated from confabulation in which the patient is not conscious of lying. See also confabulation.

M

Machiavellianism: A term that describes people who express the need for power by manipulating and exploiting others in a deceptive and unscrupulous fashion.

Macropsia: False perception that objects are larger than they really are. See also micropsia.

Magic: Primitive, superstitious practices based on the assumption that natural processes can be affected by actions which influence or propitiate supernatural agencies or in the case of sympathetic magic, by actions which resemble those which the magician wishes to induce.

Magical thinking: The individual believes that his or her thoughts, words, or action might, or will in some manner cause or prevent a specific outcome in some way that defies the normal laws of cause and effect. Example: A man believed that if he said a specific prayer three times each night, his mother's death might be prevented indefinitely; a mother believed that if she had an angry thought her child would become ill. Magical thinking may be part of ideas of reference or may reach delusional proportions when the individual maintains a firm conviction about the belief despite evidence to the contrary.

Magical thinking: is seen in children, in people in primitive cultures, and in Schizotypal Personality Disorder, Schizophrenia and Obsessive compulsive Disorder.

Magnan's sign: Formication.

Magnetic resonance imaging (MRI): A technique for imaging anatomical structures which involves placing subjects in a strong magnetic field and then, by use of magnetic gradients and brief radio frequency pulses, determining the resonance characteristics at each point in the area to be studied. Used to detect structural or anatomical abnormalities, such as brain and incipient multiple sclerosis. See also brain imaging.

Main effect: The overall relationship between a class of independent variable and the dependent variable. The term is used mainly in analysis variance.

Maintenance drug therapy: A stage in the course of chemotherapy. After the drug has reached its maximal efficacy, the dosage is reduced and sustained at the minimal therapeutic level that will prevent a relapse or exacerbation.

Major depression: A severe affective disorder characterized by one or more depressive episodes but no history of a manic episode.

Maladaptive: Referring any mental activity or behaviour that is dysfunctional or counter productive with regard to the person's ability to cope effectively with the problems and stresses of life.

Maladjustment: A poor adjustment. The term is used of people, particularly children and adolescents, whose behaviour is judged to conflict strongly with the expectations and requirements of society.

Malevolent transformation: Sullivan's term for a learned attitude in which the world of interpersonal relationships is regarded as painful and dangerous because of past interpersonal failures. It frequently leads to social withdrawal.

Malingering: Feigning disease in order top achieve a specific goal – for example, to avoid an unpleasant responsibility. See also Factitious disorder, somatoform disorder.

Mania: Mood disorder characterized by elation, agitation, hyperactivity and hyper excitability, and accelerated thinking and speaking (flight of ideas). It characterizes the manic phase of bipolar affective disorder. See also hypomania.

Table of Manias and Philias: Used as a suffix- mania refers to an exaggerated interest in or preference for something, in many instances of sufficient intensity to lead to compulsive or impulsive actions. The traditional terms for several of the impulse disorders employ the mania suffix: kleptomania, trichotillomania, pyromania.

In general, mania stresses behaviour and action, whereas the suffix 'philia' emphasizes the feeling, attitude, disposition, or preference. Another suffix, used much less frequently, is 'lagnia', which emphasizes the erotic element in the craving or activity; most words with this suffix refer to what DSM term paraphilias. Thus pyrophilia means an excessive interest in fires, pyromania refers to fire-setting, and pyrolagnia refers to fire-watching or fire-setting as an essential or contributing factor to sexual excitement in the subject.

There are, however, many exceptions to the general rule. Some mania words, in fact, do not refer to desire or need to all; intead, they describe an aversion or loathing (a function more typically performed by the 'phobia' suffix). Examples are demonomania (fear of devils) and nautomania (the sailor's fear of the sea).

Acrasia, acolasis, ogriothymia, and hyperepithymia are general terms for exaggerated interest, inordinate desire, and intemperance. Terms for more specific preoccupations or cravings, and impulsive or compulsive actions, include:

Alcohol: Acoria (although Hippocrates used it to mean moderation in eating), alcoholophilia, alcoholomania, dipsomania, dipsos avens, oenomania, oinomania, polyposia, poisomania, potomania.

Animals: Ophidiophilia (snakes), zooerasty, zoolagbia.

Bathing, washing: Ablutomania.

Beauty: Callomania (also = delusion that one is beautiful)

Bitting: Agriothymia hydrophobica, vampirism

Bloodletting: Phiebotomomania, vampirism (love bites)

Buying: Oniomania

Children: Pedophilia, philoprogeneity (one's own)

Collecting books: Biblomania

Collecting, greed: Hoarding, pleonexia, plutomania

Counting, numbers: Arithmomania

Death: Necromania, necrophilia, pseudonecrophilia (dead bodies), taphophilia (graves, cemeteries)

Destruction of other nations: Agriothymia ambitiosa

Destruction of other religions: Agriothymia religiosa

Drugs: Cocainomia (cocaine), etheromania (ether, inhalants), opiomania (opiates), toxicomania

Eating, food: Allotriophagy (unnatural food, such as thread), bulimia, opsomania (sweets), polyphagia

Enemas: Klismaphilia

Family, upbringing: Ecomania, oikiomania

Filth, excreta: Coprolagnia, coprophilia, mysophilia, urolagnia, urophilia

Fire, firesetting: Pyrolagnia, pyromania

Gift giving: Doromania

Hairbiting: Trichophagy

Hair pulling: Trichotilomania

Health, body functioning: Hypochondriasis, nosomania

Images: Iconomania (collecting or worshiping)

Imitate, mimic: Echomimia, echopraxia, philomimesia

Injury, pain: Castrophilia (castration), flagellomania (whipping or being whipped)

Machlaenomania (masochism in female), sexual masochism, sexual sadism, tomomania (desire to be operated upon), traumatophilia (self)

Lies, myths: Mythomania

litigation: Processomania

Marrying: Gamonomania

Masturbation: Chiromania, psycholagny

Murder, blood: Hemothymia, homicidomania, phonomania

Nostalgia, homesickness, need to go home: Nostomania, philopatrido-mania

Novelty: Philoneism

Odours: Osphresiolagnia, renifleur

Old person: Gerontophilia, gerophilia

Pain: Algolagnia (both sexual sadism and sexual masochism), algophilia (not necessarily sexual), lagneuomania (sexual sadism in the male)

The past: Delire ecmnesique

Plucking threads: Allotriorhexia

Power: Cratomania

Questioning: Fragesucht

Repeating action: Mania of recommencement

Sadness: Tristemania

Self: Autophilia, autosynnoia, egomania, folie vaniteuse

Sex, hypersexuality: Aphrodisiomania, acrai, brachuna

In females: Aedoeomania, andromania, clitoromania, estromania, folie uterine, hysteromania, metromania, oestromania, nymphomania, sexual erethism

In male: Don Juan complex, gynecoania, satyriasis, pronolagnia (need for prostitutes)

Elimination: Sexual vandalism (destroying any representation of genitals)

Watching: Scot (t) olognia, scop (t) ophilia, voyeurism

Solitude: agromania, claustrophilia, eremophilia, lygophilia (dark, gloom)

Speaking: Garrulosity, lalorrhea, logorrhea, logomonomania, mania concionabunda (public speaking)

Spending, buying: Asoticomania

Staling: Kleptolagnia, kleptomania, klopemania, monomanie du nol

Stealing books: Bibliokleptomania

Suicide: Thanatomania

Sunlight: Photomania

Thoughts (intrusive): Onomatomania

Thrill-seeker: Philobat

Touching: Delire de toucher, peotillomania (one's own penis), phaneromania (one's own body)

Trees: Dendrophilia

Urine, urination: Unmdinism, urolagnia, urophilia

Wandering: Drapetomania, dromomania, ecdemomania, ecdemomono-mania, eidemomania, eretodro- mamania, mania errbunds, oikogugia, planomania, poriomania, wanderlust

Words: Hellenomania (the display of erudition by excessive use of Greek or Latin terms), logophilia

Work(ing): Erasionomania

Writing: Erotographomania (love letters), graphomania, graphorrhea, metromania (veses), pornogra- phomania (abscene letters)

Mania à potu: A state, product by alcohol, characterized by extreme excitement and sometimes leading to homicidal attacks. The attack is usually brought on, in a susceptible person, by the ingestion of comparatively small amounts of alcohol. See intoxication, alcoholic.

Mania, absorbed: Manic stupor. See mania

Mania, ambitious: Obs. Delirium grandiosum; megalomania (q.v.); folie ambitieuse.

Mania, akinetic: See mania.

Mania, Bell's: (Luther V. Bell, American physician, (1806–62) Acute mania. See Bell's Mania: mania.

Mania, biting: A form of epidemic or mass hysteria reported in 15th century Germany: a nun began to bite her associates compulsively, and the impulse spread throughout convents in Germany, Holland, and other parts of Europe.

Mania, brooding: Morbid impulse to mediate long and anxiously; obsessive doubting, "We have already mentioned the important partplayed by the sadistic instinctual components in the genesis of obsessional neuroses. Where the epistemophilic instinct is a preponderant feature in the constitution of an obsessional patient, brooding becomes the principal symptom of the neurosis." (Freud, CO) see folie du doute.

Mania, Caeser: Obs, A feeling of being absolute master of life and death amount savages", (Bleuler, TP).

Mania, chattering: Obs, Uncontrollable urge to talk gibberish; pressured speech.

Mania, chronic: Term first used by Schott for the manic type of reaction that is more or less permanent. See mania.

Mania, chronic intellectual: Obs, " general disturbance of the intellect characterized by the existence of varying unsystematized delusions, accompanied by periods of mental excitement of depression, with more or less incoherence and mental weakness." (Foster, F.P. Medical Dictionary, 1892–94)

Mania, classification of: See classification of mania.

Mania, collecting: The morbid impulse to collect. It is sen in one of its most vivid forms in patients with schizophrenia, who often collect all sorts of articles, most of them useless; they stuff their clothing with trash. The collecting mania is often clearly representative of anal erotism. The symptom is also frequent in senile dementia. See coprophilia; hoarding; soteeria.

Mania concionabunda: Obs. Mania for addressing the public.

Mania, doubting: An obsessive doubting in which the patient finds it necessary to say "no" to everything. This patient will raise objections to whatever comes into his mind from within or without. For example, the names of people known intimately for years my become uncertain to the patient. He may realize intellectually that what he objects to is correct, but his emotions deny the fact. Usually, under analysis, it emerges that unconscious instinctual demands are being denied through the doubting-mania. (Hinsie, U.P.) See folie du doute.

Mania, grumbling: "The patients, indeed, display exalted self-consciousness, are pretentious and high-flown, but by no means of cheerful mood; they rather appear dissatisfied, insufferable, perhaps even a little anxious. They have something to find fault with in everything, feel themselves on every occasion badly treated, get wretched food, cannot hold out in the dreadful surroundings, cannot sled in the miserable beds, cannot have social intercourse with the other patients." (Kraepelin, E. Manic-Depressive Insanity and Paranoia, 1921).

Mania homicidal: Obs, Homicidomania, Any kind of mental disease where there is an attempt or desire on the part of a patient to kill.

Mania, incendiary: Pyromania, (1921).

Mania, inhibited: One of Krepelin's mixed states, characterized by flight of ideas, cheerful mood, and psychomotor inhibition. See mania, "The patient of this kind are of more exultant mood, occasionally somewhat irritable, distractible, inclined to jokes; when addressed they easility fall into chattering talk with flight of ideas and numerous clang associations, but remains in outward behaviour conspicuously quiet, lie still in bed, only now and then throw out a remark or laugh to themselves. It appears, however, as if a great inward tension, as rule, existed, as the patients may suddenly become very violent. Formerly I classified this 'inhibit mania' with manic stupor; I think, however, that it may be separated from that on the ground of the flight of ideas which here appears distinctly." (Kraepelin, E. Manic-Depressive Insanity and Paranoia, 1921).

Mania, Metaphysical: Obs, Folie du doute (q.v.); insanity of doubt; doubting mania.

Mania mitis: Obs. Hypomania. "The slightest forms of manic excitement are usually called "Hypomania". Mania mitis, mitissmima, also but inappropriately, mania sine delirio." (Kraepelin, E. Manic-Depressive Insanity and Paranoia, 1921).

Mania phantastica infantilis: A rare syndrome of childhood consisting of exaltation stages, fugues, confabulations or pseudologia fantastica (q.v.), immaturity, and retardation of mental development. The syndrome may occur as part of the delirious state following infections diseases, and also as a psychogenic or autochthonous reaction.

Mania, puerperal: Obs. Postpartum psychosis with manic features. "Where mania really appears in the puerperal state, it is , like every other kind of mania, only a link in the chain of attacks of maniacal-depressive insanity." (Kraepelin, E. Lectures on Clinical Psychiatry, 1913). See psychosis, puerperal.

Mania, reactive: Hypomania induced by some external cause. See reactive.

Mania, religion: Obs. As acute psychotic episode, usually schizophrenic or organic in origin, characterized by generalized hyperactivity, agitation, restlessness, and many hallucination s with a religious coloring. See ecstasy.

Mania senilis: Obs. Senile dementia (q.v.)

Mania sine delirio: Mania mitis (q.v.)

Mania, stuporous. See mania.

Mania transitoria: Obs. " This term is used to describe a somewhat rare form of maniacal exaltation, which comes on suddenly, is usually sharp in its character, and is accompanied by incoherence, partial or complete unconsciousness of familiar surroundings, and sleeplessness. An attack may last from an hour up to a few days." (Clouston. T.S. Clinical Laetures on Mental Diseases, 1904). It was also called ephemeral mania.

Mania, wandering: See wanderlust.

Mania (co) comium: Obs. Psychiatric hospital.

Maniaphobia: Fear or insanity.

Manic: Nonspecific lay term for a mentally disturbed person, often someone exhibiting violent or grossly irrational behaviours.

Manic defence: Form of defensive behaviour exhibited by persons who defend themselves against anxiety, guilt and depression by (a) Denial of the guilt, anxiety and depression (b) the operation of a phantasy of omnipotent control, by means of which they imagined themselves to be in control of all situations which might provoke anxiety or feelings of helplessness (c) Identification with objects from whom a sense of power can be borrowed and (d) Projection of bad aspects of the self on the others. According to Fairbairn, manic defence is a an emergency defence brought into operations when the non-specific techniques (paranoid, obsessional, hysterical and phobic) have failed to protect the ego against the onset of a depressive state. It is not confined to persons liable to develop mania or MDP.

Manic-depressive illness: An affective disorder characterized by severe alternations in mood that are usually episodic and recurrent. The unipolar type is characterized by either periodic episodes of manic (manic disorder) or periodic episodes of depression (depressive disorder). In the bipolar or circular type, the patient has at least one episode of each mood extreme and may alternate periodically between the two. See also Bipolar affective disorder, Major depression.

Manifest content: That part of a dream or fantasy that a person remembers and reports. In a dream it represents a disguised and symbolic expression of the latent content of the dream. See also latent content.

Manipulative skill: A skill which involves direct action with the hands, usually in terms of handling and placing of objects.

Mannerism: Stereotyped gesture or expression that is peculiar to a given person.

Mannkopf's sign: Pressure over or movement of painful part may lead to temporary increase of pulse rate from 10 to 30 beats per minute. This helps in differentiating pain or organic origin from psychogenic pain.

Mantra: In transcendental meditation, a Sanskrit syllable or word that is repeated over and over in an effort to produce total relaxation and control over one's state of consciousness.

Marihuana: Dried leaves and flowers to Cannabis sativa (Indian hemp). It induces somatic and psychic changes in a person when smoked or ingested in sufficient quantity. The somatic changes include increased heart rate, rise in blood pressure, dryness of the mouth, increased appetite, and occasional nausea, vomiting, and diarrhoea. The psychic changes include a dreamy-state level of consciousness, a sense of enhanced vividness of visual and auditory sensations, disruptions of time perception and memory-dependent, goal directed behaviour, disruptions of sequential thought processes, and euphoria and other alterations of mood. The compound believed to be responsible for most of its psychological effects is tetrahydrocannabinol (THC). In strong doses, marihuana can produce hallucinations and, at times, paranoid ideation. It is also known as pot, grass, weed, tea and Mary Jane; it is also spelled marijuana.

Marital counseling: Process whereby a trained counselor helps married couples resolve problems that arise and trouble them in their relationship. The theory and techniques of this approach were first developed in social agencies as part of family case work. The husband and wife are seen by the same worker in separate and joint counseling sessions that focus on immediate family problems.

Marital therapy: See Marriage therapy.

Marketing psychology: The psychology of economic choice and in particular the analysis of consumer behaviour.

Marriage therapy: A type of family therapy that involves the husband and the wife and focuses on the marital relationship as it affects the individual psychopathology of the partners. The rationale for the method is the assumption that psychopathological processes within the family structure and in the social matrix of the marriage perpetuate individual pathological personality structures, which find expression in the disturbed marriage and are aggravated by the feedback between partners.

Marxian personality psychology: A psychological metatheory deriving its assumptions from Marx's materialistic philosophy of history and applied to the development and social basis of personality.

Marxist activity psychology: The concept of object-related activity is the main concept of this psychology.

Masculine identity: Inner sense of gender affiliation with males. See also Feminine identity, Gender identity.

Masculine protest: Adlerian: doctrine that depicts a universal human tendency to move from a passive and feminine role to a masculine and active role. The doctrine is an extension of his ideas about organic inferiority. It became the prime motivational force in normal and neurotic behaviour in the Adlerian system. See also Adler, Alfred, Inferiority complex.

Masculinity-femininity scale: Any scale on a psychological test that assesses the relative masculinity or femininity of the testee. Scales vary and may focus, for example, on basic identification with either sex or preference for a particular sex role. Such scales are strongly influenced by cultural definitions of masculinity and femininity.

Masochism: A Paraphilia in which sexual gratification is derived from being physically or psychologically maltreated by the partner or oneself. It was first described by an Austrian novelist, Leopold von Sacher-Masoch (1836–1895). See also Sadism. Sadomasochistic relationship.

Massed practice: Extended periods of practice while learning a new skill, taken without breaks. Massed practice has been found to be less effective than distributed practice which allows for consolidation. See also spaced practice.

Master play: Play during early childhood which leads to the acquisition of new skills. This definition leaves open the question of whether children are motivated to achieve mastery, or perhaps cannot avoid learning when having fun. See play.

Masturbation: Although the word literally means genital excitement, it is only used to refer to self-induced genital excitement. Hence (a) *masturbation phantasy* – the imaginative activity accompanying masturbation (b) *Infantile masturbation*–masturbation occurring in childhood (c) *Masturbation equivalent or substitute*–Activity inferred to be an equivalent or substitute for masturbation.

Matching: The name given to ensuring that two sets of experimental materials or subjects are identical in all important respects. A matched task or test has questions carefully selected to ensure that, in each test, the questions are equivalent in difficulty, and in the type of problem posed. It is usual to select a group of subjects matched in terms of age, sex and overall intelligence levels, although other criteria may be used if required for the study.

Maternal deprivation: The result of the premature loss or absence of the mother. In a broader sense, the lack of proper mothering may constitute a form of maternal deprivation. That form of loss, separation, or deprivation may lead to severe emotional disorders in infants and children. Maternal deprivation may for example, cause analytic depression and less severe affective and psychosomatic disorders. The concept was proposed by John Bowlby and Rene Spitz.

Maternal drive: The tendency, usually presumed to be innate, to engage in caretaking behaviours such as nest building, retrieving and suckling during the infancy of offspring. The tendency is displayed by mothers, and sometimes by fathers, in many species. Use of term 'drive' implies that there is some basic need to be maternal, an assumption that should not be accepted uncritically. The term 'maternal instinct' is sometimes used instead, but this is even more likely to bring in assumptions for which there is inadequate evidence. The most misleading use of the terms comes when meanings which have been built up by studying species like rats are applied uncritically to humans.

Maternal privation: Rearing from birth without a mother. Strictly, privation means never having, while deprivation means having something taken away. Experiments of total maternal privation have been carried out on various species, though not with humans. However, these are typically classed as maternal deprivation studies, and in practice the term maternal deprivation is used for all variations of a shortage of mothering in the upbringing of young.

Maximum security unit: That part of an institution for the mentally ill reserved for those who have committed crimes or who are considered dangerous to others.

Mr Dougall, William (1871–1938): Born at chadderton in Lancashire. His main contributions were studies into the 'social psychology' and 'the psychology of collectivity'.

Mean: A statistical measurement derived from adding a set of scores and then dividing by the number of scores. See also Average.

Mean deviation: A statistical measure of the variability is set of values defined as the sum of the absolute differences between the values and the mean divided by the number of values.

Median: The value in a set of values above and below which there are an equal number of values. For example, in the series, 1,3,5,9,13 the value 5 is the median. See also Average.

Medical model: The idea that psychological disorders are specific illnesses with characteristic symptoms and predictable outcomes; the view that clusters of symptoms form syndromes that are caused by underlying specific illness.

Melancholia: A term originating in the Hippocratic tradition (4th century BC) which was used to denote generally the depressive syndrome until the end of the 19th century. While Kraepelin and others restricted its use to refer only to depression in the elderly. Freud redefined it as a morbid counterpart of normal mourning. Amidst a general decline in its use. DSM-III resurrected the term by giving it yet another meaning in which the 'distinct quality of depressed mood' precisely the contrast to normal mourning, are the prominent features. In view of this lack of precision, and the contradictory connotations, the continued use of the term is not recommended.

Melomania: Psychosis characterized by incessant singing.

Meme: A term coined by Dawkins (1976) to his proposed analogy between biological and cultural evolution to refer to the hypothetical cultural counterpart of the gene a 'unit' of cultural inheritance.

Memory: Process whereby what is experienced or learned is established as a record in the central nervous system (registration). Where it persists with a variable degree of permanence (retention) and can be recollected or retrieved from storage at will (recall). See also Amnesia, Hypermnesia, Immediate memory, Long-term memory, Paramnesia, Short-term memory.

Memory span: A well-known measure of an individual's capacity for retaining small units of meaningless information over a brief period of time. In a typical measure of memory span, a list of digits is read out to someone at a regular pace. On completion of the list, the individual is required to repeat what they have heard, either forward or backward. First observed by Miller (1955), it has been repeatedly observed that the average span available to the individual is of 7 digits, plus or minus 2; and that this can only be increased by some system for chunking the information into meaningful units. See also two process theory, levels of processing.

Memory trace: In older texts sometimes referred to as an engram, a memory trace is a hypothetical 'image' of what is to be remembered, which has been encoded and which is stored, for varying periods of time. The term memory trace is usually associated with the decay theory of forgetting, which holds that memory traces die away if not strengthened by being recalled from time to time. However, as this approach is not particularly open to empirical investigation, it has largely fallen into disfavour as an explanation of forgetting.

Menarche: The onset of menstrual function.

Mendacity: Pathological lying.

Mens rea: An intent to do harm. In a criminal case involving a defendant's mental state, an important question may be whether or not he has mens rea, the ability to form an intention to do harm.

Mental age: A construction development by Binet in his early work on the measurement of intelligence, mental age refers to the abilities of the individual by comparison with others of that society. By selecting a series of age–appropriate problems and tasks, a set of age norms; is developed, allowing each child to be assessed in terms of how far they measures up to these criteria. The level of difficulty of items at which the child starts to fail is compared to the norms. The average age of which the child starts to fail is compared to the norms. The average of children who pass the items up to this point is found, and this is regarded as the mental age of the child being tested. Binet's original formulation of the intelligence quotient involved the comparison of mental age with the child' chronological age ('real' age).

Mental disorder: A psychiatric illness or disease. Its manifestations are primarily behavioural or psychological. It is measured in terms of deviation from some normative concept.

Mental health: A state of emotional well-being in which a person is able to function comfortably within his society and in which his personal achievements and characteristics are satisfactory to him.

Mental hygiene: Conditions and practices conducive to the establishment and maintenance of mental health; field dealing with the prevention and early treatment of mental illness. See also Ortho-psychiatry.

Mental illness: Mental disorder; any serious impairment of adjustment; any psychiatric disorder listed in the American Psychiatric Association's Diagnostic and Statistical Manual of Mental Disorders or in the World Health Organizations' International Classification of Diseases.

Mental imagery: The use of imagined pictures, or other sensory images, such as sounds or smells, to represent information in the mind. Mental imagery involves recreating the apparent sensation, as part of the process of memory or thinking. See also symbolic representation.

Mental retardation (general): A condition of arrested or incomplete development of the mind which is especially characterized by subnormality of intelligence. The assessment of intellectual level should be based on whatever information is available, including clinical evidence, adaptive behaviour and psychometric findings. Mental retardation often involves psychiatric disturbances and may often develop as a result of some physical disease or injury. *Synonyms*: amentia: mental deficiency; mental subnormality; oligophrenia.

Mental retardation, mild: Mental retardation corresponding to an IQ level of 50 to 70. Individuals with this level of subnormality are educable and usually acquire sufficient instrumental and social skills to enable them to adjust to the demands of daily life with minimum impairment. *Synonyms*: feeble-minded, high-graded defect, mild mental subnormality; moron; debility.

Mental retardation, moderate: Mental retardation corresponding to an IQ level of 35 to 49. Individuals with this level of retardation usually acquire basic speech and can be trained for elementary self-care and simple occupational tasks, under supervision and guidance. *Synonym*: imbecility.

Mental retardation, profound: Mental retardation corresponding to and IQ level of below 20. Severe sensory-motor impairments are usually present, and acquisition of speech is not possible. In daily living such individuals require constant aid and supervision. *Synonym*: idiocy.

Mental retardation, severe: Mental retardation corresponding to an IQ level of 20 to 34. Individuals with this level of retardation usually suffer from impairment of motor and sensory development, and only acquire the rudiments of speech. Training in elementary self-care may be possible, though difficult and constant close supervision of daily living is required.

Metal set: A state of preparedness to perform certain kinds of mental operations rather than others. Mental sets may refer to particular kinds of problem-solving (see Learning set), or to readiness to perceive certain things rather than others (see Perceptual set), or to a preparedness to remember certain items of information in preference to others.

Mental status: General functional condition of mental and behavoiural process as determined by psychiatric assessment of a variety of areas of functioning, such as state of consciousness, mood and affect, thinking and speech; motor behaviour, general knowledge, memory, calculation, judgement, abstraction, and insight.

Mere exposure effect: The fact that repeated exposure to a neutral stimulus it sufficient to induce positive reactions to that stimulus (Zajonc, 1968).

Merycism: See rumination.

Mesmerism: Early term for hypnosis. Named after Anton Mesmer (1733–1815).

Metacognition: An overall term used to refer to the knowledge about how cognitive processes work which is often highly influential in cognitive development. The study of Metacognition includes the study of the ways in which people monitor and control their own cognitive activity, such as being aware of cognitive limitations (knowing that you don't know), or abilities (knowing that you can learn certain types of information readily). The act of looking a word up in a dictionary, for instance, is one which would be unlikely to happen without metacognition.

Metamemory: Knowledge about how one's memory work, or what its limitations are. Such knowledge often directly affects behaviour, such as a decision to write a note to yourself to remind you of something, or to adopt a specific revision technique to make remembering easier. See also metacognition.

Metapelet: The name given to a child-nurse or professional carer for children in an Israeli Kibbutz.

Such an individual carries the responsibility for the care of the children, rather than the parents and oversees their day to day experience and early learning.

Metapsychiatry: The interface between psychiatry and such psychic phenomena as parapsychology, mysticism, altered states of consciousness, and nonmedical healing.

Metapsychology: Term invented by Freud to describe what other sciences call 'general theory' i.e., statements at the highest level of obstruction. Metapsychological formulations describe mental phenomena in terms of the fictive psychiapparatus and ideally contain references to the topographical (id, ego or superego), dynamic (the instincts involved) and economic (distribution of energy within the apparatus) aspects of the phenomenon in question, Metapsychology is part of classical theory of psychoanalysis. Metapsychology is branch of theoretical or speculative psychology that deals with theories, hypotheses, or phenomena that are largely beyond the realm of empirical verification. Examples of such topics include mysticism; the origin, purpose, and structure of the mind; the philosophical nature of the mindbody interrelationship; the place of mind in the universe. See also parapsychology.

Meyer, Adolf (1866–1950): American psychiatrist known for his concept of psychobiology. See also distributive analysis and synthesis, Ergasia, Euergasia, Fabulation, Psychobiology, Syntropy.

Michigan Picture Stories: Projective type of psychological test similar to the Thematic Apperception Test, it is specifically designed for use with adolescents.

Micropsia: False perception that objects are smaller than they really are; sometimes called Lilliputian hallucination. See also Hallucination, Macropsia.

Midas syndrome: Increased sexual desire in the female associated with diminished desire and capacity in her male partner.

Middle insomnia: Waking up after falling asleep without difficulty and then having problem falling asleep again. See also Initial insomnia, Terminal insomania.

Migraine: Severe unilateral, throbbing headache that appears periodically, usually beginning during the teenage years and continuing to recur with diminishing frequency during advancing years. Classic migraine is a syndrome ushered in by a transient derangement of neurological function, often a visual disturbance, followed by hemicranial headache, nausea, and vomiting – all of which last for anywhere from several hours to 1 or 2 days. Common migraine has the same character and time course but develops without any prodrome. Patients with migraine are typically described as tense, meticulous, hard driving persons; there seems to be high frequency of associated emotional conflicts. Psychotherapy may thus play a role in its treatment.

Milieu therapy: Treatment that emphasizes appropriate socio-environmental manipulation for the benefit of the patient. The setting for milieu therapy is usually the psychiatric hospital. See also Moral treatment. Therapeutic community.

Mind: In psychoanalytic terms, mind is a nexus of activities and a sequence of adaptive response.

Minimal brain dysfunction: Behavioural syndrome of childhood characterized by learning difficulties, decreased attention span, distractibility, hyperactivity, impulsiveness, emotional lability, and, often, disturbances in perceptuomotor and language development. The psychopathological mechanisms have not been defined. Although the syndrome has been diagnosed with increasing frequency over the past 20 years, its validity as a diagnostic entity has been questioned. The term "minimal brain dysfunction" implies neurological cauzation, but in most cases there are no major unequivocal neurological signs, and there has been an unfortunate tendency to apply the term as a convenient explanatory label to any child presenting with a specific learning difficulty or behavioural dysfunction. See also attention deficit disorder, Hyperactivity.

Minnesota Multiphasic Personality Inventory (MMPI): Questionnaire type of psychological test for persons age 16 and over. It consists of true-false statements are coded in various scales that assess different dimensions of the person's personality structure and measure the closeness of fit with various psychiatric diagnostic categories. It consists of 550 items.

Minor tranquilizer: See Antianxiety drug.

Minutes of the Vienna Psychoanalytic Society: Dairy of Freud's Wednesday Evening Society (after 1910 Viena Psychoanalytic Society) as recorded by Otto Rank, the paid secretary between 1906 and 1915.

Mitchell, S. Weir (1880–1912): American neurologist known for his concept of rest treatment to cure "anaemia of the brain".

Mixoscopia: A sexual perversion in which a person attains orgasm by watching his or her love object make love with another person.

Mneme Memory: Hence mnemic image, the psychological equivalent of a memory trace.

Mnemonic: An aid to memory, which can be achieved in any way, including leaving a note for oneself. There have been several different kinds of mnemonics identified and developed over time. Many of them have to do with forming of mental images which will help the person to remember connections between item, or lists. Some mnemonics rely on the use of visual imagery, such as the method of loci or the key word technique. Other mnemonics rely on verbal processing, such as first-letter mnemonics, in which the first letter of each item spells out a new word or a sentence. For example 'Richard of York Gave Battle in Vain' for the colours of the spectrum (red, orange, yellow, etc). The famous 'knot in the handkerchief' is a mnemonic which combines visual and tactile cues to help the person to remember.

Mode: In a set of measurements, the value that appears most frequently. See also Average.

Modelling: Providing an example which can be limited, such that the imitator is able to learn new styles of behaviour. Modeling is considered to be an important aspect of social learning in children. It is often explicitly in therapy, to allow adults to vary their styles of interaction with others.

Modes of representation: Ways of coding information internally. Bruner identified a developmental sequence in representation, arguing that the first mode to develop was enactive representation, in which information is stored as 'muscle memories'. As the child's experience widens, and the environment makes increasingly complex demands, more sophisticated modes of representation are required: first iconic representation (using images) and then symbolic representation (in which information is represented by symbols).

Monomania: Morbid mental state characterized by preoccupation with one subject. It is also known as partial insanity.

Monosymptomatic hypochondriasis: It is an illness characterized by a simple hypochondriacal delusion that is sustained over a considerable period, sometimes for may years. The delusion is not secondary to another psychiatric illness and the personality remains otherwise well preserved. Also known as monohypochondriacal psychosis.

Monotropy: Bowlby's original idea of the way in which attachment develops between the young infant and its mother. Based on ideas from ethological studies of imprinting, the theory stated that the relationship which an infant formed with its mother was qualitatively different from any other relationship which it formed with other people, and that if the bond was broken, through separation, during the early years of life, then the child could suffer permanent damage. This led to the maternal deprivation debate, and produced extensive research into attachment and mother-infant interaction.

Mood: A pervasive and sustained emotion that in the extreme, markedly colours the person's perception of the world. Mood is to affect as climate is to weather. Common examples of mood include depression, elation, anger and anxiety. See also Affect, Anxiety, Elation, Depression.

Mood congruent psychotic features: A DSM term which refers to hallucinatory or delusional phenomena whose content consistently reflects the mood of a manic or depressed patient. See also Nihilism.

Mood, dysphonic: An unpleasant mood, such as depression, anxiety, or irritability.

Mood elevated: A mood that is more cheerful than normal; it does not necessarily imply pathology.

Mood, euphoric: An exaggerated feeling of well-being. As a technical term, euphoria implies a pathological mood. Whereas the individual with a normally elevated mood may describe himself or herself as being in "good spirits", "Very happy", or "cheerful" the euphoric person is likely to exclaim that he or she is "on top of the world" "up in the clouds", or to say, " I feel ecstatic" "I'm flying" or "I am high".

Mood, euthymic: Mood in the "normal" range which implies the absence of depressed or elevated mood.

Mood, expansive: Lack of restraint in expressing one's feeling, frequently with an overvaluation of one's significance or importance. There may also be elevated or euphoric mood.

Mood-incongruent psychotic features: A DSM-III term which refers to hallucinatory or delusional phenomena whose content does not consistently reflect the mood of a manic or depressed patient.

Mood, irritable: Internalized feeling of tension associated with being easily annoyed and provoked to anger.

Mood-swing: Oscillation of a person's emotional feeling tone between periods of elation and periods of depression.

Moral anxiety: In Freudian theory, anxiety that comes from a fear of the superego. As the superego has incorporated the rewards and punishments of the parents, it is able to inflict pain, and if it becomes too powerful the person may live in a chronic state of anxiety. See also neurotic anxiety.

Moral development: This should refer to the development of moral standards and behaviour. In fact the term has been taken over by a particular approach which concentrate on moral judgement. Piaget analyzed tendencies in the developing moral judgement of the child, such as a progression away from a belief in immanent justice. Lawrence Kohlberg developed Piaget's ideas and produced a scheme of six stages of moral reasoning along with the child progresses. While moral reasoning is important, the theory has been criticized both for the ways in which the stages are defined and for appearing to undervalue other aspects of moral development such as moral behaviour.

Moral insanity: This term was first introduced by Pritchard to designate that variety of insanity in which there were no delusions. The word 'moral' in the early nineteenth century meant much the same as the word 'psychological' today. By the middle of the nineteenth century the term 'moral insanity' was used to describe persons who would now be called 'psychopaths' and 'alcohol addicts.'

Moral realism: Another name given to the stage of heteronomous morality described by Piaget, in which the child accepts fully the rules which are given of it by society and those in authority. See also autonomous morality.

Moral treatment: A philosophy and technique of treating mental patients that prevailed in the first half of the nineteenth century and emphasized removal of restraints, humane and kindly care, attention to religion, and performance of useful tasks in the hospital. It is considered the forerunner of current milieu therapy.

Morbid perplexity: A condition seen in schizophrenia in association with loss of ego boundaries. The patient exhibits profound confusion about his own identity and the meaning of existence.

Morphemes: The smallest units of meaning in speech perception, can be prefixes, words, or suffixes; composed of syllables.

Morbido: Term coined by Federn (1936) to describe a form of energy belonging to the death instinct and analogous to libido.

Moses and Monotheism: Title of a book by Freud published in 1939. In this book Freud undertook a historical but frankly speculative reconstruction of the personality of Moses and examined the concept of monotheism and the abiding effect of the patriarch on the character of the jews. One of the Freud's last works, it bears the imprint of his latter day outlook and problems.

Mother superior complex: Tendency of a therapist to play the role of the mother in his relations with his patients. The complex often leads to interference with the therapeutic process. See also God complex.

Mother surrogate: Mother substitute. In psychoanalysis, the patient projects his mother image onto another person and responds to that person unconsciously, in an inappropriate and unrealistic manner, with the feeling and attitudes that he had towards his real mother.

Motivation: The force or energy associated with an internal state that propels a person to engage in behaviour to satisfy a need or desire.

Motivated forgetting: A term for the forgetting of information as a result of an unconscious unwillingness to remember it (e.g., the forgetting of an impending dental appointment, because you don't want to go). According to Freud, all forgetting was motivated forgetting in some way; either because it could lead to the recall of deeply buried childhood traumas, or because the information which was forgotten was symbolic of such trauma. Other researchers identified alternative explanations of many kinds of forgetting, but motivated forgetting is all considered valid as an explanation of some, instance of failure to recall information.

Motivators: Specific incentives or aspects of the environment which can induce certain forms of behaviour in the individual. The term has been commonly used in management theory, where it includes such items as the provision of personal career development at work, or bonus payments which would encourage those in employment to work harder.

Mourning: Reaction to a loss of a love object (important person, object, role, status, or anything considered part of one's life) consisting of a process of emotional detachment from that object which frees the subject to find other interests and enjoyments. See Grief.

Multiple delusions: Concurrent delusions. The delusions need not be interconnected.

Multiple mothering: Child care which is carried out by a number of different people, usually in succession. Infants in insititutions were often exposed to a succession of caregivers and it is widely accepted that this form of maternal deprivation resulted in long-term difficulties in forming relationships. These days considerable efforts are made to avoid the repeated making and breaking of attachments in children who have to be brought up in care.

Multiple personality: Psychiatrist Morrton Prince's term for the dissociative reaction in which a person has two or more distinctive personalities, most of them knowing nothing of the others. In DSM-III it is one of the dissociative disorders. See also Hysterical neurosis.

Multistore model of memory: The model that portrays the encoding, storage, and retrieval of information. As involving three separate though interacting memory systems; a sensory register, a short-term memory, and a long-term memory.

Munchausen's syndrome: It is a rare condition, characterized by patients who reportedly seek admission to hospital in a state of mental or physical distress, give plausible histories to support their complaints and submit themselves to painful or even dangerous investigations and therapies but then abruptly discharge themselves when discovered to have fabricated their stories an physical signs.

Mutism: Organic or functional absence of the faculty of speech.

N

Narcissism: Self love. It is linked to autoerotism but is devoid of genitality. The word is derived from Narcissus, a Greek mythology figure who fell in love with his own reflected image. In Psychoanalytic theory, it is divided into primary and secondary types. *Primary Narcissism* refers to the early infantile phase of object relationship development, when the child has not differentiated himself from the outside world. All sources of pleasure are unrealistically recognized as coming from within himself giving him a false sense of omnipotence. *Secondary Narcissism* results when the libido, once attached to external love objects, is redirected back to the self. See also Autistic thinking, Autoerotism.

Narcissistic personality disorder: Personality disorder characterized by a grandiose sense of self-importance, preoccupation with fantasies of unlimited success, exhibitionistic need for attention and admiration, exaggerated response to criticism or other perceived threats to self-esteem; and disturbance in interpersonal relationships. Diagnostic category introduced in DSM-III.

Narcoanalysis: See Narcotherapy.

Narcolepsy: Uncontrollable, recurrent, brief episodes of sleep associated with excessive daytime sleepiness, cataplexy, sleep paralysis, hypnagogic hallucinations, and often disturbed nocturnal sleep.

Narcotherapy: Psychotherapy conducted with the patient in a drug-induced stupor or semi consciousness state, as by the administration of barbiturates. It was originally used in the treatment of acute disorders arising in the setting of military combat. It includes narcoanalysis and narcosynthesis.

National Training Laboratories: Organization started in 1947, at Bethel, Maine, to train professionals who work with groups. Interested in personal development eventually led to sensitivity training and encounter groups.

Nativist: An individual or school or thought holding that the important determinants of development are directly inherited, through genetic transmission. The name implies that the emphasis is on qualities which are inborn. Although nativists do recognize that environment factors may have an effect on development, they consider such effects to be minimal, with the main explanation for individual differences being the genotype of the individual. The maturational theory of Gesell is an example of a nativist position. See also empiricist.

Natural group: Group that tends to evolve spontaneously in human civilization, such as a kinship, tribal, or religious group. In contrast are various contrived groups or aggregates of people who meet for a relatively brief time to achieve some goal.

Nature: The genetic factors contributing to behaviour and perception. Compare nature.

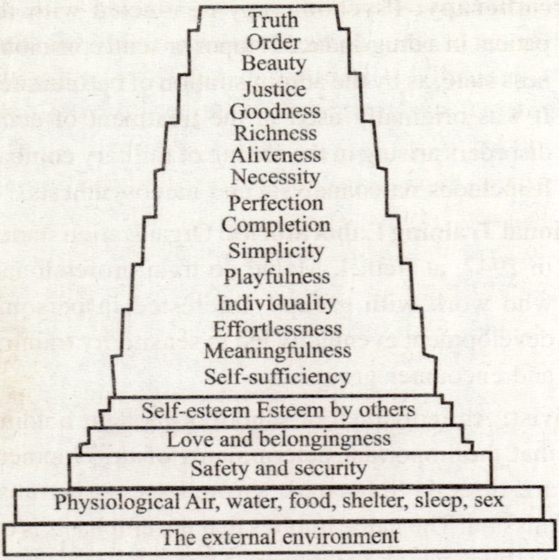

Fig. 9. Maslow's Hierarchy of human needs.

Nature-nurture controversy: The argument concerning the relative roles of the contributions of nature and nurture in the development of organisms; an enduring question in psychology; most psychologists now favour an interaction of nature and nurture. See Nature-Nurture interaction.

Nature-nurture interaction: The interplay of the genetic inheritance of an individual and environmental influences to produce the characteristics actually observed. See phenotype, reaction range.

Necromania: Pathological preoccupation with dead bodies.

Necromimesis: The delusion in which the patient believes himself to be dead and acts as though he were.

Necrophilia: Sexual attraction to or sexual contact with dead bodies.

Necrophilism: A morbid desire to be in the presence of dead bodies.

Need: Ambiguous term referring to an internal state of unsatisfaction or tension related to a wish, urge, desire, or other endogenous behavioural stimulus. Classically, it implied an innate or instinctual internal stimulus. See also Drive, Instinct, Motivation.

Need for achievement (achievement motivation): A learned motive to meet personal standards of success and excellence in a chosen area.

Need for affiliation: The motive to associate with other people, as by seeking friends, moral support, contact comfort or companionship.

Need for competence: The motive to be capable in one's activities and to master new situations.

Need for power: A learned motive to dominate or control others.

Negation: Process by which a perception or thought is admitted to consciousness in negative form e.g., the onset of a headache is registered by the thought. 'How lucky I am to have been free from headaches for so long'. Not to be confused with denial; negativism.

Negative afterimage: A visual image that persists after a visual stimulus is withdrawn and that has features which contrast with those of the stimulus (e.g., a contrasting colour).

Negative correlation: An association between increases in one variable and decreases in another.

Negative goal: Goal which an individual tries to escape from or avoid. Compare positive goal.

Negative halo: Formation of unfavourable opinions from a few negative characteristics. Compare positive halo effect.

Negative identity: Erik Erikson's term for the rebellious behaviour of adolescence when they do the opposite of what parents and others consider proper and desirable.

Negative Oedipus complex: Form of Oedipus complex in which the subject wishes to possess the parent of its own sex and regards that of the opposite sex as its rival.

Negative reinforcement: A reinforcement procedure in which a response is followed by the removal, delay, or decrease in intensity of an unpleasant stimulus; as a result, the response becomes stronger or more likely to occur.

Negative reinforcer: A stimulus or event which, when its termination is made contingent on a particular response, increases the likelihood of the response. Compare positive rein forcer, punishment.

Negative therapeutic reaction: Technical term for a fortunately rare hazard of psychoanalytical treatment viz- exacerbation of the patient's symptoms in response to precisely those interpretations which are expected to alleviate them.

Negative transfer: See transfer.

Negative transference: Transference marked by a hostile attitude toward the therapist. See transference.

Negativism: Verbal or nonverbal opposition or resistance to outside suggestion and advice. It is commonly seen in catatonic schizophrenia in which the patient resists any efforts to be moved or does the opposite of what is asked. It may also occur in organis psychoses and mental retardation.

Neoanalyst: A psychoanalytically oriented theorist who places more emphasis on social factors and less emphasis on sexuality. See psychoanalysis.

Neo-behaviourism: A revised form of behaviourism in which it is recognized that cognitive processes play a role in determining behaviour.

Neo-Freudians: A term used to describe psychoanalytic theories who accept Freud's basic ideas, but have developed them further, often emphasizing social and cultural factors in psychodynamic processes. The British neo-Freudian have concentrated on object relations which in turn had made the study of attachments an important part of developmental psychology.

Neologism: New word or phrase, often seen in schizophrenia Definitions restrict the use of the term to those new words or phrases whose derivation cannot be understood. However the term ""neologism" has also used to mean a word that has been incorrectly constructed but whose origins are nonetheless understandable for example," headshoe" to mean "hat". Those words are more properly referred to as word approximations. See also Metonymy, Periphrasis, Word approximation.

Nervous breakdown: Nonspecific term for mental disorder often implying an acute decompensation.

Network: The persons in the patient's environment with whom he is most intimately connected. It includes family members, friends, and work and recreational contacts. British psychiatrist S.H. Foulkes emphasized that psychopathology in a person is a function of his interactions within his social network and that attempts to change the person should include attempts to influence his network as well. See also Extended-family therapy. Social network debility.

Neurological amnesia: See amnesia, neurological.

Neurologist: A physician who specializes in diseases of the nervous system.

Neurology: The medical specialty that deals with organic diseases of the nervous system.

Neuropsychiatry: The medical specialty that combines psychiatry and neurology.

Neurosis: Mental disorder characterized primarily by anxiety, which may either be directly experienced and dominate the clinical picture or be unconsciously controlled and modified by various psychological mechanisms to produce other subjectively distressing and ego-alien symptoms. It was known as psychoneurosis. Although neuroses are not accompanied by gross distortion of reality or severe personality disorganization, normal functioning is impaired by the person's symptoms. Neurotic disorders have no organic basis, are relatively persistent, and are treatable.

accident (n): Traumatic (n).

acual n: Anosological category created by Freud, comprized of hypochondria, neurasthenia, and anxiety (n).

battle (n): War in.

cardiac (n): Cardioneurosis; anxiety concerning the state of the heart, as a result of palpitation, chest pain, or symptoms not due to heart disease. It may be related to some statement made by the physician which the patient misinterprets. See also neurocirculatory asthenis.

character (n): Affecting of manifested by the functioning of the entire personality rather than through discrete symptoms.

compensation (n): The development of mental symptoms motivated by the desire for, and hope of, monetary gain.

conversion hysteria (n): Conversion hysteria.

fatigue (n): Neurasthenia or psychasthenia.

military (n): A mental disorder induced by military service; see also war on and shell-shock.

neogenic (n): In existential psychiatry, the neurotic symptomatology resulting from existential frustration.

obsessive- compulsive (n): An effort to overcome anxiety by perfectionistic or magical behaviour.

occupation or professional (n): A functional disorder of a group of muscles used chiefly in one's occupation, marked by the occurrence of spasm, paresis, or incoordination on attempt to repeal the habitual movements, as in writing or playing the piano.

oral neuroses: Functional speech disorder e.g., stuttering, may be considered disorders of the oral libido.

pension (n): A type of compensation (n), motivated by the desire for premature retirement or pension.

postconcussion (n): Neurosis following cerebral concussion; a type of traumatic (n): See also neuropsychologic disorder.

posttraumatic (n): Traumatic (n).

sexual (n): A mental disorder of the sexual function, e.g., impotence.

tarda (n): Neurotic patterns developing in older people, related to organic cerebral lesions.

transference (n): In psychoanalysis, the redirection of the patient's habitual neurotic patterns toward the person of the analyst.

traumatic (n): Any functional nervous disorder following an accident or injury.

trophic (n): Trophoneurosis.

vagabond (n): Dromomania.

war (n): Battle (n): an emotional disorder induced by conditions existing in warfare; see also military (n) and shell-shock.

Neurotic disorder: A mental disorder in which the predominant disturbance is a distressing symptom or group of symptoms which one considers unacceptable and alien to one's personality. There is no marked loss of reality testing; behaviour does not actively violate gross social norms although it may quite disabling. The disturbance is relatively enduring or recurrent without treatment and is not limited to a mild transitory reaction to stress. There is no demonstrable organic etiology. In DSM-III, the neurotic disorders were included in affective disorder, somatoform, dissociative, and psychosexual disorders.

Neurotic process: A specific etiological process involving the following sequence: (1) unconscious conflicts between opposing desires or between desires and prohibitions, which cause (2) unconscious perception of anticipated danger or dysphoria, which leads to (3) use of defense mechanisms that result in (4) either symptoms, personality disturbance, or both.

Neutralization: The process by which infantile sexual and aggressive impulses and lose their infantile quality.

New beginning: Term used by M. Balint to describe the start of the process of recovery occurring in patients whose cure necessitates a regression to extreme dependence on the analyst. It corresponds to what Winnicott (1958) calls emergence of the true self.

Night hospital: A part-time hospital facility in which patients function in the outside world during the day but return to the hospital at night. See also Day hospital Partial hospitalization, weekend hospital.

Nightmare: Anxiety attack while dreaming. It is characterized by mild anxiety, good recall of dream, and mild autonomic reactions. See also Night-terror.

Night-terror: Extreme panic attack while dreaming. It is characterized by verbalizations, confusion, autonomic activity, and poor recall of dream. It is also called over nocturnes.

Nihilism: Delusion of the non existence of the self part of the self. The term also refers to an attitude of total rejection of established values or extreme skepticism regarding moral and value judgements.

Nihilistic delusion: See delusion.

Nomenclature: System of specific technical terms used to identify categories of disease.

Noncomplementary role: See role.

Non-contingent reinforcement: Reinforcement which is not dependent on a particular action or response from the organism involved. Such reinforcement is often involved in the development of superstitious behaviour.

Non-directive approach: Technique in which the therapist follows the lead of the patient in the interview, rather than introducing his own theories and directing the course of the interview. This method is applied in both individual and group therapy. See also passive therapist.

Non-parametric tests of significance: When data do not satisfy certain statical assumptions, such as being normally distributed, other specialized statistical procedures which do not require assumptions of normality must be employed. These methods are often based upon an analysis of ranks rather than on the distribution of the actual score themselves. Widely used examples are the chi-squire. Spearman rank order correlation, median, and Mann-Whitney U tests.

Non-verbal communication (NVC): Communication through signals other than those used in language. For example posture, appearance, smell and range of specific behaviours such as pupil dilation, facial expression and the pattern of eye contact. Non-verbal communication takes place through a number of different non-verbal cues, which can be combined in various ways. Some researchers have estimated NVC as being more than four times as powerful as verbal communication, though one could imagine that trying to teach the A level psychology syllabus non-verbally would be rather laborious. An understanding of the cues and use of non-verbal signals forms the basis of most social skills training.

Non-verbal cue: A signal which conveys some kind of communication to an observer without involving the use of language. Non-verbal cues are usually considered to be of seven main types: paralanguage, proxemics, posture, gesture, facial expression, eye-contact, and dress. Some theorists additionally consider that ritual and ritual symbolism should also be regarded as an important medium of non-verbal communication.

Normality: A state which is usually considered to be unremarkable: the opposite of abnormal. In attempting to identify normal and abnormal behaviour of the purposes of psychological classification, three alternative approaches are often specified. Firstly, normality is taken to be behaviour which is infrequently acknowledged. (In some cases, such as the imagined 'seeing' of a recently dead relative, the experience may actually be very common though not often openly acknowledged). A second definition of normal behaviour, is behaviour which conforms to accepted norms, or social demands. In this event, social consensus becomes a major factor in decisions concerning normality and abnormality. The third approach concentrates on statistically common behaviour, irrespective of consensus. This approach rests on the assumptions of the Gaussian (normal) distribution. The problem here is that with this approach, people who are statistically uncommon in a highly valued direction (e.g., of extremely high IQ) are also defined as abnormal.

Norms (in social psychology): A norm is a rule or standard for action. Social norms are shared definitions of desirable behaviour.

Nosology: The science of the classification of diseases.

NREM sleep: Non-REM sleep; sleep stages I through See also REM sleep.

Nuclear family: Immediate members of a family, including the parents and the children.

Null hypothesis: Research term for the hypothetical assumption that any difference observed between two groups or conditions or between a particular group and the general population is purely accidental and due to chance alone. See also Type 1 error. Type 2 error.

Number and letter peg systems: Mnemonic techniques in which to be remembered items are linked with a well-learned set of numbers or letters. Compare method of loci.

Nurse, psychiatric: Part of the mental health team, usually in an institutional setting. The nurse works with patients in the hospital milieu; today the psychiatric nurse often carries out individual, family, and group psychotherapy.

Nymphomania: Abnormal, excessive, insatiable desire in a woman for sexual intercourse. See also satyriasis.

O

Obesity: Excessive weight. Obesity is usually defined in terms of body weight being a certain percentage above the ideal weight for that person's age, sex and height. The percentage varies but is often either 15% or 30%. This vagueness is not crucial as there is no absolute standard for 'ideal weight' which is largely a cultural judgement.

Object: That towards which action or desire is directed; that which the subject requires in order to achieve instinctual satisfaction; that to which the subject relates himself (a) *Object, bad*–An object whom the subject hates or fears, who is experienced as malevolent. A bad object may be either an internal or an external object. (b) *Object cathesis*–Investment of energy is an external object, in contrast to its investment in the self. (c) *Object choice*–Narcissistic object – choice is based on identification with an object similar to the subject. Anaclitic object-choice is based on the subject's difference from the subject. (d) *Object constancy*–the ability to maintain a lasting relationship with a specific single object; or inversely, the tendency to reject substitutes for a familiar object. (e) *Object external*–An object recognized by the subject as being external to himself. (f) *Object good*–An object whom the subject loves, who is experienced as benevolent. A good object may be either internal or external. (g) *Object internal*–Object representation which has acquired the significance of an external object. They are derived from external objects by introjection's (h) *Object libido*–Libido which is invested on objects, as opposed to narcissistic libido which is invested in the self (i) *Object loss*–The loss of usually, a good external object. The event which precedes introjection's and/or mourning. (j) *Object love*–Love of an object which is recognized as a person other than oneself, in contrast to self-love and identification. (k) *Object, need satisfying*–An object whom the subject 'loves' solely on accounts of its capacity to satisfy needs and whom the subject fails to recognize as a person. The term is only used when discussing the nature of infants attachment to its mother. (l) *Object, part* – An object which is part of a person e.g., a penis or a breast (m) *Object relationship* – The relation of the subject to his object, not the relation between the subject and the object which is an interpersonal relationship (n) *Object (relations) theory*–Psychoanalytical theory in which the subject's need to relate to object occupies the central position; in contrast to instinct theory, which centres around the subject's need to reduce instinctual tension (o) *Object-representation* – The mental representation of an object. (p) *Object transitional*–object which the subject treats as being half-way between himself and another person. (q) *Object whole*–An object whom the subject recognizes as being a person with similar rights, feelings, needs etc., as himself.

Object concept: The idea that objects have a continuing existence, whether the individual is paying attention to them or not. Although this has been disputed by philosophers, the operational concept is an important one for the young child to develop in its interactions with the world; and the way in which this happens has been extensively studies as part of cognitive development.

Object constancy: The perceptual process by which adjustment is made to the fact that objects have a continuing existence even when not being attended to. See also object concept, size constancy, shape constancy.

Object permanence: See object concept.

Object relations: The emotional bonds between one person and another, as contrasted with interest in and love for the self; usually described in terms of capacity for loving and reacting appropriately to others.

Object relations theory: A psychoanalytic theory developed primarily by Melanie Klien and W. Ronald Fairbarin in Britain as a reaction against Freud' concentration on instincts. Objects are the people, parts of people or things to whom the individual relates. Infants are believed to relate only to separate parts of people, such as the mother's breast. The ability to perceive the parts as belonging to a whole person, with both their good and bad aspects, has to be learned. Only a whole person can be recognized as having their own feelings, needs, etc., which ought to be respected, so only a whole person can be the object of a mature relationship. Psychological disturbance in adults is believed to result from problems in object relations in childhood, with the more severe conditions reflecting problems earlier in development, hence the emphasis by Klein on the breast as the first, crucial, part object. Therapy is directed to resolving the relationship with bad or persecutory objects internalized by the patient so that they can make mature relationships with people and not just use them as vehicles for their own gratification.

Objective test: A test which can be marked without any need for subjective judgements. For example, multiple-choice tests and intelligence tests are regarded as objective by most psychologists.

Observational learning: Learning which occurs as a result observing the behaviour of others. As such observational learning includes the two processes of imitation and identification, and is an important component of social learning theory.

Obsession: Persistent and recurrent idea, thought, or impulse that cannot be eliminated from consciousness by logic or reasoning. Obsessions are involuntary and ego-dystonic. See also compulsion.

Obsessional thinking: This term refers not to obsessional thoughts but to form of thinking displayed typically by obsessional characters and accepted by them as a valid form of mental activity. Its function is to reconcile ambivalent attitudes and it tends therefore to consist of highly abstract formulations designed to reconcile contradictions or of statements typically linked by 'buts' which tend to cancel one another out.

Obsessive-compulsive disorder: A neurotic disorder characterized by the persistent recurrence of obsessions and compulsions.

Obsessive compulsive personality: A personality disorder characterized by perfectionism, over conscientiousness, and excessive inhibition with regard to self expression and relaxation. It is also called anankastic personality. In DSM III the condition was called compulsive personality disorder.

Occam's razor: A scientific principle which states that, given choice between two possible solutions or theoretical explanations for a given problem, the simple one of the two should be adopted.

Occupational neurosis: A selective inhibition of the performance of specific, usually highly skilled actions, motor or mental, that are essential to a subject's occupation. In the absence of organic pathology. Examples are writer's cramp, musician's cramp, or accountant's sudden difficulty with mental arithmetic. Such dysfunction is usually a manifestation of an underlying anxiety state, and the term with its implication of an independent status for the disorder, should be avoided.

Occupational psychiatry: Area of psychiatry concerned with mental illness in industry, including the psychiatric aspects of absenteeism, vocational adjustment, operational fatigue, and accident proneness.

Occupational psychology: The use of psychological knowledge and principles in the study of people at work, or in any productive occupation. Occupational psychology and industrial psychology are closely linked, but occupational psychology has a wider range than just the study of people in industrial situations, as it includes such occupations as that of housewife, novelist, and unemployed person.

Occupational therapy: A form of therapy in which the patient engages in useful, purposeful activities in a therapeutic social setting involving interaction with other patients and hospital personnel.

Oceanic feeling: Phrase used by Romain Rolland in a letter to Freud to describe the mystical, cosmic emotion which (according to Roland) is the true source of religious sentiments.

Oedipus complex: Constellation of feelings, impulses, and conflicts in the developing child that concern sexual impulses and attraction toward the opposite-sex parent and aggressive, hostile, or envious feelings toward the same-sex parent. Real or fantasied threats from the same-sex parent result in the repression of those feelings. The development of the Oedipus complex coincides with the phallic phase of psychosexual development. One of Freud's most important concepts, the term was originally applied only to the male. See also Electra complex. Totem and Taboo.

Oligophrenia: Mental retardation.

Omission of reinforcement/omission training: An instrumental conditioning/operant conditioning procedure in which positive reinforcement is withdrawn following a response. The effect of this procedure is to decrease the likelihood of the response which leads to removal of positive reinforcement, compare punishment, negative reinforcement.

Omnipotence: Omnipotent phantasies are phantasies that the subject is omnipotent. Omnipotence of thought refers to the belief that thoughts can of themselves alter the external world.

Onanism: Coitus interruptus: The term is sometimes used interchangeably with masturbation.

Oneiromancy: Divination by means of dreams; not to be confused with dream interpretation which makes no claim to be predictive and uses the dream solely as evidence of the dreamer's state of mind. Oneirology is a rarely used word for the scientific study of dreams.

Oneirophrenia: A syndrome described as occurring in acute schizophrenic illness, with some clouding of consciousness and dream-like (oneiroid) state with vivid scenic hallucinosis, catatonic features and diminished contact with the real world. Comment: The claim for an independent status of this syndrome has not found general support. The term was first introduced by Mayer Gross in 1924 (as 'oneiroid state') and then used in 1945 by Meduna and McCulloch. See also: dream-like state.

One-trial learning: A very rapid form of learning, through classical conditioning, in which just one experience or event is sufficient for a lasting learned association to occur. Most examples of one-trial learning have to do with food or pain, and are thus regarded as linked to very basic survival mechanisms. If consumption of a specific food is followed by vomiting, or if contact with a specific stimulus is followed by a painful experience, then a strong avoidance behaviour will result which is highly resistant to extinction. The forms of one trial learning that are specific to the species and which seem to have a biological basis are examples of prepared learning. One-trial learning has also been associated with instances of superstitious learning.

Ontogenetic: Pertaining to the development of an individual person. See also Phylogenetic.

Open hospital: Mental hospital without locked doors or physical restraints.

Open system: A system which is open to receive energy or information. Open systems are therefore able to develop, and will tolerate new structures within them, as opposed to a closed system.

Operant: Any unit of behaviour which has an effect (of any kind) on the environment. Also known as operant behaviour, it is the basis of the conditioning of voluntary behaviour. Unless behaviour which has some kind of effect in the environment is produced spontaneously, the law of effect cannot come into play, and the behaviour will continue to be emitted more or less randomly.

Operant chamber: A simple box often called a 'skinner box', with a device which can be worked by an animal in the box to control reinforcement.

Operant conditioning: A process of stimulus-response learning of voluntary behaviour, which occurs as a result of the consequence of actions produced by an organism (animal or human being). The idea is that the learning of an appropriate action or operant is likely to be reinforced (strengthened). If the increases the action is followed by a pleasant consequence (see law of effect). This increases the probability that the action will occur again. Reinforcement in operant conditioning can be positive or negative. If positive, the action is directly rewarded; if negative, it is indirectly rewarded by the removal or avoidance of something unpleasant. The other major class of conditioning is called classical conditioning. See also primary and secondary reinforcement, reinforcement schedules, shaping.

Operant strength: This is a term used to describe how strongly a response acquired through operant conditioning has been learned. There are two main measures of operant strength; resistance to extinction and response rate.

Operations: Manipulations of objects or concepts. The major use within psychology is in Piaget's theory which is largely about the different kinds of cognitive operations, particularly logical manipulations, which are carried out by children at different ages. See concrete operations and formal operations.

Operational definition: The meaning of a concept when it is translated into terms amenable to systematic observation and measurement, e.g., temperatures defined by a thermometer reading under standard conditions.

Opponent-process theory: A hedonistic view of motivation and emotion which says that many emotional motivating states are followed by an opposing, or opposite state. Compare drive theories, incentive theories and incentive motivation, optimal-level theories.

Oppositional disorder: A mental disorder of childhood that is characterized by pervasive negativism, continuous argumentativeness, and an unwillingness to comply with reasonable suggestions and persuasion.

Oral: Appertaining to the mouth (a) *Oral character*–Character displayed by persons with fixations at the oral stage. Typical oral character traits are optimism and pessimism, generosity, moodiness, depression, elation, talkativeness, greed and the tendency to engage in wishful thinking (b) *Oral erotism*–Sensuous please derived from the mouth (c) *Oral sadism*–Pleasure in hurting by biting. Pleasure in phantasies of biting and eating destructively (cannabilism) (d) *Oral stage*–In classical theory of psychoanalysis, the first stage of both libidinal development and ego development, in which the mouth is the main source of pleasure and hence the centre of experience.

Oral dyskinesia: See Tardive dyskinesia.

Oral phase: The earliest stage in psychosexual development. It lasts through the first 18 months of life. During this period the oral zone is the centre of the infant's needs, expression, and pleasurable erotic experiences. It has a strong influence on the organization and development of the child's psyche. See also Anal phase, Genital phase, Infantile sexuality, Latency phase, Phallic phase, Psychosexual development.

Oral triad: Term used by Lewin (1946) for the conjoined wishes to be suckled by, sleep with and be devoured by the breast, wishes which, in his view underlie the psychopathology of mania.

Order effect: An experimental effect which arises as a result of the order in which two tasks are presented. Order effects are of two main kinds: practice effects, where the subject becomes more skilled are a given task as a result of practice, and so performs better in later conditions of the experiment: and fatigue effects, where the subject becomes tired or bored as the study progresses, and so performs worse in later experimental conditions. See also counter-balancing.

Orectic: To do with desire or appetite. The term is only likely to be encountered as an opposite of cognitive.

Organ neurosis: Used by psychoanalysts as a synonym for psychosomatic disorders. It has also been used for anxiety states in which the anxiety symptoms have become restricted to one physical system, e.g., cardiac neurosis, in which the anxiety symptoms are held to be due to a cardiovascular disorder.

Organic brain syndrome (OBS): See Organic mental disorder.

Organic mental disorder: Mental disorder caused by transient or permanent brain dysfunction attributable to specific organic factors. The organic mental disorders include delirium, senile and presenile dementias and substance-induced disorders.

Orgasm: The culminating-point in sexual intercourse, the moment at which tension affects are replaced by discharge affects. The word is occasionally used to refer to an equivalent moment in pre-genital acts, hence gastrointestinal orgasm for satiation of the oral instinct; and by still further extension, pharmacotic orgasm (Rado 1933) for the response to addictive drugs.

Orgasmic dysfunction: Failure to achieve orgasm through physical stimulation.

Orientation: State of awareness of oneself and one' surrounding in terms of time, place, and person.

Orienting reflex: A set of physiological and behavioural changes which occur in response to an unexpected stimulus which attracts the attention of the individual. The orienting reflex includes a positioning of the body towards the sound of other stimulus, keeping the body very still, a dilation of the blood vessels in the head, EEG changes and alterations to muscle tone, heart rate and breathing. This combination of physiological changes means that the individual is more prepared to receive the stimulus. The opposite pattern, when a stimulus is being excluded, is called the defensive reflex.

Origence: A personality characteristic of creative thinkers; resistance to conformity and an emphasis on individualized interpretation and expression are features of this personality dimension.

Orthodox sleep: Ordinary, quiescent sleep which does not involve rapid eye movements (REM), or the experience of dreaming. Orthodox sleep occurs at lightly or deeply asleep, and which each show characteristic RRG patterns. Stage 1 sleep is entered first, and is the lightest form of sleep with a fairly regular EEG pattern. Some dreaming may take place during this stage. The sleeper then progresses through the stages to the deepest level of stage 4 in which the EEG is very irregular with large spikes. In this stage it is very difficult to awaken the sleeper and in children, bed-wetting, night terrors and sleepwalking my occur. The pattern changes through the period of sleeping. See sleep cycles. Orthodox sleep is also called NREM (non rapid eye movement) sleep. See also paradoxical sleep.

Orthophrenia: Soundness of mind; also the curing of a disordered mind.

Orthopsychiarty: An interdisciplinary approach to the study and practice of maintaining or restoring mental health. It involves principles derived from psychiatry, psychology, sociology, social work, medicine, and other fields. Particular emphasis is placed on preventive techniques to promote healthy mental development and growth; the essential focus is on metal hygiene. See also Mental Hygiene.

Osphresisophilia: Morbid attraction to or interest in odours and smells.

Othello syndrome (morbid jealousy): Delusion of infidelity on part of sexual partner. Normal phenomena are interpreted to fit in with conviction. The common causes are alcoholism, organic psychosis, schizophrenia, obsession personality etc.

Other-directed person: A person who is readily influenced and guided by the attitudes and values of other people. See also Inner-directed person.

Overanxious disorder: An anxiety disorder of childhood or adolescence characterized by excessive worrying and fearful behaviour that is grossly disproportionate to the magnitude of the real environmental stress or threat.

Overcompensation: A conscious or unconscious process in which a real or imagined physical or psychologic deficit generates exaggerated correction. Concept introduced by Adler.

Overdetermination: The concept that phenomena which as dreams and neurotic symptoms reflect the operation of multiple causative factors, particularly with regard to symbolic meaning or significance.

Over-extension: The tendency, found particularly in young children acquiring a language, to apply words too widely, e.g., calling all men 'Daddy".

Over-homosexuality: Behaviourally expressed homosexuality, as distinct from unconscious homosexual wishes or conscious wishes that are held in check. See also Homosexuality, Latent homosexuality.

Overvalued idea: An unreasonable and sustained belief or idea that is maintained with less than delusional intensity. It differs from an obsess ional thought in that the person holding the overvalued idea does not recognize its absurdity and thus does not struggle against it. As with a delusion, the idea or belief is not one that is ordinarily accepted by other members of the person's culture or subculture.

Example: A patient with a long-standing hand-washing compulsion thought there might be danger in shaking hands with people, because they might have recently been inculcated against smallpox and be infectious. Although she acknowledged that the danger might not be real, she could not accept reassurances that there was medically no danger.

P

Paired-associate learning: A learning task which involves the association, or linking together, of two stimuli, usually words. This form of learning task was extremely popular in the study of memory throughout the 1950s and 1960s, but of recent years has been criticized for its artificiality.

Pairing: Presenting two stimuli in such a way that they always occur together.

Palinopsia: It is the persistence or recurrence of visual images after the stimulus object has been removed. It may occur in patients in delirious states that follows metabolic abnormalities resulting from hepatic or renal failure, anoxia, infection, drug intoxication or withdrawal and also in dementia, schizophrenia and manic depressive psychosis.

Pandemonium model: A hierarchical model of cognition, first proposed in the late 1960s, which an interesting example of bottom-up processing. It has been mainly concerned with feature-recognition in perception, and the way in which the identification of features can be combined to result in meaningful percepts. The model proposes a hierarchical organization of 'subdemons', 'cognitive demons' and 'decision demons'. There are myriads of sub-demons, each of which is tuned into detecting specific aspects of a stimulus, such as specific letters in a word. When a stimulus occurs, the appropriate sub-demon shrieks. The more similar the stimulus is to the demon's template, the louder it shrieks. The decision demon at the next level in the hierarchy is faced with the task of deciding which the shrieking-subdemons best represents the stimulus, taking into account other shrieking subdemons responding to subsequent stimuli (hence the name of pandemonium model). As the overall picture becomes more complex, general cognitice emons come into action, which operate at a higher level, and represent complete concepts or schemata. Because of the idea of competition between the demons at each level, this model is well able to cope with the explanation of our response to ambiguous stimuli but some consider it to be weak in explaining some of the more general aspects of active cognition.

Panic: An acute, intense attack of anxiety associated with personality disorganization. The anxiety is overwhelming and accompanied by feelings of impending doom. See also aspects of active cognition.

Panic attack: An episode of acute intense anxiety occurring in panic disorder, schizophrenia, major depression, and somatization disorder.

Panphobia: Fear of everything.

Pantomine: Gesticulation; psychodrama without the use of words.

Papez circuit: A neural circuit identified in 1957 by the neuroanatomist J.W. Papez. It consists of the mammillary bodies in the hypothalamus, anterior thalamus, cingulated gyrus, entorhinal cortex, hippocampus and their interconnecting fibers. It is believed to be important in mediating emotional experience and behaviour. (Fig. 10)

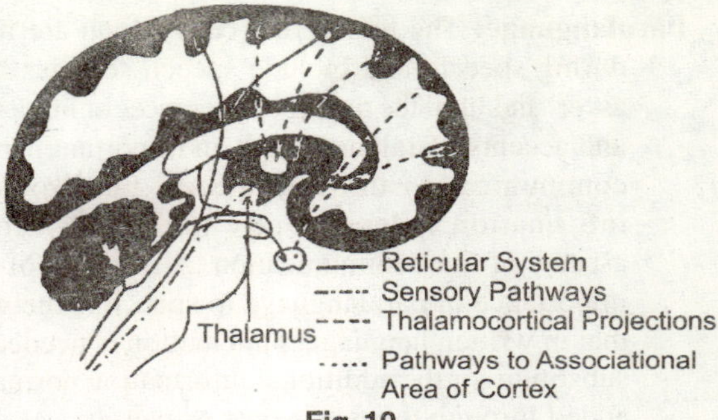

Fig. 10.

Paradox: A situation in which two or more rules combine to give an impossible outcome, like the Cretan who said 'all Cretans are liars'. Paradoxes have been much studied in logic and mathematics but for psychologists the chief interest is in those that trap people into apparently crazy behaviour. See double bind for an example. Some therapists believe that many symptoms result from paradoxes in the person's life and so are best treated with a 'counter-paradox' designed to free them. A common example would be to instruct the person to have their 'un-controllable' symptoms at a particular time. If they have the symptom then it shows they can control it. If they do not have the symptom it shows the symptoms can be prevented, i.e., it is constrollable. As with any other powerful therapeutic technique, paradoxical injunctions can be ineffective and potentially harmful unless they are used with respect and sympathetic understanding for the patient.

Paradoxical sleep: A name given to the type of sleep in which rapid eye movements occur (it is also called REM sleep), during which dreaming occurs. It was named paradoxical in the 1960s as a result of the discovery that EEG patterns shown in this type of sleep suggested that the sleeper was only lightly sleeping and would wake easily; whereas in reality they proved very difficult to wake by some stimuli (like ioud noises) but easy to waken by more meaningful events like having their name spoken. See also sleep cycles; orthodox sleep.

Paralanguage: The non-verbal cues which are used during speech, and include speech sounds, such as 'er' and 'um' the timing of utterances or inflection and accents. Paralanguage is an important part of communication through speech, but provides information independently the actual verbal aspects of the communication. A measure of the importance of paralanguage to speech is the way that in written language, punctuation is needed to substitute for the additional information normally added through tones of voice or pauses.

Parallel processing: The processing of information in such a way that more than one set of operations is happening simultaneously. Models of parallel processing were introduced to cognitive psychology in an attempt to account for the extremely rapid ways in which people can search for information, taking several features into account apparently all at the same time.

Parameter: Any quantitative value that a variable can take.

Parametric study: One which examines the effects on a dependent variable of variations, usually across a broad range, in the value of the independent variable.

Parametric tests of significance: Tests based on the assumption that the form of the distribution of the observations is known, usually a so-called normal distribution, widely used tests based on such as assumption include analysis of variance, t-test, and Pearsonian correlation coefficients.

Paramnesia: Disturbance of memory in which reality and fantasy are confused. It is observed in dreams and in certain types of schizophrenia and organic mental disorders. It includes phenomena such as déjà vu and deja entendu, which may occur occasionally in normal persons. See also confabulation, Jamais vu.

Paranoia: A rare condition characterized by the gradual development of an intricate, complex, and elaborate system of thinking based on (and often proceeding logically from) misinterpretation of an actual event. A person with paranoia often considers himself endowed with unique and superior ability. Despite its chronic course, this condition does not seem to interfere with thinking and personality. To be distinguished from schizophrenia, paranoid type.

Paranoia conjugal: Paranoia characterized by delusions of jealously. With no evidence or with irrelevant evidence, a spouse or a lover becomes convinced that his or her partner is being unfaithful.

Paranoia querulans: A state characterized by a quarrelsome irritability associated with a conviction of injustice and persecution, some times of delusional intensity, arising from real or imaginary wrongs, insults or injuries, and often leading to incessant litigation. *Synonym*: litigious paranoia.

Paranoiac: A person with paranoia.

Paranoid delusion: See delusion.

Paranoid disorder: A mental disorder characterized by persecutory or grandiose delusions and related disturbances in mood, thought, and behaviour. In DSM-III the paranoid disorders include paranoia, shared paranoid disorder, acute paranoid disorder, and a typical paranoid disorder.

Paranoid ideation: Thinking that is dominated by suspicious persecutory, or grandiose content.

Paranoid personality disorder: A personality disorder characterized by rigidity, hypersensitivity, unwarranted suspicion, jealousy, envy, an exaggerated sense of self-importance, and tendency to blame and ascribe evil motives to others.

Paranoid schizophrenia: A schizophrenic disorder characterized by the presence of persecutory or grandiose delusions often accompanied by hallucinations.

Paraphasia: Type of abnormal speech in which one word it substituted for another; the irrelevant word generally resembles the required one in its morphology, meaning, or phonetic composition. The inappropriate word may be either a legitimate one used incorrectly, such as "clover' instead of 'train' or a bizarre nonsense expression. Such as 'treen' instead of 'train'. Paraohasic speech may be seen in organic aphasias and in mental disorders, such as schizophrenia. See also Metonymy, Neologism, Word approximation.

Paraphilia: Type of psychosexual disorder. The term refers to sexual deviation characterized by persistent and recurrent sexual fantasies, often of an unusual nature, without which imagery erotic arousal or orgasm is not attained. The fantasies generally involve themes of suffering, humiliation, sexual activity with nonconsenting partners, or preference for a nonhuman object for sexual arousal. The paraphilias include fetishism, transvestism, zoophilia, pedophilia, exhibitionism, voyeurism, sexual masochism, and sexual sadism.

Parapraxis: A faulty act, blunder, or lapse of memory such as a slip of the tongue or misplacement of an article. According to Freud, these acts are caused by unconscious motives.

Paraprofessional: A nonprofessionally trained person who works in a mental hospital. The paraprofessional may have a degree in the arts or from some professional school other than those serving the mental health group but has not obtained a degree in one of the usual mental health professions.

Parapsychology: Branch of psychology that deals with extranormal events and behavioural phenomena that are not accounted for or explained by the tenets and laws of present-day conventional science. Examples include clairvoyance, precognition, telepathy, and psychokinesis. See also extrasensory perception. Metapsychology, Psychokinesis.

Parataxic distortion: Sullivan's term for distortions in judgement or attitude in interpersonal relations based on patterns set by earlier experience. Previously developed ways of coping with significant people in a person's life are applied by the person in later interpersonal integrations. See also Transference.

Parathymia: A schizophrenic distortion of mood in which the affective state is inappropriate to the patient's circumstances and / or behaviour. See also incongruity of affect; mood, inappropriate; mood, incongruous.

Parens patriae: In the context of mental illness, this term refers to the constitutional power of the state to involuntarily commit those mentally ill persons who are in need of care and treatment for their mental illness.

Paresis: Weakness of organic origin; incomplete paralysis; term often used instead of general paralysis.

Paresthesia: Abnormal tactile sensation, often described as burning, picking, tickling, tingling, or creeping.

Partial hospitalization: A system of treating mental illness in which the patient is hospitalized on a part-time basis. See also Day hospital, Night hospital, weekend hospital.

Partial reinforcement: Reinforcement in a operant conditioning process which is not given every time the desired behaviour is shown, but only some of the time. This is also known as intermittent reinforcement, and produces a somewhat slower but stronger form of learning which is more resistant to extinction. See also reinforcement schedules.

Partial insanity: See Monomania.

Participant observation: A research technique in which the research takes a full role in the group being studied, often without the knowledge of the other members. In this way the distortion produced by the presence of an observer is minimized, and the researcher can obtain a fuller appreciation of the experiences of the group. See observational study.

Passive-aggressive personality disorder: A research technique in which the research takes a full role in the group being studied, often without the knowledge of the other members. In this way the distortion produced by the presence of an observer is minimized, and the researcher can obtain a fuller appreciation of the experiences of the group. See observational study.

Passive therapist: Therapist who remains inactive but whose presence serves as a stimulus for the patient in the group or individual treatment setting. See also active therapist, Nondirective approach.

Pastoral counseling: Use of psychotherapeutic principles by a clergyman helping parishioners with emotional problems.

Pathobiology: Psychoanalytical study of a historical character based on the available biographical evidence and not on direct clinical observation. This genre, of which Freud's Leonardo da Vinci is a good example and Freud and Bullit's study of Wilson (1967) a bad one, suffers from the grave limitation that one of the clinical criteria of correct interpretation, the patient's (ultimate) agreement with it, is not forthcoming.

Pathognomonic: Term applied to a sign or symptom specifically diagnostic of a particular disease entity.

Pathological gambling: Compulsion to gamble. It is one of the disorders of impulse control.

Pattern perception: The way in which different perceptual features of shapes or figures are recognized as belonging together and forming a pattern of stimuli, rather that being separate and discrete. Without pattern perception, our subjective experience would be simply of patches of light and dark or of patches of colour, without any linking of the stimuli into meaningful units. The basis of pattern perceptions is figure-ground organization the inherent tendency for our perpetual system to organize sensory data into meaningful figures set against backgrounds. This organizational principle results in pattern perceptions, and is evident in the perception of other sensory modes, such as music or speech perception, which, involve pattern perception in linking and distinguishing the different components of the information.

Pavlovian conditioning: Respondent conditioning. See conditioning.

Pavlov, Ivon Petrovich (1849–1936): Russian neurophysiologist noted for his research on conditioning. Awarded Nobel Prize in Medicine (1904).

Pavlov's theory of schizophrenia: A theory propounded by Pavlov, who held that the symptoms of schizophrenia are the result of a state of inhibition of the cerebral cortex.

Pavor nocturnes: See Night-terror.

Peak experience: The rare experience of feeling for a moment complete and at one with oneself and the world. Maslow regarded peak experiences as important, but not essential, aspects of self actualization.

Pecking order: Hierarchy or sequence of authority in an organization or social group.

Pederasty: Homosexual anal intercourse between men and boys with the latter as the passive partners. The term is used less precisely to denote male homosexual anal intercourse.

Pedophillia: A paraphilia involving sexual activity of adults with children as the objects. It may involve any form of heterosexual or homosexual intercourse.

Peer group: A small group of friends or associates who share common values, interests and activities. Also, used for virtually all persons of the same age e.g., school tend to be age-graded.

Peer review: Review of physician services by a panel of other physicians. See also Professional standards Review Organization. Utilization review committee.

Penetrance: In genetics, the frequency with which genes for a particular trait are actually expressed in the phenotype of those possessing them.

Penis and Phallus: Strictly speaking, the penis is an anatomical term referring to the male generative organ, the phallus, an anthropological and theological term referring to the idea or image of the male generative organ i.e., the penis is an organ with biological functions, the phallus is an idea venerated in various religions as a symbol of the power of nature. Hence Jung's (probably apocryphal) remark that the penis is only aphallic symbol. Boys are said to go through a Phallic Phase during which they are not only preoccupied with the penis but also with the idea of potency, virility, manliness and strength and power generally.

Penis Awe: Term used by Phyllis Greenacre to describe the emotion evoked by the sight of the penis in certain patients, some of whom describe is an being surrounded by a halo.

Penis envy: Envy of the penis occurring either in women in respect of men generally or in boys in respect of adult males. According to Freud, penis envy is universal in women, is responsible for their castration complex and occupies a central position in the psychology of women.

Peotillomania: False masturbation, pseudo masturbation; a nervous tic consisting in constant pulling at the penis.

Percept: The conscious awareness of element in the environment by the mental processing of sensory stimuli. The term is sometimes used in a broader sense to refer to the mental process by which all kinds of data- intellectual and emotional, as well as sensory-are organized meaningfully. See also Apperception, Hallucination, Illusion.

Perceptual constancy: The way that a person's perception adjusts itself so that the world is seen as constant, despite the changes in stimulation produced at the sense organs. The perceptual constancies enable us to perceive events more accurately in terms away they are. There are many forms of perceptual constancy, of which the most studied have been size constancy, shape constancy, colour constancy, and location constancy.

Perceptual defence: The idea that the perceptual system is more likely to receive information which is not threatening, and has higher thresholds for perceiving information which is challenging or threatening to the individual, meaning that such information is less likely to be detected or recognized.

Perceptual set: A state of readiness or preparedness to perceive certain kinds of information rather than other kinds. Perceptual set is a powerful phenomenon, which links closely with selective attention and which can be affected by arrange of circumstances, such as prior experience, emotion, motivation, culture and habit.

Perfectionism: Practice of demanding of other or of oneself a higher quality of performance than is required by the situation.

Period prevalence: Research term for the total number of cases of a disease known to have existed during a specified time period. See also Point prevalence.

Perplexity: Persistent repetition of words, ideas, or subjects so that, once an individual begins speaking about a particular subject or uses a particular work, it continually recurs. Perseveration differs from the repetitive use of 'stock words' or interjections such as 'you know' or 'like'. Perseveration is most commonly seen in Organic Mental Disorders, Schizophrenia, and other psychotic disorders.

Person perception: The application of methods for studying and understanding perception to the perception of people. Person perception is fundamental in the process of understanding other people, and often, by implication, ourselves. It has been found to have the usual features of perception when its operating in conditions in which the object is complex and the conditions are difficult. That is, it is highly influenced by set and expectations, and by the needs, fears and wishes of the observer. Person perception is an active and highly researched area within psychology, involving the study of attribution; of non-verbal communication; of interpersonal attitudes; and social memory.

Personal constructs: A unique set of ideas about the world and the people in it, which each individual develops and uses to make sense of the world, and to function effectively in it. Personal constructs were proposed by George Kelly (1955) as the individual theories which people use to generated hypotheses in order to explain their experience Kelly's model of the person was of 'man as-scientist' that the person was actively making sense of the world by formulating hypotheses about it, and then testing them, much as a scientist investigates their chosen subject area. By identifying the special, personal set of constructs which the individual uses, a therapist would be far better placed to understand that person and to assist them with their problems in living. Kelly's was thus an idiographic theory, concerned with the uniqueness of the individual and how he understood his world. The form of assessment known as the repertory grid, which Kelly developed, allows the therapist to utilize the individual's own constructs in analyzing their experience.

Personal space: The distance which people keep between themselves and others during everyday activities. The distance will vary depending on the individual's culture, on the circumstances, and on their relationship with the other person; we tend to position ourselves more closely to intimate friends than we do to strangers. Personal space is a manifestation of proxemics, and an important non-verbal cue; it is often described in terms of territoriality.

Personality: Characteristic configuration of behaviour-response patterns that each person evolves as a reflection of his individual adjustment to life.

Personality, dependent: A personality disorder, with or without asthenic features, with a low degree of self-esteem, a persistent tendency to avoid the assumption of responsibility, and an inclination to subordinate personal drives to those of other people. See also: asthenic personality disorder.

Personality disorder: Mental disorder characterized by inflexible, deeply ingrained, maladaptive patterns of adjustment to life that cause either subjective distress or significant impairment of adaptive functioning. The manifestations are generally recognizable in adolescence or earlier. The types of personality disorders include paranoid, schizoid, schizotypal, histrionic, narcissistic, antisocial, borderline, avoidant, dependent, compulsive, passive-aggressive, and atypical.

Personality disorder, affective: A condition characterized by lifelong predominance of a pronounced mood which may be persistently depressive, persistently elated, or alternately one then the other. During periods of elation there is unshakable optimism and an enhanced zest for life and activity, whereas periods of depression area marked by worry, pessimism, low output of energy and a sense of futility. Such individuals are prone to manic depressive psychosis but it does not occur inevitably. *Synonym*: cycloid personality; cyclothymic personality; depressive personality; dysthymic personality; hyperthymic personality.

Personality disorder, anankastic: A lifelong pattern of personality organization characterized by feeling of personal insecurity, doubt and incompleteness leading to excessive conscientiousness, stubbornness and caution. There may be insistent and unwelcome thoughts or impulses which do not attain the severity of an obsessive compulsive disorder. There is perfectionism and meticulous accuracy and a need to check repeatedly in an attempt to ensure this. Rigidity and excessive doubt may be conspicuous. *Synonym*: compulsive personality, obsessional personality.

Personality disorder, asthenic: Personality disorder characterized by passivity and a weak or inadequate response to the demands of daily life. Lack of vigour may show itself in the intellectual or emotional spheres; there is little capacity for enjoyment. *Synonyms*: inadequate personality; passive personality.

Personality, explosive: Personality disorder characterized by instability of mood with liability intemperate outbursts of anger, hate, violence or affection. Aggression may be expressed in words or in physical violence. The outbursts cannot readily be controlled by the affected person, who is not otherwise prone to antisocial behaviour. *Synonyms*: aggressive personality; emotional instability (excessive).

Personality disorder, hysterical: A personality pattern characterized by shallow, labile affectivity, dependency on others, craving for appreciation and attention, suggestibility and theatricality. There is often sexual immaturity, e.g., frigidity, and over-responsiveness to stimuli. Under stress, hysterical symptoms (neurosis) may develop. *Synonyms*: histrionic personality; psycho infantile personality.

Personality disorder, schizoid: Personality disorder in which there is withdrawal from affection, and social and other contacts, with autistic preference for fantasy and introspective reserve. Behaviour may be slightly eccentric or indicate avoidance of competitive situations. Apparent coolness and detachment may mask as incapacity to express feeling.

Personality disorder with predominantly sociopathic or a social manifestations: Personality disorder characterized by disregard for social obligations, lack of feeling for others, and impetuous or callous unconcern. There is a gross disparity between behaviour and the prevailing social norms. Behaviour is not readily modifiable by experience, including punishment. People with this personality are often affectively could and may be abnormally aggressive or irresponsible. Their tolerance to frustration is low; they blame others or offer plausible rationalizations for the behaviour which brings them into conflict with society. *Synonyms*: amoral personality; antisocial personality disorder; a social personality; moral insanity; socio pathic personality.

Personality dynamics: An approach to understanding behaviour in terms of the active interplay of aspects of the personality structure. Freud's account of personality in terms of interactions between the id, ego, and super-ego is the classic example.

Personality eccentric: A personality disorder characterized by an overvalued private system of beliefs or habits which are exaggerated in nature, sometimes fantastic and held with fanatical conviction.

Personality fanatic: A personality pattern dominated by overvalued ideas that are held tenaciously and may be extensively elaborated without qualifying for delusional status. Individuals may pursue their idea combatively in defiance of social norms or adopt more private, often eccentric ways of life.

Personality hyperthymic: A variant of personality characterized by cheerfulness and high level of activity without the morbid overtones of hypomania. Hyperthymia and dysthymia constitute the cyclothymic personality type which is associated with manic-depressive disease. See also affective personality disorder.

Personality immature: A personality disorder characterized by conduct and emotional response that suggest a failure or lag in psychobiological development. A constitutional basis for this anomaly has been suggested by electroencephalographic abnormality in the form of slow, paroxysmal theta or delta wave activity, mostly in the temporooccipital areas of the brain, which is commonly associated with behavioural disorders of children and criminals. The validity of this correlation is not universally accepted.

Personality, multiple: A rare condition in which an individual exhibits two or more relatively separate, alternating personalities. Dissociation, suggestibility, and role playing are all regarded as psychopatholigically significant factors in the genesis of the disorder. It is usually viewed as hysterical but has been reported in organic states, especially epilepsy.

Personality, passive-aggressive: A personality disorder characterized by a pattern of aggressive feelings expressed covertly by various forms of passivity, e.g., stubbornness, sullenness, or procrastinating or inefficient or inefficient behaviour.

Personality, psychasthenic: A form of personality disorder characterized by an asthenic physique, a low level of energy, a proneness to fatigue, lassitude, lack of conative drive, and sometimes an over sensitivity associated with obsessional traits, Comment: The term drives from the concept of neurasthenia, introduced by Beard in 1869.

Personality traits: Features of an individual's personality. Traits are descriptive terms that are within normal limits.

Personology: Term borrowed by Marjorie Brierley from General Smuts to describe the study of the personality 'not as an obstruction or bundle of psychological abstractions, but rather as a vital organism, as the organic psychic whole which par excellence it is' (smuts) and used by her to distinguish the science of personality from Metapsychology, the two differing in that the former retains the person and his experience while the latter conceives of it as the result of the interaction of personal structures.

Pervasive developmental disorder: A disorder characterized by severe distortions in the development of social skills, language, and contact with reality. Many psychological functions are involved, and a child with a pervasive developmental disorder displays abnormalities that are not normal for any stage of development. Infantile autism is a pervasive developmental disorder. See also Specific developmental disorder.

Perversion: Deviation from the expected norm. In psychiatry, it commonly signifies sexual perversion. See also Psychosexual disorder.

Perverted logic: See Evasion.

Phallic overbearance: Domination of another person by aggressive means. It is generally associated with masculinity in the negative aspects.

Phallic phase: The third stage in psychosexual development. It follows the anal stage and last from about age 2 or 3 to about age 6. During this period, sexual interest, curiosity, and pleasurable experiences are centered on the penis in boys and the clitoris in girls. The resolution of Oedipus complex is the dominant developmental conflict during this stage; it is thus also referred to an Oedipal stage. See also Anal phase, Genital phase, Infantile sexuality, Latency phase, Oral phase, Psychosexual development.

Phantasy: See Fantasy.

Phantom limb: False sensation that an extremity that has been lost is, in fact, present.

Phenomenology: The study of events or happenings in their own right, rather than from the point of view of inferred causes. It is associated with existential psychiatry and reflects the theory that behaviour is determined by the way the person perceives reality, rather than by external reality in objective terms. The word came into use in philosophy after publication of Hegel's "phenomenology of the spirit".

Phenomenon, Napalkov: (A.V. Napalkov, Russian neurophysiologist). In exception to the usual; conditioned reflex experiments occurring in some phobic patients in which the conditioning stimulus (e.g., a traumatic event) does not immediately produce a fear reaction; instead the fear increases in time rather than being extinguished as it ordinarily would during exposure to the unreinforced conditioning stimulus.

Phenotype: The outward, observable expression of person's genetic constitution. See also Genotype.

Pheromone: Chemical signal that a person releases into the external environment and that affects the behaviour or physiological states of other persons.

Phi phenomenon: An illusion of movement brought about by the sequencing in illumination of adjacent lights. If one light comes on when the other goes off, and the light next to it goes on when that goes off, what is perceived (assuming it happens reasonable quickly) is an impression of one light moving across from the location of the first one to the location of the last. This phenomenon is widely used in illuminated advertising signs, and can sometimes be very convincing. Should the lights be arranged in a circle, the perceived circular motion is seen as describing a circle of smaller diameter than the actual arrangement of the lights. It is thought that the phi phenomenon is a manifestation of the Gestalt psychologists' principle of closure occurring with dynamic stimuli rather than with static ones.

Phobia: An obsessive, persistent, unrealistic, intense fear of an object or situation. The fear is believed to arise through a process of displacing an internal (unconscious) conflict to an external object symbolically related to the conflict. See also displacement. Some of the common phobias are (add "abnormal fear of" to each entry):

achluophobia: Darkness.

acrophobia: Heights.

agoraphobia: Open spaces or leaving the familiar setting of the home.

ailurophobia: Cats.

algophobia: Pain

androphobia: Men

autophobia: Being alone or solitude.

bathophobia: Depths.

claustrophobia: Dogs.

erythrophobia: Blusing; sometimes used to refer to the blushing itself.

gynophobia: Women.

hypnophobia: Sleep.

mysophobia: Dirt and germs.

panphobia: Everything.

pedophobia: Children.

xenophobia: Strangers.

Phobic disorder: An anxiety disorder characterized by intense specific fear of an object or situation. It is also called phobic neurosis. Phobic disorder is frequent in childhood. In DSM the phobic disorders include agoraphobia with and without panic attacks, social phobia, and simple phobia.

Phoneme: A basic unit of spoken language; a speech sound. Phonemes are not the same as syllables: a one-syllable word, like 'cat' for instance, is made up of three distinct phonemes, which are combined to produce the syllable, or morpheme.

Phonemics: The study of regularities and distinctive patterns in the combination of phonemes in spoken language.

Phrenology: The study of the bony conformation of the skull in the belief that it is related to mental faculties and traits.

Phyloanalysis· Term adopted by Trigant Burrow to describe type of behaviour analysis conducted in groups. Burrow was a pioneer in the study of human behaviour in groups, but his chief interest was in understanding human evolutionary status, rather than in developing techniques of group psychotherapy. Because the earlier term for his work, "group analysis" led to confusion with analytic group psychotherapy, Burrow dropped the term and spoke, instead, of phyloanalysis.

Phylogenetic: Pertaining to the development of the species. See also Ontogenetic.

Physical disorder: A disorder of body function whose manifestations are not primarily behaviou:al or psychological.

Physiological correlate: A physical change which accompanies a behavioural or psychological response. The term is used to avoid making assumptions about causality. It may be recognized, for instance, that a cognitive event such as concentration or sleep is accompanied by physiological correlated is adopted as a description.

Physiological need: Identified by Maslow as ebbing the lowest level in his hierarchy of needs; physiological need are the requirements for physical functioning, such as the needs for food, water, etc.

Physiological psychology: The study of the way in which human behaviour and cognition are influenced or performed by processes which take place physically within the body. The term 'physiological' is preferred to 'biological' because such influences are usually exerted by whole systems of physical functioning operating together, such as is demonstrated in the fight or flight response, or the sensory information processing systems. Physiological psychology is often seen as being inherently reductionist as it explains behaviour in terms of the actions of neurons and chemicals, but many physiological psychologists maintain an interaction's approach to the subject, in which physiological factors are sent as contributing to or influencing behaviour, but necessarily determining it.

Piaget, Jean (1896–1980): Swiss psychologist noted for his research on cognitive development in children. Piaget divided the development of intelligence into three major periods: sensorimotor (birth to 2 years), concrete operations (2 to 12 years), and formal operations (12 to through adult life). See also categorical thought, Formal operations, syncretic thought.

Piblokto: A culture-specific syndrome seen in Eskimos, usually women. The affected person screams, cries, and runs naked through the snow, sometimes with suicidal or homicidal tendencies.

Pica: An eating disorder consisting of the cravind and eating of unusual foods or other substances. Seem in variety of medical conditions, pregnancy, and emotional disturbances.

Pickwickian syndrome: Condition characterized by obesity, hypoventilation, and hypersomnia.

Pilomotor response: The response of the hair of the body standing on end at times of extreme fear or rage. In many animals, this forms an impressive signal, resulting in the animal looking much larger and, presumably, more fearsome to a would-be attacker. It is also sometimes used to fluff-up the hair to provide added protection from cold. In human being, owing to the shortness and near-invisibility of much body hair, the pilomotor response simply results in the skin appearance known as goose-pimples, as the contraction of the small muscle at the base of each hair pulls the surrounding skin into a small bump.

Fig. 11. The pilomotor response.

Pinel, Philippe (1746–1826): French reformer in the field of mental illness. He is known for his work in abolishing physical restrains on hospitalized patients.

Placebo: An inactive substance or preparation that is given as though it were pharmacologically active medicine. Its major use is in controlled studies to determine the efficacy of medicinal preparations; any beneficial or deleterious effects of the placebo may be ascribed to psychological factors. The term may also refer to any type of treatment that has no specific effects on the particular illness involved.

Placebo, active: The presence or absence of side effects may allow the patient to identify whether he is receiving drug or placebo (for example, dry mouth may be associated with chlorpromazine). An active placebo is one which may mimic the side effects, but does not have the specific and assumed therapeutic pharmacologic action of the drug under investigation.

Placebo effect: Phenomenon in which a person exhibits a clinically significant response to a pill containing a therapeutically inert substance or a treatment without specific effect on the person's condition. Placebo effects are not limited to subjective reports; physiological functions may be objectively influenced.

Play therapy: A type of therapy used with children in which the child reveals his problems on a fantasy level with dolls, clay, and other toys. The therapist intervenes opportunely with helpful explanations about the patient's response and behaviour in language geared to the child's comprehension. See also Activity group therapy.

Pleasure principle: In psychoanalysis, the principle by which the id seeks immediate tension reduction by either direct or fantasied gratification. It is also known as the pleasure-pain principle. Developmentally, the pleasure principle antedates the reality principle. See also Reality principle.

Pleonexia: A psychiatric disorder in which the patient has an excessive desire to acquire wealth or objects.

Pluralism: In psychiatry, the notion that multiple factors affect behaviour.

Point prevalence: Research term for the total number of cases of a disease known to have existed at a given point of time. See also Period prevalence.

Polymorphous perverse sexuality: Psychoanalytic conceptualization of sexuality in the human infant, for whom sexual gratification can be achieved by homosexual, heterosexual, or inanimate stimulation of several body zones. All humans, therefore, have the potential to develop sexual perversions in adulthood, depending on how the sexual drives are channeled developmentally.

Polyphagia: Pathologic overeating. Also known as bulimia.

Polysomnography: The all-night recording of a variety of physiologic parameters (e.g., brain waves, eye movements, muscle tonus, respiration, heart rate, penile tumescence) in order to diagnose sleep related disorders.

Positive regard: Linking, affection or love for another person. The term was used by Carl Rogers to describe what he considered to be one of the two basic needs of the human being; the need for positive regard from others. This, he thought, could be conditional upon appropriate behaviour or unconditional, but as a basic need, it would have to be satisfied. Roger's form of therapy requires that the therapist provides the client with unconditional positive regard. See also self-actualization.

Positive reinforcement: Reinforcement which provides something that the organism wants likes or needs- a reward of some kind. See also negative reinforcement.

Positivism: A belief that reliable information can only be obtained about events that can be observed directly. It therefore claims that science should only deal with observables and not hypothetical constructs. Behaviourism in its more primitive forms has been the clearest example of a positivistic approach within psychology. An even more restrictive version, called logical positivism, claims that a hypothesis can only by regarded as scientific if there is a way in which it can potentially be disproved by empirical observation. Logical positivism has been largely abandoned or superseded, but it was always more popular among philosophers of science than among psychologists, who mostly just got on with the job of studying hypothesized psychological process such as motivation. August Comte was its founder (1758–1857).

Postconcussional syndrome: States occurring after generalized contusion of the brain, in which the symptom picture may resemble that of the front lobe syndrome or that of any neurotic disorders, but in which in addition, headache, giddiness, fatigue, insomnia and a subjective feeling of impaired intellectual ability are usually prominent. Mood may fluctuate, and quite ordinary stress may produce exaggerated fear and apprehension. There may be marked intolerance of mental and physical exertion, undue sensitivity to noise, and hypochondriacal preoccupation. The symptoms are more common in people who have suffered from neurotic or personality disorders, or when there is a possibility of compensation. This syndrome is particularly associated with the closed type of head injury when signs of localized brain damage are slight or absent, but it may also occur in other conditions. *Synonyms*: post-traumatic brain syndrome, nonpsychotic; status post commotion cerebri.

Post-hypnotic amnesia: The forgetting of information as a result of a suggestion made while the subject was under hypnosis, and which occurs after the hypnotic state has finished. Post-hypnotic amnesia is often described by subjects as feeling like 'tip-of-the-tongue' forgetting can also last for several days.

Post-hypnotic suggestion: A suggestion made to someone while they are in a hypnotic state, which concerns behaviour which they will undertake once the hypnotic fugues over. In the case of relatively trivial forms of behaviour, this is often performed by the subject, who typically says that they 'just felt like doing it'. Post-hypnotic suggestion has sometimes been presented by Hollywood film makers as being so powerful that it could force a subject to act against their will, but thus represents part of the Hollywood mythology of hypnotism, which bears little resemblance to the real thing. It is not possible to force someone to do anything against their will, either during hypnosis or through post-hypnotic suggestion; the state of hypnosis itself necessarily involves the willing cooperation of the subject throughout.

Postpartum psychosis: A psychotic reaction, usually depression, after childbirth.

Posttraumatic stress disorder: An anxiety disorder that occurs after and as a result of a disturbing event in the patient' life. It may be acute, chronic, or delayed.

Postural echo: A non-verbal signal which often indicated friendliness or that two people are in substantial agreement. While the participants are engaged in a soçial exchange (such as a converzation) they may be seen to be adopting (usually unconsciously) the same posture; or mirroring each other's posture if they are face-to-face. It may be used consciously by therapists and salesmen to produce a feeling of rapport in the client.

Posture: A powerful non-verbal cue which is commonly used to indicate attitudes or emotions. It is about the positioning of the body, the relative arrangement of the limbs. Posture is commonly, though usually unconsciously, taken as a communicative signal, and make a considerable difference to how a verbal message is understood. See also postural echo, non-verbal communication.

Posturing: Strange, fixed, and bizarre bodily positions held by the patient for an extended time. See also catatonia.

Posturology: The study of posture. In psychoanalysis the study of the ways in which character, defences, sexual attitudes and conflicts are revealed in posture. Its logical companion, gesturology, does not occur.

Potency: A male's ability to perform the sexual act; specifically, the capacity to achieve and maintain an erection during coitus.

Potomania: Morbid impulse for intoxicating drinks.

Poverty of content of speech: Speech that is quantitatively adequate but qualitatively inadequate because it imparts minimal, vague, or repetitious information.

Poverty of speech: See Laconic speech.

Power Law: A law propounded by S.S. Stevens which states that the subjective strength of a stimulus is equal to the physical strength of the stimulus raised to a power (squared, cubed etc.) Like Fechner's law, the power law relates to the fact that as a stimulus becomes stronger, bigger changes are required in order to have the same psychological effect. The power law differs from Fechner's law in the mathematical expression of the relationship.

Power semantics: It is concerned with the use of language in maintaining and consolidating differential power in a society and the manipulation of people by means of language.

Practice effect: An experimental effect in which apparent changes in the dependent variable happen as a result of the subject gaining practice in the task during the course of the experiment, and therefore improving their performance. Practice effects are usually controlled by counterbalancing the order of presentation of the conditions of the study.

Pragmatics: An approach in studying language which concentrates on the functions that language performs rather than on the structure of the language itself (linguistics).

Pratt, Joseph H.: Boston physician born in 1842 and generally considered to be the first pioneer in group psychotherapy in America. He formed discussion groups amount patients with tuberculosis to deal with the physical aspects of their disease. Later, those groups began discussing the emotional problems that stemmed from the illness.

Preconscious: One of the three divisions of the psyche in Freud' s topographic model, the preconscious includes all mental contents that are not in immediate awareness but that can be consciously recalled with effort. See also Conscious, Unconscious.

Predictor variable: The test or other form of performance which is used to predict the person's status on a criterion variable. For example scores on the Scholastic Aptitude Test might be used to predict the criterion "finishing college within the top 33% of graduating class." Scores on the Scholastic Aptitude Test would be predictor scores.

Pregenital stages: In psychoanalysis, the first stages of psychosexual development namely, the oral and the anal stages which occur before genitals have begun to exert the predominant influence on sexual behaviour. See also Anal phase, Genital phase, Infantile sexuality, Oral phase, Phallic phase, Psychosexual development.

Prejudice: Preconceived adverse judgement or opinion formed without just grounds or sufficient knowledge. Elements of irrational suspicion or hatred are often involved, as in racial prejudice.

Premature ejaculation: Ejaculation occurring before or immediately after vaginal intromission during coitus. Broader definitions take into consideration the ability of the man to delay ejaculation during coitus for a sufficient length of time to satisfy a normally responsive female partner.

Premenstrual tension syndrome: A group of physical and psychological symptoms which is varying combinations characteristically recur in women in the second, luteral phase of the menstrual cycle and subside during the first 11–12 days of the cycle. The commonest symptoms include tension, irritability, depression, painful breasts, fluid retention and backache. The relationship of mental ill-health and hormonal disturbances to this syndrome remains unclear. See also psychogenic dysmenorrhoea.

Pre-moral stage: The first of Kohlbr's three stages of moral development, in which moral judgements are seen entirely instrumentally, in terms of whether or not the individual is likely to be detected and /or punished.

Premorbid: Occurring before the onset of disease.

Pre-operational stage: The second of Piaget's stages of cognitive development. During this stage children are unable to think in terms of logical concepts such as conservation or reversibility and they are dominated by perceptual features of their world. The stage starts from about 2 years of age, at the end of the sensori-motor stage, when object permanence is first seen. It ends at about 7 years when the child starts the stage of concrete operations.

Presenile dementia: In DSM, called primary degenerative dementia, presenile onset; examples include Alzheimer's disease and Pick's disease.

Pressure of speech: An increase in the amount of spontaneous speech; rapid, loud, accelerated speech. It is also called pressured speech. Occurs in mania, schizophrenia, and organic disorders. See also Communication disorder, Logorrhea.

Prevalence: Total number of cases of a disease existing a given point in time (point prevalence) or during a specified time period (period prevalence). See also Incidence.

Preventive psychiatry: Branch of preventive medicine dealing with mental disorders. Encompassed within its scope are measures to prevent mental disorders (primary prevention); measures to limit the severity of illness, as through early case finding and treatment (secondary prevention); and measures to reduce disability after a disorder (tertiary prevention).

Primal repression: See Repression.

Primal scene: In psychoanalysis, the real or fantasied observation by a child of sexual intercourse, particularly between his parents.

Primal therapy: A system of psychotherapy developed by Arthur Janov. The patient undergoes a short period (2 to 3 weeks) of intensive individual therapy, preceded by a 24 hour period of isolation and followed by a few months of group therapy with other post primal patients. During the therapy the patient is encouraged to experience a series of what Janov calls primal, in which the patient relieves the prototypical traumatic events that originally crystallized his suffering and thereby created his neurosis.

Primary degenerative dementia, presenile onset: See Alzheimer's disease. Pick's disease, Presenile dementia

Primary gain: Reduction of anxiety achieved by a defense mechanism; relief from tension or conflict through neurotic illness. See also Secondary gain.

Primary prevention: See preventive psychiatry.

Primary process: In psychoanalysis, the mental activity directly related to the functions of the id and characteristic of unconscious mental processes. The primary process is marked by privative, prelogical thinking and by the tendency to seek immediate discharge and gratification of instinctual demands. It is seen in infancy and in dreams.

Primary reinforcer: See Reinforcement.

Prince, Morton (1854–1929): American neurologist and psychiatrist known for his study of multiple personalities.

Principal diagnosis: The condition established after study to be chiefly responsible for the admission of the patient to the hospital or for outpatient treatment.

Principle of closure: Probably the most powerful of the Gestalt principles of perceptual organization, the principle of closure refers to the perceptual tendency towards complete forms and shapes. So a set of disconnected lines is likely to be seen as indicating an incomplete shape if this is at all possible, rather than simply being taken as independent stimuli. The principle of closure also extends into the perception of movement, in the form of stroboscopic motion and the phi phenomenon.

Principle of parsimony: See Occam's razor.

Principle of proximity: One of the Gestalt principles of perceptual organizations, which states that stimuli which occur close to one another will tend to be perceived as grouped together, all other things being equal.

Principles of similarity: One of the Gestalt principles of perceptual organization which states that similar will tend to be perceived as grouped together, all other things being equal.

Prison psychosis: Psychotic reaction to incarceration or to the prospect of incarceration. See also Ganser's syndrome.

Privilege: Legal term referring to the legal right of a patient to prevent his physician from testifying about information obtained in the course of treatment. It is the legal formulation of the ethical principle of confidentiality. In some states, information obtained in the course of the doctor-patient relationship is considered privileged communication.

Privileged communication: The laws of evidence in some jurisdictions provide that certain kinds of communication between persons who have a special confidential or fiduciary relationship will not be divulged. The psychotherapist-patient and doctor-patient relationship is, in some states, considered privileged communication. But the law is in a state of flux and there are many exceptions – e.g., a patient who sues, basing the suit in whole or in part on psychiatric considerations, may waive privilege. It is important to realize that the privilege belongs to the patient not to the therapist, and can be waived only by the patient unless otherwise provided by the law of legal proceedings.

Proactive interference: When information which has already been learned interferes with the learning of new material. Proactive interference is particularly common when someone is trying to learn a set of similar tasks within a relatively short period of time. It may account for the primacy effect.

Process schizophrenia: Unofficial term for schizophrenia attributed more to endogenous factors than to specific environmental influence. See also Reactive schizophrenia.

Prodrome: An early symptom of a disease. It often serves as a warning or premonitory sign of the approach of a morbid condition.

Programmed learning: A technique for applying operant conditioning to classroom learning. The information is broken down into small units, and presented to the student in such a way that one unit leads naturally on to the next. Each unit involves some kind of simple test question. If the student gets it right, they move onto the next state; if they get it wrong, they go back over the relevant material again. The idea is that this approach maximizes positive reinforcement (in the shape of correct answers) for the student, thus maximizing interest in and application to the learning process. As an example of pure operant conditioning, programmed learning has been criticized on the grounds that knowledge of results is a cognitive rather than a behavioural reinforcement. In classroom practice, the absence of social interaction between student and teacher has often presented its own difficulties, and programmed learning has tended to be introduced in a manner that is far more limited than was previously envisaged.

Projection: Unconscious defense mechanism in which a person attributes to another those generally unconscious ideas, thoughts, feelings, and impulses that are in himself undesirable or unacceptable. Projection protects the person from anxiety arising from an inner conflict. By externalizing whatever is unacceptable the person deals with it as a situation apart from himself. See also Blind spot, Schreber case.

Projective set: A type of psychological test with loosely structures test material that requires the subject to reveal his own feelings, personality, or psychopathology. Examples include the Rorschach Test and the Thematic Appreciation Test.

Prosocial behaviour: The opposite of antisocial behaviour; prosocial is used to refer to behaviour which involves helping others or making a positive gesture towards them in some way. It is commonly used in discussions of bystander intervention and altruistic behaviour.

Proprioception: See Kinesthetic sense.

Prosopagnosia: An inability to recognize familiar faces that is not due to impaired visual acquity or level of consciousness.

Prototaxic: A term introduced by Harry Stack Sullivan to refer to primitive illogical thought processes. See Primary process.

Pseudo aggression: A neurotic defense in which the patient denies his basic masochistic feelings and displays them, instead, as false aggression.

Pseudo authenticity: False or copied expression of thoughts and feelings.

Pseudo collusion: Sense of closeness, relationship, or cooperation that is not real but is based on transference.

Pseudocyesis: It is defined as the conviction of a non-pregnant woman that she is pregnant, occurring with symptoms associated with pregnancy. It excludes delusions of pregnancy during psychosis, feigned pregnancy in malingering, endocrinal disorders like the galactorrhoea amenorrhoea syndrome and pelvic or abdominal tumors causing symptoms of pregnancy.

Pseudodementia: A dementia-like disorder that can be reversed by appropriate treatment and is not caused by organic brain disease. The term is also used to describe a condition in which the patient shows an exaggerated indifference to his surroundings in the absence of a mental disorder. It also occurs in depression and factitious disorders.

Pseudofamily: See Care-giver

Pseudologia fantastica: A disorder characterized by uncontrollable lying in which the patient elaborates extensive fantasies that he freely communicates.

Pseudo mutuality: Phenomenon displayed by married couples and families in which the members are united by their capacity to satisfy each others neurotic needs.

Pseudoschizophrenia: A group of disorders resembling schizophrenia in some of their clinical features but belonging to different diagnostic categories. According to Rumke the 'pseudoschizophrenias' include manic-depressive illness, organic states, severe hysterical reactions, obsessive-compulsive conditions, and schizoid and paranoid personality disorders. See also: latent schizophrenia.

Psychalgia: See psychogenic pain disorder.

Psychasthenia: Obsolete term used by Janet to describe a syndrome characterized by fears and phobia.

Psyche: The mind. The psychoanalytical literature, following Freud, uses psyche and mind synonymously. However whereas 'mind; tends to be used in contrast to 'body', 'psyche' isusually contrasted with 'soma'.

Psychiatric nurse: See Nurse, psychiatric.

Psychiatric social worker: See Social worker, psychiatric.

Psychiatrist: A medical doctor whose speciality is the study and treatment of mental disorders.

Psychiatry: The branch of medicine that deals with diagnosis, treatment and prevention of mental disorders.

Psychic determinism: Freudian concept that all mental phenomena have specific antecedent causes, often operating on an unconscious level.

Psychic energizer: Any Antidepressant drug.

Psychoactive drug: Any drug that alters mental or behavioural processes.

Psychoanalysis: A theory of human mental phenomena and behaviour, a method of psychic investigation and research, and a form of psychotherapy originally formulated by Sigmund Freud. As a technique for exploring the mental processes psychoanalysis includes the use of free association and the analysis and interpretation of dreams, resistances, and transferences. As a form of psychotherapy, it uses the investigative technique, guided by Freud's libido and instinct theories and by ego psychology to gain insight into a person's unconscious motivations, conflicts, and symbols and thus to effect a change in his maladaptive behaviour. Several schools of thought are loosely referred to as psychoanalytic at present. Psychoanalysis is also known as analysis in depth and its practitioners are known as psychoanalysts. See also Reconstructive psychotherapy.

Psychoanalyst: A psychotherapist, usually a psychiatrist, who has had training in psychoanalysis and who uses its techniques in a treatment setting.

Psychoanalytic group psychotherapy: A method of group psychotherapy pioneered by Alexander Wolf and based on the operational principles of individual psychoanalytic therapy. Analysis and interpretation of a patient's transference, resistances, and defenses are modified to take place in a group setting. Although strictly designating treatment structures to produce significant character change, the term encompasses the same approach in groups conducted on more superficial levels for smaller goals.

Psychobiology: Term introduced by Adolf Meyer and referring to the study of the human being as an integrated unit, incorporating psychological, social and biological functions.

Psychodrama: Psychotherapy method originated by J.L. Moreno in which personality make-up, interpersonal relationships, conflicts, and emotional problems are expressed and explored through dramatization. The therapeutic dramatization of emotional problems includes (1) protagonist or patient, the person who presents and acts out his emotional problems with the help of (2) auxiliary egos, persons trained to act and dramatize the different aspects of the patient that are called for in a particular scene in order to help him express his feelings. and (3) the director, leader, or therapist, the person who guides those involved in the drama for a fruitful and therapeutic session. See also Hypnodrama, Improvization, Reenactment, Role playing, self realization. Theater of spontaneity.

Psychodynamics: The systematized knowledge and theory of human behaviour and its motivation the study of which depends largely upon the functional significance of emotion. Psychodynamic recognize the role of unconscious motivation in human behaviour. The science of psychodynamics assumes that one's behaviour is determined by past experience, genetic endowment, and current reality.

Psychogenic: Produced or caused by mental factors, rather than organic factors. It usually refers to a symptom or an illness.

Psychogenic amnesia: A dissociative disorder characterized by the sudden inability to recall information stored in memory in the absence of an underlying organic mental disorder. When associated with travel to another locate and the assumption of a new identity, the condition is called psychogenic fugue.

Psychogenic dysmenorrhoea: Abdominal pain or cramps occurring during menstruation (and not as part of the premenstrual tension syndrome), for which underlying psychological causes have been postulated without being convincingly demonstrated. See also: premenstrual tension syndrome.

Psychological cyclical vomiting: Sudden attacks of vomiting in children, which. In the absence of gastrointestinal disease, last for several days and cease abruptly, with a tendency to reoccur after intervals of several weeks or longer. Emotional difficulties are thought to underline the disturbance.

Psychogenic fugue: A dissociative disorder characterized by periods of total amnesia in which one travels and assumes a new identity. See also Fugue, psychogenic amnesia.

Psychogenic hiccough, psychogenic cough: Hiccough (singultus), the involuntary spasm of the inspiratory muscles followed by an abrupt closure of the glottis, can be a normal transient occurrence after eating or drinking or, when persisting or reoccurring frequently, a symptom of a somatic disease. Psychogenic cauzation has been surmised, but not proved, in cases where no physical cause is found. In contrast, a dry, unproductive cough in the absence of respiratory or central nervous system disease, is more readily accepted to be a neurotic symptom or an isolated psychogenic tic.

Psychogenic pain disorder: A disorder in which the predominant feature is the complaint of pain on the absence adequate physical findings and in which there is evidence that psychological factors play a causal role. It is also known as psychalgia.

Psychohistory: As approach to history that examines events within a psychological framework. If attempts to connect individual and collective ideas and emotions with wider historical currents.

Psychokinesis: Phenomenon in which directed thought processes influence physical events. See also parapsychology.

Psycholexicology: The psychological study of words and their meanings (believed to be coined by Geroge A. Miller).

Psycholinguistics: The exploration of the psychological factors involved in the development and use of language.

Psychologic autopsy: Post-mortem evaluations of the psychodynamics leading to a person's suicide.

Psychological defence system: See Defence mechanism.

Psychologist: A person trained in psychology, usually with a graduate degree (M.A. Ph.D.).

Psychologist, clinical: A psychologist with additional training and experience in a clinical setting who specializes in the evaluation and treatment of human mental disorders.

Psychology: Traditionally defined as 'the science of mind' but of recent years, and increasingly, the science of behaviour'. Qualifies of 'psychology' refer either to specialized branches of the subject-abnormal, normal, animal, human, child, genetic (developmental, industrial, social, clinical, academic, educational – or to different systems of thought – behaviouristic Gestalt, psychoanalytical), Freudian, Jugian, adlerian. Term was coined by Gockel.

Psychometry: The science to testing and measuring mental and psychologic ability, efficiency potentials, and functioning, including psychopathologic components.

Psychomotor: Combined physical and mental activity.

Psychomotor agitation: Generalized physical and emotional overactivity in response to internal and/or external stimuli, as in hypomania.

Psychomotor retardation: Slowing of mental and physical activity, common in depression.

Psychopathic personality: See Antisocial personality disorder.

Psychopathology: See abnormal.

Psychopharmacology: The study of the mental and behavioural effects of drugs.

Psychophysiological disorder: See psychosomatic disorder.

Psychopolitics: A relatively new term that has been applied in two different contexts. According to one usage, it describes the psychological dimension of political behaviour, such as the reciprocal influence on persons of political environments and their societies. According to another image, it refers to specific tactics of politicians that are intended to yield benefits to them through the use of psychological strategies.

Psychosexual development: A series of stages from infancy to adulthood, relatively fixed in time, determined by the interaction between a person's biologic drives and the environment. With resolution of this interaction, a balanced, reality-oriented development takes place; with disturbance, fixation and conflict ensure. This disturbance may remain latent or give rise to character logic or behavioural disorders. The stages of development are:

(a) **Oral:** The earliest of the stage of infantile psychosexual development, lasting from birth to 12 months or longer. Usually subdivided into two stages: The oral erotic, relating to the pleasurable experience of sucking, and the oral sadistic, associated with aggressive biting. Both oral eroticism and sadism continue into adult life in disguised and sublimated forms, such as the character traits of demandingness or pessimism. Oral conflict, as a general and pervasive influence, might underlie the psychologic determinants of addictive disorders, depression, and some functional psychotic disorders.

(b) **Anal:** The period of pregenital psychosexual development, usually from one to three years, in which the child has particular interest and concern with the process of defecation and the sensations connected with the anus. The pleasurable part of the experience is termed anal eroticism. See also anal character.

(c) **Phallic:** The period from about 2.5 to 6 years, during which sexual interest curiosity, and pleasurable experience center about the penis in boys, and in girls, to lesser extent, the clitoris.

(d) **Oedipal:** Overlapping some with the phallic stage, this phase (ages four to six) represents a time of inevitable conflict between the child and parents. The child must desexualize the relationship to both parents in order to retain affectionate kinship with both of them. The process is accomplished by the internalization of the images of both parents, thereby giving more definite shape to the child's superego. With this internalization largely completed, the regulation of self-esteem and moral behaviour comes from within.

Pyschosexual disorder: A disorder of sexual functioning that is caused, wholly or partly, by psychological factors. See also Ego-dystonic homosexuality, Gender identity disorder, Paraphilia, Psychosexual dysfunction.

Psychosexual dysfunction: A psychosexual disorder characterized by an inhibition in sexual desire or a psychophysiological functions. In DSM the psychosexual dysfunctions include inhibited sexual desire, inhibited sexual excitement, inhibited female orgasm, inhibited sexual desire, inhibited sexual excitement, inhibited female orgasm, inhibited male orgasm, premature ejaculation, functional dyspareunia, functional vaginismus.

Psychosis: A mental disorder in which a person's thoughts, affective response, ability to recognize reality, and ability to communicate and relate to others are sufficiently impaired to grossly interfere with his capacity to deal with reality. The classical characteristics of psychosis are: impaired reality testing, hallucinations, delusions, illusions. The term was first used by Feuchtersleben in 1846.

Psychosis, reactive: A term employed to designate a group of psychoses causally related to a preceding external event, e.g., personal loss, bereavement, insult, natural disaster. The psychoses are mostly of brief duration, often but not always remitting with the recession of the provoking factor. Their form and content tend to reflect the nature of the precipitant and to fall into three broad clinical categories; disorders of consciousness (confusional), disorders of affect (depression), and delusional disorders (paranoid). This classification of the reactive psychoses, originally delineated by Wimmer (1916) as psychogenic psychoses, is widely but not universally accepted. In ICD, the term refers to a small group of psychotic conditions that are largely or entirely attributable to a recent life experience. The term should not be used for the wider range of psychoses in which environmental; factors play some (but not major) part in etiology. *Synonym*: psychogenic psychosis.

Psychosis reactive depressive type: A depressive psychosis which can be similar in its symptoms to manic-depressive psychosis, depressed type, but is apparently provoked by a saddening stress such as bereavement or a severe disappointment or frustration. Compared with manic-depressive psychosis, depressed type, there may be less clinical variation of symptoms and the delusions are more often understandable in the context of the life experiences. There is usually a serious disturbance of behaviour, e.g., major suicidal attempt. *Synonyms*: reactive depressive psychosis; psychogenic depressive psychosis.

Psychosis reactive, excitative type: An affective psychosis similar to manic depressive psychosis, manic type, but apparently provoked by emotional stress.

Psychosocial deprivation: Deprivation of social and intellectual stimulation. It is believed to be causative factor in mental retardation and emotional disorders in children.

Psychosocial development: Developmental progress of a person with regard to social relations and social reality as primarily described by Eric Erikson. Specified developmental tasks characterize successive chronological periods from infancy through maturity. The major tasks and their periods are: trust versus mistrust (infancy), autonomy versus doubt (toddler), initiative versus guilt (preschool), industry versus inferiority (school age), identity versus identity diffusion (adolescence), intimacy versus isolation (young adulthood), generativity versus self absorption (adulthood), integrity versus despair (mature age).

Psychosocial dwarfism: Shunted growth and failure to thrive in childhood which are reversible and have been attributed to the psychological effects of distorsions of the parent-child relationship. The evidence for a primary psychological cauzation is not disputed, and inadequate food intake, usually masked by psychosocial problems in the family, is thought to be the principal factor. *Synonym*: deprivation dwarfism.

Psychosocial stressor: A factor is judged to be a significant contributor to the development of exacerbation of a psychiatric disorder. Examples include marriage, death of a spouse, illness, work problems, change in residence, and natural disaster.

Psychosomatic disorder: A disorder characterized by physical symptoms caused by psychological factors. It usually involves a single organ system inverted by the autonomic nervous system. The physiological and organic changes stem from a sustained emotional disturbance. It was previously known as psycho physiological disorder. In DSM, it is called psychological factor affecting physical condition. See also Anaclitic therapy.

Psychotherapist: A person trained to treat mental, emotional, and behavioural disorders. See also Active therapist; Passive therapist; Psychiatrist, psychoanalyst, psychologist, clinical: psychotherapy.

Psychotherapy: A form of treatment for mental illness and behavioural disturbances in which a trained person establishes a professional contract with the patient and through definite therapeutic communication, both verbal and nonverbal, attempts to alleviate the emotional disturbance, reverse or change maladaptive patterns of behaviour, and encourage personality growth development. Psychotherapy is distinguished from such other forms of psychiatric treatment as the use of drugs and electroshock therapy. See also Brief Psychotherapy.

Psychotic: A person suffering from a psychosis. See also Psychosis

Psychotic depressive reaction: Psychosis distinguished by depressed mood precipitated by some event, usually in a person who had not previously demonstrated severe depression. In DSM, called major depressive disorder, single episode with mood-congruent psychotic features.

Puerperal psychosis: See Postpartum psychosis.

Punishment: The application of some kind of penalty or unpleasant event in order to suppress an unwanted form of behaviour. Although punishment is commonly used as a means of behavioural control, there is some evidence to suggest that it is of limited value by comparison with more directive approach such as the direct rewarding of desired behaviour which occurs in operant conditioning. Note that punishment is not a form of negative reinforcement. See physical punishment, psychological punishment.

Q

Quaalude: A sedative hypnotic (methaaualone) which is frequently abused because of its alleged aphrodisiac properties.

Quadrangular therapy: A type of marital therapy that involves four people: the married pair and each spouse's therapist.

Q-sort: A test often utilized in conjection with client-centered therapy, to evaluate the individual's self-esteem in their own terms. The Q-sort consists of set of cards, each of which provides a short statement about character or personality, which may be positive, neutral or negative. Clients are asked to sort the cards into piles which express how closely the statements fit with the individual's own self-concept e.g., 'very like me', 'unlikeme' etc. When all the cards have been sorted, the client is asked to sort them again, but this; in terms of their ideal self; 'myself as I would like to be'. The similarity or otherwise; between the two sets of card-sorts provides a correlation coefficient indicative of the individual's esteem. Among other uses, the Q-sort has been employed in studies of the efficacy of client-centered therapy.

Qualitative difference: A difference in kind, not simply in amount. If two things are qualitatively different, it implies that arithmetic comparisons between them are not appropriate, as they are of a different nature, like chalk and cheese. See also quantitative difference.

Quantitative variable: An object to observation which varies in manner or disagree in such a way it may be measured.

Quantity: In this Project for a Scientific psychology which has written in 1895 but only published posthumously in 1950. Freud used 'Q' to represent whatever it is that distinguishes activity from rest in the nervous system and which is capable of being quantified. Q was conceived as being attached to neurons and of being capable of passing from one neurone to another.

Quantum: Literally 'an amount' but usually, as in quantum physics the discrete unit into which a quantifiable entity is divisible. The classical theory postulated the existence of quanta of psychic energy which are generated in the Id, which are capable of being discharged in action and of being bound (attached) to those mental structures which constitute the Ego.

Quota sampling: A system of obtaining a sample for a study which involves identifying a set of representative sub-groups within the population, and taking a number of subjects from each of these sub-groups. The size of each sub-group in the sample depends on its proportional size in the original population. For instance, in a study of student attitudes to their Technical College, the sample would be picked to represent the same proportions of different types of students as were found in the college as a whole-if 10% of the students were on same day-release courses, then 10% of the sample would be drawn from the day-release students. See also sampling.

R

Race differences: Group differences between different races identified by use of psychometric tests. Because these tests usually measure something valued by European culture, and because their objectivity has been overestimated, findings of lower scores, for example on intelligence tests, of ethnic minority groups have been used as the basis for claims of racial superiority. These claims have then led to a rather more careful inspection of the evidence and it is now recognized that neither race nor intelligence can be defined or measured with enough accuracy to justify claims about the relationships between them.

Racism: Discrimination, prejudice or unfair practice towards someone which occurs purely on the basis of their ethnic group or skin colour.

Random: A statistical term that means occurring by chance or without attention to selection or planning. A random sample of a given population consists of a group of subjects selected in such a manner that each member of the population has an equal probability of being selected for the sample.

Random sample: A group of subjects selected in such a way that each member of the population from which the sample is derived has an equal or known change (probability) of being chosen for the sample.

Range: A statistical measure of the variability of a set of values defined as the difference between the largest value and the smallest value.

Rank, Otto (1884–1939): Austrian psychoanalyst, one of Freud's earliest followers and the long-time secretary and recorder of the minutes of the Vienna Psychoanalytic society. His works include—The Trauma of Birth and The Myth of the Birth of the Hero. He split with Freud on the significance of the birth trauma, which he used as a basis of brief psychotherapy.

Rapid eye movement (REM) sleep: A form of sleep in which the body remains comatose, except for the eye muscles, which move rapidly and continuously. When woken from REM sleep, subjects often report dreaming, and if an external stimulus, such as being lightly sprayed with cold water, is applied at this time, the dream content is likely to reflect the stimulus; in their case the subject might dream of being out in the rain. REM sleep occurs in phases throughout the night. Each phase usually lasts about 20 minutes, before the subject passes on the one of the deeper, quiescent levels of sleep. The phases become longer and more frequent during the course of sleep. Over the life span the time spent in REM sleep drops from about 8 hours in the newborn to about 1.5 hours in the elderly. The function of REM sleep is disputed, with theories ranging from those that see it as functional either in physiological restorative processes or as the phase in which the information acquired during the previous day is processed, to theories that it is left over from a previous stage of evolution. REM sleep is also known as paradoxical sleep.

Rapport: Conscious feeling of harmonious accord, sympathy, and mutual responsiveness between two or more persons. Rapport contributes to an effective therapeutic process in both group and individual settings. See also Countertransference, Transference.

Rapture of the deep syndrome: Psychosis seen in scuba and deep-sea divers. It is also known as nitrogen narcosis because of its association with excessive blood nitrogen levels. Sensory deprivation may also contribute to this acute, self-limited mental disorder.

Rat Man: Nickname given in a analytical literature of the patient described by Freud in his paper "Notes upon a case of Obsessional Neurosis" (1909).

Rational-emotive therapy (RET): A form of cognitive psychotherapy development by Albert Ellis. It is based on the idea that people make common logical errors, e.g., believing that it is necessary to be competent in every way, to have everyone love you, and to have whatever you want immediately. RET takes the form of persuading the client, by cognitive, emotional and behavioural means, to see persuading the client, by cognitive, emotional and behavioural means, to see things differently (correctly) so that their behaviour will be less destructive.

Rationalization: An intelligence test which is designed to be culture fair. The test consists of a series of grids or matrices of 8 patterns from which the 9th can be deduced logically, and a set of patterns of which one is the missing 9th pattern and therefore the correct answer. The special feature of the test is that it is entirely non-verbal and it is even possible to administer it to someone with whom the tester shares no language at all. Despite the attempt of Raven to make the test independent of culture, it still reflects some cultural assumptions and experience. Three examples of these assumptions are: 1. solving a puzzle whenever it is presented to you. 2. geometric shapes can be manipulated according to rules. 3. familiarity with two-dimensional representation (line drawings). In many cultures manipulation of and or interest in abstract forms of this kind are not regarded as particularly desirable human activities.

Ray, Issac (1807–1881): One of the original 13 founders of the American Psychiatric Association. He is famous for his treatise on Medical Jurisprudence of Insanity (1837).

Reactance: The tendency of people to be made uncomfortable by any restriction of their freedom of choice. Once such pressure is perceived people will often act in opposition to it.

Reaction: This is used rather loosely for any changes in the psychological state which is brought about by external events which do not damage the brain. Jaspers has defined a reactive psychiatric illness as 'one in which there is a clear relation between the illness and the alleged cause; the content of the illness is the same as the cause, and if the cause can be reversed the illness will disappear'.

Reaction formation: An unconscious defense mechanism in which a person develops a socialized attitude or interest that is the direct antithesis of some infantile wish or impulse that he harbours either consciously or unconsciously. One of the earliest and most unstable defense mechanisms, it is closely related to repression; both are defenses against impulses or urges that are unacceptable to the ego.

Reaction range: A broad range of potential reactions to deprived, average, and enriched environments set by a person's heredity.

Reaction time: A measure of how quickly a person can produce an accurate response to a stimulu. Reaction time has been used by psychological researchers in a wide range of investigations, including ageing, decision-making, drug effects and vigilance. It provides a rapid and reliable measure, which is highly sensitive to disturbance by additional or extraneous factors.

Reactive depression: This term is used by many English-speaking psychiatrists in a rather ill-defined way. It can mean a state of unhappiness which has occurred as a response to some psychological trauma or, in other words, excessive normal unhappiness. It can also mean a depressive illness which has been provoked by a psychological upset or in which the symptoms fluctuate in response to environmental changes.

Reactive disorder: Mental disorder judged to be a reaction to one or more life events or circumstances, without which the disorder would not have occurred. See also Brief reactive psychosis. Reactive depression. Reactive schizophrenia.

Reactive schizophrenia: Unofficial term for schizophrenia attributed primarily to predisposing or precipitating environmental factors. See also Process schizophrenia.

Reality adaptation: The process of becoming adapted to the external environment. According to classical theory, the infant is totally maladapted and obeys the Pleasure-principle without reference to external reality.

Reality anxiety: In Freud's classification of anxiety, he included those situations in which the anxiety is justified by a real external threat. See moral anxiety.

Reality principle: According to Freud, mental activity is governed by two principles; the pleasure principle and the Reality principle, the former leading to relief of instinctual tension by hallucinatory wish-fulfillment the latter to instinctual gratification by accommodation to the facts of and the objects existing within the external world. According to Freud's original formulations, the reality principle is acquired and learned during development, whereas the pleasure principle is acquired and learned during development, whereas the pleasure principle is innate and primitive.

Reality testing: Fundamental ego function that consists of tentative actions that test and objectively evaluate the nature and the limits of the environment. It includes the ability to differentiate between the external world and the internal world and to accurately judge the relation between the self and the environment. Falsification of reality, as with massive denial or projection, indicates a severe disturbance of ego functioning and/or the perceptual and memory processes upon which it is partly based.

Recall: The process of bringing a memory into consciousness. Recall is often used to refer to the recollection of facts, events and feelings that occurred in the immediate past.

Recency effect: A learning effect in which the items which occurred most recently in a sequence are more likely to be recalled than those which occurred earlier on.

Receptor: The term is usually used to mean sense receptor, a specialized cell or group of cells which picks up sensory information, either from within (see proprioceptors) or outside of the body, and converts it into electrical impulses for transmission to the central nervous system. So, for example, the light-sensitive rod and cone cells of the eye are receptors, as are the hair cells in a the organ of Corti in the ear, and the pressure-sensitive cells in the skin.

Receptor site: A location on the dendrite of a neurone, opposite a synaptic knob, which is sensitive to and readily absorbs a specific chemical. The appropriate chemical is released into the synaptic cleft from vesicles on the synaptic knob of the opposing neurone, and functions as neurotransmitter, rendering the receiving neurone more or less ready to fire. Receptor sites may also pick up chemicals with a similar structure, and many psychoactive drugs have their effect by being taken up at receptor sites appropriate for other chemicals: the hallucinogens LSD and psilocybin are picked up at receptor sites sensitive to the neurotransmitter serotonin, while opiates such as herein and morphine are picked up at sites appropriate for the enkephalin and endorphins.

Recidivism: Repeated legal offences, such that the person concerned, the recidivist appears in court on several occupations, not just once. A certain amount of work on juvenile delinquency reported by Rutter suggests that recidivism links very strongly with a continually stressful home life, at least for teenagers.

Reciprocal altruism: Helping behaviour which occurs is a social context such that an individual, person or animal who receives help, in turn helps the individual who originally helped him. Reciprocal altruism often occurs over extended periods of time, and may not be recognized by a short-term ethological study.

Reciprocal inhibition and desensitization: A kind of behaviour therapy in which a person is conditioned to associate comfortable, supportive surroundings with anxiety-producing stimuli, thus decreasing the anxiety associated with those stimuli.

Reciprocal linking: The name given to a positive relationship between two or more people in which each participant likes the other(s). Positive feelings which are received from someone are reciprocated, i.e., the same degree of positive feeling is directed towards that person.

Recognition: The second form of remembering identified by Ebbinghaus, and one which is used extensively by human beings. Ebbinghaus, working with lists of nonsense syllables, demonstrated that material which cannot be recalled may nonetheless be recognized as having been in a previously learned set of information, if it is presented to a subject.

Reconstruction: Also sometimes known as red integration, this is the third of the four basic forms by which memory may be demonstrated, according to the work of Ebbinghaus. Once subjects to recognize or recall the items learned, they are often able to re-construct the list in its original sequence, if provided with the relevant items. Although they will not experience a specific memory of the list, one particular sequence often 'feels more right' than any other arrangement.

Reconstructive psychotherapy: A form of therapy that seeks not only to alleviate symptoms but also to produce alternations in maladaptive mental and behavioural patterns and to develop new adaptive approaches to problems in living. That aim is achieved by bringing into conscious awareness insight into conflicts, fears, and inhibitions. See also Psychoanalysis.

Recreational drugs: which are consumed primarily for enjoyment or appreciation of their effects, rather than for medicinal purposes. These include legal drugs such as alcohol, nicotine, and caffeine and illegal drugs such as marijuana, amphetamines and heroin. The use of recreational drugs in some form occurs in all known human societies, and in some cultures includes the use of very powerful hallucinogens such as mescaline. In general, the more powerful drugs are consumed within some kind of ritualized setting, while less potent ones such as marijuana are taken more casually. Within Western societies, however, the rituals are confined to subcultural habits, and are not often used as a framework for the experience of the drug itself.

Reductionism: A form of argument which takes the view that an event, behaviour or phenomenon can be understood as being nothing but its behaviorists that human experience could be seen as nothing but combination of S-R links; or the view that behaviour may be understood as nothing but the action of 'selfish genes' are both reductionist arguments. Although often superficially appealing, reductionist argument ignores other levels of explanation, such as cognitive explanation or experimental/social factors in understanding the phenomenon, and as such provide a limited understanding of the event under study. Note that even if the most extreme reductionist position is true and all human functioning is the result of the activities of sub-atomic particles, it would be nonsense to try to explain a human activity such as a joke in these terms.

Redundancy: A term used mostly in information theory for the extent to which a message does not provide new information.

Reenactment: In psychodrama, the acting out of a past experience as if it were happening in the present, so that a person can feel, perceive, and act as he did the original time.

Registration: See Memory.

Regression: Unconscious defense mechanism in which a person undergoes a partial or total return to earlier patters of adaptation. Regression is observed in many psychiatric conditions, particularly schizophrenia.

Regressive-reconstructive approach: A psychotherapeutic procedure in which regression is made an integral element of the treatment process. An original traumatic situation is reproduced to gain new insight and to effect personality change and emotional maturation. See also Psychoanalysis. Reconstructive psychotherapy.

Rehabilitation: All methods and techniques used in an attempt to achieve maximal function and optimal adjustment in a given patient; the physical, mental, social and vocational preparation of a patient for the fullest possible life compatible with his abilities and disabilities. In as much as the process aims also to prevent relapses or recurrences of the patient's condition, it is sometimes called tertiary prevention.

Rehearsal: The repetition of information for the purpose of improving subsequent retention.

Reich, Wilhelm (1897–1957): Austrian psychoanalyst who emigrated to the United States in 1939. He is best noted for his theory of neurosis, which he believed was associated with incomplete release of tension and energy during orgasm. He coined the term "orgone" for a kind of universally pervasive physical and biological energy that was typified by the pent-up libidinal energy that sought free expression and release through orgasm.

Reification: Treating ideas or concepts as if they were objects or facts. For example, starting from the fact that people can be seen to behave more or less intelligently, and going on to assume that there is a 'thing' called intelligence. It is easy to slip into reification when talking about cognitive processes, for example in Broadband's filter model there is a box labeled 'filter' which is used to indicate a process. The mistake is to represent it as if it must be a mechanism. Another form of this error is psychology is to define a possible phenomenon and then assume it is a fact which then has to be explained. For example, there was a long period in which different theories were proposed to account for some children being obedient and other disobedient, before researches observed real children and found that none were either consistently obedient or consistently disobedient. The fact that were have a good explanation for something (say, male aggressiveness) does not prove that thing exists. See also labeling.

Reik Theodor (1888–1969): Psychoanalyst and early follower of Freud, who considered Reik one of his most brilliant pupils. Freud's book The Question of Lay Analysis was written to defend Reik's ability to practice psychoanalysis without medical training. Reik made many valuable contribution to psychoanalysis on the subjects of religion, masochism, and therapeutic technique. See also Third ear.

Reincarnation: The belief those after death people are reborn either as another person or in some other animate form.

Reinforcement: Process whereby any event or stimulus contingent on an operant response increases the probability of that response's recurring. Positive reinforcement refers to the process whereby a stimulus (the positive rein forcer) increases the frequency of performance of whatever response it follows. Negative reinforcement involves an aversive stimulus (the negative reinforcer), the termination of which increase the frequency of the response that terminates it. Stimuli that possess reinforcing characteristics are called primary reinforcers—for example, food. Stimuli that acquire reinforcing characteristics by being paired with primary reinforcers are called conditioned reinforcers—for example, money. See also Conditioning, Schedule of reinforcement, Token economy.

Reinforcement contingencies: The circumstances under which reinforcement will be given. These may vary naturally or be systematically carried, as in the case of behaviour shaping.

Reinforcement schedule: A particular pattern of applying partial reinforcement. There are four main types of reinforcement schedule, each of which produces a distinctive effect on the pattern of responding. Schedules may either fixed or variable; if fixed, then reinforcement is given according to a predetermined pattern; if variable, it is given according to a randomized sequence which average out at a particular number. Reinforcement may also depend on the number of responses that has been made since the last reinforcement, or the time interval which has elapsed since the last reinforcement was given. The four schedules are: fixed-ratio, fixed-interval, variable ratio and variable-interval. Fixed-ratio reinforcement produces a rapid rate of response but a low resistance to extinction. Fixed-interval reinforcement produces a low rate of response and a low resistance to extinction. Variable ratio produces a high rate of response with a high resistance to extinction. Variable-interval produces a steady regular rate of response and a high resistance to extinction.

Reinforcer: Something which strengthens a learned response; which makes a learned response more likely to occur again. In classical conditioning, the reinforcer is simply the repetition of the pairing of the unconditioned and conditioned stimuli. In operant conditioning the reinforcer is the event that occurs after the operant behaviour, making it more likely to occur again, and which may be either positive or negative.

Relatedness: Sense of sympathy and empathy with regard to other; sense of oneness with others. It is the opposite of isolation and alienation.

Relative refractory period: The period after a neurone has fired when it will only respond to a stimulus of unusual strength. This occurs after the absolute refractory period, when it will not fire at all, and reflects the cell's renewal of resources after the production of the burst of electrical energy in the form of the electrical impulse.

Relative risk: Epidemiological measure of the risk of developing a disorder in a specified subset of the population as compared with the total population or a different subset of it. Comparison is usually made between groups exposed and groups not exposed to a particular hereditary or environmental factor to gain information about the role of the factor in the disorder in question. Relative risk is then expressed as a ratio of the frequency of the disorder in exposed persons to its frequency in those not exposed.

Relative threshold: The degree by which a stimulus must increase in order for the increase to be perceived. The threshold is set at the point where 50% of changes of that magnitude are perceived, and changes in direct proportion to the intensity of the initial stimulus. The law known as *Fechner's law* expresses this relationship. See just noticeable difference.

Relaxation training: A range of techniques to bring about a relaxed state in the subject. Usually used as a component in therapy, for example in maintaining a relaxed state in a phobic patient as they approaches the feared object. Many of the techniques used in psychotherapy are based on methods developed for meditation, such as yoga, or are variations on hypnotic induction procedures.

Edmund Jacobson popularized the approach with a procedure in which the subject concentrates on, and relaxes, groups of muscles in turn. Biofeedback can also be used.

Relearning method: A method to measure retention that compares the time required to relearn material with the time used in initial learning of the material.

Relearning savings: The fourth (weakest) level of remembering identified by Ebbinghaus in his work on the memorization processes. He found that there were situations where all traces of memory of a specific set of times appeared to have been lost, in that the set could not be recalled, recognized, or reconstructed; but when the set of items was encountered again, it would take less time to re-learn than a comparable set which had not previously been learned.

Reliability: The extent to which the same test or procedure will yield the same result either over time or with different observers. The most commonly reported reliabilities are (1) *test-retest reliability* – the correlation between the first and second test of a number of subjects; (2) *the split-half reliability* – the correlation within a single test of two similar parts of the test; (3) *interrater reliability* the agreement between different individuals scoring the same procedure or observations, and (4) *alternate form*, high correlation between two forms of the same test.

Reliability paradox: A very reliable test may have low validity precisely because its results do not change i.e., does not measure true changes.

Religion: For Freud's view that religious ideas are illusions, fulfillment of the oldest, strongest and most urgent wishes of mankind, where he interprets belief in God as a response to recognition of human helplessness. Freud also described 'neurosis as an individual religiosity and religion as a universal obsessional neurosis'.

Remission: Significant improvement or recovery from a disorder; it may or may not be permanent.

Remote memory: See Long-term memory.

Remotivation: A group treatment technique used with withdrawn patients in mental hospitals.

REM sleep: Stage of sleep during which dreaming occurs and the sleep exhibits coordinated rapid eye movement (REM). The electroencephalogram demonstrates a desynchronized pattern of cerebral activity. It accounts for one-fourth to one-fifth of total sleep time.

Reparation: The process (Defence mechanism) of reducing guilt by action designed to make good the harm imagined to have been done to an ambivalently invested object; the process of re-creating an internal object which is phantasy has been destroyed. In Kleinian writings, there is a tendency to regard all creative activity as reparative and to consider reparation one of the normal processes by which the individual resolves his inherent ambivalence towards objects.

Repertory grid: A technique developed by George Kelly, for utilizing a person's personal constructs to examine the significant people in his world, and to identify actual or potential sources of psychological discomfort or stress. The repertory grid is an idiographic technique, which enables a therapist to see the patient's world as they see it, a valuable first step in most forms of therapy. The repertory grid is also used more generally in research to indicate how people perceive and understand their worlds.

Repetition–compulsion: Term used by Freud to describe what he believed to be an innate tendency to revert to earlier conditions. The concept was used by him in support of the Death-instinct concept. Since the animate develops out of the inanimate, there is, innate drive, the death-instinct, to return to the inanimate. The concept was also used to explain the general phenomenon of Resistance to therapeutic change.

Repetitive pattern: Continual attitude or mode of behaviour characteristic of a person and performed mechanically or unconsciously.

Repression: An unconscious defense mechanism in which unacceptable mental contents are banished or kept out of consciousness. A term introduced by Freud, it is important in both normal psychological development and in neurotic and psychotic symptom formation. Freud recognized two kinds of repression: (1) *repression proper* – the repressed material was once in the conscious domain; (2) *primal repression* – the repressed material was never in the conscious realm. See also Suppression. Freud distinguished manifestations of the impulse are kept unconscious. According to Freud, all ego development and adaptation to the environment are dependent on primary repression, in the absence of which impulses are discharged immediately by hallucinatory wish-fulfillment. On the other hand, excessive secondary repression leads to defective ego development and the emergence of symptoms, not sublimations.

Repressive-inspirational group psychotherapy: A type of group therapy in which discussion is intended to bolster the patients' morale and help them avoid undesired feeling. It is used primarily with large groups of seriously regressed patients in institutional settings.

Residential treatment facility: A center where the patient lives the receives treatment appropriate for his particular needs. A children's residential treatment facility ideally furnishes both educational and therapeutic experiences for the emotionally disturbed child.

Residual: The phase of an illness that occurs after remission of the florid symptoms or the full syndrome. Example: the residual states of infantile autism, attention deficit disorder and schizophrenia.

Residual schizophrenia: Schizophrenia in which the patient no longer is psychotic but does have some remaining signs of the illness.

Resistance: A conscious or unconscious opposition to the uncovering of unconscious material. Resistance is linked to underlying psychological defense mechanisms against impulses from the id that are threatening to the ego.

Resistance to extinction: How long a learned response will carry on without any further reinforcement. Resistance to extinction is often used as a measure of operant strength, in other words, to indicate how strongly something has been learned.

Respondent conditioning (classical conditioning, Pavlovian conditioning): Elicitation of a response by a stimulus that normally does not elicit that response. The response is one that is mediated primarily by the autonomic nervous system (such as .. or a change in heart rate). A previously neutral stimulus is repeatedly presented just before an unconditioned stimulus that normally elicits the response. When the response subsequently occurs in the presence of the previously neutral stimulus, it is called a conditioned response, and the previously neutral stimulus a conditioned stimulus.

Response bias: The tendency that subjects have to produce experimental responses which are socially desirable, or that they think the experimenter expects. For example, a study involving comparing reactions to sexually explicit material with reactions to neutral material may show a difference which results from the subject's unwillingness to appear overly concerned with sexual matters; or from their embarrassment. If this is not directly the topic under study, it will result in a response bias which could obscure other experimental findings.

Response generalization: The tendency to produce a learned response in conditions which are similar, though not identical to those under which the response was learned. In general, the more similar the conditions are, the stronger the response will be, known as the generalization gradient.

Response rate: How frequently a response or unit of behaviour occurs in a set period of time. Response-rate is often used as a measure of operant strength, or as an indicator of how strongly something has been learned.

Restitution: Either (1) the defensive process of reducing guilt by making amends to an ambivalently invested object or (2) the process by which schizophrenic or paranoid patient constructs delusions which restore to him a sense of significance.

Restricted affect: See Affect, restricted.

Retardation: A reduction or slowing down of mental and physical activity, as often observed in depression; psychomotor retardation. See also Mental retardation, Psychomotor.

Retention: See Memory.

Retrieval: A term used to refer to the process of remembering thing, in which the information is sent as being 'retrieved' or brought back from, some kind of storage system.

Retroactive interference: When new information which is being learned interferes with the ability to recall information which was learned previously. For example, a tennis player who takes up squash may find their tennis deteriorates for a while. See also proactive interference.

Retroflexion: A psychoanalytic term used notably by Rado to describe the turning of rage onto oneself.

Retrograde amnesia: The form of amnesia (memory disorder) where the person is unable to remember thing which happened before the event which rendered them amnesiac. Retrograde amnesia usually occurs after some form of brain damage, but can happen in a minor way after concussion. It is not uncommon for people who have been in an accident involving severe concussion to lose all memory of the few minutes leading up to the accident. See also amnesia.

Retrospective falsification: Unconscious distortion of past experiences to conform to present emotional needs.

Reversal: 1. An instinctual vicissitude. According to classical theory, instincts are capable of undergoing reversal so that sadism can change into masochism, voyeurism and exhibitionism etc, the reversal being usually, though not always from active to passive.

2. Defence mechanism which exploits the possibility of reversal. According to Anna Freud, Reaction Formation is a defence in which the ego avails itself of the instinct's capacity for reversal.

Reversibility: The operation of returning something to its original state by reversing the process which transformed it in the first case. The concept of reversibility plays an important part in Piaget's theory of cognitive development. Understanding that an operation in reversible allows one to understand important aspects of the world. Examples are: if a ball of plasticine can be rolled out into a sausage shape, it can also be rolled back into a ball. If A is larger than B, then B is smaller than A. If 3 squared is 9, then the square root of 9 is 3, Piaget saw an understanding of reversibility as an essential part of concrete operations; in particular it is necessary before conservation can be acquired.

Reward: Something which is provided for an organism, animal or human, after a desired piece of behaviour has occurred and which takes the form of something that the orgasm wants, needs, or likes. The concept particularly important in the theory of operant conditioning, where reward form positive reinforcement for learned behaviour.

Ribonucleic acid (RNA): A chemical substance involved in cellular protein synthesis. Its structure is coded for by DNA. In turn, RNA determines the sequence of amino acids in the synthesized protein molecule. It may play a critical role in memory. See also Deoxyribonuclei acid (DNA).

Ribot's law: In a demanding illness, the memory for recent events is lost before the memory for remote events (memory regression).

Right to refuse treatment: Legal doctrine holding that a person, even when involuntarily committed to a hospital, may not be forced to submit to any form of treatment against his will unless a life and death emergency exists.

Right to treatment: Legal doctrine that a facility is legally obligated to provide adequate treatment for an individual when the facility has assumed the responsibility of providing treatment.

Risky shift: A term which describes the fact that groups often take riskier decisions than the individual members of the group would take. This was first put forward by Stomer in 1961.

Ritual: Formalized activity practiced by a person to reduce anxiety in obsessive compulsive disorder. It also refers to ceremonial activity of cultural origin.

Ritualistic behaviour: Automatic behaviour of cultural or psychogenic origin.

Robotics: The area of research which involves the development of mechanical systems which can perform a set of actions in a way comparable to that of a human being. Many highly successful robotic system have been developed and applied, particularly in the manufacturing industries. They have involved considerable research not just into movement systems but also into the development of such techniques as optical scanning devices, which can identify and respond to anomalies or changes in the appearance of the material being manufactured. As such robotics is often considered to form one branch of the research into artificial intelligence.

Rogers, Carl R. (1902–1987): A psychologist, a founder of humanistic psychology and known for developing a client-centered approach to psychotherapy, which permits the patient to take the lead in the focus, pace, and direction of therapy; coined the term "self-actualization" to describe self-discovery and personal growth.

Role: Pattern or type of behaviour developed under the influence of significant people in the person's environment. When the behaviour pattern conforms with the expectations and demands of other people, it is said to be a complementary role. If it does not conform with the demands and expectation of others, it is known as a non-complementary role.

Role behaviour: Behaviour which is considered to be appropriate for someone who is playing a specific social role. For instance, someone playing the role of a shop assistant is expected to behave in certain ways, to be smart, and alert, and to demonstrate specific behaviours such as asking if a customer needs to be served or requires information about prices, etc. Other kinds of behaviour of which the person may be equally capable, such as ballroom dancing, are completely inappropriate to the social role of shop assistant. See also role expectation.

Role confusion: In Erikson's developmental theory, a state in which the identity is not well defined. It may be regarded as a temporary state (this can occur at any time of life but is particularly common during adolescence) or as the long-term consequence of having failed to establish a clear identity during adolescence. See psychosocial stages.

Role count: The sum total of social roles which an individual plays. The concept becomes particularly important in the case of those who have recently retired; the process or retirement results in a drastic reduction the number of social roles played by the individual, and some researchers consider that it is important for the retired person to replace at least some of those social roles in alternative social activities.

Role expectation: The implicit but nonetheless very clear ideas which members of a society have concerning the ways that people ought to behave when they are playing a social role in that society. Behaviour which does not conform, at least in general terms, to role expectations will usually meet with social sanctions of some kind, for example the exclusion of the person from the group.

Role play: Taking a particular role temporarily and behaving, as nearly as possible, like a person who actually holds that role. Role play is widely used in training situations and is an effective way of helping people understand what it feels like to have the given role, and allows them practice the role before being fully committed to it. It has been found that acting a role often shifts a person's opinions towards those they have been working with. Preparatory role play may also help reduce anxiety and improve performance in stressful situations such as interviews.

Role playing: Psychodrama technique in which a person is trained to function more effectively in his real-life roles. In the therapeutic setting of psychodrama. The protagonist is free to try and to fail in his role, for he is given the opportunity to try again until he succeeds. New approaches to feared situations can thus be learned and applied outside the therapeutic setting.

Rorschach test: A projective test in which the subject is asked his associations in response to a series of inkblot pictures.

Rosenthal effect: The finding by Robert Rosenthal and others that one's expectations can have an effect on an outcome that is being observed. Used particularly in connection with the finding that when teachers were told that a group of children were very bright, those children performed better than a similar group that the teachers had been told were all dull. The term is also used for various forms of experimenter effect and self-fulfilling prophecy.

Rumination: A rare eating disorder of early childhood characterized by recurrent regurgitation of food in the absence of nausea, retching, or associated gastro intestinal disorder. The regurgitated food is either ejected from the mouth or reached and reswalloed. It is also called merycism.

Rush, Benjamin (1745–1813): The father of American psychiatry. His book, Medical Inquiries and Observations upon the Diseases of the Mind (1812) was the only American textbook on psychiatry until the end of the 19th century.

S

Sadism: A paraphilia in which sexual gratification is achieved by inflicting pain or humiliation on the partner. The French writer Danatien Alphonse Francois Sade, usually called the Marquis de Sade (1740–1814) was the first to describe this condition. See also Masochism, Sadomacsochistic relationship.

Sadomasochistic relationship: A relationship in which the enjoyment of suffering by one person and the enjoyment of inflicting pain by the other person are important and complementary attractions in their ongoing interaction. See also Masochism, Sadism.

Safety need: The second level of Maslow's hierarchy of needs, safety needs refer to needs for security, shelter and freedom attack. These needs become important once basic physiological needs have been satisfied. Once the safety needs in turn have been satisfied, according to Maslow, the next level of needs, social needs, become important.

Salience: Something which is particularly noticeable or likely to be perceived. The salience of an object or event may be due to its physical properties, such as brightness and clarity; or it might arise because the object or event relates to needs, emotional states or meanings on the part of the perceiver.

Salmon, Thomas W. (1876–1927): American psychiatrist; mental hygiene, military psychiatry.

Sanatorium: An institution where patients are treated for chronic physical or mental diseases or where they are attended to during a period of recuperation.

Sandler's triad: A symptom group consisting of low self-esteem with confusion of identity, sadomasochistic behaviour towards military authorities and impotence, seen frequently as an essential part of camptocormia.

Sapphism: See Lesbianism.

Satiation: Satiation is defined operationally as the point at which an animal will no longer seek food. It is usually used in investigations of hunger or other motivational states and it implies that the underlying need is temporarily satisfied.

Satyriasis: Morbid insatiable sexual needs or desires in a man. It may be caused by organic or psychiatric factors. See also Nymphomania.

Scapegoat theory: The idea that prejudice arises from people seeking to blame others for their own negative circumstances. According to scapegoat theory, poor living conditions, economic depression and frustrating situations lead people to react in hostile ways to others; and this reaction is likely to focus on any individuals who are present but don't belong to the person's own peer group. Scapegoat theory has been put forward as an explanation for the growth of racism and sexism during times when economic circumstances are severe.

Scattering: One of the schizophrenic thinking disorders in which association are sometimes irrelevant or tangential, with the result that speech production are occasionally incomprehensible.

Schachter-Singer theory: A theory of the relationship between felt emotion and bodily conditions, it states that felt emotion is based on the interpretation of the reason for bodily arousal. Compare James Lange theory, Cannon-Bard theory.

Schedule of reinforcement: Scheme of intermittent reinforcement in which a response is not reinforced every time it occurs. Four broad classes of intermittent schedules are based on either the number of responses required before an opportunity for reinforcement is presented or the passage of a certain amount of time before a given performance is reinforced: (1) *fixed-ratio schedule,* in which a constant number of responses must occur between reinforcements; (2) *variable-ratio schedule,* in which the average number of responses between reinforcements is constant but there is a wide variation around that average in the number of responses between each reinforcement: (3) *fixed-interval schedule,* in which certain fixed amount of time must pass between opportunities for reinforcement: and (4) *variable-interval schedule,* in which the average time between reinforcement opportunities is fixed but the actual interval is variable. See also Reinforcement.

Scheid cyanotic syndrome: Scheid attempted to explain sudden death in excited manic patients and in catatonic states as a somatic condition somehow related to a somatic febrile or toxic etiology of the psychosis itself. Some believe that such deaths are due to physiological exhaustion secondary to pathologic over activity.

Schema: A hypothetical model of the way that information is stores by the brain. It is used to direct action, and in understanding the relationships between events. A schema would include all the information relation to a particular event or type of event, including representations of previous actions; theoretical and practical knowledge about the event; ideas and opinions about it, etc. The concept of schemata has formed a major part of the theory of cognitive development put forward by Piaget, and the cognitive theory of Neisser. The idea of schemata and their extension and development through experience, provides a useful model for understanding how many different levels of comprehension can be involved in both new and familiar situations. See also anticipatory schema.

Schilder, Paul (1886–1940): American neuropsychiatrist. He started the use of group psychotherapy at New York's Bellevue Hospital, combining social and psychoanalytic principles. He is best known for his work on the psychology of body image.

Schism: Hostility between parents is said to lead to schizophrenic daughter.

Schizoaffective disorder: A psychotic disorder with sign and symptoms compatible with both an affective disorder and a schizophrenic disorder.

Schizocaria: An acute form of schizophrenia, sometimes called catastrophic schizophrenia, in which the patient's personality deteriorates rapidly.

Schizoid personality disorder: A diagnostic category for persons with defects in the capacity to form social relationships but without order striking communicative or behavioural eccentricities.

Schizoidia: Schizoidism; also used synonymously with schizophrenic spectrum disorders to refer to a variety of abnormalities that are found among non-schizophrenic relatives of schizophrenic patients.

Schizophasia: A variety of schizophrenia in which there is gross speech disorder which is often in marked contrast to the intelligence shown by the patient's general behaviour.

Schizophrene: One affected by schiophrenia.

Schizophrenese: The associational defects of the schozophrenic patient as manifested in his speech.

Schizophrenia: Psychotic mental disorder characterized by disturbances in thinking, mood, and behaviour. The thinking disturbance is manifested by a distortion of reality, sometimes with delusions and hallucinations, accompanied by fragmentation of associations that results in characteristic disturbances of speech. The mood disturbance includes ambivalence and inappropriate or constricted affective responses. The behaviour disturbance may be manifested by apathetic withdrawal or bizarre activity. Formerly known as dementia preox, schizophrenia as a term was introduced by Eugen Bleuler. The causes of schizophrenia remain unknown. The types of schizophrenia include disorganized, catatonic, paranoid, undifferentiated, and residual. See also Affect, blunted; Ambulatory schizophrenia; Bleuler, Eugen; Burned-out schizopherenic; Catatonia; Hebephrenia; Latent schizophrenia; Schizoaffective disorder; Schizophreniform disorder.

Schizophrenia, latent: A term introduced by Bleuler (1911) to designate a cluster of abnormal personality traits which he attributed to an underlying schizophrenic process though positive evidence of schizophrenia was lacking. Closely related concepts are 'borderline' schizophrenia and the 'schizotypal' personality disorder. In ICD-9, the term is not recommended for general use but a description is provided for those who believe it to be useful: a condition of eccentric or inconsequent behaviour and anomalies of affect which give the impression of schizophrenia though no definite and characteristic schizophrenic anomalies, present or past, have been manifest. *Synonyms*: borderline schizophrenia; pseudoneurotic schizophrenia; pseudops- ychopathic schizophrenia; schizotypal personality disorder; schizophrenia larvata.

Schizophrenia, paraphrenic: A term applied occasionally to paranoid schizophrenic illness of relatively late onset in which the clinical picture is dominated by systematized expansive or fantastic delusions. In Leonhard's schema paraphrenia is the preferred term for all paranoid forms of schizophrenic psychosis within the 'systematic' group of the disorder.

Schizophrenia, prepsychotic: A phase that precedes the onset of a schizophrenic illness and in which the patient deviates from the premorbid state without exhibiting the characteristic symptoms of the illness *Synonym*: prodromal schizophrenia.

Schizophrenia, residual: A chronic form of schizophrenia in which the symptoms that persist from the acute phase have mostly lost their sharpness. Emotional response is blunted and thought disorder, even when gross, does not prevent the accomplishment of routine work. *Synonyms*: chronic undifferentiated schizophrenia; Restzustand (schizophrenic); schizophrenic residual state; Schizophrenic defect state.

Schizophreniform disorder: In DSM, a disorder similar to schizophrenia except that it lasts less than 6 months but more than 1 week.

Schizotypal personality disorder: Diagnostic category for persons who exhibit various eccentricities in communication or behaviour, coupled with defects in the capacity to form social relationships. The term emphasizes a possible relationship with schizophrenia. See also Latent schizophrenia, Schizoid personality disorder.

Schnauzkrapnf: Term coined by Karl Luding Kahlbaum (1828–99) for protrusion of the lips such that they resemble a snout. The condition is found almost exclusively in the catatonic form of schizophrenia.

School phobia: A young child's sudden fear of and refusal to attend school. It is usually considered a manifestation of separation anxiety.

Schreber case: One of Freud's cases. Daniel Paul Schreber's published autobiographical account, entitled Memoirs of a Neurotic (1903), was analyzed by Freud in 1911. The analysis of those memoirs permitted Freud to decipher the fundamental meaning of paranoid processes and ideas, especially the relationship between repressed homosexuality and projective defenses.

Scopophilia: Pleasure in looking. Listed by classical theory as one of the infantile, component – instincts. The spelling 'scoptophilia' dates from a mistake made by Freud's first translators.

Scotoma: In psychiatry, a figurative blind spot in a person's psychological awareness. In neurology, a localized visual field defect. See also Blind spot.

Scotomization: Defensive process by which the subject fails (consciously) to perceive circumscribed areas either of his environmental situation or of himself (derived from Scotoma, a blank area in the visual field).

Screen memory: A childhood memory which is in itself trivial but which can be treated as a dream, interpretation of its manifest content revealing a significant latent content.

Screening: Initial patient evaluation that includes medical and psychiatric history, mental status evaluation and diagnostic formulation to determine the patient's suitability for a particular treatment modality.

Secondary gain: The external gain derived from any illness, such a personal attention and service, monetary gain, disability benefits, and release from unpleasant responsibility. See also primary gain.

Secondary process: In psychoanalysis, the form of thinking that is logical, organized, reality oriented, and influenced by the demands of the environment; it characterizes the mental activity of the ego. See also Abstract thinking, Primary process, Reality principle.

Sedative: A drug that produces a calming or relaxing effect through central nervous system depression. Some drugs with sedative properties are barbiturates, chloral hydrate, paraldehyde, and bromide. See also Hypnotic.

Selection bias: The inadvertent selection of a non-representative sample of subjects or observations. A classic example is a 1936 Literacy Digest poll which predicted London's election over Roosevelt because telephone directories were used as basis for selection respondents.

Selective attention: Attention which is channeled towards certain stimuli and ignores the presence of others. The most well-known example of this is when someone is concentrating on one particular converzation among a large amount of background noise, some of which may be actually louder than the converzation being attended to. This was dubbed the cocktail party effect in the 1950s, and gave rise to a considerable amount of research, often involving dichotic listening tasks and split-span tasks. The research eventually gave rise to several different filter theories, which eventually showed that there is a considerable amount of unconscious semantic processing even of unattended information.

Self: (1) The individual's perception or awareness of herself or himself – of his or her body, abilities, personality traits, and ways of doing thing. (2) The executive functions by means of which an individual manages, copes, thinks, remembers, perceives, and plans.

Self-actualization: See Actualization.

Self-analysis: Investigation of one's own psychic components. It plays a part in all analysis, although to a limited extent, since few people are capable of sustaining independent and detached attitudes to the degree necessary for this approach to be therapeutic.

Self-awareness: Sense of knowing oneself, particularly in terms of insight into one's own psychodynamics. Self-awareness is a major goal of most psychotherapies.

Self concept: The sum total of the ways in which the individual sees her or himself. Self-concept is often considered to have two major dimensions: a descriptive component, known as the self-image, and an evaluative component, known as self-esteem, although in practice the term is more commonly used to refer to the evaluative side of self-perception.

Self-consciousness: An exaggerated awareness of one's own behaviour, feelings and appearance, combined with a belief that other people are equally aware, interested, and critical. Self-consciousness is often particularly extreme during adolescence.

Self-disclosure: The process through which one person lets himself or herself be known by another.

Self-discovery: In psychoanalysis, the freeing of the repressed ego in a person who has been brought up to submit to the wishes of the significant others around him.

Self-esteem: The personal evaluation which an individual makes of her or himself; their sense of their own worth, or capabilities. Excessively low self-esteem is regarded as indicating a likelihood of psychological disturbance, and is particularly characteristic of depression. There are several simple questionnaires which have been developed for measuring self-esteem, as well as more sophisticated tests such as the Q-sort.

Self-fulfilling prophecy: A distortion of a event or situation that eventually leads an individual to behave as he is expected to behave by others in his social setting. The classic example of the self-fulfilling prophecy in action came from work by Rosenthal, in which undergraduate students were given a set of experimental rats to train in maze-running. Despite the fact that there were no observable behavioural differences between the rats at the start of the experiment, the students were told that they could expect some to be very quick at learning the maze, while others would be very slow. The rats performed according to these predictions, because the predictions had induced expectations on the part of the students which affected how they handles the animals during training. Further studies by Rosenthal and his colleagues demonstrated the power of expectations held by teachers towards their pupils, and the self-fulfilling prophecy is now considered to be a major social influence which needs careful control in psychological investigations. See also experimenter effects.

Self-image: A person's conception of his own identity, personality and worth as a person.

Self-perception theory: The idea that we gain knowledge about ourselves by observing our own behaviour. e.g., 'I must have been hungry because I ate an extra sandwich'. Overtly such an approach may appear native, yet there is considerable evidence to suggest that people do make attributions about their own behaviour based on how they have seen themselves acting or reacting. This was given by Bem (1972).

Self-persuasion: The modifications of a person's beliefs to become consistent with what they observe about their own behaviour.

Self-realization: Psychodrama technique in which the protagonist enacts, with the aid of a few auxiliary egos, the plan of his life, no matter how remote it may be from his present situation. For instance, an accountant who has been taking singing lessons, hoping to try out for a musical comedy part in summer stock and planning to make the theater his life's work, can explore the effects of success in that venture and of possible failure and return to his old livelihood.

Self-reference: Term denoting a person's repeatedly referring the subject under discussion back to himself.

Self-schema: A cognitive generalization about the self, derived from past experience that organizers and guides the processing of self-related information contained in the invidual's social experiences. (Markus,1977).

Self-system: Sullivan's term for a personalty system designed to ward off anxiety and preserve a positive view of the self.

Semantic: To do with meaning, the intended communication or meaning which underlies any utterance or signal. The word semantic usually used in contrast with syntactic, referring to the structure of the communication (e.g., sentence structure). Such contrasts are particularly useful in examining the use of language in communication.

Semantic conditioning: A conditioning process which uses a stimulus-response form of learning like operant or classical conditioning, in which the individual is trained to respond to the meaning of a word or phrase. Although the perception of meaning is a cognitive rather than a behavioural event, studies of semantic conditioning are report to show all the characteristics of behavioural conditioning, such as generalization, discrimination, etc. However, there is a certain amount of evidence to indicate that semantic conditioning only 'works' if the subjects catch on to what the study is about, and decide to cooperate.

Semantic differential: A method of measuring the connotative meaning of words and concepts. See connotative meaning.

Semantic memory: A long-term memory store containing the meanings of words, and concepts and the rules for using them in language. Compare episodic memory.

Semantic relations grammar: A theoretical approach to understanding the way in which very small children put word together, which emphasizes the meaning, or intention, underlying the utterance. The short sentences and limited utterances of the child are viewed as telegraphic speech, signalling the most important parts of the communications, and only becoming more refined in terms of additional words or word endings later on. The theory was developed by Roger Brown in opposition to the view of language acquisition developed by Chomsky, which largely ignored what the child was intending to communicate and concentrated instead on the structure of the utterance. See also Psycholinguistics.

Semiotics: The study of pattern in communication of all kings, including language, ritual, non-verbal communication, animal communication, etc. Although primarily concerned with the meanings within such communication, the study of semeiotics also sees the form of the communication as providing important clues to that meaning. In other words, a clear distinction between meaning and form is not considered appropriate, as the form will influence the meaning, and the intended meaning will affect the choice of the form. For example, a reminder to staff in an office from the boss about switching off unnecessary lights could be delivered as a spoken communication, a hand-written memo, or a formally typed memo. Although the words might be identical, the form affects the meaning of the communication.

Senile dementia: Dementia secondary to diffuse cerebral atrophy associated with advancing age. The onset is insidious, and progression is slow and gradual. No specific therapy is known. In DSM, called primary degenerative dementia, senile onset.

Senzation: Feeling or impression when the sensory nerve endings of any of the six senses – taste, touch, smell, sight, kinesthesia, and sound – are stimulated.

Sense of self: A person's feeling of individuality, uniqueness, and self direction.

Sensitive period: A time period during development in which a given capacity or form of learning can be acquired more easily. Sensitive periods are distinguished from critical periods by the fact that the capacity can be acquired outside the set period, though with greater effort.

Sensitivity training group: Group in which members seek to develop self-awareness and an understanding of group processes, rather than to gain relief from an emotional disturbance. See also Encounter group, Personal growth laboratory, T-group.

Sensori-motor stage: The first of Piaget's four stages of cognitive development, in which the immediate cognitive task which the child faces concerns the decoding of sensory information, and the coordination of motor action. The first step in achieving this, according to Piaget, is the reduction of the infant's egocentricity to the point where it can distinguish between 'me' and 'not-me', and has formed its first schema, the body-schema. Another important milestone during this period is the development of object constancy. See also pre-operational stage, concrete operational stage, formal operational stage.

Sensorium: Hypothetical sensory center in the brain that is involved with a person's clarity of awareness about himself and his surroundings, including the ability to perceive and process ongoing events in light of past experience, future options and current circumstances. It is sometimes used interchangeably with consciousness.

Sensory deprivation: Lack of external stimuli and the opportunity for the usual perceptions. Sensory deprivation may be produced experimentally or may occur in real-life contexts – for example, deep-sea diving, solitary confinement, loss of hearing or eyesight – and may lead to hallucinations, panic, delusions and disorganized thinking. See also Deprivation, emotional.

Sensory extinction: Neurological sign operationally defined as failure to report one of two simultaneously presented sensory stimuli, despite the fact that either stimulus alone is correctly reported. It is called sensory inattention.

Sentiment: A configuration of emotional dispositions oriented about one cognition (of object, person, group or symbol) and existing as a structured, relatively abiding element in individual character and social tradition.

Separation anxiety: The fear and apprehension noted in infants when removed from the mother (or surrogate mother) or when approached by strangers. Most marked from sixth to tenth month. In later life, similar reactions may be caused by separation from significant persons or familiar surroundings.

Separation-individuation: Psychologic awareness of one's separateness, described by Margaret Mahler as a phase in the mother-child relationship that follows the symbiotic stage. In the separation individuation stage, the child begins to perceive himself as distinct from the mother and develops a sense of individual identity and an image of the self as object. Mahler described four subphases of the process: differentiation, practicing, rapprochement (active approach toward the mother, replacing the relative obliviousness to her that prevailed during the practicing period), and separation – individuation proper (awareness of discrete identity, separateness, and individuality). See also symbiosis.

Serial-position effect: The observation that in memory experiments using a list of items to be remembered, items at the beginning and end of the list of remembered best.

Serial processing: The processing of information one item at a time. Many early cognitive models assumes serial processing in, for instance, problem-solving or the decoding of language, although recent evidence suggests that, in fact, information is often processed on several levels simultaneously (parallel processing).

Serial reproduction: A technique for investigating constructive memory developed by Barlett, in which a first account is reproduced from memory, and so on. In this way, errors and alterations which occur in the accounts become cumulative, and therefore easier to classify and categorize. One everyday example of the use of serial reproduction is in the game 'Chinese whispers', in which a sentence or phrase is passed along a line of people, each person passing the message on by whispering into the ear of the next person. By the time the message reaches the end of the line, it has usually become completely distored.

Serotonin: Hydroxytryptamine (abbreviated 5-HT), an endogenous indolamine synthesized from dietary tryptophan and found in the gastrointestinal tract, the platelets, and the central nervous system. There is compelling evidence that is monoamine serves as a neurotransmitter substance in the central nervous system. It may play an important role in such diverse functions as sleep, sexual behaviour, aggressiveness, motor activity, perception (particularly pain), and mood. Dysfunction in central serotonergic systems has been proposed as a cause or factor in various mental disorders, including schizophrenia and the affective disorders.

Set: A state of preparedness or readiness for a particular type of experience. Set may be demonstrated with most forms of cognitive process, but the most striking examples of it are perceptual set and learning set. In each case, information which is relevant to the prepared state is picked up far more quickly and easily that information which is not relevant.

Set-weight: A pre-determined body weight, which seems to form the 'natural' weight of the animal concerned. The idea of set-weight arose from studies of the hypothalamus, in which it was observed that rats with lesions in particular areas of the hypothalamus would eat more than usual. At first it was thought that these areas represented 'feeling centres', but later findings showed that the increased intake only lasted until they had reached a certain body weight. At that point the rats would adjust their food intake to stay at that level. Experimental lesions in other areas of the hypothalamus produced effects in the opposite direction: rats would cease to eat until their body weight had dropped to a certain point, whereupon they would resume eating but eat only enough to maintain the new body weight. It has been suggested that similar mechanisms might be implicated in the case of obesity in humans.

Sexism: Discrimination against a person on the basis of their sex. It is often more subtle than racism because it is likely to be based on assumptions about sex differences which are widely held in society. As many of these assumptions have been developed to justify an unfair treatment of women (see rationalization), sexism is often taken to mean discrimination against women.

Sex-role behaviour: Behaviour which is influenced by the person's beliefs about what is appropriate for members of their own sex. The term can also be used to refer to behaviour which conforms to society's definition of appropriate gender behaviour.

Sex-role learning: The processes by which a child or adolescent acquires an understanding of what is appropriate behaviour for their own sex, as opposed to appropriate behaviour for members of the other sex. Sex-role learning starts very early in life, and three-ears-olds have quite a clear ideas of which gender related behaviours their parents think are appropriate.

Sex stereotypes: Beliefs which are held in the culture about sex differences and appropriate sex-role behaviour. Like all stereotypes they make a useful starting point to know what to expect from a person, but easily become misleading if used in preference to observing what the person is actually like.

Sexual abuse: A form of child abuse in which children are involved inappropriate sexual activities, mostly with adults, and which is know to be psychologically damaging. Typical consequences involve distoring the child's ability to form appropriate relationships: limiting their ability to express affection in non-sexual ways; sometimes producing a high level of sensitivity to sexual cues, and tendency to misinterpret ordinary interactions as sexual in content. Cases of child abuse are sometimes detected by signs of unhappiness and an inability to concentrate at school. Since most cases of child sexual abuse involve incest the victims are often afraid of the consequences, and are therefore reluctant to disclose the abuse. Help for individuals who have been victims of sexual abuse depends on the age at which it is identified, and may include play therapy, family therapy, individual psychotherapy, or self-help groups.

Sexual delusion: See Delusion.

Sexual deviation: A mental disorder characterized interests and behaviour other than what is culturally accepted. Sexual deviations include sexual interest in objects other than a person, such as bestiality; bizarre sexual practices, such as necrophilia; and other sexual activities that are not accompanied by copulation. See also Bestiality, Exhibitionism, Masochism, Paraphilia, Psychosexual disorder, Sadism.

Sexual drive: One of the two primal drives or instincts (the other is the aggressive drive) according to Freud's dual-instinct theory formulation in 1920. Also known as life instinct or Eros, it operates under the pleasure-unpleasure (pleasure-pain) principle, and its main goal is to preserve and maintain life. Its unconscious psychic energy is known as libido. See also Aggressive drive, Death instinct, Life instinct.

Sexual identity: Biologically determined sexual state. See also Gender identity.

Sexual masochism: See Masochism.

Sexual orientation disturbance: See Ego-dystonic homosexuality.

Sexual sadism: See Sadism.

Shaman: A healer in a primitive tribe who uses supernatural or spiritual powers to cure the sick.

Shame: An emotion resulting from the failure to live up to self-expectations. See also guilt and superego.

Shaping: An operant conditioning technique used in behaviour therapy. A behavioural goal is reached in stepwise fashion through selective reinforcement of closer and closer approximations of the desired behaviour.

Shared paranoid disorder: A paranoid disorder in which a paranoid delusional system develops as a result of the person's close relationship with a paranoiac. The two persons share at least some delusions. If the person with the shared paranoid disorder is separated from the person with the established paranoid psychosis, the delusions diminish or disappear as a rule. Term introduced in DSM-III. See also Folie a deux.

Shell shock: Obsolete World War I term for an acute mental disorder arising as a consequence of combat experience.

Shinekeishitsu: A syndrome described by Japanese psychiatrists consisting of obsessions, compulsive perfectionism, social withdrawal, multiple somatic complaints and neurasthenia.

Short-term memory: The reproduction, recognition, or recall of perceived material after a period of 10 seconds or longer has elapsed after the initial presentation. It is also known as recent memory. See also Immediate memory, Long-term memory, Memory.

Shyness disorder: See Avoidant disorder.

Sibling rivalry: Competition among siblings for the attention, affection, and esteem of their parents or for other recognition or reward.

"Sick role": An identity adopted by an individual as a "patient" that specifies a set of expected behaviours, usually dependent.

Sign: Objective evidence of a disease or disorder. See also Symptom.

Sign, echo: A speech disorder observed in epileptic patients characterized by the repetition of a word in some part of a sentence.

Sign, eyelash: In a case of unconsciousness due to functional disease, such as hysteria, stroking the eyelashes will make the lids move, but no such reflex will occur in case of organic brain lesion such as apoplexy, fracture of the skull, or other severe traumatism.

Sign, eye-roll: An index of susceptibility to hypnosis developed by psychiatrist Herbert Spiegel; the subject is directed to roll his eyes upward as far as possible and at the same time to lower his eyelids slowly. The amount of white space showing under the corneas is scored from zero (no space or "eye-roll") to five. Low scores are not hypnotizable; they tend also to be critical, controlling personally types who favour thinking over feeling. The readily hypnotizable high scorers tend to be uncritical and gullible people who are "feelers" rather than "thinkers".

Sign, Magnan: Formication; "cocaine bug", a tactile hallucination found in some cocaine abusers consisting of the feeling that small animals are moving in or under the skin. The phenomenon was first described by Magnan and Saury in 1889. It is relatively rare and when it does appear it is usually in association with intravenous use of the drug.

Sign, mirror: A symptom seen frequently in schizophrenic patients, who tend to stand in front of a mirror or other shining surface for unduly long time. The mirror sign is generally regarded as an expression of the patient's autistic withdrawal.

The same sign can also occur in advanced organic dementia (e.g., Alzheimer's disease): The patient sits for hours in front of a mirror, talking to his own reflection; because of complete loss of personal identity, the patient does not realize that the reflection is his own.

Sign, Rosenbach's: (Ottomar Rosenbach, German physician, 1851–1907). Inability of neurasthenics to close the eyes immediately and completely on command.

Sign, Rumpf: (Theodor Rumpf, German physician, 1862–1923). In cases of neurasthenia pressure over a painful point will accelerate the pulse from 10 to 20 beats/minute.

Sign, Schuele's: (Heinrich Schuele. German psychiatrist, 1839–1916). See omega melancholium.

Sign, Stiller's: (Berthold Stiller, Budapest physician, 1837–1922). The presence of floating tenth rib as indicative of a neurasthenic tendency; called also costal stigma.

Signal anxiety: Attenuated anxiety that functions as an early warning system for the ego. It derives from the normal capacity to anticipate a potentially dangerous situation and react to it by deploying emergency defenses before it becomes intense. Signal anxiety may progress to a full-fledged anxiety attack or even to a panic state if the early warning is not heeded or if available defenses prove insufficient. A situation becomes traumatic when the influx of stimuli is too great for the psyche to master or discharge.

Signal-detectability theory: A theory about how weak signals are detected despite the presence of background noise. By making simplifying assumptions, (in particular that only the level of noise and the level or signal are to be considered, and that when both are present the levels simply add to the total sensation, rather than interacting or canceling each other out) in has been possible to produce a mathematical analysis of the process of detecting signals. This approach has been effective in certain restricted cases, and much of the theory is incorporated in the receiver-operating characteristic curve.

Signal-detection task: A task used to investigate how long to subject can perform effectively, when asked to identify one particular type of signal appearing at random intervals amid other distracting stimuli. The task might be auditory: a tone lasting a bit longer than other tones which are sounded at intervals, for instance; or it might be visual, such as the detection of one special shape appearing among other shapes. Some signal detection task are replications of the displays which a radar operator would scan, allowing researchers to identify potential source of error, and to investigate possible alleviating measures.

Significance level: The arbitrarily selected probability level for rejecting the null hypothesis, commonly 05 or .01.

Significant differences: When statistical tests show that a given difference is not likely to have occurred by chance. In many behavioural studies, the likelihood of an event occurring less frequently than 1 in 20 times ($p<.05$) is considered the minimal acceptable significance level. The determination that a given difference between two groups is significant merely serve to identify the likelihood that it was not a chance event. In no way does this prove that the demonstrated systematic difference is necessarily due to the reasons hypothesized by an investigator. Systematic factors not considered by the investigator can sometimes be responsible for significant differences.

Simple phobia: A phobic disorder characterized by fear and avoidance of an object or situation not included in agoraphobia or social phobia.

Simulation: Any process of modeling imitating an actual, real-life event. The term is used in psychology to refer to: apparatus which mimics a real situation in which training can be more safely carried out, as in aeroplane cockpit simulators; people who act as if they have psychological or physical conditions, as in faking epileptic seizures; and in computer simulation.

Simultanagnosia: Impairment in the perception or integration of visual stimuli appearing simultaneously.

Simultaneous conditioning: A variant of classical conditioning in which the unconditional stimulus is presented at exactly the same time as the conditioned stimulus. See also trace conditioning, delayed, conditioning.

Sisyphus reaction: The behaviour pattern of joyless striving in work and home life, setting the stage for major illness or myocardial infarction.

Situational attribution: In attribution theory, this refers to explaining a person's behaviour or experiences as arising from the situation that they are in rather than from the personality or other internal characteristic of that person (which would be dispositional attribution). See also attributional error.

Situationism: The view that behaviour is more a product of a particular situation than a product of enduring characteristics of a person such as traits.

Sixty-nine: A slang expression referring to fellatio and/or cunnilingus practiced simultaneously by two persons, the head of each being near the feet of the other.

Sjobering, Henrik: (1879–1956) Swedish psychiatrist described certain personality types and reactions to stress as based on constitutional phychological variables and cerebral lessions.

Skew: Overprotective, intrusive and dominant mother and over compliant, submissive father is said to lead to schizophrenic son. (given by Lidz, Cornelison, Fleck et al. 1957).

Skinner box: A device developed by B.F. Skinner for investigating operant conditioning. A typical Skinner Box will contain little other than a lever, a food delivery chute, and a signal light. When a hungry small animal such as a laboratory rat is placed in the box, its exploratory behaviour eventually results in its pressing the lever; at which point a food pellet is delivered. This reinforces the lever-pressing action, rendering the animal more likely to repeat it. This process results in the learning of lever-pressing as a means of obtaining food, although the experience of one of the authors suggests that this only happens if the animal feels inclined to co-operate, and is not inevitable. The preliminary phase of getting the animal to push the lever for the first time will be quicker if a behaviour shaping procedure is employed. The signal light can be used as a discriminatory stimulus; and the Skinner Box may be set to deliver partial reinforcement according to a reinforcement schedule.

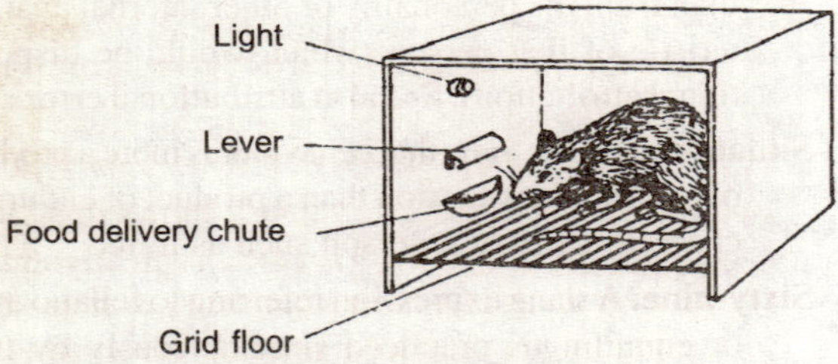

Fig. 12. Skinner Box.

Skills: An acquired ability to carry out more or less complex psychomotor, acts in various domains, including the visuospatial, symbolic, linguistic, numeral, social, learning and specific.

Slater, Eliot, Trevor Oakeshort: (1904–1983) British psychiatrist, one of the founding fathers of 20th century biological psychiatry, best known for his studies of the genetics of schizophrenia and manic depressive illness. Physical Methods of Treatment (1944, with W. Sargant); Clinical Psychiatry (1954, with Mayer Gross and M. Roth; (The Genetics of Mental disorders (1971, with V. Cowie).

Slavsom, S.R.: American theoretician who pioneered in group psychotherapy based psychoanalytic principles. Many of his concepts derived from his work with children, including his introduction and development of activity group therapy. See also Activity group therapy, Collective experience.

Sleep: A recurred temporary period of relative unconsciousness, characterized by a reversible ceszation of the person's waking sensorimotor activity and accompanied by characteristic electroencephalographic changes. Sleep is divided into REM (rapid eye movement) and non-REM (NREM) periods; four stages of NREM sleep, based on EEG findings, are recognized. See also REM sleep.

Sleep cycles: Pattern of sleeping which involve changes in EEG recordings produced by a sleeper, and corresponding differences in how easy the person finds it to wake up. During a typical night, sleepers pass through the different levels of sleep in a cyclic fashion between five and seven times. Levels 1 and 2 are light sleep characterized by irregular EEG patterns; the deeper levels 3 and 4 shows regular wave patterns in EEG recordings. Typically, the sleeper will cycle through the levels every 40 to 80 minutes, and then enter REM sleep for a period before starting a new cycle. During a period of normal sleep, deeper stages become shorter and then cease completely, while the REM stage becomes, longer. See also rapid eye movement sleep; orthodox sleep.

Sleep terror disorder: Condition occurring in stage 4 sleep manifested by panic, confusion, and poor recall for the event. Contrast with nightmares.

Sleep-walking: A state of automatism occurring in the course of normal sleep, most commonly in childhood, and sometimes related to emotional disturbance. Episodes of sleep-walking are characterized by repetitive and purposeless movements with a low level of awareness and critical skill which can lead to self-injury; there is complete amnesia for the events subsequently. The incidents occur during sleep stages 3 and 4 but not during rapid-eye-movement (REM) sleep. *Synonym*: somnambulism.

Social adaptation: Adjustment to the whole complex of interpersonal relationships; the ability to live and express oneself in accordance with society's restrictions and cultural demands. See also Adaptational approach.

Social breakdown syndrome: The signs and symptoms indicating that the long term institutionalization of a mental patient has itself contributed to the patient's symptoms. Examples include the development of progressive social and vocational incompetence, excessive passivity, and learning the chronic sick role.

"Social clock": A society's timetable for the "right" ages to marry, have children start work, retire, and have other adult experiences.

Social cognition: An area in social psychology that studies social influences on thought, memory, perception, and other cognitive processes.

Social control: Influence exerted on a person or a group of persons to conform to the demands or expectations of a society or any of its representative institutions, agencies, or organizations.

Social drift hypothesis: Given by Goldberg and Morrison that the schizophrenics drift down the social scale.

Social exchange theory: The idea that social relationships may be viewed as a kind of economic system in which the people engaged in a relationship become dependent on each other for the quality of the outcomes they experience from the relationship; involves comparison levels (CL) and comparison levels for alternatives (Clalt).

Social facilitation: The finding that performance is usually improved by the presence of others. Simple and well rehearsed tasks are most likely to be facilitated, so if the presence of others is a source of arousal, the phenomenon follows the Yerkes-Dodson law.

Social inhibition: In social groups, the retardation action caused by the presence of other people.

Social instinct: See Herd instinct.

Social interaction: A process in which two people or animals directly influence each others' behaviour. Social interactions is the core phenomenon of social psychology, and the complex regulation of forms of social interactions is an important part of the young child's socialization.

Social interest: To Alfred Adler, the ability to feel empathy, to co-operate, and to be connected to others.

Social learning theory: An approach to child development which states that children develop through learning from the other people around them. Social learning theory emphasizes the process by which children come to adopt the rules, norms and assumptions of their society, e.g., operant conditioning, imitation, and identification. In general, social development is seen as a continuous learning process, rather than as happening in stages and may theories consider it to continue throughout adult life.

Social loafing: The rendency of group members under some conditions, to reduce their efforts and "loaf"; one result of the diffusion of responsibility.

Social modes: Campbell's term for the acquisition of information from other people; learning from other people; useful in understanding conforming. Compare personal modes.

Social motivation: See social motives.

Social motives: Learned motives, such as the need for affiliation, power, competence, or achievement, that are acquired from social experiences.

Social needs: The third level in Maslow's hierarchy of needs is concerned with group identity and membership, love, and positive interaction with others. According to Maslow, social needs become important once the basis physiological needs and the safety needs have been satisfied. Once the social needs have been adequately met, aesthetic needs become important. At the top of the hierarchy is self-actualization, which Maslow considers to be possible only once all other levels of need are satisfied. Many psychologists criticize this model of human needs on the grounds that it does not account for many instances of human behaviour which 'higher' needs are apparently put before basic ones, the classic example being the case of the 'starving poet'; there are also may examples of pro-social behaviour in the face of physical deprivation.

Social network therapy: A type of therapy in which the therapist assembles all the persons – relatives, friends, social relations, work relations who have emotional or functional significance in the patient's life. All or some of the Social network may be assembled at any given time. See also Extended-family therapy.

Social norms: Forms of behaviour which are widespread within a society and/or are widely accepted appropriate. Often, it is the second condition which is more important; for example, there are probably far more people in our society who abuse children than the number who work professionally for their welfare and protection. Yet concern for children, rather than abuse of them, is still accepted as the norm. Acceptance of a person in a society is usually based on the extent to which the person follows, or at least expresses agreement with, the norms.

Social perception: The way we view other people, based on information obtained about others and attributions we make about the causes of their behaviour.

Social perspective: A current viewpoint in psychology which emphasizes the social interactions among people and the social influences which affect behaviour. See social psychology.

Social phobia: A phobic disorder characterized by a fear of being observed by others. The social phobias include fears of public speaking, blushing, eating in public; writing in front of others, and using public elevators.

Social psychiatry: Branch of psychiatry interested in ecological, sociological and cultural variables that engender, intensify, or complicate maladaptive patterns of behaviour and their treatment.

Social psychology: The branch of psychology which is particularly concerned with the nature and form of social interaction and how people come to influence each others' behaviour. It also includes the study of social perception, including attitudes and attribution.

Social skills training: A practical procedure by means of which new forms of social behaviour can be learned or existing behaviour modified. The aim of this training is to help clients to organize or improve their social skills, namely behavioural sequences that conform to social norms and which enable people to achieve desired social goals more efficiently and acceptably.

Social therapy: A rehabilitation form of therapy with psychiatric patients aimed at improving social functioning. Occupational therapy, therapeutic community, recreational therapy, milieu therapy, and attitude therapy are forms of social therapy.

Social worker, psychiatric: A skilled professional, trained in social work, who works with psychiatrists, usually in an institutional setting. The psychiatric social worker evaluates family, environmental, and social factors in the patient's illness; may work in intake and reception with new patients; and may follow up and counsel after discharge. All those activities are incorporated in the technique of case work. Psychiatric social workers also carry out individual, family and group psychotherapy and participate in community organizations.

Socialization: The process by which a child becomes integrated into society by adopting its norms and values, acquiring the necessary skills of social interaction, and learning to adopt an acceptable role.

Sociobiology: The systematic study of the biological basis of social behaviour. The field was pioneered by E.O. Wilson.

Sociogram: Diagrammatic portrayal of the relationship of every person to every other person in a group situation.

Sociology: The scientific study of group behaviour and social organization.

Sociometry: The study and measurement of the interpersonal psychological structure of a group or society.

Sociopath: Obsolete term for a person with an antisocial personality disorder.

Sociotherapy: Any treatment modality whose primary emphasis is on socio environment and interpersonal factors – for example, the therapeutic community.

Sodomy: Anal intercourse. Legally, the term may include other sexual deviations as well, such as bestiality.

Solipsism: Correctly, philosophical theory that only the self is knowable or that the apparent external world consists of our own thoughts.

Soma: The body.

Somatic delusion: See Delusion.

Somatic hallucination: See Hallucination.

Somatization disorder: A somatoform disorder characterized by recurrent and multiple physical complaints with no apparent physical cause. It is also known as Briquet's syndrome.

Somatoform disorder: A mental disorder characterized by physical symptoms but no organic cause. The production of the symptoms is linked to psychological factors or conflicts but is not under voluntary control. In DSM the somatoform disorders include somatization disorder, conversion disorder, psychogenic pain disorder, and hypochondriasis. See also Factitious disorder, Malignering, Munchausen syndrome.

Somnambulism: Sleepwalking. More frequently seen in males than in females, it is most common in children, who generally outgrow it. In adults it is often associated with other psychiatric disturbances, such as schizoid personality disorder and schizophrenia. In DSM, it is included in sleepwalking disorder.

Somnolence: Pathological sleepiness or drowsiness from which the patient can be aroused to a normal state of consciousness.

Sopor: A state of marked drowsiness in which the patient can make purposeful reactions to some stimuli.

Sorcery: It refers to the deliberate alteration of events through magic and rituals for good or evil purposes. Sorcery syndromes characterized by anxiety and fears of preoccupation have been described in Australian aborigines. In India, a kind of sorcery called *Bhanamati* has been practiced for some centuries in South India. The causes can be due to psychiatric illnesses (i.e., conversion disorders, somatization disorder, anxiety disorder, dysthymia, schizophrenia etc) or physical illnesses.

Southard, Elmer Ernst (1876–1920): American psychiatrist, social psychiatry, industrial hygiene.

Spasmophilia: (1) A neuropsychiatric syndrome, described by Joyeux in 1958, consisting of moderate anxiety, irritability, hypermotility, insomnia, dysfunction in various organ systems (gastrointestinal, cardiovascular, genital, skin) and positive Chvostek sign. All the symptoms may be precipitated or aggravated by hyperventilation. (2) In general and constitutional medicine, a syndrome characterized by under secretion of the parathyroids.

Special child: A term adopted to refer to all children whose qualities or abilities are well outside the normal range. It represents an attempt to avoid the automatically negative implications of terms like mentally handicapped and retarded and to make an association between children who need special resources because of some disadvantage and those who need special attention because they are exceptionally gifted in some way. More recently, the expression 'children with special needs' has been adopted to reduce the possibility of labelling.

Specific developmental disorder: A disorder characterized by delays in the development of specific psychological functions involved in social skills and language. A child with a specific developmental disorder acts as though he were passing through a developmental stage earlier than in appropriate for his years. In DSM the specific developmental disorders include developmental reading disorder, developmental arithmetic disorder, developmental language disorder, and developmental articulation disorder. See also Pervasive developmental disorder.

Spectrophobia: The hysterical phobia for mirrors and the dread of catching sight of one's own face in a mirror had in one case a 'functional' and 'material' origin.

Speech act: A term introduced by Buhler (1934) and subsequently taken up by Austin (1962) who stresses that in saying things speakers are actually doing things.

Speech disturbance: A term that encompasses any of a variety of language and communication disorders not due to impaired function of speech muscles or organs of articulation. See also Communication disorder, Language disorder.

Speech therapy: The profession which helps people who have some problem with verbal communication. Speech therapists use many techniques from psychology, particularly behavioural methods, and are increasingly paying attention to social factors in the disruption of communication.

Spitz, Rene A. (1887–1974): Austrian born psychoanalyst; development studies; pioneer in applying research methods to Freud's analytic concepts of child development.

SST: (1) Social skill training (2) Self-statement training, a cognitive approach to the treatment of agoraphobia that aims to replace self defeating cognitions with positive self-statements in confronting and coping with the feared situation.

Stammering and stuttering: Disorders in the rhythm of speech, in which the individual knows precisely what he or she wishes to say, but at the time is unable to say it because of an involuntary, repetitive prolongation or ceszation of a sound. *Synonyms*: logoneurosis; logospasm.

Standard deviation (SD): Statistical measure of variability within a set of values so defined that, for a normal distribution, about 68 per cent of the values fall within one SD of the mean, and about 95 per cent lie within two SD's of the mean. It is sometimes represented by Q, the Greek letter sigma.

Standard error of the mean (SEM): Statistical measure of how variable – that is, how reliable – a mean value calculated on the basis of a given samples is as an estimate of the true mean of the population from which the sample was selected. It is obtained by dividing the standard deviation of the population by the square root of the number of measures in the sample.

Stanford-Binet Intelligence Scale: A primarily verbal test of intellectual functioning administered individually to children and adults. It emphasizes problem solving and is one of the most widely used I.Q. tests. See also Intelligence quotient.

Startle reaction: A reflex response to a sudden intense stimulus, consisting of a diffuse motor response involving flexion movements of the trunk and extremities (hence, in German, Zusammenschreken-reflex) and associated with a sudden increase in alertness. It occurs in normal persons and in acute anxiety disorders.

State-dependent learning: Learning which is demonstrated most effectively when the individual is in the same physiological state as when it was originally learned. For instance, information learned when a subject is under the influence of alcohol is often most readily recalled at times when the subject is again under the influence. State-dependent learning may similarly be demonstrated with a range of drugs, including amphetamines and tranquilizers.

States in creative thinking: A pattern of steps that is frequently involved in the solution of problems by talented and creative people, the stages are preparation, incubation, illumination, evaluation, and revision.

Statistical inference: The process of using a limited sample of data to infer something about a large population of potentially obtainable data which has not been observed.

Statistical significance: Research term referring to an experimental result, based on a sample of observations, that demonstrates an outcome or effect of sufficient magnitude alone in less than 5 per cent. See also Type 1 error.

Status: Relative position, rank, or standing of a person in a group of a group in reference to other groups or in reference to some larger grouping.

Status epilepticus: Continuous epileptic seizures. See also Epilepsy.

Stedman, Charles H.: (1805–66) American Psychiatrist; one of the original thirteen founders of Association of Medical Superintendents of America (forerunner of American Psychiatric Association).

Stekel, Wilhelm (1868–1940): Viennese psychoanalyst who suggested the formation of the first Freudian group, the Wednesday Evening Society. A man given to intuition, rather than to systematic research, his insight into dreams proved stimulating and added to the knowledge of symbols. Nevertheless, his superficial wild analysis proved incompatible with the Freudian school. He introduced the word "Thanatos" to signify death wish.

Steppingstone theory: The assumption that use of gateway drugs (such as alcohol and marihuana) predisposes to use and abuse of other classes of ("harder") drugs.

Stereotyped movement disorder: A disorder characterized by recurrent, involuntary, repetitive gross motor movements. In DSM the stereotyped movement disorders include transient tic disorder, chronic motor tic disorder, and Gilles de la Tourette's disease.

Stereotype: Continuous mechanical repetition of speech or physical activities. It is observed in cases of catatonic schizophrenia.

Stilted speech: Excessively formal, stiff, stylized, or pompous speech; overly polite, distant, or antiquated speech.

Stimulant: A drug that stimulates the central nervous system to produce increased psychomotor activity. Methylphenidate, caffeine, and the amphetamines are examples.

Stimulus: Any event, internal or external to the person, that elicits some kind of nervous system activity or response.

Stimulus discrimination: The form of discrimination shown in stimulus response learning, in which a response will occur to one specific stimulus, but will not occur in the presence of a similar stimulus. Unlike stimulus generalization which occurs without prior training, stimulus discrimination is learned by the organism through reinforcement. Responses made in the presence of one stimulus are reinforce, those made to the other are not. In this way, the organism comes to discriminate between the two.

Stimulus generalization: When a learned response is produced to a Stimulus different from the one to which it war originally learned. Stimulus generalization often shows the generalization gradient that the response is strongest to those stimuli which are most similar to the original one.

Stimulus-response learning: Learning which occurs as a result of the association between a Stimulus and some kind of behavioural response. In general, there are thought to be two basic forms of Stimulus – response learning; classical conditioning and operant conditioning. Some psychologists classify one-trial learning, in which such an association is formed as a result of only one learning trial or experience, as third form; others regard it as a special form of classical conditioning.

Stockholm syndrome: A syndrome in which captives identify with, and have sympathy for, their captors on whom they are very dependent for survival. First described in a Stockholm bank robbery where hostages were so affected by their captor bank robbers. Also seen in terrorist-hostage situations. The major defense mechanism as described by Anna Freud was known as identification with the aggressor.

Stransky, Erwin (1877–1962): Viennese neurophsychiatrist pupil of Wagner von Jauregg; first to publish text book in Germany on mental health; concept of intrapsychic ataxia, the dissociation of the thymopsyche from the noopsyche, as the essential characteristic of schizophrenia.

Strephosymbolia: A type of reading and writing disability characterized by confusion between similarly formed but oppositely oriented letters (as in b and d, p and q) and a tendency to reverse the order of letters and words. Commonly seen in Attention Deficit Disorder.

Stress: A term introduced into human physiology by Cannon in the early 1920s to denote all physical, chemical and emotional stimuli which exceed a certain critical threshold and disrupt the equilibrium of the internal milieu of the organism. In the 'general adaptation syndrome' described by Selye (1950) the term changed its meaning and became a common denominator for the nonspecific responses of the organism to such stimuli. In current usage it is used interchangeably to describe various aversive stimuli of excessive intensity; the physiological, behavioural and subjective response to them; the context mediating the encounter between the individual and the stressful stimuli; or all the above as a 'system'. The term is clearly overstretched and should be used sparingly.

Stress immunity: Failure to react to emotional stress.

Structuralism: An approach to theory in which psychological phenomena are explained as the natural outcome of the way the organism is structures. The proposed structures may be physical and open to direct examination (e.g., accounts of aggression based on interpreting brain structure) or hypothetical. Examples of the latter are Freud's personality structure and Piaget's cognitive structures. Structural approaches in anthropology and sociology are concerned with the social structures within which people function, though these are often taken to be outward manifestations of mental structures. The term is also applied to attempts to understand how language works by examining its structure. Structural theories are contrasted with functional approaches.

Structured interactional group psychotherapy: A type of group therapy developed by Harold Kaplan and Benamin Sadock in which the therapist provides a structural matrix for the group's interactions, the most important of which is that a different member of the group is the focus of the interaction in each session.

Study skills: The set of techniques, strategies and behaviour patterns which form a structured approach to learning; often based on psychological theory, but also on experiences acquired and transmitted less formally. Study skills can be related to the theoretical area of recognition, but is usually treated as a separate topic in its own right. It includes such features of effective study as reading skills, effective revision techniques, organizing study time, and examination strategies.

Stupor: State of decreased reactivity to stimuli and less than full awareness of one's surroundings. As a disturbance of consciousness, it indicates a condition of partial coma or semicoma. In psychiatry, it is also used synonymously with mutism and does not necessarily imply a disturbance of consciousness, in catatonic stupor the patient is ordinarily well aware of the nature of his surroundings.

Stuttering: A speech disorder characterized by repetitions or prolongations of sounds, syllables, or words or by hesitations and pauses that disrupt the flow of speech. It is also known as stammering.

Subconscious: Obsolete term for the preconscious and the unconscious.

Subjectivity: State in which evaluation and interpretation are influenced by one's own feeling and thinking.

Sublimation: An unconscious defense mechanism in which the energy associated with unacceptable impulses or drives is diverted into personally and socially acceptable channels. Unlike other defense mechanisms, sublimation offers some minimal gratification of the instinctual drive or impulse.

Substance use disorder: The DSM-IV term for drug dependence. See also Drug dependence.

Substitution: An unconscious defense mechanism in which a person replaces an unacceptable wish, drive, emotion, or goal with one that is more acceptable.

Sudden infant death syndrome (SIDS): Also called cot death or crib death. Babies appear to go through a vulnerable period around 2 to 4 months and during this time a significant number are found dead in their cots, having shown little or no sign of illness or any other warning sign. Some research suggests that it may be associated with a failure to learn how to restart breathing early in life following apnea, but most research has concentrated on possible medical causes. Cot deaths are of major concern to psychologists because they are relatively common and an extremely distressing form of bereavement.

Suggestion: The process of influencing a patient to accept an idea, belief, or attitude suggested by the therapist. See also hypnosis.

Suggestibility: State of uncritical compliance with influence or uncritical acceptance of an idea, belief, or attitude. It is commonly observed among persons with hysterical traits.

Suicide: The act of self-inflicted, self-intentioned taking of one's own life. Although the underlying factors that lead a person to take his or her own life may not necessarily by fully understood by that person, the act of suicide is considered to be both voluntary and intentional.

Sullivan, Harry Stack (1892–1949): American psychiatrist and psychoanalyst know for his research in the psychotherapy of schizophrenia and for his view of complex interpersonal relationships as the basis of personality development.

Summation: The cumulative effect of several neurons transmitting information to one neurone at the same time. If a single synaptic transmission is received, from one other neurone only, it is unlikely to be enough to produce a response in the next cell. But the total effect brought about by several receptor sites receiving the neurotransmitter at the same time will produce the effect.

Superego: In psychoanalysis, the part of the personality structure that represents the internalized values, ideals and moral attitudes of society. Its psychic functions are expressed in guilt, self-critism, and conscience. It develops through the child's identification with his parents, and the severity of its prohibition of the demands is said to be related to the intensity and extent of resolution of the Oedipus complex. It has a rewarding function, referred to as the ego ideal, and a critical and punishing function, which evokes the sense of guilt. See also Conscience, Ego, Id.

Supportive psychotherapy: A type of psychotherapy that aims to reinforce a patient's defenses and help suppress disturbing psychological material. Supportive psychotherapy utilizes such measures as inspiration, reassurance, suggestion, persuasion, counseling, and reduction. It avoids probing the patient's emotional conflicts in depth. See also psychotherapy.

Suppression: Conscious act of controlling and inhibiting an unacceptable impulse, emotion, or idea. Suppression is differentiated from repression in that repression is an unconscious process.

Surface contact: The second level of involvement in the growth of relationships; interactions are governed by general cultural norms specifying appropriate behaviour and social etiquette. Compare unilateral awareness, stage of mutuality.

Surface structure: The actual expression in speech of the core ideas in the deep phrase structure; the deep phrase structure is converted into the surface structure by transformation rules. See transformational grammar.

Surrogate: Substitute; one who takes the place of another.

Susto: Culture-specific mental syndrome seen in Latin America. It is characterized by an intense fear of evil supernatural forces; Fallen fontanel syndrome.

Symbiosis: A dependent, mutually reinforcing relationship between two persons. It is generally a normal, constructive characteristic of the infant-mother relationship, but it can also occur in a destructive context, as between two mentally ill persons who reinforce each other's pathology or in mother-infant relationship that induces in the child's intense separation anxiety, autism, and severe regression (symbiotic psychosis).

Symbiotic psychosis: A condition seen in two-to four year-old children with an abnormal relationship to a mothering figure. The psychosis is characterized by intense separation anxiety, severe regression giving up of useful speech, and autism.

Symbolic representation: The third of the modes of representation described by Bruner, in which information is stored as symbols, such as numbers, words, or signs. Bruner argues that this mode of representation enables the child to organize and categorize information, and to perceive relationships which might not otherwise have been readily identifiable. As such, he regards the development of symbolic representation, especially through the use of language, as being of paramount importance in cognitive development. See also enactive representation, iconic representation.

Symbolization: A general mechanism in all human thinking by which some mental representation comes to stand for some other thing, class of things, or attribute of something. This mechanism underlies dream formation and some symptoms, such as conversion reactions, obsessions, and compulsions. The link between the latent meaning of the symptom and the symbol is usually unconscious.

Sympathy: A feeling or capacity for sharing in the interests or concerns of another. Many arise when there is no emotional attachment to the person towards whom one is sympathetic, since the feelings of the sympathetic person remain essentially internal. Contrast with empathy.

Symptom: Any abnormality indicative of a mental or physical disorder experienced by the patient but not observable by a physician. See also Sign.

Symptom formation: Unconscious psychic process in which a repressed impulse is indirectly released and manifested through a symptom. Symptom formation may be regarded as a kind of compromise, reflecting a partial satisfaction of both the forbidden impulse and the ego reaction against it.

Symptom substitution: Phenomenon in which a set of Symptoms that are removed directly in therapy, without regard for the unconscious conflicts responsible for their formation, are replaced by new Symptoms. It has constituted a theoretical objection to such modalities as behaviour therapy and hypnotherapy.

Symptomatic psychosis: A physically induced usually short lived psychotic state accompanying infections, systemic, visceral and endocrine disease, and pregnancy and the puerperium. The clinical features are most often those of clouded consciousness, a dysmnesia state, depression, or psychomotor excitement, but syndromes resembling closely the ; 'functional' psychoses have also been described, Causal factors can include metabolic and toxic disturbances and a constitutional predisposition. In ICD-9 an additional code had been added to identify the associated physical or neurological condition. *Synonym*: transient organic psychotic conditions.

Syncretic thought: Piaget's term for prelogical, egocentric, solipsistic thinking that characterizes early childhood mentation. See also Primary process.

Syndrome: Recognizable constellation of symptoms and signs.

Syndrome, air pollution: Symptoms associated with exposure to air pollutants, such as headache, fatigue, irritability, depression, and impaired judgement.

Syndrome, amotivational: Passivity, lack of interest, loss of drive, "dropping out, and difficulties in attention and concentration, described by some as the usual effect of long-term marihuana use. Some use the phrase a motivational states to refer to deficit symptoms in schizophrenia. See symptoms, deficit; symptoms, negative.

Syndrome, angry woman: A personality disorder described in house wives consisting of a morbidity, critical attitude to others, perfectionism, obsessive neatness and punctuality, marital maladjustment, proneness to alcohol or drug abuse, periodic outbursts of unprovoked anger, and serious suicide attempts.

Syndrome, battered child: Term coined by pediatrician C.H. Kempe in the 1960s denoting physical injuries to children secondary to intentional acts of omission or to repeated, volitional, excessive beatings, by a parent or caretaker. Other than the obvious immediate dangers to the child's life and adequate physical growth, it is possible that such cruelty and abuse may constitute a long-term hazard in that it predisposes to a psychic development along the lines of delinquency and violence.

Syndrome, body-packer: Drug overdose as a result of the ingestion of multiple small packages of contraband drugs (most commonly cocaine) in order to transport them. Rupture of the package or leaking from semipermeable wrappings (such as condoms) results in acute drug intoxication and, often, death.

Syndrome, Briquet's: Hysterial, so-named because P. Briquet was the first to describe hysteria systematically, in 1859, some use the eponym to refer specifically to the polysymtomatic form of hysteria with many visits to different physicians, excessive medications, excessive hospitalizations, and excessive surgery. Criteria for the diagnosis of Briquet's syndrome include (1) vague or dramatic medical history beginning before the age of 35 years. (2) a history of multiple symptoms (usually not less than 20) severe enough to interfere significantly with the patient's life and/or to require medication or a visit to a physician, and (3) a lack of any medical explanation for the symptoms. See hypochondriasis.

Syndrome, buffoonery: "The buffoonery syndrome is not always easily separated from catatonic states. In this syndrome the entire picture is taken up with playing demonstrative striking tricks, and with giving wrong answers; like the Ganser twilight state in probably only occurs as a reaction to a situation from which unconsciously one wants to escape through insanity." (Bleuler, TP)

Syndrome, Capgras's: The delusional belief in the existence of identical doubles of significant others or of oneself or both such as the delusion that one's spouse has been replaced by one or more imposters. The syndrome was first described in 1923 by J. Capgras and Reboul-Lachaux and is also known as illusions of doubles or illusions of false recognition. It is to be distinguished from autoscopy, defects of memory, perception, or recognition, hallucination, illusion and prosopagnosia. The Capgras delusion is a negative misidentification that denies the genuineness of a known person (through admitting of a resemblance), in contrast, Fregoli's phenomenon (the illusion de Fregoli, the illusion of a negative double) is a positive misidentification, consisting of a belief that a prosecutor has assumed the guise of various people whom the subject encounters in his daily life. (Fregoli was an actor famed for his ability to alter his appearance.) See syndrome, intermetamorphosis.

Syndrome, Cinderella: Simulation of neglect, or false accuzation of neglect by a child, such as an adopted child's allegation (unfounded) that her stepmother made her do all the household chores and then left her unclothed in a snowdrift while the stepmother went off to the movies with her other children.

Syndrome, clinical poverty: Consisting of slowness, underactivity, reduced emotional responsivity, and impaired ability to communicate (as manifested, for example, in a wooden expression, monotonous voice, lack of gesturing, poverty of speech content). The clinical poverty syndrome is a type of long-term impairment or disability that tends to persist in may schizophrenics even after acute symptoms have subsided.

Syndrome, Cotard's: (Jules Cotard, French neurologist, 1840–87) Delire de negation(s); the nihilistic delusion(s) found in severe depression, when the patient feels his head or bowels have been destroyed, his family has been exterminated, he is penniless, etc.

Syndrome, deliberate self-harm: Conscious and willful inflicting of painful, destructive, or injurious acts on one's own body without intent to kill. Typically the subject feels mounting tension and an impelling impulse to act, followed by a feeling of relief after the injury has been inflicted on the self. The most frequent amputation (e.g., tongue or ear), biting, burning, enucleation of the eye, genital mutilation including castration, removal of the tongue, head banging, ingestion of medications and other objects, jumping from heights, hair pulling, and insertion of foreign bodies into the urethra.

The syndrome most commonly begins in late adolescence and continues for many years. It probably occurs most often in borderline or schizophrenic patients, in order to (1) relieve feelings of depersonalization; (2) lessen inner tensions; (3) solve genital conflicts' (4) reassure the subject that he or she is alive by seeing his own blood; (5) deny inability to control the body by planning its destruction. Also called para-suicide, self-attack, self-mutilation, symbolic wounding. See suicide, attempted.

Syndrome, Delilah: Promiscuity in a woman for whom seduction of the partner is equated with rendering him weak or helpless, something she would like to have achieved with her dominating and exploitative father.

Syndrome, displaced child: A form of separation phenomenon, often precipitated in a child by the birth of a sibling. Symptoms include a mixture of irritability, discouragement, jealousy of siblings, and feelings of rejection by other children.

Syndrome, effort: Neurocirculatory asthenia.

Syndrome, Ekbom's: Restless legs syndrome (q.v.); when it occurs spontaneously it is often associated with low serum iron. Akathesia as a side effect of neuroleptic administration is similar in appearance and may also be associated with iron deficiency. Even though not anemic, such patients show low serum iron and percentage saturation, and high total iron-binding capacity. Further, the lower the serum iron the more severe the Akathesia.

Syndrome, fetal alcohol: A pattern of retarded physical and mental growth, with associated cranial, facial, limb, and cardiovascular anomalies, that is found in 30 to 50% of the offspring of severely alcoholic mothers. Damage to the fetus by maternal alcoholism is one of the most common recognizable causes of mental retardation. The affected children do not typically "catch up" in their growth patterns, even when given a nutritionally adequate diet. The basis for the syndrome is believed to be a direct toxic effect of alcohol and/or one of its intermediate breakdown products on the fetal brain.

Syndrome, fragile X: A chromosomal disorder consisting of a gap or constriction at the distal end of the long arm of the X chromosome at Xq28, resulting in the appearance of an X chromosome with a satellite and a tendency to break easily.

The fragile X chromosome is definitely associated with mental retardation in males. Macroorchidism is a strong phenotypic indicator of the presence of a fragile X and of retardation.

The disorder is believed to occur in 1 of ever 2,000 to 3,000 male births, making it second only to Down's syndrome as a cause of retardation, even though relatively few females are affected. A male born to a mother with fragile X chromosome has a 50% chance of manifesting the disorder.

There may be an association between fragile X chromosome and dyslexia (primary learning disability) but contrary to earlier claims there is little evidence for an association between fragile X and autism.

Syndrome, Freud's: P. Janet coined this expression: " The mania for repression .. is still an interesting symptom; and it explains certain remarkable phenomena, such as monstrous and acrilegious longings. It will continue to form a part of mental pathology under the name of 'Freud's syndrome'."

Syndrome, Ganser: (Sigbert J.M. Ganser, German psychiatrist, 1853–1931) One of factitious disorder; the Ganser twilight syndrome is factitious disorder with psychological symptoms, while the Munchhausen syndrome is factitious disorder (chronic) with physical symptoms. The Ganser syndrome is also known as "the nonsense syndrome" or syndrome of deviously relevant answers; it is held, hope to be treated leniently by the court in virtue of their malady. It is described by many investigators as a hysterical reaction. The patient seldom does anything correctly. When shown a watch reading 3:30, the patient may say it read 5:00; when shown a glove he says it is a hand; he designates a 50-cent piece as a dollar bill; calls a key a lock. But in addition to such approximate answers, which may be seen also in hysterical pseudodementia, behaviour, with episodes of excitement or stupor, as though the subject were acting out an artificial psychosis (neuromimesis).

Syndrome, general adaptation: The various changes in the body in response to and/or as defense against stress. Selye distinguishes three stages in this syndrome; the alarm reaction, in which adaptation is not yet acquired; the stage of resistance in which adaptation is optimal; and the stage of exhaustion, in which the acquired adapta- tion is lost again.

Syndrome, Gjessing's: (jes'ing) Recurrent episodes of catatonic stupor or excitement occurring in schizophrenics and associated with phasic variations in the nitrogen metabolism; first described by R. Gjessing in 1938. The syndrome is related to inadequate metabolism of dietary protein, leading to periods of nitrogen retention that are concurrent with hyper – or – hypokinetic episodes. Dietary regulation is sometimes enough to control such patients: in others, thyroid administration increases nitrogen output with corresponding improvement in mental state.

Syndrome, holiday: Sadness, anxiety, or other emotional pain – reflected in increased rates of suicide, hospital admissions, and deaths in automobile, accidents occurring during the period between Thanksgiving and New Year's Day. The syndrome appears to be an expression of unmet dependency needs triggered by the reminiscing and loving aspects of the holiday season.

Syndrome, hyperventilation: Formerly termed Da-Costa's syndrome, effort syndrome, irritable heart, neurocirculatory asthenia, soldier's heart, war neurasthenia.

Syndrome, intensive care: Psychosis appearing in patients in postoperative recovery units or in intensive care units. Significant factors contributing to the development of such a complication include the following: (1) the physical conditions of the unit itself – often impersonal, highly mechanized, unfamiliar, isolated, windowless, and in certain ways a type of sensory deprivation experience; (2) the physical condition of the patient within the unit is usually immobilized to a severe degree and in considerable discomfort; (3) the nature of the underlying pathology, including the medical-surgical complications and the age of the patients, and the effects these have on brain function; (4) the effects of medication and operative procedures on brain function; and (5) the premorbid level of functioning, including personality structure and genetic-constitutional factors.

Syndrome, intermetamorphosis: Delusional conviction that various people in one's environment have been transformed physically and psychologically into other people. Intermetamorphosis differs from Fregoli's phenomenon, which also involves false identification, in that it includes false physical resemblance in addition to false recognition. See syndrome, Capgras's.

Syndrome, Main's: The ability of a patient (usually a female psychotic who is a nurse or is otherwise closely related to the field of medicine, and part of whose productions include recounting long-continued incestuous relationships) to extort "frantic sympathy and remarkable therapeutic privilege" from her attendants, and to imbue "doctor or nurse with a vivid sense of private significance for the patient, of being peculiarly attuned to her." The syndrome was first described by T.F. Main in 1957.

Syndrome, maternal deprivation: The psychobiologic response to withdrawal or withholding of the emotional, affection, cognitive, or other supplies needed for proper development that ordinarily are provided by the mother. Most typically, it appears in children without mothers who are reared in institutions, in children who for one reason or another are separated from the mother at an early age, and in children whose mothers are incapable of providing consistently suitable emotional support for their children. See depression, anaclitic; deprivation, emotional.

Syndrome, Munchhausen: A name suggested by Asher in 1951 to refer to patients who wander from hospital to hospital ("hospital hoboes"), feigning acute medical or surgical illness and giving false and fanciful information about their meditation of the affected in their thirties or forties. Early symptoms are blank facies, an unblinking stare, loss of initiative, short attention span, loss of remote memory, failure to understand verbal orders, difficulty in walking because of spasticity, and dysarthria. Extrapyramidal and cerebellar signs, if present at all, appear late in the course of the disorder. No specific treatment is applicable, and although no underlying metabolic disorder, a specific enzyme defect, probably limited to the metabolism of nervous issue, is suspected.

Syndrome, night-eating: A type of eating disorder that occurs in some obese patients consisting of nocturnal hyperphagia, incomnia, and morning anorexia. The syndrome tends to appear episodically, and during such periods weight control is especially difficult or even impossible for the patient. A second type of eating pattern found in obese patients is binge eating consumption at irregular intervals of large quantities of food in an orgiastic manner. A third pattern is eating without saturation, seen most frequently in patients with central nervous system disturbances, and characterized by overeating without relationship to stress situations and without regular periodicity.

Syndrome, nonsense: Popular synonym for Ganser syndrome (q.v.).

Syndrome of approximate answers: See answers, syndrome of approximate; syndrome Ganser.

Syndrome, persecution: Described in war refugees with concentration camp experience or those who are persecuted in flight; consists of pervasive anxiety, over-reactivity, irritability, chronic depression, psychosomatic disturbance, and defense by means of dehumanization and unconscious identification with the aggressor. The social contacts and marriages of those with the syndrome are likely to be confined to others who have had similar experiences. See neurosis, traumatic; post-traumatic stress disorder.

Syndrome, phantom lover: Erotomania (q.v.).

Syndrome, pickwickian: Alveolar hyperventilation syndrome: obesity associated with hypersomnolence (especially, daytime sleepiness, hypoventilation, and polycythemia, and often also with twitching movements, cyanosis, periodic respira tions, congestive heart failure, arterial hypoxia and hypercapnia and rightward axis deviation on electrocardiogram. The syndrome may sometimes be reversed by weight loss. Although the pathophysiology of the syndrome is poorly understood, the drowsiness, sleep, and muscular twitching appear to be related to hypercapnia, while poly- cythemia and cyanosis appear to be related to arterial hypoxia. See eating disorders; syndrome, Kleine-Levin.

Syndrome, post-torture: A Dutch study of refugees from nine countries examined symptoms immediately following torture, complaints at the time were widely divergent. Psychic problems were particularly pronounced. There is not enough evidence to justify the term post-torture syndrome, an analogy with post-concentration camp syndrome. The question remains if a clearly developed syndrome will appear with passage of time.

Syndrome, premenstrual (PMS): Changes in mood, behaviour, cognition and somatic functioning seen in some women in relation to the menstrual cycle. Symptoms usually begin a few days before the onset and end shortly after the onset of a menstrual period; most frequently reported symptoms are anxiety, irritability, depressed mood, breast tenderness, abdominal discomfort, and a feeling of distention. It is generally assumed that endocrine abnormalities are a major factor in producing the syndrome, but evidence for the assumption is no stronger than the evidence implicating psychological factors as the major cause. See late luteal phase dysphoric disorder.

Syndrome, prisoner of war (POW): Psychopathologic manifestations occurring in prisoners of war, presumably a reaction to capture and imprisonment. Various types of reaction have been described, among them a syndrome of withdrawal, apathy, and sometimes death, which has been likened to the anaclitic depression reported by Spitz in hospitalized or otherwise deprived children.

Syndrome, psychomimic: Symptoms without organic basis that resemble the illness of another, typically, the latter illness has been fatal to an ambivalently related person, and the psychomimic syndrome often occurs on or near the anniversary of the other's death.

Syndrome, Puerto Rican: Fighting sickness; male de palea; a culture-specific syndrome consisting of an initial brooding period followed by agitation and striking out against anyone the subject encounters.

Syndrome, savant: A rare disorder in which severe developmental or psychiatric handicap is combined with islands of remarkable ability, usually artistic or memory-related, that stand out in sharp contrast to the otherwise permeating disability.

Syndrome, silver cord: A family constellation consisting of a passive or absent father and a dominating mother, believed by some to be significantly related to the subsequent of schizophrenia. See mother, schizophrenogenic.

Syndrome, social breakdown: The deterioration in social abilities, interpersonal relationships, and general behaviour that frequently accompanies organic and functional psychoses (and especially the schizophrenias). The term emphasizes the belief that such personality distortions, rather than being a inherent part of the psychotic process, are instead a reaction to the patient's environment; the male patient who is isolated from women will no longer make attempts to be attractive to the oppositive sex, the person who is deprived of all purposeful activity or removed from any meaningful occupation will have no reason to keep tract of time, etc. The social breakdown syndrome occurs in many situations – mental hospitals, prisons, concentration camps, etc. See psychiatry, community.

Syndrome, Strauss: See impulse disorder, hyperkinetic.

Syndrome, survivor: Any number of symptoms, including depression, insomnia, anxiety, psychosomatic illness, nightmares etc. that are believed to be based upon guilt feeling over being a sole – or nearly sole – survivor of a disaster in which others perished who were emotionally close, such as parents, siblings, spouse, or friends. The survivor syndrome is a type of post-traumatic stress disorder (q.v.). See neurosis, traumatic.

Syndrome, temporal lobe: A constellation of characteristic interictal personality changes observed in may patients with temporal lobe epilepsy, consisting of changes in sexual behaviour, religiosity, a tendency toward extensive or compulsive drawing and writing, preoccupation with detail and clarity, and a profound sense of righteousness.

Syndrome, vulnerable child: Symptoms often noted in child who, though he has survived an acute episode of severe illness, continues to be treated by his parents as if his life were still in considerable danger.

Syndrome, acute: Bleuler differentiated between the acute and chronic forms of schizophrenia. The acute syndromes are transitory states of various kinds that may occur as simple exacerbations of the chronic state or as reactive episodes, in response to emotionally charged experiences. The acute syndromes occur more frequently in the early years of the disease process; they may last for hours only, or they may persist for years. Subsequent memory for these episodes varies, but complete amnesia for them is unusual. Bleuler listed the following acute syndromes; melancholic conditions, manic conditions, catatonic states, delusions (amentia in the terms of the Viennese school), twilight states. Benommenheit, confusional states, fits of anger, anniversary excitements, stupor, deliria, fugue states, and dipsomania. See schizophrenia.

Syndrome, culture-specific: Behaviour disorders that appears to be limited to certain societies and have no counterpart in current Western nosology. Among such syndromes are amok, amurakh. Arctic hysteria, bangungut, berserk, copying mania, delahara, echul, falling out, fighting sickness, grisi siknis. Hsieh-Ping. Imu, jumpers, juramentado, kimilue, koro, lata, mal de pelea, menerik, miryachit, olonism. Oriental nightmare-death syndrome, piblokto, pseudoamok syndrome, Puerto Rican syndrome, susto, Tropenkoller, voodoo death, wihtigo psychosis, and windigo psychosis.

Syneidesis: (sin-I-de sis) This Greek word was proposed by Monakow to replace the English conscience. Monakow suggest that conscience is not a specifically human phenomenon and does not belong to the sphere of consciousness, but is a characteristic of all living beings in any stage of development. This concept is at variance with prevailing psychiatric opinion, which believes that conscience is a product of the interaction of the child with frustration-producing elements in the child's environment. See conscience.

Synergism, sexual: A sexual excitation that arises from a combination of various stimuli acting simultaneously. The manifold pleasurable stimulation of the surface of the body to unpleasant, or even painful, processes within the organism. Freud considered that perhaps every important physical process contributes to the genesis of sexual excitement. Even the combination of the two opposed instinctual tendencies – love and hate – may arouse sexual excitement; sexual synergism can be aroused provided the intensity of discomfort and pain does not pass a certain limit. According to the individual sexual constitution, this synergism manifests itself in different ways.

Synesthesia: Condition in which the stimulation of one sensory modality is perceived as sensation in a different modality, as when a sound produces a sensation of colour.

Syntaxic mode: The mode of perception that forms whole, logical, coherent pictures of reality that can be validated by others.

Syntaxic thought: Sullivan's term for logical, goal-directed, reality-oriented thinking. See also Secondary process.

Syntropy: A term used by Adolf Meyer to characterize healthy or wholesome relationships.

Systematic desensitization: A form of behaviour therapy developed by Joseph Wolpe and others in which anxiety-evoking stimuli are presented to the patient while he is in a state of deep muscle relaxation in an attempt to weaken the bond between the stimuli and the anxiety. The technique has proved particularly useful in the treatment of phobias. See also Reciprocal inhibition and desensitization.

T

Taboo (Tabu): (1) Anthropological term for the setting apart of an object or person or for the absolute prohibition of some class of acts on the ground that it would be a violation of the culture's whole system of thought i.e., an object is taboo if, it is untouchable, an act is taboo if it is unthinkable in terms of the culture's structure. (2) Any action which is prohibited by authority or by social pressure can be described as 'taboo'. In Psychoanalysis the taboos mentioned are incest and on killing the totem animal. Tachylogia: See Logorrhea.

Tachyphasia: Extreme rapidity of flow of speech occurring in anxiety states, mania and certain organic states.

Tacit knowledge (in social psychology): A term used to refer to the wide variety of things a person has to know or assume in order both to make sense of other peoples' utterances and activities, and to produce ones that are intelligible to others.

Talion: Retaliation. In psychoanalysis, the talion principle refers to the fear that all injury, intentional or accidental will be punished in kind – that is, an eye for an eye and a tooth for a tooth.

Tangentiality: A disturbance in which the person replies to a question in an oblique, digressive, or even irrelevant manner and the central idea is not communicated. The term has been used roughly synonymously with loosening of associations and speech derailment, but in DSM it refers only to answers to questions and not to spontaneous speech. Failure to communicate the central idea distinguishes tangentiality from circumstantiality, in which the goal idea is reached in a delayed or indirect manner. See also Circumstantiality, Communication disorder.

Tarasoff decision: A California court decision which essentially imposes a duty on the therapist to warn the appropriate person or persons when he becomes aware that his patient any present a risk of harm to a specific person or persons.

Tarantism: Dancing mania; specifically, what appears to have been a culture-specific syndrome in Italy in the 16th and 17th centuries, consisting of compulsive dancing as a way to undo the bite of tarantula.

Target patient: Group member on whom attention is focused by other members; the patient under discussion is structured interactional group psychotherapy.

Task of Emotional Development (TED): Group whose main energy is devoted to reaching some goal, as in finding a solution to a problem, creating a specific product, or pursuing in some other manner any activity that is essentially goal directed. Distinguished from this type of groups is the experimental group, which is mainly concerned with sharing whatever happens in a more spontaneous, less directed fashion.

TAT: See Thematic Apperception Test.

TED: See Tasks of Emotional Development.

Teeth grinding: Habitual clenching or grinding of the teeth, unrelated to mastication, and occurring in either sleep or the waking state. The subject usually lacks full awareness of the symptom. The causes can be multiple but release of emotional tension through muscular contractions is commonly implicated. *Synonym* bruxism.

Telegraphic speech: Concise speech which leaves out redundant words, as in a telegram, but gets the essential meaning across. Telegraphic speech is used by children of around 2 years, who typically combine only 2 or 3 words at a time in each utterance. Indeified as such by Roger Brown, it formed the basis of his approach to language acquisition, which rejected the prevailing structural approaches to infant speech and instead focused on the child's communicative intentions. The overall approach was known as semantic relations grammer.

Telemetry: Sending measurements over a distance, usually using radio frequencies. Telemetry is used to monitor the physiological responses of freely moving subjects such as athletes, children at play, and migrating birds.

Teleology: The study of purpose, also the claim that a phenomenon exists for a purpose (extrinsic teleology) or has a purpose of its own (immanent teleology).

Telepathy: Extrasensory perception of the mental activities of another person.

Temperament: Inherent, constitutional predisposition to react in a certain way to stimuli. Variations is temperament are evident very early in life.

Tender mindedness: A personality characteristic put forward by William James, and later elaborated by H.J. Eysenck: characterized by a gently, optimistic and idealistic approach to the world. Its opposite, tough mindedness, is characterized by a harsher, more pessimistic approach.

Tension: Physiological or psychic arousal, uneasiness, or pressure toward action; an unpleasuarable alteration in mental or physical state that seeks relief through action.

Tension headache: A sensation of tightness, pressure, or dull pain which may be generalized or, more typically, have a 'band-like' quality. As a transient disturbance, it is commonly associated with the stresses of everyday life but, when persistent, may be presenting feature of an anxiety state or a depressive illness.

Terminal insomnia: Early morning awakening or waking up at least 2 hours before planning to. See also Initial insomnia and Middle insomnia.

Territoriality: Ethological concept referring to the fact that in many species of animals, individuals establish areas which they defend against introducing members of their own species. This behaviour-pattern presumably fulfils two functions: spreading of the species over the available environment and reducing the occasions for fighting members of the same species.

Test: A systematic procedure to measure or assess some characteristic, ability, or skill of a subject, such as intelligence or personality traits. A Normative-referenced test is one that compares the performance of the individual subject with a group whose performance on the test is used as a standard. A criterion-referenced test is one in which the standard is a specified set of performances or actions; the subject is evaluated as to whether he does or does not meet the criteria, without comparing his performance to that of a group (e.g., can the patient dress himself, or can be not?). See reliability; validity.

Test, ability: Any evaluation of presently existing potentiality or capacity to function; a test of maximal performance in any area.

Test, ACE: The American Council of Education intelligence test, designed for use with secondary school and college students.

Test, achievement: Any evaluation of what gains the subject has made in an area following training and instruction.

Test, analogies: A test of ability to comprehend relationships, usually by asking the subject to name the fourth term that bears the same relation to the third as the second does to the first. Example: Ship is to water as automobile is to what?

Test, aptitude: A test of the probable level of future performance that will be reached following further maturation and/or training.

Test, Arthur Point Scale: A non-verbal performance measure of intellectual ability, consisting of 10 subjects, mainly of the formboard variety. The test is most reliable within the 7 to 13 year age range and is of particular value when the subject's verbal capacity is compromised by foreign language handicap, speech or hearing defect, or personal and cultural factors.

Test, Bender Visual-Motor Gestalt: A projective technique consisting of nine geometrical figures that are copied by the subject; devised by Lauretta Bender and first described by her in 1938. Its chief applications are to determine retardation, loss of function, and organic brain defects in children and adults, and in the study of personality deviations that show regressive phenomena. It is of limited usefulness in the study of neuroses and psycho-somatic disorders.

Test, Bero: (ba'ro) Behn-Rorschach test; a set of plates prepared by Behn with the assistance of Rorschach. Zullinger provided the norma of the Bero test.

Test, beta: A set of mental tests used in the U.S. Army in 1917–18, designed for illiterates. Instructions are given in signs and the material is pictorial in character, in contrast to alpha tests, which are carried out verbally.

Test, block design: A performance test in which the subject tries to match standard designs using coloured blocks ; used as a measure of intelligence and as an indicator of deterioration in brain damage and in the schizophrenias.

Test, cancellation: Any test in which the subject is instructed to strike out one or more specified symbols may be particular letters, numbers, words, or geometrical figures.

Test, chi-square: A statistical test, developed originally by Karl Pearson, that measures the significance of differences occurring between groups.

Test, Cornell Word Form (CWF): A modification of the word-association technique devised to distinguish "normals" from subjects with neuropsychiatric and psychosomatic disorders in a way not apparent to the subject. The test is used primarily in industrial psychology. It consists of a list of stimulus words, each of which is followed by two response words. The subject is asked to encircle whichever of the two words seems to him to be the most related to the stimulus word; e.g., mother – mine, woman.

Test, draw-a-person: A method of personality analysis based upon the interpretation of drawings of the human figure. Although figure drawings had been used by many workers in the field, it was Karen Machover who in 1949 outlined a system of interpretation that was correlated with clinical diagnostic categories.

Test, drawing-of-a-man: See test, Goodenough.

Test, fact-hand: A test of diffuse cerebral dysfunction devised by Bender. The subject, whose eyes are closed, is touched simultaneously on the cheek and the dorsum of the hand; retesting is done with the eyes open. Results are considered positive if the subject fails consistently to identity both stimuli within 10 trials. By the age of 7, normal children respond with a negative test. Positive results are seen not only in cases of cerebral dysfunction in children and adults, but also in schizophrenic children. See tactile sensation, double simultaneous.

Test, Fink-Green-Bender: See tactile sensation, double simultaneous.

Test, Gesell development: "The Gesell Schedules consist of a series of 27 age level recorded observations and reactions to standardized situations from birth through the first five years of life. At each age level an inventory of activities is divided into four categories of behavious: (1) Motor; (2) Adaptive; (3) Language; and (4) Personal-Social. Each of these categories of behaviour is evaluated by observing the infant or child in a number of standardized situations." (Masserman, J.H The Practice of Dynamic Psychiatry, 1955).

Test, good and evil: See responsibility, criminal.

Test, Goodenough: A test of a child's intellectual level of development based upon the subject's drawing of a human figure. The test was introduced in 1926 by Florence Goodenouth, who standardized the children's drawings and thereby produced a simple and satisfactory test of intelligence.

Test, House-Tree Person (HTP): A type of projective test in which the subject is asked to draw a house, a tree, and a person.

Test, Janet's: (Pierre Janet, French physician, 1859–1947) A test for the determination of tactile sensibility; the patient answers "yes" or "no" when touched by the examiner's finger.

Test, Kent EGY: A series of 10 questions used for a quick estimate of intelligence.

Test, Knox cube: A performance test, of particular value when the subject suffers from a language handicap or barrier, in which the subject taps a series of four cubes in various prescribed sequences.

Test, Kohnstamm: The Kohnstamm maneuver is often used to demonstrate suggestibility to a subject being prepared for hypnotic trance induction. It is a normal neurophysiologic reaction, elicited by having the subject press his extended arm as strenuously as possible against a wall for approximately two minutes, after which the arm will rise automatically with or without a suggestion to that effect.

Test, Kohs block-design: An intelligence test in which the subject copies a design using small, multi-coloured cubes.

Test, Lowenfeld: See test, mosaic.

Test, Machover: See test, draw –a-person.

Test, Minnesota Multiphasic Personality Inventory (MMPI): A personality questionnaire consisting of 550 statements concerning behaviour, feelings, social attitudes, and frank symptoms of psychopathology. To each question, the subject must answer T (true), F (false), or ? (cannot say), and his answer sheet is then scored by various keys that have been standardized on different diagnostic groups and personality types. The MMPI was originally constructed by psychiatrist, J.C. McKinley, and a psychologist, Starke Hathaway.

Test, mosaic: A projective technique, introduced by M. Lowenfelf and further developed by F. Wertham, which imploys a set of 300 colored pieces (black, blue, red, green, yellow, and off-white) in six shapes (squares, diamonds, oblongs, and three different sized triangles). The subject is presented with the test objects on a tray and is asked to make anything he wants on the board. The designs made by adults and children have been correlated with diagnostic categories, and individual designs can be interpreted on the basis of these correlations.

Test, myokinetic psychodiagnosis: A test devised by Mira that consists of drawings of patterns with both the right and the left hands. The left-hand drawings are believed to reveal genotypic reactions and the right-hand drawings are said to express more superficial phenotypic reactions. Comparison of the drawings is made to diagnose various conditions and character traits.

Test, organic integrity (OIT): A modification of the Casgrandie test for colour-dominance and form-dominance perception, described by H.C. Tien. The OIT is said to be a rapid test for organic brain disease; it is based on the theory that central nervous system damage will interfere with ability to perceive form.

Test-person: The subject who is examined by the association method.

Test, PMA: A test of seven traits believed by Thurstone and Thurstone to account for most of the variance in primary mental abilities (PMA). These traits are: V (verbal comprehension), W (word fluency), N (number), S (space), M (associative memory), P (perceptual speed), and R (reasoning) or I (induction).

Test, progressive matrices: An intelligence test in which the subject is asked to choose, from several alternatives, the one part that will complete the abstract design presented to him. The test is made up of 60 such designs.

Test, projective: A type of psychologic test in which the test material presented to the subject is such that any response will necessarily be determined by his own prevailing mood or underlying psychopathology. See method, projective.

Test, psycholinguistic: See Illinois Test of Psycholinguistic Abilities.

Test, right and wrong: See responsibility, criminal.

Test, Rorschach: (Hermann Rorschach, Swiss psychiatrist, 1884–1922) A projective test consisting of ten inkblots of varying designs and colors, which are shown to the subject one at a time with the request of interpret them. Its purpose is to furnish a description of the dynamic forces to personality through an analysis of the formal aspects of the subject's interpretations. The test yields information as to the intellectual and emotional processes, the degree of personality integration, variability in mental functioning, and the degree to which the subject responds to environmental influenced and to his inner promptings. The test not only is used to obtain a picture of the subject's personality, but also serves as an aid in problems of differential psychiatric diagnosis and prognosis.

Test, sociometric: The sociometric test is an instrument with which to measure the amount of the organization shown by social groups. It requires an individual to choose associated for any group of which he is or might become a member. The test reveals that the underlying attraction-repulsion pattern of a group differs widely from its visible structure and the groups tested upon the basis of different criteria tend toward diversity of structures. These structures have been revealed when the criteria of the test have been applied to home groups, work groups, and school groups.

Test, spider's web: A test of the biological effects of various body fluids (urine, serum, etc.) on the pattern of a spider's web. It has been found, for example, that schizophrenic urine gives different and more marked pattern changes than does non-schizophrenic urine.

Test, spontaneity: The spontaneity test proceeds by throwing the subject into standard life situations in which he improvises freely while acting opposite members of the group to whom he has been found emotionally related as revealed by the sociometric test, either through attraction or repulsion. The situations may express such emotions like anger, fear, sympathy, dominance or any other emotions. They may express such as father, employer, or any other roles.

Test, Stanford-Binet: "The revised Stanford-Binet Intelligence Scale is the test most frequently used in the individual examination of children. It consists of 120 items, plus several alternative tests that are applicable to the age range between two years and adulthood. The tests have a variety of activities of graded difficulty, both verbal and performance designed to tap a variety of intellectual functions such as memory, free association, orientation in time, language comprehension, knowledge of common objects, comprehension, knowledge of common objects, comparison of concepts, perception of contradictions, understanding of abstract terms, the ability to meet novel situations and the use of practical judgement. In addition to many other varieties of function, there are also tests of visual-motor coordination." The score is expressed in months of mental age, which is divided by the chronological age (in months) and then multiplied by 100 to give the intelligence quotient.

Test, Szondi: A projective test, developed by Szondi in Switzerland in the 1940s, which consists of six sets of pictures, each set containing eight photographs. These eight photographs are of eight different psychobiologic conditions-homesexual, sadist, epileptic, hysteria, catatonic schizophrenic, paranoid schizophrenic, manic-depressive depressed, manic-depressive manic. The subject chooses from each set the two pictures he likes most and the two he dislikes the most. The eight different conditions portrayed are presumed to be extreme pathologic representatives of the eight basic emotional needs. The test is interpreted in terms of the degree of tension, and the subject's attitude to this tension, in each of these eight need-systems. The need-systems are as follows: the need for tender, feminine love (h factor); the need for aggression and masculinity (s factor); the mode of dealing with crude, aggressive motions (e factor); the need to exhibit emotions (hyfactor); narcissistic ego-needs (k factor); the expansive tendencies of the ego (p factor); the need for acquiring and mastering object (d factor); and the need to cling to objects for enjoyment (m factor). Although the Szondi test can be used clinically, as a projective technique, without reference to the viewpoint that let to its development, the basis of the test is Szondi's theory of genotropism (q.v.).

Test, thematic apperception (TAT): A projective technique, originally described by Morgan and Murray in 1935, which focuses primarily on the dynamics of interpersonal relationships. In its present form (the third set to be used since 1935), it consists of a series of 31 pictures that depict a number of social situations and interpersonal relations. In clinical practice, 10 or 12 of the pictures are usually selected by the examiner on the basis of which of the total 31 are most likely to elicit information on the subject's problems. The selected pictures are then presented to the subject's relationship to authority figures, to contemporaries of both sexes, and in terms of the compromises between and the needs to the id, the ego, and the superego. There are various method of interpreting results; the one advocated by Murrary is the need-press method (see method, need-press). L. Bellak recommends interpretation in terms of the following 14 categories: main theme, main hero, attitudes to parental figures, figures introduced, objects introduced, objects omitted, attribution of blame, significant conflicts, punishment for crime attitude to hero, signs of inhibition (in aggression, sex, etc.), outcome, pattern of need gratification, and plot. It is to be noted that the TAT is only incidentally a diagnostic tool and is not primarily designed for nosologic classification.

Test, Wada dominance of 3–4 minutes: described by J. Ehrenwald (Archives of General Psychiatry 7, 1962), who theorizes that it is a measure of ego strength in that it "causes a temporary breakdown of the synthetic and integrative functions of the ego touched off by the dissociation of the visual and postural components of the patient's experiences of the body image and of the outside world."

Test, Wada dominance: A method for determining the side of cerebral dominance by intracarotid injection of amobarbital, introduced by J. Wada in 1949.

Test, Wechsler-Bellevue: An intelligence test, that most widely used test in the average adult, consisting of five verbal tests, five performance test, and an additional vocabulary test. The 11 subtests are as follows: general in formation, general comprehension, arithmetic, digit span, similarities, vocabulary, picture arrangement, picture completion, block design, object assembly, and digit symbol. The subtests are scored on the basis of sped and accuracy, and results can be transplanted into standard scores that give verbal IQ, the performance IQ, and the full-scale IQ.

Test, Word-in-context: A test of capacity for verbal reasoning in which the subject is asked to determine the meaning of a given word by reading selected passages of prose.

Test, Z: See test, Zulliger.

Test, Zulliger: A brief Rorschach-type test of particular value for rapid screening of a group of patients; administration time averages ten minutes.

Testamentary capacity: In the executing of a legally valid will, the basic required legal elements are: (a) the approximate monetary value and nature of the estate should be known by the testator; (b) he should know the natural heirs to his bounty (that is, a spouse or other blood related persons to whom the estate would ordinarily be expected to go); (c) he should know that the instrument (will) that he is signing is, in fact, a will; and (d) he should know the beneficiaries of the will.

Tests, alpha: A series of mental tests, first used in the United States military service (1917) to determine the relative mental ability of recruits. There are eight different types of test: for directions, arithmetical ability, practical judgement, synonyms and antonyms, correct arrangement of sentences, completion of series of digits, analogies, and information. The tests are designed particulary for group application and for rapid mechanical scoring.

Tests, Binet-Simon: (be-na' semaw N') (Alfred Binet, French psychologist, 1857–1911, and Theodore Simon, French physician, 1873–1861). Tests of intellectual capacity, which is expressed as the intelligence quotient (IQ), introduced in France in 1905 as a result of studies made to determine whether children could be educated as the new laws required. The Standford revision of the tests for use with American children was made in 1916, although they had already been introduced into the United States of Goddard in 1910.

Tests, Brunet: (broo-na') A development scale designed for use with infants as young as 1 month.

Tests, Buhler: A development scale designed for use with infants from birth up to school age.

Tests, sorting: A method of psychological testing in which the subjects into groups on the basis of similarity or some other abstract relationship. Such sorting or Zurodnung tests are particularly associated with Kurt Goldstein. Vigotsky, Hanfmann, and Kaanin. Patients with cortical lesions, particularly, show impairment of abstract behavious as measured by these tests. Schizophrenics, too, do poorly on these tests; but performance is more varied than in ordinary brain damage cases, for the schizophrenic tends to project himself into the test objects and animate and embellish them.

T-group (training group): A group that emphasizes training in self-awareness and group dynamics.

Thanatology: The study of death and the matters leading up to it and following it.

Thanatos: The name of the Greek god of death, which was used by Freud to refer to the death instinct; a concept which he developed in order to account for the interpersonal and intrapersonal aggression of World War I. See also Death Instinct.

Theater of Spontaneity (Stegreiftheater): Improvizational theater in Vienna that played an important role in the development of psychodrama by J.L. Moreno as a therapeutic technique in group psychotherapy.

Thematic Apperception Test (TAT): A projective psychological test in which the subject supplies interpretations of a series of ambiguous life situation drawings, based on his own feelings and attitudes and reflecting his unconscious conflicts and defensive structure. See also Michigan Picture Stories.

Theory: A general statement predicting, explaining, or describing the relationships among a number of constructs.

Theory of the humours: A type theory of personality originating in the second century BC, and popular throughout the Middle Ages. It identified four main types of personality, each of which was supposed to come about through the action of particular body fluids. The four types are: choleric, thought to result from an excess of yellow bile; sanguine, from blood; melancholic, from black bile, and phlegmatic, from phlegm. That this was a popular theory can be seen in the way that many words have retained meanings which derive directly from that theory. It was this view of the origins of human personality which led to the word humour, which had meant bodily fluid, coming to mean 'mood' or 'temper'.

Therapeutic agent: Anything – a person or a drug – that promotes healing.

Therapeutic alliance: Conscious contractual relationship between therapist and patient in which each implicitly agrees that they need to work together to help the patient with his problems. It involves a therapeutic splitting of the patient's ego into observing and experiencing parts. A good therapeutic alliance is especially necessary for the contribution of treatment during phases of strong negative transference. See also Working alliance.

Therapeutic community: Institutional treatment setting designed with an emphasis on the importance of socioenvironmental and interpersonal influences in the therapy, management and rehabilitation of the hospitalized mental patient. See also Milieu therapy.

Therapeutic crisis: Turning point in the treatment process. An example is acting out, which, depending on how it is dealt with, may not lead to a therapeutic change in the patient's behaviour. See also Therapeutic impasse.

Therapeutic group: Group of patients joined together under the leadership of a therapist for the purpose of working together for psychotherapeutic ends-specifically, for the treatment of each patient's mental disorders.

Therapeutic impasse: Deadlock in the treatment process. Therapy is in a state of imminent failure when there is no further insight or awareness and when sessions are reduced to routine meetings of patient and therapist. Unresolved resistances and transference and countertransference conflicts are among the common causes of the phenomenon. See also Therapeutic crisis.

Therapeutic role: Position in which one aims to treat, bring about an improvement, or provide alleviation of a distressing condition or state.

Therapeutic window: The well-defined range of blood levels associated with optimal clinical response to antidepressant drugs, such as nortiptyline. Levels above or below that range are associated with a poor response.

Therapist: See Psychotherapist.

Thinking: See Cognition.

Thinking compulsion: See Intellectualization.

Thinking through: The mental process that occurs in an attempt to understand one's own behaviour and gain insight from it.

Third ear: Ability to make use of intuition, sensitivity, and awareness of subliminal cues to interpret clinical observations of individual and group patients. First introduced by the German Philosopher Friedrich Nietzsche, the term was later used in analytic psychotherapy by Theodor Reik.

Thompson, Clara: (1893–1958) American psychoanalyst; associated with Harry Sullivar and his modification of psychoanalysis (interpersonal relationships).

Third nervous system: Burrow's conception of a nervous system based on function, rather than anatomy.

Thought, abstract: See Abstract thinking.

Thought broadcasting: Feeling that one's thoughts are being broadcast or projected into the environment. Seen in schizophrenia.

Thought, concrete: See Concrete thinking.

Thought control: See Delusion of control.

Thought deprivation: See Blocking.

Thought disorder: Any disturbance of thinking that affects language, communication, or thought content. Thought disorder is the hallmark feature of schizophrenia. Its manifestations range from simple blocking and mild circumstantiality to profound loosening of associations, incoherence, and delusions. See also Communication disorder, Language disorder.

Thought disorder, content: Disturbance of thinking in which the person exhibits delusions that may be multiple, fragmented, and bizarre.

Thought disorder, formal: A disorder in the form of thought, as distinguished from the content of thought. It is characterized by a failure to follow semantic and syntactic rules that it not consistent with the person's education, intelligence, or cultural background.

Three-cornered therapy: See Co-therapy.

Three Essays on the Theory of Sexuality: Title of a book by Freud published in 1905. It applied the libido theory to the successive phases of psycho-sexual maturation in the infant, child, and adolescent. It made possible the integration of a vast diversity of clinical observations and promoted the direct observation of child development.

Tic: Involuntary, spasmodic, stereotype movement of a small group of muscles. Predominantly psychogenic, tics are seen most prominently in moments of stress or anxiety. They are rarely the result of organic disease.

Time and motion: A method of analyzing working pattern developed by F.W. Taylor down work sequences into sequences of actions with maximum economy and minimum effort. Taylor showed how productivity in industry could be dramatically increased, and his work is often considered to be the foundation of ergonomics. Although it is still used from time to time today, it has proved to be of only limited value on the factory floor; people have an understandable aversion of being treated as if they were robots.

Time perception: The subjective of the passage of time, which is found not to correspond precisely with objective time. Time perception has been studied experimentally to determine the effect of various forms of cognitive tasks, and of psychoactive drugs.

Timidity: Inability to assert oneself for fear of some fancied reprisal, even in the absence of objective evidence of potential harm.

Tip of the tongue phenomenon: A phenomenon of memory in which the individual experiences the feeling of knowing the desired information but is temporarily unable to bring it to consciousness.

Toe-walking: Walking on the toes rather than on the whole foot; toe-walking has been reported in approximately 20% of childhood schizophrenics.

Toilet training: The program of teaching a child to control his bladder and bowel functions. The attitudes of both parent and child regarding the period may have important psychological implications for the child's later development.

Token economy: A program applying principles of operant conditioning to the management of an institutional setting, such as a ward or a classroom. The reinforcement of desirable behaviour is provided in the form of tokens and credits (conditioned reinforcers) that may be exchanged for a variety of positive reinforces, such as food, television time, and a weekend pass. See also Reinforcement.

Tolerance: Phenomenon in which, after repeated administration, a given dose of a drug produces a decreased effect, or increasingly larger doses must be administered to obtain the effect observed with the original dose. See also Drug dependence.

Topological psychology: The psychological geometry formulated by Lewin (1936) to represent diagrammatically certain structural concepts of field theory.

Torpedoing: The application of intense electrical currents to the bodily region involved in hysterical conversions.

Totem: Anthropological term for animal, plant of other object which is venerated by a particular tribe or community and which it treats as a symbol of itself or as its protector. In Freud's Totem and Taboo (1911), the speculative theory, the totem symbolizes the primal. Father who was murdered when his sons rebelled against his mastery of the primal Horde.

Totem and Taboo: Title of a book by Freud published in 1913. In it he applied his psychoanalytic concepts to the data of anthropology. He was able to afford much insight into the meaning of trail organizations of customs, especially by invoking the Oedipus complex and the characteristics of magical thought as he had discovered them from studies of the unconscious. See also Oedipus complex.

Tourette's disease: See Gilles de la Tourette's disease.

Toxic psychosis: A psychosis caused by toxic substances produced the body or introduced into it in the form of chemicals or drugs. See also Substance-induced organic mental disorder.

Trainable: Capable of achieving a certain degree of self-care and social adjustment at home and vocational usefulness in a closely supervised setting. The term describes the moderately mentally retarded. See also Educate, Mental retardation.

Trainer: Professional leader or facilitator of a sensitivity training or T-group, teacher or supervisor of a person learning the science of practice or group therapy.

Training group: See T-group.

Trait: An aspect of personality, such as sociability, impulsiveness, conveniently, etc. See also trait theory.

Trait theory: A theory of personality in which personality is considered to consist of a collection of differing, usually measurable traits. One of the best known examples, is that of R.B. Cattell whose personality inventory measures 16 different personality factors (and so is called the 16PF).

Trance: A state of focused attention and diminished sensory and motor activity seen in hypnosis, hysterical neurosis, dissociative types (see under neurosis), and ecstatic religious states.

Transaction: Interaction that arises in an encounter between two or more persons. Eric Berne, the founder of transactional analysis, defined a transaction as involving a stimulus from an ego state of one person and the corresponding response from a ego state of another person.

Transactional analysis: Eric Berne's system of psychodynamic psychotherapy that focuses on the interactions – that is, transactions – between the patient and the therapist in the treatment session and between the patient and others in his social environment. The system includes four components: (1) Structural analysis of intrapsychic phenomena; (2) transactional analysis proper, the determination of the currently dominant ego state (parent, child or adult) of each participant; (3) game analysis, identification of the games played in their interactions and of the gratifications provided; and (4) script analysis, uncovering of the causes of the patient's emotional problems. Transactional analysis is used in both individual and group psychotherapy.

Transference neurosis: A phenomenon occurring in psychoanalysis in which the patient develops a strong emotional attachment to the therapist as a symbolized nuclear familial figure. The repetition and the depth of that misperception or symbolization characterize it as a transference neurosis.

Transient situation disturbance: Self-limited mental disorder of any severity occurring in response to an overwhelmingly stressful situation. In DSM-III replaced by adjustment disorder. See also Adjustment disorder.

Transsexualism: A gender identity disorder in which a person has a desire to be of the opposite sex. Some transsexuals, many of whom have adopted the role of the opposite sex since childhood, have successfully undergone sex-changing surgical procedures, accompanied by intensive hormonal therapy and psychotherapy.

Transvestism: A paraphilia characterized by dressing in the clothing of the opposite sex for the purpose of sexual arousal. It is usually seen in men with a strong desire to appear as women. It is also spelled transvestitism.

Trauma: In psychiatry, a significant upsetting experience or event that may precipitate or aggravate a mental disorder.

Traumatic neurosis: A neurosis occurring after severe physical or psychological trauma. A useless term, best avoided.

Trend of thought: Thinking that centers on a particular idea associated with an affective tone.

Triad: Interactional relationship among three persons. Its prototype, the father-mother-child relationship, may evolve projectively in group therapy.

Triad, anal: The group of three prime, or outstanding traits of the so-called anal character: (1) Obstinacy (2) Parsimony (3) Pedantic orderliness.

Trichotillomania: Compulsion to pull out one's hair.

Tuke, William (1732–1819): British pioneer in the treatment of mental patients without the use of physical restraints.

Tumescence, Penile: Erection of the penis. Nocturnal penile tumescence (NPT) is associated with over 90% of REM sleep episodes and is thus useful aid in differentiating between psychogenic (where NPT is ordinarily preserved) and impotence due to organic impairment (where NPT is typically reduced or absent).

Turning against the self: One of the four instinctual vicissitudes described by Freud (1915), the other three being Reversal into its opposite. Repression and Sublimation, listed by Anna Freud (1937) as one of the mechanisms of Defence.

Twin research: A powerful method of investigating the relative degree of phenotypic variance that can be attributed to genetic factors and to transmissible and nontransmissible environmental factors. For example, the dissimilarities between monozygotic twins are compared with the behavioural variations occurring in non-twin siblings or dizygotic twins.

Type A personality: A temperament characterized by excessive drive, competitiveness, a sense of time urgency, impatience, unrealistic ambition, and need for control. Believed to be associated with a high incidence of coronary artery disease.

Type B personality: A temperament characterized by a relaxed, easy-going demeanor; less time-bound and competitive than the A personality.

Type 1 error: Research term referring to the rejection of the null hypothesis when it is true – that is, concluding erroneously that an observed effect or result is significant when, in fact, it is not and can be explained solely on the basis of the operation of chance factors. When the statistically calculated probability (P value) of making a type I error on the basis of an experimental result is less than 0.05, the result is considered statistically significant. The type of error and the arbitrarily chosen 0.05 level of significance are sometimes called alpha (α). See also Null hypothesis, SaListical significance, Type 2 error.

Type 2 error: The failure to reject a false null hypothesis – that is, concluding that any difference or effect demonstrated in an experiment is no greater than that expected by chance alone when, in fact, there is an actual difference or effect. It is also called a beta (β) error. See also Null hypothesis, Satistical significance, Type 1 error.

Type theory: A theory of personality in which people are classified according to common characteristics. Sheldon grouped people according to types of physique, their somatotype, with personality characteristics supposedly associated with particular kinds of bodily build. Jung also grouped people according to personality type, most famously introversion and extroversion. The theory of the humours provides another example of an early type theory of personality. A more restricted approach in the study of personality is the 'narrow-band' approach, the identification of a single type such as the authoritarian personality.

U

Unconditional positive regard: A prerequisite for mental health and personal growth, according to Carl Rogers. Rogers identifies two basic human needs: the need for positive regard, from other people, and the need for self-actualization. The person must satisfy both of these needs, but if their only positive regard is conditional upon 'good' or appropriate behaviour, then much of their behaviour will be directed towards obtaining that approval. This means that they will not feel free to explore their own potential and their need for self-actualization because of the fear of engendering social disapproval. Most people, however, have at least one person at some time in their life who gives them unconditional positive regard. In that relationship, they can be sure of the person's affection and warmth, and this means that they can feel free to develop and explore new aspects of themselves. Unconditional positive regard is usually provided by parents, during childhood, though Rogers believes that it is not tied to the early years of life. The formation of such a basis of unconditional positive regard is at the heart of Roger's client-centered therapy.

Unconditioned response: A response which occurs automatically to a particular stimulus, and not have to be learned. For example, pulling the hand away from a burningly hot surface is an unconditioned response: it happens as a reflex, without the need for conscious recognition of what is happening. See also unconditioned stimulus, conditioned response, conditioned stimulus, classical conditioning, conditioning.

Unconditioned stimulus: A stimulus which automatically produces a response in an organism (animal or human being). The term 'unconditioned' means 'not learned': a stimulus of this kind will operate by reflex, or automatically, with no learning being necessary. It forms the basis for classical conditioning as the new, conditioned stimulus becomes linked with the unconditioned one. See conditioning.

Unconscious: 1. (Noun) In psychoanalysis, the topographic division of the mind in which the psychic material is not readily accessible to conscious awareness by ordinary means. Its existence may be manifested in symptom formation, in dreams, or under the influence of drugs. 2. (Noun) In popular but more ambiguous usage, any mental material not in the immediate field of awareness. 3. (Adjective) In a state of unawareness, with lack of response to external stimuli, as in a coma. See also Conscious, Preconscious.

Unconscious motive: A motive of which the person is unaware but which continues to have an effect on behaviour. For example, a student may underachieve during exams owing to an unconscious rebellion against parental pressure to succeed; although consciously, she or he will be trying to do as well as possible, the chosen revision strategies are ineffectual, relying on rote learning or simply reading through notes, and this ensures that they do not do as well as they could. Unconsciously, they have shied away from being too successful. Human behaviour is often influenced by such unconscious motives; and disentangling them such that the individual becomes aware of what is going on can be one of the main tasks of psychotherapist.

Underachieve: One who fails to perform at the level of his known potential or capability.

Undersocialized: Characterized by the absence of adequate social bonds to others. See also Conduct disorder.

Undifferentiated schizophrenia: A schizophrenic disorder in which the psychotic symptoms are prominent but do not fall into the other schizophrenic subtypes.

Ultradian rhythm: See Biological rhythm.

Ululation: The incoherent crying of psychotic or hysterial patient.

Undoing: An unconscious defense mechanism by which a person symbolically acts out in reverse something unacceptable that has already been done or against which the ego must defend itself. A primitive defense mechanism, undoing is a form of magical expiatory action. Repetitive in nature, it is commonly observed in obsessive – compulsive disorder.

Unilateral awareness: The first level of involvement in the growth of relationships; a person notices another and may make judgements evaluating the characteristics of the other. Compare surface contact, stage of mutuality.

Unipolar psychosis: An effective disorder characterized by recurrent episodes of depression or, much more rarely, recurrent manic states. See also Bipolar affective disorder, Manic depressive illness.

Unprepared behaviours: Responses which can be acquired by an animal species when learning procedures are applied. Compare prepared behaviours, contra prepared behaviours.

Uranomania: The delusion that one is of divine or celestial origin.

Uranophobia: Fear of heaven.

Uxoricide: Killing of a wife by her husband.

V

Vaginismus: Painful vaginal spasm, usually psychogenic, that occurs during coitus, causing dyspareunia. It may have its onset during preparation for intercourse, making penile insertion impossible.

Validity: The extent to which a test measures what it is designed to measure. Types (a) *Predictive* (ability of the test to predict outcome); (b) Content (whether the test selects a representative sample of the total tests for that variable; (c) *Construct* (how well the experiment tests the hypothesis underlying it).

Vampirism: The phenomenon of the vampire, an ancient, ubiquitous and fascinating activity in which an individual is involved in the ingestion of blood, necrophilic activity and necrosadism. The psychiatric conditions that seemed to have a close relation with it are schizophreniform disorders, hysteria, severe psychopathic disorders and mental retardation.

Variable: In research, any characteristic or factor that may assume different values. The terms "independent variable" and "dependent variable" indicate a relationship of cause and effect, respectively.

Variable-interval schedule: See Schedule of reinforcement.

Variable-ratio schedule: See Schedule of reinforcement.

Variance: A statistical measure of the variability within a set of observations. It is defined as the sum of the squared deviations from the mean divided by the number of observations. It equals the standard deviation squared. Analysis of variance is a technique for testing experimental results for significance; it is used when more than two sample means are to be compared. See also Analysis of variance.

Variation: A statistical term referring to the manner in which persons in a population vary among themselves with respect to a given quality or trait. Three common measures of variation are the range, the variance, and the standard deviation. A knowledge of variation in a population is important because it indicate how useful the mean value is as a representative figure. Variability of persons also affects the precision of sample estimates.

Veblem, Thorstin: Born in rural Winconsin, USA in 1857, he gave "The theory of the leisure class."

Vegetatove: Pertaining to functions that are largely physiological concerned with the growth, nutrition, or general physical health and homeostasis of the organism. In depression, the term is applied to characteristic symptoms, such as sleep disturbance (especially early morning awakening), decreased appetite, constipation, weight loss, and loss of sexual response. Vegetative nervous system is an obsolete term for autonomic nervous system.

Veraguth, fold of: (Otto Veraguth, German neurologist, 1870–1940) Contraction upward and lackward of the inner third of upper eyelid, thus changing and arch of upper lid into an angle. Veraguth described this change as a characteristic sign of depressed type of manic-depressive psychosis.

Verbal amnesia: See Amnesia, neurological.

Verbal deprivation hypothesis: The idea put forward by Bernstein and others, that the form of language learned by a child could represent a disadvantage when it came to learning or handling abstract forms of information. Bernstein argued that restricted codes of language, with their relatively limited vocabularies and reliance on shared assumptions on the part of the listener, meant that would find the kind of conceptual and abstract learning which they encountered in school inherently more difficult than children who used elaborated codes. This idea was hotly disputed by many researchers, notably Labov, who demonstrated that children who used highly restricted codes of handling abstract and theoretical concepts, as long as those concepts were introduced in a setting in which the children felt relaxed.

Verbal memory: This term is used in two main ways. Firstly to mean the storing of mental images by using words as a form of coding for information. In this case, verbal memory is simply meant as a variation of symbolic representation, with all the associated features and advantages. Secondly, the term is used to mean memory for words. Much laboratory research on memory, especially in the early years, concentrated initially on asking subjects to memorize list of words, partly because subjects were able to state clearly exactly what they remembered, which was not always easy with visual or auditory images. But there is considerable recent evidence to suggest that this form of learning is qualitatively different from the way that people remember connected prose or speech, and even more different from everyday memory. In its most general sense, verbal memory includes memory for speech and prose.

Verbomania: Meaningless and stereotyped repetition of words or phrases. It is also known as cataphasis. It is a symptom seen in schizophrenia. See also Perseveration, Logorrhea.

Verstehende psychologie: An approach to psychology applying the method of verstehen i.e., under standing mental processes in others through observation of physical processes and analogy to one's own (directly accessible) mental processes. The term was coined by Jaspers.

Vicarious learning: Learning through observing what happens to others. Vicarious learning was particularly investigated by Bandura in studies of imitation in children. He found that children who saw others being rewarded for aggressive acts were more likely to imitate them. Behaviour patterns may be acquired or abandones as a consequence of seeing other people being rewarded or punished for them. See also identification.

Vienna Psychoanalytic Society: An outgrowth of the Wednesday Evening Society, an informal group of Freud's earliest followers. The new name was acquired and a reorganization took place in 1910, when the society became a component of the newly formed International Psychoanalytical Society. Alfred Adler was president from 1910 to 1911, and Freud was president from 1911 until it was disbanded by the Nazis in 1938.

Vineland Social Maturity Scale: Psychological test assessing capacity for independent functioning.

Visceral learning: See Biofeedback.

"Visual cliff": An apparatus for testing depth perception in young animals and babies.

Visual hallucination: See Hallucination.

Visual illusions: Figures which appear to be other than they really are, as a result of the ways in which the brain interprets information. Visual illusions have been extensively studied by psychologists, as it is thought that investigations of the errors of perception can throw light on how normal perceptual processes work. The visual illusions most commonly studied by psychologists fall into three main categories: *geometric illusions,* usually in the form of simple line drawings, *illusions of movement,* such as the phi phenomenon or the waterfall effect, and *colour illusions.*

Voice-recognition systems: Computer systems which can analyse the distinctive features of the human voice, and respond to key words which have been spoken. The development of voice-recognition systems forms a major area of research in the field of artificial intelligence, but represents no easy task, owing to wide differences in articulation shown by different people. Some success has been achieved in the development of systems which can 'learn' patterns of speech used by a particular person. This is usually achieved by the individual concerned reading out a set of key words and phrases, which the computer system uses as a baseline for identifying their characteristic speech patterns, and retains for when next receiving information from that person.

Volitional: Self-initiated.

Volubility: See Logorrhea.

Volly principle: In the auditory system, and in several others sensory systems, the intensity of a stimulus is signaled by means of the rate at which electrical impulses are fired to the brain. This signal can be achieved by each neurone firing very rapidly but owing to the absolute and relative refractory periods, there is a limit to how fast each neuron can fire. In the case of very intense stimuli, the neurons fire in relays or volleys: a set of neurons will fire, closely followed by another set, and then other. In this way, the brain receives a series of impulses at a rate which would not be possible for the neurons if each were firing singly.

Voluntary control: Deliberate bringing about of an activity or refraining from an activity The person exercising the control is aware of the nature of the activities and of the end to be achieved.

Volunteer bias: Individuals who volunteer for some procedures are not generally representative of the total population. Self selected patients who seek out treatment based upon newspaper publicity, for example, are likely to do significantly better than random patients who are simply offered the treatment.

Von Domarus principle: A theory to explain schizophrenic thinking which is characterized by the idea that two things are identical merely because they have identical predicates or properties. First proposed by Eilhard von Domarus in 1946.

Vorbeireden: One who is at cross purposes with another; applied to the person with Genser syndrome who seems to miss the point of questions put to him by talking around or past them and giving nonsensical or approximate answers.

Voyeurism: A paraphilia in which sexual excitement, frequently with orgasm, is obtained by looking at others naked, disrobing, or engaging in sexual activity.

W

WAIS: See Wechsler Adult Intelligence Scale.

Waterfall effect: A special case of a negative after-effect involving the perception of steady movement. If someone looks steadily at movement which occurs consistently in one direction, such as gazing at a waterfall, then, when they look away at a stable background, they experience an illusion of movement in the opposite direction. In the case of the waterfall, this involves the impression that the bank or surroundings are moving steadily upwards; if the effect is as a result of the movement of a train, then the train may seem to be moving backward when it stops at a station.

Watson, John B. (1878–1958): American psychologist the founder of the behaviourism school of psychology.

Waxy flexibility: See Catalepsy.

Weber, Max (1864–1920): A German sociologist, with Durkheim, as one of the two founder of modern sociology. He wrote, "The Protestant ethic and the spirit of capitalism". He divided social action into four types – Zweckrational (rational action in pursuit of a goal). Wertrational (rational action with reference to a value), emotional and traditional.

Weber's law: A law discovered by Ernst Weber in the early years of psychology, during which psychophysics was being developed. The law stated that the amount by which a stimulus needs to be changed in order for the change to be noticeable (the just noticeable difference) is a constant proportion of the strength of the stimulus. The value of this constant proportion is know as Weber's constant. In practical terms, the implications of Weber's law is that stronger stimuli will need to increase or reduce by greater amounts than do smaller stimuli, before they are perceived as different. See also Fechner's law, power law.

Wechsler Adult Intelligence Scale (WAIS): Intelligence test assessing intellectual functioning in adults.

Wechsler Intelligence Scale for Children (WISC): Intelligence test assessing intellectual functioning in children aged 5 to 15.

Wechsler Preschool and Primary Scale of Intelligence (WPPSI): Intelligence test assessing intellectual functioning in children aged 4 to 6½.

Wednesday Evening Society: A small group of Freud's followers who in 1902 started meeting with him informally on Wednesday evenings to receive instructions in psychoanalysis. As the society grew in numbers and importance, it evolved in 1910 into the Vienna Psychoanalytic Society.

Weekend hospital: A form of partial hospitalization in which the patient spends only weekends in the hospital and functions in the outside world during the week. See also Day hospital, Night hospital, Partial hospitalization.

Weltanschauung: (German) World outlook; conception of reality; philosophy of life.

Weyer, Johann (1515–1588): Dutch physician considered by some to be the first psychiatrist. His interest in human behaviour led to his writing De Praestigiis Daemonum (1563), a landmark in the history of psychiatry.

White, William Alanson (1870–1937): American psychiatrist famous for his early support of Psychoanalysis and his contributions to forensic psychiatry.

White-out Syndrome: A psychosis that occurs in Arctic explorers and mountaineers who are exposed to a lack of diverse stimuli in the snow-clad environment.

Windigo: A culture-specific syndrome seen in Canadian Indians. It is characterized by a delusion of transformation into or possession by a windigo (wihtigo), a feared supernatural cannibalistic monster.

Wish fulfillment: In the psychoanalytic theory of dreams, the dream is supposed to be a disguised expression of sexual or aggressive urges or wishes; for this reason, the dream is sometimes said to be fulfilling a wish or urge.

Witchcraft: It is commonly, referred to the believed use of supernatural means for evil ends. Also see sorcery.

Withdrawal: Pathological retreat from interpersonal contact and social involvement; extreme decrease of intellectual and emotional interest in the environment. It may be seen in schizophrenia and depression.

Withdrawal syndrome: Stereotyped constellation of signs and symptoms that appears when the person stops taking a drug on which he had become physically dependent. It is also known as abstinence syndrome. Specific clinical features are characteristic for the particular drug. See also Alcohol withdrawal syndrome, Delirium tremens, Drug dependence.

Wittels, Fritz (1880–1950): Austrian Psychoanalyst. One of Freud's early followers, Wittels wrote a biography of him in 1924 during a period of enstrangement, when he was under the influence of Wilhelm Stekel. Later, a reconciliation took place, and Freud conceded that some of Wittel's interpretations were probably correct.

Wolf-Man: Sobreiquet given in the analytic literature to the patient described by Freud in his " From, the History of an Infantile Neurosis" (1918).

Word approximation: The use of conventional words in an unconventional or inappropriate way (metonyms) or of new words that are developed by conventional rules of word formation – for example, "hand shoes" for gloves and "time measure" for clock. It is distinguished from a neologism, which is a new word whose derivation cannot be understood. See also Metonymy, Neologism, Paraphasia.

Word association test (WAT): It provides someone with a stimulus word and ask for the first word that comes to mind, e.g., say 'table' and the response may well be 'chair'. It reveals people's verbal habits, the structure of their verbal memory, thought processes and occasionally even emotional 'states and personality'. It was given by the British scientist Galton.

Word recognition threshold: A measure of the minimum degree of exposure of a word necessary for a subject to identify it. The normal procedure is to vary the time during which the word is exposed; other conditions could involve presenting the word more or less faintly, or at different distances. The threshold is usually taken to be the point at which the word is recognized 50% of the time, as the exposure necessary will vary on each individual occasion. Recognition thresholds are usually measured using a tachistoscope.

Word salad: An incoherent, essentially incomprehensible mixture of words and phrases commonly seen in far-advanced cases of schizophrenia. See also Incoherence.

Working alliance: In group therapy, the collaboration between the group as a whole and each patient for the purpose of promoting the mental health and emotional maturation of the members with the help of the therapist. See also Therapeutic alliance.

Working through: In psychoanalysis, the repeated and varied examination of a conflict, neurotic trend, or other problem for the purpose of increasing insight into unconscious processes and effecting adaptive personality changes. Free association, resistance, interpretation, and working through constitute fundamental facets of the psychoanalytic process.

Writer cramp: A painful spasm of the muscle of the hand and the fingers used in writing, which appears at the start or shortly after the beginning of the writing act, and tends to recur. See also: occupational neurosis. First described by Sir Charles Bell (1933). *Synonyms*: graphospasm; scriveners's palsy, occupational cramp, craft palsy.

Wundt, Wilhelm (1832–1920): Philosopher, physiologist, psychologist studied the domain of 'folk psychology'. (Volkerpsychologie); and four stage theory of 'cultural evolution' – primitive, totemic, heroic – deistic and humanistic.

X

X: A term normally used to represent a raw score in a set of data; also used for any unknown score or the value of an independent variable.

X: An abbreviation often used to refer to the mean of a set of scores.

X-linkage: Mode of genetic transmission in which a tract or gene is linked to the X chromosome. Has been implicated in some cases of bipolar disorder.

Xenophobia: An irrational and excessive fear of strangers or strange (foreign) cultures, which can often become converted into intense, Jingoistic patriotism and/or recial or cultural prejudice.

Y

Yavis: A term used to describe the typical patient considered suitable for psychoanalysis. The term stands for 'young, attractive, verbal, intelligent and successful'. Patients who don't fit these criteria are frequently allocated to other less expensive forms of treatment, e.g., behaviour therapy. Although this idea is only semiserious. It contains more than a grain of truth in terms of the types of patients which many psychoanalysts prefer to treat.

Yavis syndrome: According to Schofield (1964), young male American psychiatrists tend to select for psychotherapy female patients who display the 'YAVIS' syndrome, being Young. Attractive, Verbally fluent, Intelligent and Successful and having the same social background and aspirations as themselves. This ironic comment on the American psychiatric and psycho-analytic scene is part of a general attract on the tendency to expand professional time and skill on patients who are not ill in any clinical sense at the expense of research on the major psychiatric disorders.

Yerkes-Dodson Law: An expression of the relationship between a person's state of physiological arousal, and their performance of a task or job. When plotted on a graph, it takes the form of an inverted U curve. Up to a point, increased arousal improves performance, but beyond that point further increases in arousal will cause performance to deteriorate. Furthermore, the shape of the curve will vary with the complexity of the task, simple tasks being less affected by high arousal and showing a wider flatter curve and complex tasks reaching their optimal level at a relatively lower state of arousal, increasing and falling off more sharply.

Yerkish: An artificial 'language' developed during experiments in chimpanzee language training at the Yerkes primate laboratory in Georgia, U.S.A. Initially developed for use with a chimpanzee named Lana, it consists of a series of symbols used in a fairly arbitrary fashion to stand for concepts and conjunctions. There is considerable debate as to just how far Yerkish can be regarded as a language rather than just an arbitrary set of symbols.

Yoked control: An experimental set-up which the experimental group and the control group are paired, such that any member of the experimental group has one of the control group receiving exactly the same experiences. The pairs are linked (yoked) in such a way that what happens to other, e.g., if one receives a reward or punishment the other does too. This makes it easier for the experimenter to ensure that any differences which arise between the two are produced by the independent variable.

Young-Helmholtz theory: The idea that human colour vision depends on activity in three different kinds of cones-one kind which absorbs short wavelengths of the visible spectrum most readily, a second kind which absorbs middle wavelengths, and a third kind which is most sensitive to relatively long wavelengths.

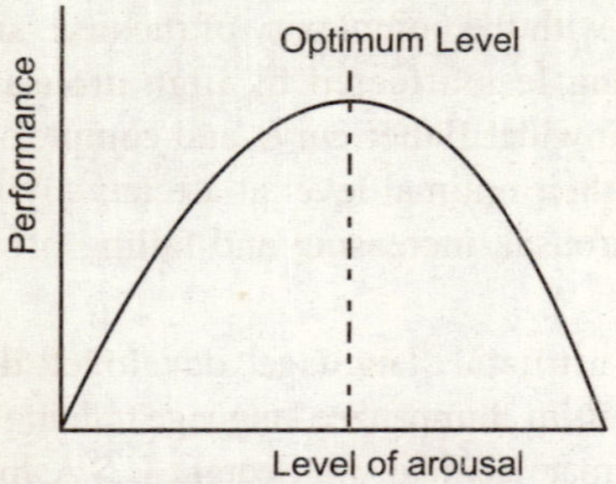

The Yokes-Dodson Law

Youth: The period of studenthood which may follow adolescence and which precedes full incorporation into the adult world.

Z

Zeitgeber: A German word meaning 'time-giver'. The term occurs in studies of biological rhythms, referring to environmental events that provide the organism with a precise timing to which their innate rhythms can be attached. For example many animals are born with a rhythm of approximately 24 hours (the circadian rhythm). The daily alternation of light and dark is a seitgeber which enables the circadian rhythm to adjust to precisely 24 hours.

Zeutgeist: The 'spirit of the times', the social and cultural climate within which an even occurs or a theory is developed. Scientific theories are very rarely, if ever, independent of their cultural climate and the form that a theory takes and the information which counts as acceptable evidence for a theory can vary dramatically from one period to the next. By and large, those scientific theories which become popular tend to be the theories which 'fit' the Zeitgeist best.

Zener cards: A standard set of card used in experimental studies of extrasensory perception.

There are usually 25 cards, each bearing one of 5 simple symbols; cross, wave, circle, star or square.

In a typical experiment subjects are asked to guess which pattern is on a card that another subject (out of sight) is looking at. They are also sometimes called Rhine cards.

Zero-sum game: In games theory, the class of games in which a fixed quantity of resources is distributed between the players, so that for anyone to do better someone else must do worse. Zero-sum games are of particular interest to social psychologists because it has been found that people operate according to the same principles even when they are not in a zero-sum situation. That is, people will often work hard to ensure that others do worse than themselves even if this has no effect on their own gains and in some cases may even mean sacrificing them.

Zollner illusion: A particularly powerful visual illusion in which parallel lines appear to converge as a result of being crossed by short diagonal lines set at angles to the main ones.

Zooerasty: Kraft-Ebing's term for the paraphilia consisting of sexual intercourse with an animal.

Zoolagnia: Sexual attraction to animals.

Zoophillia: A paraphilia in which animals are used to produce sexual excitement. See also Bestiality.

Zoophobia: Fear of animals.

Z-score (standard score): A number that indicates how far a given score is above or below the mean, using the standard deviation of the distribution as the unit of measurement.

Appendix–I

TECHNICAL MENTAL ILLNESS GLOSSARY (BHATIA, 1991) (English to Hindi)

Aberration	विपथन
sex a.	लिंग विपथन
sexual a.	यौन विपथन
Abreaction	भावविरेचन युक्ति
Acalculia	परिकलन अक्षमता
Acute	तीव्र
Addict	व्यसनी
Addiction	व्यसन
Adjustment	समायोजन
Affect	भाववृति
blunt a.	भुथरा भाव
elated a.	उल्लासित भाव
flat a.	समतल भाव
incongruous a.	बेमेल भाव
labile a.	अस्थिर भाववृति
perplexed a.	व्यग्र भाव
sad a.	उदास/ खिन्न भाव
shallow a.	उथला भाव
Affective	मर्मस्पर्शी
After-image	अनुबिम्ब
Age	वय
mental a.	मानसिक वय
Aggressive	आक्रामी
Aging	कालप्रभावन/ वयोवृद्धि
Agoraphobia	अवकाश भीति/ बाह्य-भीति (खुले स्थान का डर)
Alcohol	ऐल्कोहॉल/ मधसार/ मद्य
Alcoholic	ऐल्कोहॉली/ मद्यव्यसनी
Alcoholism	मदात्यय/ पानात्यय

Allopsychic	परमानसिक
Ambivalence	उभयभाविक/उभयवृतिता
Amimia	इंगिताभाव
Amnesia	स्मृतिलोप
anterograde a.	घटनोतर स्मृतिलोप
psychogenic a.	भाधिज स्मृतिलोप
retrograde a.	घटनापूर्व स्मृतिलोप
verbal a.	वाचिक/शब्द स्मृतिलोप
Analeptic	सजीवक/ऐनैलेप्टिक
Analysis	विश्लेषण
Anergic	अनूर्ज
Angor animi	मरणातंक/आसन्नमृत्यु आतंक
Anorexia	अरूचि/अरोचक
Anti	प्रतिरोधी
anti-convulsant	आक्षेपरोधी
antiepileptic	अपस्मारोधी
antisterility	प्रतिबंध्यता
Anxietas presenilis	जरापूर्व चिंता
Anxiety	चिन्ता/उत्कण्ठा/व्यग्रता
a neurosis	चिन्ताधि
Anxious	चिन्तित
Apathetic	उदासीन
Apathy	भावहीनता/विराग
Aphasia	वाचाघात
Aphonia	स्वरहानि
Appetite	क्षुधा/बुभुक्षा
Apperception	अभिबोध
Apprehension	आशंका
Approximation	सन्निकटन
Apraxia	चेष्टा अक्षमता/एप्रैक्सिया
Areflexia	अप्रतिवर्तता
Asexual	अलैंगिक
Asocial	असामाजिक
Aspermia	अशुक्रता
Assessment	निर्धारण
Astereognosis	विन्यास ज्ञानहीनता/ ऐस्टीरियोग्नोसिस
Asthenia	अवसन्नता/दुर्बलता
Astasia-Abasia	गति अक्षमता/ऐस्टेसिया-ऐबेसिया
Ataxia	पूर्वजता
Attention	ध्यान

Attitude	संस्थिति/वृति
Aura	पूर्वाभास
gustatory a.	स्वाद पूर्वाभास
motor a.	गति पूर्वाभास
olfactory a.	गंध पूर्वाभास
psychical a.	मनोविकारी पूर्वाभास
sensory a.	संवेदी पूर्वाभास
visceral a.	आशयिक पूर्वाभास
visual a.	दृष्टि पूर्वाभास
Autistic	स्वपरायण
Automatic	स्वचालित
a obedience	स्वचालित आज्ञापालन
Automatism	स्वचालता
post epileptic a.	अपस्मरारोत्तर स्वचालता
Autopsychic	स्वमानसिक
Autosuggestion	आत्मसुझाव
Bedwetting	शय्यामूत्रण
Behaviour	व्यवहार/आचरण
abnormal b.	अप्रसम/असामान्य व्यवहार
differential b.	विभेदी आचरण
social b.	सामाजिक व्यवहार
Behaviourism	आचरणवाद
Bestiality	तिर्यग्योनिगमन
Beverage	पेय
intoxicating to	मादकपेय
Biochemical	जीवरासायनिक
Biosocial	जीवसामाजिक
Bradykinesis	मन्दगतिक्रम
Bradyphrenia	मदोमन्दता/मनः श्यानता
Bulimia	अतिबुभुक्षा
Cannabis	कैनेबिस (भंग, चरस, गांजा)
Cannibalism	नरभक्षण
Castration	वन्ध्यकरण/बीजग्रंथि उच्छेदन
Catalepsy	पेशी प्रतिष्टंभ/कैटालेप्सी
Cataplexy	केटाप्लेक्सी/भयजन्य निश्चलता
Catathymic	केटाथाइमिक
Catatonia	तान प्रतिष्टम्भ/कैटाटोनिया
Cathartic	विरेचक
Catharsis	विरेचण
emotional c.	आवेश विरेचण

Cause	कारण
predisposing c.	पूर्वप्रवर्तक कारण
precipitating c.	अध:पतन कारण
specific c.	विशिष्ट कारण
Character	गुण/लक्षण
anal erotic c.	गुदाकामुक लक्षण
cultural c.	संवर्धी गुण
dominant c.	प्रभावी गुण
recessive c.	अप्रभावी गुण
Chorea	लास्य/कोरिया
huntington c.	हंटिंग्टन कोरिया
syndenham's c.	सिडेनहम कोरिया
Chronic	चिरकारी
Clinic	निदानशाला
child guidance c.	बालनिदानशाला
Clonic	अवमोटन
Cognition	बोध
Coma	सन्यास/कोमा
c. vigil	सजग सन्यास
Comatose	सन्यस्त
Compensation	सम्पूर्ति
Compensatory	क्षतिपूरक
Complex	संकर/सम्मिश्र/काम्प्लेक्स
electra c.	इलेक्ट्रा काम्प्लेक्स/मातृ विद्वेषवशात् पितृ आसक्ति
inferiority c.	हीनमन्यता
oedipus c.	इडिपस सम्मिश्र
Concentration	सान्द्रता/सान्द्रण
Concept	धारणा/संकल्पना
Conflict	संघर्ष
Consciousness	संज्ञा
loss of c.	संज्ञालोप
Convulsion	आक्षेप
clonic c.	अवमोटी आक्षेप
hysterial c.	हिस्टीरिया आक्षेप
jacksonian c.	जैक्सोनी आक्षेप
tetanic c.	धनुस्तम्भी आक्षेप
tonic c.	तानी आक्षेप
Coprolalia	मलवाच्यता/ कोप्रोलेलिया
Cry	चीत्कार
Culture	संवर्ध

Day-dreaming	दिवा स्वप्न
Delinquency	अपचार
Delinquent	बालापचारी
Delirium	प्रलाप
d. tremens	सकम्प प्रलाप
Delusion	विभ्रम/भ्रान्ति/मिथ्याविश्वास
nihilistic d.	श्र: नास्तित्व भ्रान्ति
d. of grandeur	वैभव भ्रान्ति
hypochondriac d.	रोग भ्रमि भ्रान्ति
d. of influence	प्रभाव भ्रान्ति
d. of persecution	अभिद्रोह भ्रान्ति/उत्पीड़न भ्रान्ति
religious d.	धार्मिक भ्रान्ति
d. of self-reference	स्वत: निर्देश भ्रान्ति
somatic d.	दैहिक/कायिक भ्रान्ति
Delusional	भ्रान्तिमय
Dementia	मनोभ्रंश
presenile d.	जरापूर्व मनोभ्रंश
Dementia precox	अन्तराबन्ध/कालपूर्वमनोभ्रंश
Dependence	निर्भरता
Depersonalisation	अवैयक्तिकीकरण
Depressant	अवसादक
Depressed	अवनमित
Depresio apathetica	भावहीन अवसादक
Depression	आवदाब/गर्त/अवसाद
affective d.	भाववृतीय अवसाद
agitated d.	सोद्वेग
reactive d.	अतिक्रियात्मक अवसाद
simple d.	साधारण
Depressor	विपर्यय/अवनमनी/अवसाद
Derealisation	अवास्तविक-अनुभति
Desensitisation	विसुग्राहीकरण
systematic d.	व्यवस्थित/क्रमबद्ध/संहत/संस्थित विसुग्राहीकरण
Development	परिवर्धन
chronological d.	कालक्रमिक परिवर्धन
d. of milestones	परिवर्धन मार्गशिला
Disorientation	स्थिति भ्रांति
Distractibility	ध्यानान्तरण
Drinker	मद्यप
Dyskinesia	अपप्रवाह
tardive d.	टारडिव अपप्रवाह

Dysthymia	डिस्थाइमिक
Eccentric	उत्केन्द्रक/सनकी
Echolalia	शब्दानुकरण
Echopraxia	क्रियानुकरण
Ecstasy	अत्यानन्द
Ego	अहम्
disintegration of e.	अहम् विघटन
e. ideal	आदर्श अहम्
super e.	परम अहम्
Egocentricity	अहम् केन्द्रिता
Egotistical	अहंकारी
Emotion	आवेश
Encephalopathy	मस्तिष्कविकृति
Encopresis	असंयतपुरिषता
Enuresis	असंयतमूत्रता
Epilepsia partialis continua	सतत आंशिक अपस्मार
Epilepsy	अपस्मार/मिरगी/एपिलेप्सी
akinetic e.	अगतिक अपस्मार
focal e.	विकारस्थानी अपस्मार
focal motor e.	विकारस्थानी प्रेरक अपस्मार
idiopathic e.	अज्ञातहेतुक अपस्मार
jacksonian e.	जैक्सोनी अपस्मार
major e. (grandmal)	गुरु अपस्मार
minor e (petitmal)	लघु अपस्मार
myoclonic e.	पेशीअवमोटनी अपस्मार
psychomotor e.	मन: प्रेरक अपस्मार
reflex e.	प्रतिवर्ता अपस्मार
temporal e.	शंखखण्ड अपस्मार
Epileptiform	अपस्माररूपी
Erotic	कामोत्तेजक
Eroticism	कामुकता
anal e.	गुदा कामुकता
Erotomania	कामोन्माद
Euphoria	सुखाभास
Euthansia	सहज मृत्यु
Eutonia	सुदेहाभास
Examination	परीक्षा
mental state e.	मानसिक दशा परीक्षा
Excitement	उत्तेजना
catatonic e.	केटाटोनिक उत्तेजना
Exorcism	भूतापसरण

Expression	मुखाकृति/भावाकृति
vacant e.	शून्य भावाकृति
Face	आनन
mask like f.	निर्व्यजक आनन
Facies	मुखाकृति, पृष्ठक
apathetic f.	उदासीन मुखाकृति
Fainting	मूर्च्छा
episodic f.	प्रासंगिक मूर्च्छा
Falsification	मिथ्याकरण
retrospective f.	पश्चावलोकी मिथ्याकरण
Fatigue	शान्ति/क्लान्ति
Feeling	अनुभूति
f. of passivity	परवशान भूति
f. of unreality	अवास्तविकता अनुभूति
Fellatio	मुखमैथुन
Fetishism	वस्तुकामुकता
Fixation	स्थिरीकरण/बंधन
anal f.	गुदा स्थिरीकरण
genital f.	जननांगी स्थिरीकरण
oral f.	मुख स्थिरीकरण
Flagellation	कशाभन्यास, कशाघात
Folie à deux	द्वि साहचर्य मानसरोग
Folie à trios	त्रिसाहचर्य मानसरोग
Folie circulaire	चक्री मानसरोग
Folie raisonmante	कुतर्क मानसरोग
Formication	पिपिलिकासरणानुभूति
Free	अवाध/अयुक्त/मुक्त
f. association	अयुक्त समागम
Fugue	फयूग/स्मृतिभ्रंश जनित
Gait	चाल
cerebellar g.	अनुमस्तिष्कीय चाल
festinating g.	अपत्वरित चाल
highsteppage g.	उच्चपगक्षेपण चाल
scissor g.	कर्तरी चाल
shuffling g.	पादघर्ष चाल
wadding g.	डगमगाती चाल
Gerontology	जरा विद्या
Globus	गोलक
g. hystericus	ग्लोबस हिस्टेरिकस
g. pallidus	पाण्डुर गोलक

Habit	आदत/अभ्यास
h. spasm	अभ्यासाकर्षटिक
Habituation	अभ्यस्तता
Hallucination	विभ्रम
auditory h.	श्रवण विभ्रम
functional h.	क्रियात्मक विभ्रम
gustatory h.	स्वाद विभ्रम
hypnagogic h.	निद्रापूर्व विभ्रम
hypnopompic h.	निद्रोतर विभ्रम
microptic h.	वामन विभ्रम
olfactory h.	घ्राण विभ्रम
reflex h.	प्रतिवर्त विभ्रम
tactile h.	स्पर्श विभ्रम
visual h.	दृष्टि विभ्रम
Hallucinogens	विभ्रमजनक औषधियां
Headache	शिरोवेदना
Health	स्वास्थ्य
mental h.	मानसिक स्वास्थ्य
Hebephrenia	हेबिफ्रेनिया
Hemiplegia	पक्षाघात
hysterical h.	हिस्टीरिया पक्षाघात
Heterosexuality	इतरलिंगी कामुकता
History	इतिवृत
case h.	रोगीवृत
family h.	पारिवारिक वृत
h. of past illness	पूर्वरोग वृत
h. of present illness	वर्तमान रोग वृत
h. sheet	इतिवृत पत्र
h. taking	इतिवृत लेना
menstrual h.	आर्तव वृत
obstetric h.	प्रसूतिवृत
personal h.	व्यक्तिवृत
socio-economical h.	सामाजिक-आर्थिक वृत
Hospital	चिकित्सालय
mental h.	मानसिक चिकित्सालय
Hygiene	स्वस्थ वृत
personal h.	वैयाक्तिक स्वस्थवृत/ वैयाक्तिक स्वास्थ्य
Hyperactivity	अतिसक्रियता

Hyperkinesis	अतिगतिक्रम
Hypersomnia	अतिनिद्रा
Hyperventillation	अतिसंवातन
hysterial h.	हिस्टीरिया अतिसंवातन
Hypomania	अल्पोन्माद
Hysteria	हिस्टीरिया
anxiety h.	चिंता हिस्टीरिया
conversion h.	रूपान्तरित हिस्टीरिया
dissociation h.	वियोजन हिस्टीरिया
Hysteroid	हिस्टीरियासम
Iatrogenic	चिकित्सक प्रेरित
Idea	विचार
autochthonous i.	निराधार विचार
flight of i.	कल्पना की उड़ान
self accusatory i.	आत्मद्रोषरोपी विचार
i. of influence	प्रभावजन्य विचार
i. of reference	संबंधी विचार
Identity	तद्रूपता/अभिज्ञान
Idiopathic	अज्ञातहेतुक
Idiot	जड़बुद्धि
Illusion	भ्रम
Image	प्रतिबिम्ब
mental i.	मानसिक प्रतिबिम्ब
real i.	वास्तविक प्रतिबिम्ब
virtual i.	आभासी प्रतिबिम्ब
Imago	पूर्णकीट/इमैगो
Imbecile	मूढ़
Impotence	षण्ढता
functional i.	क्रिया षण्ढता
organic i.	ऐन्द्रिय षण्ढता
psychic i.	मनः षण्ढता
Incongruity	असामंजस्य
Incontinence	असंयति
Incurable	असाध्य
Inhibition	संदमन
competitive i.	स्पर्धी संदमन
reciprocal i.	अन्योन्य संदमन
Insanity	विक्षिप्ति/पागलपन/मानसरोग
communicated i.	साहचर्य मानसरोग
impulsive i.	संवेदी मानसरोग
moral i.	नैतिक मानसरोग

Insecurity	असुरक्षा
Insight	अन्तर्दृष्टि
Insomnia	अनिद्रा
Instability	अस्थिरता
emotional i.	भावात्मक अस्थिरता
sense of i.	अस्थिरता ज्ञान
Instinct	प्रवृति/सहज प्रवृति
death i.	मृत्यु प्रवृति
herd i.	समूह प्रवृति
life i.	जीवन प्रवृति
sexual i.	यौन प्रवृति
Intellect	प्रज्ञा
Intelligence	बुद्धि
Intelligence quotient	बुद्धिलब्धि
Intelligence scale	बुद्धिमाप
Intensity	तीव्रता
Intention	चेष्टा
Intercourse	परस्पर व्यवहार/संपर्क
sexual i.	सम्भोग
Interest	रुचि
Intersex	मध्यलिंगी/उभयलिंगी
Intoxicant	मादक
Intoxication	मादकता
pathological i.	विकारी मादकता
Introjection	अन्तर्ति वेशता
Introspection	अन्तर्निरीक्षण
Introversion	अन्तर्मुखता
Introverted	अन्तर्मुखी
Intuition	अन्त: प्रज्ञा/सहज प्रज्ञा
Invalidism	अशक्तता
Irreversible	अपरावर्ती
Judgement	निर्णय
Kinesthesia (Kinesthesis)	गतिसंवेदना
Lability	अस्थिरता
emotional l.	भावात्मक अस्थिरता
Latent	गुप्त/प्रच्छन्न
Lethal	घातक
Level	तल
l. of attention	ध्यान तल
Libido	कामलिप्सा

Liar	मिथ्याभाषी
pathological l.	विकारी मिथ्याभाषी
Lisping	अस्फुट वाक्
Macropsia	बृहतदृष्टता
Malingering	छलरूग्णता
Mania	उन्माद/ व्यसन
acute m.	तीव्र उन्माद
chronic m.	चिरकारी उन्माद
delirious m.	प्रलापी उन्माद
Manifestation	अभिव्यक्ति
hysterical m.	हिस्टीरिया अभिव्यक्ति
Mask	मास्क
Masochism	स्वपीड़न रति/स्वपीड़क
Maturation	परिपक्वता/परिपाक
Mature	पक्व/ प्रौढ़
Maturity	प्रौढ़ता
Medicine	औषध/ भेषज/आयुर्विज्ञान
preventive m.	निरोधक आयुर्विज्ञान
psychosomatic m.	मनोकायिक आयुर्विज्ञान
social m.	सामाजिक आयुर्विज्ञान
Melancholia	विषण्णता/मेलेंकोलिया
involutional m.	प्रत्यक् कालिक विषण्णता
Memory	स्मृति
immediate	निकटतम/प्रत्यक्ष
m.	तात्कालिक स्मृति
recent m.	अभिनव स्मृति
remote m.	दूरवर्ती/ सुदूर स्मृति
Mental	चिबुक/मानसिक
Mentalis	अधरउन्नमानिका
Micropsia	ह्रस्वदृष्टिता
Migraine	माइग्रेन
complicated m.	जटिल माइग्रेन
ophthalmoplegic m.	नेत्रपेशीघाती माइग्रेन
simple m.	साधारण/सामान्य माइग्रेन
Mind	मन
Multifactorial	बहुघटकीय
Narcissism	स्वरूप कामुकता
Narcoanalysis	तन्द्राविश्लेषण
Narcolepsy	तन्द्रालुता
Narcosis	सुषुप्ति

Negativism	नकारात्मकता
Neologism	व्यर्थशब्द निर्माण
Nervousness	अधीरता
Neurasthenia	तन्त्रिकावसाद/तन्त्रिका दौर्बल्य
Neurologist	तन्त्रिका विज्ञानी
Neurosis	विक्षिप्ति
anxiety n.	चिन्ता विक्षिप्ति
cardiac n.	हृद् विक्षिप्ति
cultural n.	सांस्कृतिक विक्षिप्ति
hypochondrical n.	रोग भ्रम विक्षिप्ति
hysterical n.	हिस्टीरिया विक्षिप्ति
occupational n.	व्यवसायज विक्षिप्ति
phobic n.	भीती विक्षिप्ति
traumatic n.	अभिघातज विक्षिप्ति
Nightmare	दुःस्वप्न
Nightterror	स्वप्न भीति
Nocturnal	नैश
Nosology	रोगवर्गीकरण विज्ञान
Numbness	सुन्नता
Obesity	स्थूलता
endogenous o.	अंतर्जात स्थूलता
exogenous o.	अतिभोजो स्थूलता
Objective	वस्तुपूरक
Object libido	विषय लिप्सा
Obsessive	बाध्य
compulsive	मनोग्रस्त
neurosis	विक्षिप्ति
Opium	अहिफेन/अफीम
Oppositional	सम्मुखी
Orientation	दिग्विन्यास/अभिविन्यास
Orogenital	मुखजननेन्द्रिय
Papilloedema	अक्षिविम्बशोफ
Paralysis	अंगघात/लकवा
congenital spastic p.	सहज संस्तम्भी अंगघात
facial p.	अर्दित/आनन घात
p. agitans (parkinsonism)	सकम्प अंगघात
Todd's p.	टॉड अंगघात
Paramnesia	अपस्मृति
reduplicate p.	पुनरावर्ती अपस्मृति

Paranoia	संविभ्रम, व्यामोह
Parapraxia	चेष्टाविपर्यय
Parental	पैतृक
Pathogenesis	रोगजनक/विकृतिजनक
Pathological	वैकृत/विकृतिजन्य
Pathophysiology	विकारी-शरीर क्रिया
Patient	रोग/मरीज
indoor p.	अन्तरंग रोगी
mental p.	मनोरोगी
outdoor p.	बहिरंग रोगी
Perception	प्रत्यक्ष/अवगम/बोध
loss of p.	अवगम हानि
sense p.	इन्द्रिय प्रत्यक्ष
space p.	दिक् प्रत्यक्ष
visual p.	चॉक्षुक प्रत्यक्ष
Periodicity	आवर्तिता
Perseveration	सतत प्रसक्ति
Personality	व्यक्तित्व
cyclothymic p.	चक्रीय विक्षिप्ति संबंधी व्यक्तित्व
epileptic p.	अपस्मारी व्यक्तित्व
hysterical p.	हिस्टीरिया व्यक्तित्व
multiple p.	बहु व्यक्तित्व
pathological p.	वैकृत व्यक्तित्व
psychopathic p.	मनोवैकृत व्यक्तित्व
prepsychotic p.	मनोविक्षिप्तिपूर्व व्यक्तित्व
split p.	विखण्डित व्यक्तित्व
syntonic p.	संतुलित व्यक्तित्व
Phantasy	स्वैरकल्पना
Phobia	भीति
Pica	अखाद्य खाने की इच्छा/ विपर्यस्त क्षुधा
Poisoning	विषाक्तता
Posture	सस्थिति/आसन/स्थिति
erect p.	उच्छित स्थिति
sitting p.	आसीन
Prevention	निवारण/निरोध
level of p.	निवारण स्तर
primary .	प्राथमिक निवारण
secondary p.	द्वितीयक निवारण
tertiary p.	तृतीयक निवारण
Principle	तत्व/सिद्धांत/नियम

pleasure pain p.	सुखदर्द सिद्धांत
reality p.	वास्तविकता सिद्धांत
Prognosis	प्राग्ज्ञा/पूर्वानुमान
Projection	प्रक्षेपण/प्रक्षेण
false p.	मिथ्या प्रक्षेप
Pseudocrisis	कूट-संकट
Pseudocyesis	कूट-सगर्भगता
Pseudologia phantastica	विकारी मिथ्याभाषण
Pseudoparesis	कूट-आंशिकघात
Psychasthenia	मनोदौर्बल्य
Psychiatric	मनोविकारी
Psychiatrics	मनोविकार विज्ञान
Psychiatrist	मनोविकार विज्ञानी
Psychiatry	मनोविकार चिकित्सा
clinical p.	लाक्षणिक मनोविकार चिकित्सा
Psychic	मन:/मानसिक
Psychoanalysis	मनोविश्लेषण
Psychogenic	भाधिज
Psychological	मनोविज्ञान संबंधी
Psychologist	मनोविज्ञानी
Psychology	मनोविज्ञान
Psychometrist	मनोमितिज
Psychomotor	मन: प्रेरक
Psychopath	मनोविकृत
Psychopathology	मनोविकृती
Psychosis	मनोविक्षिप्ति
affective p.	भाववृतीय मनोविक्षिप्ति
battle exhaustion p.	युद्ध परिक्लान्ति विक्षिप्ति
epileptic p.	अपस्मारी मनोविक्षिप्ति
involutional p.	प्रत्यक्कालिक मनोविक्षिप्ति
manic depressive p.	उन्माद अवसादी मनोविक्षिप्ति
postictal p.	अपस्मारोत्तर मनोविक्षिप्ति
presenile p.	जरापूर्व मनोविक्षिप्ति
puerperal p.	प्रसूति मनोविक्षिप्ति
schizophrenic p.	विखण्डित मनोविक्षिप्ति
senile p.	जरा मनोविक्षिप्ति
Psychosomatic	मन: कायिक मनोविक्षिप्ति
Psychosurgery	मन:शल्यचिकित्सा
Psychotherapy	मनश्चिकित्सा

Pyknolepsy	पिक्नोलेप्सी
Pyknotic	संघनित
Pyromania	दहनोन्माद
Quality	गुण
affective q.	आवेशी गुण
Reaction	प्रतिक्रिया/अभिक्रिया
alarm r.	चेतावनी/ सतर्कता/ प्रतिक्रिया
anamnestic r.	पुनः स्मरण प्रतिक्रिया
conditioned r.	औपाधिक प्रतिक्रिया
defence r.	रक्षा प्रतिक्रिया
emotional r.	भावात्मक प्रतिक्रिया
perplexity r.	व्यामोह प्रतिक्रिया
primary r.	प्राथमिक प्रतिक्रिया
psychotic r.	मनोविक्षिप्ति
Reception	अभिग्रहण
r. order	अभिग्रहण आदेश
Reciprocal	अन्योन्य
r. inhibition	अन्योन्य अवरोध
Reflex	प्रतिवर्त
Regression	प्रतिक्रमण
Relationship	सम्बन्ध
cause-effect r.	कार्य-कारण सम्बन्ध
Relaxation	शिथिलन/ शान्ति
progressive r.	प्रगतिशील शिथिलन
Repression	दमन/ निग्रह
Resistance	प्रतिरोध
Responsibility	उत्तरदायित्व
criminal r.	अपराध उत्तरदायित्व
Retardation	मन्दता/ मन्दन
mental r.	मन्दबुद्धि
speech r.	वाक् मन्दता
Rhythm	ताल-अनुक्रम
Rigidity	कठोरता/ दृढ़ता
functional r.	क्रियात्मक कठोरता
organic r.	कायिक कठोरता
Sadism	परपीड़नकामुकता
Sadistic	परपीड़नकामुक
Schizoid	आतराबन्धी
Schizophasia	निरर्थक शब्दोच्चारण
Schizophrenia	विखंडित मनस्कता

Sedative	शामक
Self	स्वत:
Self retaining	स्वधारक
Senescence	जरा/जीर्णता
Senile	जराजन्य
Sensation	संवेदन/संवेदना
Sense	संवेद/ज्ञान/बोध
Sensitive	सुग्राही/सूक्ष्मग्रही
Sensitivity	सुग्राहीता/सूक्ष्मग्रहीता
Sensorium	संवेदन-क्षेत्र
Sensory	संवेदी
Sequelae	अनुगम
Sex	लिंग
s. age	लिंग वय
s. reversal	लिंग परिवर्तन
Side effects	अनुबंधी प्रभाव
Situation	स्थिति
Somatic	दैहिक/कायिक
Somatopsychic	कायमानसिक
Somnolence	तन्द्रा
Spasm	आकर्ष/ऐंठन/उद्वेष्ट
Spasmodic	आकर्षी/उदवेष्टकर
Spasticity	संस्तम्भता
Specificity	विशिष्टता
Speech	वाक्/ उच्चारण
distorted s.	विकृत वाक्
muffled s.	वस्त्ररूद्धवाक्
scanning s.	सविराम उच्चारण
(stacatto) slurring s.	स्खलित उच्चारण
Spell	दौर
breath holding s.	श्वास--धारण दौरण
Sperm	शुक्राणु

Appendix–II

TABLE OF PSYCHOLOGIC TESTS

Test	Type	Assesses	Age of Patient	Method	Administration
Alexander's Performance Scale	Intelligence	Cognitive functioning and Motor development	Below 10 years (3 to 6½ years)	Performance on 3 subtests	Individual
Babcock Levy Test	Intelligence	Cognitive functioning and motor development	1-Adult	Performance on 9 categories of subtests	Individual
Bayley Scales of Infant Development	Infant development	Cognitive functioning and motor development	1–30 months	Performance on subtests measuring cognitive and motor development	Individual

Test	Type	Assesses	Age of Patient	Method	Administration
Beck Depression Inventory	Personality	Measures depression	Adult	Performance on self report format	Individual
Behaviour Problem Checklist	Behaviour checklist	Child's Psychopathology	4–16 years	Behaviour assessed on 55 items on 3 point severity	Interview guardian
Bender Visual-Motor Gestalt Test	Projective visual-motor development	Personality conflicts Ego function and structure Organic brain damage	5-Adult	Patient's reproduction of geometric figure	Individual
Benton Visual Retention Test	Objective performance	Organic brain damage	Adult	Patient's reproduction of geometric figures from memory	Individual
Bhatia's Performance Scale	Intelligence	Cognitive functioning and motor development	Boys 11–16½ years	Performance on 5 subtests	Individual

Test	Type	Assesses	Age of Patient	Method	Administration
Brief Cognitive Rating Scale	Personality assessment	Cognitive assessment on 5 axes	Over 65 years	Assessment on 5 axes with 7 subtests	Individual
Brief Psychiatric Rating Scale	Symptomatology	Symptomatology and global pathology	Adult	Assessment on 18-dimension rating scale	Individual
California Personality Inventory	Personality inventory	Personality structure	Adolescent Adult	Performance on 17 scales	Individual
Cattell Infant Intelligence Scale	Infant development	General motor and cognitive development	1–18 months	Performance on developmental tasks	Individual
Cattell's 16 PF	Personality inventory	Personality conflicts (Personality factors)	Adults	Performance on self report format	Individual
Child Behaviour Checklist	Behaviour checklist	Child's Psychopathology	4–16 years	Behaviour assessed on 118 items	Interview knowledgeable informat

Test	Type	Assesses	Age of Patient	Method	Administration
Children's Apperception Test (CAT)	Projective	Personality conflicts	Child	Patient's makes up stories after viewing pictures	Individual
Draw-A-Person Draw-A-Family House-Tree	Projective	Personality conflicts Self-image (DAP) Family perception (DAF) Ego functions Intellectual functioning (DAP) Visual-motor coordination	2-Adult	Patient's drawings on a blank sheet of paper	Individual
Eysenck Personality Questionnaire	Personality inventory	Personality structure	Adult	Performance on a self-report format	Individual
Frostig Development Test of Visual Perception	Visual perception	Eye-motor coordination Figure ground perception	4–8 years	Performance on paper and pencil test measuring five aspects of	Individual or group

Test	Type	Assesses	Age of Patient	Method	Administration
		Constancy of shape Position in space Spatial relationships		visual perception	
Gesell Developmental Schedules	Preschool development	Cognitive, motor, language and social development	1-60 months	Performance on developmental tasks	Individual
Global Assessment of Functioning Scale	Mental health illness continuum	Psychological; social and occupational functioning	Adult	Functioning assessed on code 0–100 from observation and report	Individual
Goldstein's Colour Cancellation Test	Intelligence	Cognitive functioning and motor development	Adult	Performance copying coloured designs	Individual
Goldstein's Test of Organicity	Projective Visual-motor development	Organic brain damage	Adult	Performance on 4 subtests	Individual

Test	Type	Assesses	Age of Patient	Method	Administration
Grant's Multiphasic Personality Questionnaire	Projective	Personality conflicts	Adult	Answers on 100 items	Individual
Halstead-Reitan Neuropsychological Battery and other measures	Brain functioning	Cerebral functioning and organic brain damage	6-Adult	Various subtests measure aspects of cerebral functioning	Individual
Hamilton Anxiety Rating Scale	Personality assessment	Assessment of anxiety	Adult	Assessment on 7 items	Individual
Hamilton Depression Rating Scale	Personality assessment	Objective assessment of depression and its severity	Adolescent-Adult	Assessment on 17 major and 4 minor items	Individual
Holzman Inkblot Technique	Projective	Personality conflicts Ego function and structure Defensive structure	3-Adult	Performance on 45 inkblot plates	Individual

Test	Type	Assesses	Age of Patient	Method	Administration
Illinois Test of Psycholinguistic Ability (ITPA)	Language ability	Auditory, vocal, visual-motor channels of language, receptive, organizational and expressive components	2–10 years	Performance on 12 sub-tests measuring various dimensions of language functioning	Individual
Knox Cube Imitation Test	Intelligence	Intelligence below 10 years age Concentration and memory in adults	1 month adult	Performance on tests measuring cognitive and motor development	Individual
Louisville Fear Survey	Symptom checklist	Fear and anxiety behaviour	4–16 years	Assessed on 81 items	Interview guardian
Maudsley Medical Questionnaire	Development	Personality conflicts (and neurotic tendencies)	Adult	Answer on 40 questions	Individual

Test	Type	Assesses	Age of Patient	Method	Administration
Michigan Picture Stories	Defensive structure	Personality conflicts	Adolescent	Patient makes up stories after viewing stimulus pictures	Individual
Million Clinical Multiaxial Inventory	Personality inventory	Personality structure Diagnostic classification	Adolescent Adult	Performance on 11 scales (175 items)	Individual
Minnesota Multiphasic Personality Inventory (MMPI)	Paper and pencil; personality inventory (566 items)	Personality structure Diagnostic Classification	Adolescent Adult	Personality profile reflecting, nine dimensions of personality Diagnosis based upon actuarial prediction	Group
Otis Quick Scoring Mental Abilities Tests	Intelligence	Intellectual functioning	5-Adult	Performance on verbal and non-verbal dimensions of intellectual functioning	Group

Test	Type	Assesses	Age of Patient	Method	Administration
Proteus Maze Test	Development	Cognitive functioning Visuo-motor coordination	3-Adult	Tracing a figure with pencil without lifting it	Individual
Rorschach	Projective	Personality conflicts Ego function and structure Defensive structure Thought processes Affective integration	3-Adult	Patient's associations to inkbolts	Individual
Rosenzweig Picture Frustration Study	Projective	Personality conflicts	4–13 years	Responses on items/situations	Individual, Group (above 9 years)
Sack's Sentence Completion Test	Projective	Personality conflicts Ego function and structure Defensive structure	Adult	Performance on incomplete items provided	Individual

Test	Type	Assesses	Age of Patient	Method	Administration
Schedule for Affective Disorder and Schizophrenia	Symptomatology	Symptoms of affective disorders and schizophrenia	Adult	Structured interview of patient	Individual
Senior Apperception Test (SAT)	Projective	Personality conflicts	Over 65	Patient makes up stories after viewing stimulus pictures	Individual
Stanford-Binet	Intelligence	Intellectual functioning and development tasks	2-Adult	Performance on problem solving	Individual
Tasksa of Emotional Development (TED)	Projective	Personality conflicts	Child and Adolescent	Patient makes up stories after viewing stimulus pictures	Individual
Thematic Apperception Test (TAT)	Projective	Personality conflicts	Adult	Patients makes up stories after viewing stimulus pictures	Individual

Test	Type	Assesses	Age of Patient	Method	Administration
Vineland Social Maturity Scale	Social Maturity	Capacity for independent functioning	0–25 + years	Performance on developmental tasks measuring various dimensions of social functioning	Interview Patient or guardian of patient, occa-ssional self-report
Wechsler Adult Intelligence Scale (WAIS)	Intelligence	Intellectual functioning	16-Adult	Performance on 10 sub-tests measuring various dimensions of intellectual functioning	Individual
Wechsler Intelligence Scale for Children (WISC)	Intelligence	Intellectual functioning Thought processes Ego functioning	5–15	See above	Individual
Wechsler Preschool Primary Scale of Intelligence (WPPSI)	Intelligence	Intellectual functioning Thought processes Ego functioning	4–6½ years	See above	Individual